Women and Farming

Rural Studies Series

†Available in hardcover and paperback.

Women and Farming

Changing Roles,
Changing Structures

edited by Wava G. Haney
and Jane B. Knowles

Westview Press / Boulder and London

Rural Studies Series, Sponsored by the Rural Sociological Society

Cover photo: Martha Buelke, Dodge County, Wisconsin, about 1899. Photograph by William Buelke, courtesy of State Historical Society of Wisconsin (Buelke Collection).

This Westview softcover edition is printed on acid-free paper and bound in softcovers that carry the highest rating of the National Association of State Textbook Administrators, in consultation with the Association of American Publishers and the Book Manufacturers' Institute.

Published in 1988 in the United States of America by Westview Press, Inc., 5500 Central Avenue, Boulder, Colorado 80301

Library of Congress Cataloging-in-Publication Data
Women and farming.
   (Rural studies series)
   "[Papers from] the Second National Conference on
American Farm Women in Historical Perspective, held in
Madison, Wisconsin, on October 16–18, 1986"—Foreword.
   Includes index.
   1. Women in agriculture—United States—Congresses.
I. Haney, Wava G.   II. Knowles, Jane B.   III. National
Conference on American Farm Women in Historical
Perspective (2nd: 1986: Madison, Wis.)   IV. Series:
Rural studies series (Boulder, Colo.)
HD6073.A292U68   1988   331.4′83′0973   88-17170
ISBN 0-8133-7605-X

Printed and bound in the United States of America

The paper used in this publication meets the requirements of the American National Standard for Permanence of Paper for Printed Library Materials Z39.48-1984.

6   5   4   3   2

THIS BOOK IS DEDICATED WITH HONOR, RESPECT AND AFFECTION TO

Kathryn F. Clarenbach
Professor, University of Wisconsin-Madison
and University of Wisconsin-Extension

and

Eugene A. Wilkening
Professor Emeritus, University of Wisconsin-Madison

TABLE OF CONTENTS

LIST OF TABLES AND FIGURES

PREFACE

Changes in the structure of U.S. agriculture have profound implications for the roles of farm women. The Second National Conference on American Farm Women in Historical Perspective held in Madison, Wisconsin, on October 16-18, 1986, considered many aspects of this theme. In this book, twenty essays from that conference discuss work, family, community, and political roles of farm women and the ways farm, family, and public policy affect farm women's roles. Collectively, they build on earlier studies to advance both our understanding of farm women's lives and our understanding of agricultural systems. Each of these, in turn, can lead to better public policy and a fuller and more exciting research agenda for the future.

During the three day conference, nearly 200 scholars and farm women explored such topics as: farm women in the political arena, black women and farming, farm women within family structures, farm women's roles in communities, labor allocation on and off the farm, images of farm women, the financial crisis and mental stress, women as independent farmers, intergenerational land transfer, changing economic power and resource control, technology and changing roles of farm women, women and the land, farm women in farm organizations, and farm women in cross-cultural perspective. These essays highlight the major issues raised in our collective consideration of women and farming in historical and comparative perspective.

Wava G. Haney and Jane B. Knowles

ACKNOWLEDGEMENTS

Many individuals and organizations pooling their resources and skills created a successful Conference and produced this book. Six faculty, staff, and students of the University of Wisconsin System together with the editors collaborated over a two-year period to plan the Conference and handle the post-Conference details. A very special thanks is extended to Marian Thompson, Karen P. Goebel, Lorna Clancy Miller, Eugene A. Wilkening, Mary Neth, and Alice Anderson who energetically and cooperatively took responsibility for specific parts of the planning and enthusiastically endured the course. Thanks also to Jeanne Dosch who served as administrative assistant to the Committee for a few months immediately before and after the Conference.

The Conference was sponsored by a number of units of the University of Wisconsin System together with the Wisconsin State Historical Society. We are particularly grateful for the support received from the College of Agricultural and Life Sciences of the University of Wisconsin-Madison and for the assistance of the University of Wisconsin-Extension and the University of Wisconsin Centers. In addition to the support received from their offices, several individuals in these units contributed to the quality and operation of the Conference. We especially thank Leo M. Walsh, Dean of the College of Agricultural and Life Sciences; Kenneth H. Shapiro, Director of International Agricultural Programs and Associate Dean of the College of Agricultural and Life Sciences; Stephen C. Smith and Frank W. Kooistra, Associate Deans of the College of Agricultural and Life Sciences; Gene F. Summers, Chair, and Jess C. Gilbert, Assistant Professor, Department of Rural Sociology; and S. Jane Voichick, Program Leader, Family Living Education, University of Wisconsin-Extension. In addition, Marlene Skaife, Program Assistant, and Nancy Kanaskie, Specialist in the Department of Rural Sociology, UW-Madison and the secretarial staffs of Family Living Education, UW-Extension; International Agricultural Programs and the Land Tenure Center, UW-Madison; the University of Wisconsin Center-Richland and the University of Wisconsin Center-Baraboo handled many Conference details efficiently and pleasantly. The Department of History and the Women's Studies Program of the College of Letters and Sciences, UW-Madison, and the School of Family Resources and Consumer Sciences, UW-Madison, also provided support services to the Committee.

A grant from the Wisconsin Humanities Committee funded the participation of several humanists and underwrote other Conference expenses. The Cudahy Fund provided scholarships for farm women from six Wisconsin farm organizations: Rural Wisconsin, Wisconsin Farm Bureau Federation, Wisconsin Farm Unity Alliance, Wisconsin Farmers Union, Wisconsin Grange, and Wisconsin

National Farmers Organization. The Evjue Foundation, the Farm Foundation, the North Central Regional Center for Rural Development, and International Agricultural Programs, UW-Madison, also provided substantial grant monies to underwrite participation by scholars presenting papers and farm women panelists and discussants. The College of Agricultural and Life Sciences, UW-Madison, provided funds for programmatic expenses. The State Historical Society provided facilities, services in kind, and special exhibits for the Conference. Finally, Dow Chemical U.S.A., Farmers Union Central Exchange, Inc. (Cenex), JI Case, Wisconsin Power and Light Foundation, Inc., John Deere and Company, and Cremer Foundation, Inc., all contributed funds to sponsor participation by farm women.

The anthology itself owes much to the cooperation of the authors. They have responded to several reviews and requests for revisions, sometimes on short notice, in the spirit of sisterhood. The authors and the editors have benefitted from the comments of two anonymous reviewers and the editor of the Rural Studies Series, Fred Buttel, as well as substantive suggestions and excellent editorial work by copy editor, Cathy Loeb.

In the final stage of production, Brian Larson expertly converted symbols from an array of software programs into a readable manuscript and Carol Feyen numbered and renumbered the subject and name indices. Support from JoAnn Hinz and the University of Wisconsin Centers Office of University Relations allowed us the possibility to perfect technical aspects of the document.

Rural women from the Andean Highlands to Sub-Saharan Africa and the Caribbean Islands to America's Dairyland have taught us much about women's lives and women's concerns. The personal and professional life of one of us was shaped by the model of three farm women - Ruth Taylor Gillespie, Estella Gillespie Awwiller, and Avanell Coriell Haney - and her professional insights were informed by the lives of Carol G. Thompson, Glenna G. St. Clair, and Barbara H. Baker whose off-farm work makes a difference on three part-time Ohio farms.

Surviving a four-year project required tolerance, understanding, and support of family members and co-workers. A special thanks to Emil and Tanya Haney and Richard, Katherine, and Jon Knowles as well as to colleagues at UW-Madison and the UW-Centers.

Finally, the joy of this project was working together and in collaboration with other scholars from a variety of disciplines on a mutually important set of research and policy issues.

W.G.H. and J.B.K.

INTRODUCTION:
MAKING "THE INVISIBLE FARMER" VISIBLE

Two decades of research on women's lives have made women's contributions to culture and society visible. In the United States, women continued to play a vital role in production even as their consumer role increased (Ryan 1975; Hartmann 1976; Tilly and Scott 1978; Weinbaum and Bridges 1979). In addition, they remained the guardians of the reproduction of social institutions even as they built the base for new institutions and for many of the movements that transformed established ones (Ryan 1975; Smith 1975-76; Wertheimer 1977).

Until recently, however, most of the historical work has focused on the urban experience. Consequently, it has stressed the development within the emerging commercial, industrial economy of separate domains for women and men, and the consequences of men's dominance in the public sphere and women's banishment to the realm of home and kin.

Despite the persistence of family-centered production units in the agricultural sector, early studies of the farm and farm family typically followed these urban-based models (Joyce and Leadley 1977). However, in the early 1980s when scholars began to look at the lives of farm women, it became clear that a different paradigm was needed. The new model would have to account for the way a production system based on household as well as corporate units framed women's lives and for the way the transformations underway in agriculture bound them.

Hence, the early theoretical work underscored the integration of the family farm system and the overlap in farm women's farm and family roles, together with the link between changes in the structure of agriculture and the market and nonmarket activities of women and men (Elbert 1981; Flora 1981; Haney 1983). Subsequent historical (Jensen 1981 and 1986; Sachs 1984; and Jones 1985) and contemporary (Rosenfeld 1985) studies have helped to sharpen and expand these perimeters. The essays in this collection synthesize and chart new theoretical paths while uncovering new dimensions of farm women's lives in the past and the present. Collectively, they expose us to the regional, racial, ethnic, religious, and social class diversity among farm women in the United States and briefly compare these experiences to those of their Third World sisters.

The anthology not only contributes to the development of a more accurate historical record but also demonstrates the potential for farm women's participa-tion in reshaping food and agricultural policy and rural community development strategies. Thus, while the volume is significant for scholars and students of agricultural history and contemporary rural society, its relevance is not limited to academicians. The essays are also important to farm women, farm families, and practitioners interested in farm economics, farm policy, and the rural commu-nity.

Historical studies of farm women are documenting women's contributions to America's agricultural, industrial and commercial development. They show clearly not only that farm women actively molded agricultural history, but also that their work shaped the industrial town and city (cf. Bender 1974). Hence, women's history would have us reconsider the relative contributions of our foremothers and forefathers to the entire process of nation-building. Feminist theory helps us understand why farm women's efforts were accorded little public value, despite their enormous contribution to the survival of family farm agriculture and the growth and development of rural institutions and communi-ties. In addition, the new research makes clear the saliency of policy concerns about farm women's control over traditional factors of agricultural production – land, other capital, and women's own labor.

The recent urban-oriented literature has identified occupational segregation and wage discrimination as key policy concerns. Women's access to employment in traditionally male occupations like the professions, management, and the trades, together with the elimination of a gender-based wage structure, has been the target of over a decade of debate that has resulted in some change. Since many farm families rely on the off-farm wages of women, policy changes origi-nating with the women's movement and the scholarship it has encouraged cer-tainly are important to farm women.

FARM WOMEN AND POLICYMAKING

The focus on women and farming at the Second National Conference on American Farm Women in Historical Perspective clarified women's relation to factors of agricultural production and refined our understanding of women's roles in farm families and rural communities. These essays, which began their lives as presentations at that conference, evoke a vivid awareness of the historical and cross-cultural continuity in rural women's problems.

The essays elucidate gender-based patterns that define women's options in agricultural production and rural community life as well as their opportunities to accomplish individual goals that may conflict with farm family goals. The es-says also describe the ways women have affected and continue to affect agricul-tural production, family farm survival, and rural institutions.

These essays, therefore, lay the groundwork for policy making in three ar-eas: (1) agricultural policies that recognize and support women's roles in farm-ing; (2) rural community development policies that take into account women's roles in community building; and (3) gender policies that give women more control over their lives.

Agricultural policy

Policy discussions of women and farming must begin with the issue of women's control over factors of production. That issue, in turn, begins with land. Jensen (1984, 1) summarized the American experience this way: "The study of women in agricultural development begins with the inescapable reality, that women have seldom had control over the land they have labored on." There were exceptions, but their numbers were quite small. Initially law, and then custom, restricted ownership and control of land by women. Although women inherited land upon the death of their parents and their spouses, law and custom prevented married women from holding land directly (and most rural women married). Therefore, when women did inherit land, brothers or husbands typically became the guardians of their sisters' and wives' landholdings, and sons frequently served in the same capacity for their widowed mothers. Even after women organized and gained the right for married women to hold title in their own name, men continued to control most of the agricultural land. As Jensen (1984, 3) concludes, "[this gave] a solid patriarchal base to agriculture in most regions for most of American history."

Even when women held formal title to land and other collateral, farmed, managed, and disposed of land – as more women evidently did beginning in the late nineteenth century – private or public lenders seldom granted them credit for the purchase of farmland on their own signatures. Thus, except for the Homestead Act permitting access to land by single women and widows, women had to depend upon spousal and intergenerational land transfer. These laws and customs emanating from the patriarchal structure served to create farm women's invisibility in the agricultural production record. That invisibility helped to perpetuate assumptions about women's contributions to farming that restricted land owning by women into the modern period. Without land as collateral, women were left out of the capitalization of American agriculture as well. Information in these essays undermines the assumption that only men were farmers. Therefore, this research should help to foster land and agricultural credit policies that accord the same treatment to farm women's and farm men's assets and to their management potential.

Systematic attention to women's relationship to land ownership and control also helps us understand the implications for women and for the agricultural unit of different types of land inheritance systems and of land ownership and control arrangements. Farm women and farm households may vary in their long-term interests and goals. Research on the consequences of various land arrangements can help us sort out the ways particular land systems confine or open alternatives for women and for the unit. For example, what are the relationships between equal inheritance patterns in intergenerational land transfer and the possibility for intergenerational farm continuity and expansion? What are the implications of family corporate models for women's control over land, labor, and capital and for equal inheritance patterns? The essays in this volume open the discussion on some of these emerging policy issues.

Until the 1930s, most American women lived in the countryside and provided labor that produced subsistence for their families and profitable returns on the landowner's investment. Within the context of the farm household, married and single women produced and processed agricultural goods for use by the farm family and for sale in local, regional, and sometimes national markets. Single women hired out for wages as domestic servants in the towns or on neighboring farms and, especially during harvests, as farm laborers. The wages of these farm women, and of those single farm women who populated the early industrial labor force and taught most of the rural school children, as well as the profits from the sale of farm women's products, were frequently invested in land owned by their fathers, husbands, or brothers. Women also provided a major component of the agricultural labor for the two other systems of labor control common in American history – tenancy and slavery. Both of these labor systems led to the ownership of large tracts of agricultural land by a few white men. Most of this labor has only recently been brought into the public record; early policies were based on the notion that agricultural work was male work. Therefore, public policies discriminated against farm women.

The federal estate tax is a prime example of such discriminatory policies. The patriarchal structure of land ownership and a public record kept only on the farm labor and management activities of men lent support to federal law that defined farmers as male. Even if the wife was formally a joint tenant with her husband, the entire estate was regarded as his. If the husband was the first to die, the entire estate was considered a gift to the wife and taxed accordingly. On the other hand, if the wife died first, her husband paid no federal estate tax. This "widow's tax," as Laura Lane of the *Farm Journal* named it, was successfully challenged by farm women activists who drew on the research documenting labor and management activities of farm women and thus the fallacy of the rationale supporting the tax (Lane 1984). This example is testimony to the value of scholarship in changing the lives of contemporary farm women.

Attention to farm women's farm labor has also helped change the approach to farmers by providers of private and public agricultural services. Farm service providers like agribusiness and the extension service have begun to define the agricultural production unit as including the farm household and thus have started to incorporate farm women into their promotional and educational programs in new ways. Farm women's new visibility in agriculture seems also to be a factor in the recent efforts to recruit women for technical and university agricultural programs and as agricultural service agents and technical advisors. These changes, in turn, seem to be encouraging more women to farm independently. Several essays in this anthology address the diversity of farm women's work, as well as the manifest and latent consequences for farm women's economic roles of agricultural policies, economic and technological trends, and normative prescriptions for men's and women's work.

As with land ownership, women were excluded from the political process first by law and then by custom. However, with the emergence of populist reform movements in the late nineteenth century, some farm women, like their urban counterparts, began to defy tradition. Farm women were active in early farm organizations – the Farmers' Alliance and later the Grange – and in third party movements, all of which grew out of financial crises in agriculture (Miller and Neth, Chapter 20, this volume; Wagner 1984; Starr 1984). In fact, women's presumed moral superiority, together with the casting of reform issues in moralistic tones, enabled women to carve out niches in these organizations and movements. Women used a great variety of communication forms – speeches, letters to newspaper and farm magazine editors, novels, songs, poems, and essays – to mobilize farmers and their supporters in towns and cities on the issue of farmers' discontent with farm economics and with macroeconomic policies such as unregulated credit, farm-to-market transport rates, coinage, and international trade.

By the beginning of the twentieth century, a second wave of rural protest developed. It split along two lines. One movement by large prosperous farmers focused on making farming more scientific and more businesslike. Their goal was to increase farm income by coordinating producer organizations' efforts to promote and market products with government technical aid provided by the extension service to increase agricultural production. The second movement brought rural people, including many farmers, extension workers, and university faculty, together around the broader issue of the quality of rural life. Knowles (page 304, this volume) summarizes the involvement of farm women in these two movements: "While it is too simplistic to think of these diverging streams of thought as representing 'masculine' vs. 'feminine' points of view, it is unmistakably the case that women's concerns about the quality of farm life only found significant expression in the second, newer sort of agricultural protest." In speeches, essays, letters, and especially through a new innovation of social science, the survey, farm women raised their voices to protest conditions within the farm family and in rural communities (Jones 1984; Knowles, Chapter 17, this volume).

Rural community development policy

Essays in this volume show a clear continuity in farm women's concerns. In the nineteenth and again in the twentieth century, the themes of farm women, individually and as members of movements and organizations, have been family welfare and farm economics. Thus, the essays point to the need to incorporate concern for women and the concerns of women into rural development policies as well as into the economic policies discussed earlier. Of particular importance to rural development professionals are the data showing women's traditional and emerging roles in rural community life. Through their informal community work in gender, family, and neighborhood networks, women have spun and woven the social fabric of rural community life and created a sense of sharing and mutuality (Neth, Chapter 19, this volume). But women have not only built the base of informal community life. Through their activities in formal women's organizations, they have been important in shaping the social and economic base of local rural institutions. However, community development has heretofore paid little attention to either of these processes. For this reason, development professionals have often missed issues of particular importance to rural women, rural families, and rural communities while operating in such a way as to stifle women's formal and informal leadership, and thus their contributions to rural economic and community development.

Gender related policy

Farm women have concentrated on farm women *qua* women only to a very limited degree. However, again, there seems to be a continuity in the concerns they have raised. And again, rural policymakers and practitioners can benefit from listening to women's stories. Two issues appear repeatedly in the letters of farm women preserved in historical archives and in the speeches of contemporary farm women. One is the need for the providers of agricultural services to recognize the multiple and overlapping roles of farm women – particularly their involvement in the farm enterprise and in the rural community. The other is a desire to be recognized as capable leaders by the male-dominated agricultural leadership and by policymakers and providers of agricultural and rural services.

By including essays that look beyond the experience of the United States, the book can help policymakers in advanced capitalist countries as well as in developing countries to better understand the differential impact of public policies on women and men. The essays show the negative, though perhaps unintended, impacts on women of government policies on concerns ranging from legal rights to property – and hence access to credit and capital formation – to expansion of cash cropping, use of capital-intensive agricultural technology, and the general growth of resource-extensive agriculture. By giving visibility to the enormous economic contribution of women to agricultural systems in every country of the world, the essays can help policymakers to see that the inclusion of women can combine equity and efficiency.

SCHOLARSHIP ON FARM WOMEN: NEW INSIGHTS, NEW QUESTIONS

While thus far we have emphasized the contributions this anthology can make to agricultural policy development and rural social change, we certainly feel it is equally germane to agricultural scholarship. Together, the essays advance the state of the art in at least six areas: (1) examination of continuity in farm women's work and flexibility in farm women's roles; (2) documentation of micro-level elements – farm, family, and individual social characteristics – that frame women's lives; (3) exploration of some of the areas of competition and conflict, as well as complementarity, in the needs and goals of the family farm, the farm family, and the farm woman; (4) documentation of macro-level elements – economic and agricultural policies and structural transformation in agriculture – that circumscribe farm women's lives; (5) exploration of farm women's attempts to alter public policy; and (6) comparison of the impact of changing roles and changing structures on women in agricultural systems in developed and developing countries.

Multiple roles of farm women

The integration and flexibility of farm women's roles, systematically detailed in several essays, are perhaps best illustrated by an upstate New York farm woman who, throwing up the lid of her washing machine, invited one social scientist "to sort out farm wash from home wash" (Elbert, Chapter 14, this volume). Or, by a Wisconsin dairy farm woman who said that while she was regularly responsible for certain daily and seasonal tasks on the farm, "much of my farm work is the result of filling in for my husband whose seed business and farm related meetings take him away – often at milking time, or for my son whose school activities interfere with the evening milking" (Haney and Wilkening 1984). Farm women's integration of farm and household work, as well as the ways they have augmented the income of their families, shows up in the historical and the contemporary data. For example, Elbert's research found that New York farm women urged Cornell University's first home economics extension program to teach them skills they could use at home to earn cash for farm family survival. The Harmon essay and the McCarthy, Salant, and Saupe essay document the range and extent of farm women's off-farm employment today, as well as its pertinence to farm viability.

A number of essays explain the distinct but overlapping aspects of farm women's work, detailing both their productive and reproductive roles. Productive roles discussed include non-wage agricultural production, self-employment in either the formal or informal market sectors, and wage or salary work off the farm. Farm women's reproductive roles analyzed in this volume include household production, human capital production, and volunteer community-building activities (cf. Cloud, Chapter 16, this volume for a discussion of all but one of these categories). Perhaps even more importantly, the essays begin to sort out the way region, race, ethnicity, religion, social class, and farming system shape the particular composite of women's economic roles and limit women's economic options. Moreover, consideration of farm women's economic roles is not confined to married women or women whose husbands also farm. The Rosenfeld and Tigges essay explores the characteristics and roles of independent women farmers interviewed as part of a recent national survey.

Farm women, farm and family

The collection also identifies the characteristics of the farm, the family, and the women themselves that influence farm women's options. Many of the essays treat specific cases. But because of the variety of situations analyzed in this volume (from sharecropping to tribal tenure arrangements, from patriarchial to more egalitarian family authority structures, from low-income black to middle-income white women, and from labor-intensive to resource-intensive production), the rich diversity as well as the vast sameness of farm women's lives is exposed.

The essays affirm previous research that identified farm characteristics like size and commodity as important to women's farm work. However, variables explored extensively in the developing country literature are treated more fully in these essays. For example, essays by Jones, Garkovich and Bokemeier, Flora, and Virginia Fink show that farm characteristics like tenure and management structure as well as type of technology and the degree of its use affect farm women's agricultural options and their work and family roles generally.

Family characteristics – particularly the content of family goals, family definitions of men's and women's roles, the nature of the family decision-making structure, and the stage in the family life cycle – are also consequential to women's options. As has been evident from previous research, individual characteristics like age and educational level influence women's options and their choices. However, analyses presented in this volume point to issues of race and social class as worthy of much greater attention by rural social scientists.

Conflict and complementarity within farm families

But the essays do more than simply identify factors that meaningfully influence the options of farm women. This scholarship begins to challenge the presumed harmony between farm and family goals and between farm and farm women's goals, the assumed complementarity in men's and women's roles, and the lack of competition between farm men and women for control of income and decision making. Since these scholars ask questions about possible areas of conflict and tension, their analyses begin to map out the conditions that give rise to contradictions and conflict within farm families and between the family and the firm, as well as those that lead to harmony and complementarity. The essay by Salamon and Davis-Brown is especially important to this discussion.

Farm women, agricultural policy and agricultural structure

Sorting out the relative influence of these endogenous factors yields a more complete understanding of the agricultural system and the role of farm women in the persistence of family farm agriculture. But there are also exogenous factors that affect the organization of agriculture, and thus women's options. On this question, Flora's essay shows us how macroeconomic and agricultural policies have played key roles in determining women's access to property rights, and thus credit and capital accumulation, as well as women's control over their labor. A number of other essays show how transformations in the structure of agriculture change women's relationship to the traditional factors of agricultural production – land, labor, and capital.

Women's role in policy making

Since the populist period of the late nineteenth century, farm women have been actively involved in public organizations focused on farm issues. However, scholars have heretofore done little to systematically document the role women played in the early farm organizations or in the rural populist movement. Several essays in this volume advance our understanding of the roles farm women have played in mobilizing farm and nonfarm support around particular agricultural issues and the diversity as well as consistency in farm women's policy positions.

Cross-cultural perspectives on farm women

An equally fruitful area for research is women's productive roles in agricultural systems around the world. The comparative approach of Cloud and Flora raises new questions about the nature of the structural transformation in U.S. agriculture in the late nineteenth and early twentieth century and the differential impact it may have had not only on farm women and farm men but also on farm women from different social classes, regions, and racial and ethnic groups. Just as importantly, historical and comparative explications inform the paradigms used to explore the present.

THE ORGANIZATION OF THE COLLECTION

The essays are organized around six themes: (1) the impact of social and economic change on farm women; (2) portraits of farm women's lives; (3) farm women's economic roles; (4) farm women and resource control; (5) farm women in historical and comparative perspective; and (6) farm women's community and political roles.

The three essays in Section I establish a historical record of black, Indian, and white women's struggles with major social and economic upheavals. The section begins with Jacqueline Jones's comparative treatment of the sharecropping system and its implications for poor black and white women's farm and family roles. Dolores Janiewski's case study of public and private efforts to transform the food production system, and thus the gender roles, of Native American peoples, and Deborah Fink's case study of Nebraskan farm families during the Depression show farm women's resilience, as well as the impact of social change on their roles. In addition, each essay gives us a different view of how ignorance of women's agricultural roles can often bring unintended and unanticipated results.

Section II gives us portraits of farm women's lives painted from their own words, as well as images created by writers and scholars who saw farm women as interesting and important figures. Through oral autobiographies of women from a New York dairy farm community, Nancy Grey Osterud captures farm women's sense of themselves, their relationship to the land, and the ways they integrated their farms, families, and community roles. Seena Kohl's and Julia Hornbostel's essays use historical writings and fiction, respectively, to explore the significance of class, race, and gender in the lives of farm women of the past.

While several essays in this volume consider the work of farm women briefly, those in Section III make it their central focus. Carolyn Sachs's theoretical treatment of farm women's work roles shows that they do not fit the urban-based model of separate spheres and therefore require a new theoretical approach. The two essays that follow Sachs's treat specific cases of women's on- and off-farm work. McCarthy, Salant, and Saupe analyze the determinants of Wisconsin farm women's off-farm employment, while Harmon's study develops profiles of multiple job-holding Kentucky farm women. Using data from the first national Farm Women Survey, Rachel Rosenfeld and Leann Tigges's essay bridges Section III and IV by focusing on the work of farm women who have greater control over production resources – independent farm women.

Technology and resource control are the central focus of the next three essays. Using case materials from two ethnoreligious communities in Illinois, Sonya Salamon and Karen Davis-Brown lead off Section IV with an essay that considers the very timely question of whether equitable patterns of farmland transfer are compatible with farm efficiency and intergenerational farm continuity. Lorraine Garkovich and Janet Bokemeier's essay then explores the way the mechanization of agriculture has shaped farm women's economic roles. The section closes with Virginia Fink's case study of how increased use of agricultural and household technology has affected the work of southeastern Ohio farm women.

The next section of the book puts the lives of U.S. farm women in comparative and historical perspective. Collectively, the essays of Elbert, Flora, and Cloud bring together the themes that have emerged in the scholarly study of farm women's economic roles, succinctly summarizing current knowledge and suggesting a new research agenda. Sarah Elbert's keynote address opens this integrative and contextual look at farm women in the United States. Through her own historical and contemporary work on farm women, Elbert discusses the theme of the conference – how the transformation of agricultural systems affect farm women's roles and how farm women can influence those transformations.

Flora's essay follows. Her analysis of the historical and comparative literature on the intersection of macro policy and women's roles treats the impact of agricultural policy on farm women. Flora's essay, together with that of Kathleen Cloud, pulls together comparative literature on women in agricultural production to show a convergence in factors found to influence women's participation in farming. The two essays provide some direction to the ongoing debate in rural historiography on whether agriculture development in America is a unique case or whether it shares common characteristics with other development experiences. While this debate is, in effect, backward looking to the comparative experiences of the United States and Europe, Cloud's essay both changes the focus to women and extends the debate to encompass the current experiences of Third World countries.

The anthology closes with an area of recent interest to both scholars and farm women – farm women's roles in the public life of rural communities. Section VI focuses in the first three essays on farm women's political and community roles historically. Jane Knowles's essay shows us that farm women's interest in agricultural policy is not new. Her analysis of survey materials collected by universities and governmental agencies at the turn of the century underscores the continuity in farm women's issues throughout the twentieth century. MaryJo Wagner's essay shows a different kind of continuity in farm women's lives – that between their private and public selves. In her case study of women and children in the Populist Party, she shows how farm women combined their family and community roles to politically socialize their children. The integrative theme in farm women's lives continues in Mary Neth's essay, that shows how farm women built the base of rural communities. Through their kin and friendship networks women organized the special events and celebrations of the community, built systems of sharing and exchange, and thus created the traditions, the meaning, and the sense of belonging necessary to and common in rural communities.

The final essay brings us the insights of farm women themselves. The experiences and views of Naioma Benson, Connee Canfield, Nancy Vogelsberg-Busch, and Denise O'Brien, each of whom participated in the opening panel at the conference, are quoted extensively in Lorna Clancy Miller and Mary Neth's essay on farm women's response to current agricultural policies and reasons for the emergence in the past decade of a variety of new farm organizations, including organizations of farm women. It seems appropriate that these four farm women who set the tone for three exhilarating days of debate, dialogue, and discussion at the conference by sharing their insights from their personal and public lives should get the last word in this volume dedicated to the twin values of un-fettered scholarship and democratic policy making.

Wava G. Haney, Jane B. Knowles
Madison, Wisconsin, January 1988

BIBLIOGRAPHY

Bender, Thomas. 1974. *Toward an Urban Vision: Ideas and Institutions in Nineteenth-Century America.* Lexington, Ky.: University of Kentucky Press.

Elbert, Sarah. 1981. "The Challenge of Research on Farm Women." *Rural Sociologist* 1 (Nov.): 387-90.

Flora, Cornelia Butler. 1981. "Farm Women, Farming Systems, and Agricultural Structure: Suggestions for Scholarship." *Rural Sociologist* 1 (Nov.): 383-86.

Haney, Wava G. 1983. "Farm Family and the Role of Women." In *Technology and Social Change in Rural Areas*, ed. Gene F. Summers, 179-93. Boulder, Colo: Westview Press.

Haney, Wava G., and Eugene A. Wilkening. 1984. "From Kerchiefs, Pails, and Cans to Plaid Collars, Record Books, and Farm Office: Technology, Policy, and Wisconsin Dairy Farm Women in the Twentieth Century." Paper presented at the American Farm Women in Historical Perspective Conference, at the New Mexico State University, Las Cruces, N. Mex., February 2-4.

Hartmann, Heidi. 1976. "Capitalism, Patriarchy, and Job-Segregation by Sex." *Signs* 1 (Spring): 137-69.

Jensen, Joan. 1984. "Women in Agricultural Development: Introduction." Department of History, New Mexico State University. Photocopy.

_____. 1986. *Loosening the Bonds: Mid-Atlantic Farm Women, 1750-1850.* New Haven, Conn: Yale University Press.

_____. ed. 1981. *With These Hands: Women Working on the Land.* New York: Feminist Press.

Jones, Jacqueline. 1985. *Labor of Love, Labor of Sorrow: Black Women, Work and the Family from Slavery to the Present.* New York: Basic Books.

Jones, Lu Ann. 1984. "The Pursuing Phantom of Debt: The Diary of Nannie Haskins Williams." Paper presented at the American Farm Women in Historical Perspective Conference, at the New Mexico State University, Las Cruces, N. Mex., February 2-4.

Joyce, Lynda M., and Samuel M. Leadley. 1977. "An Assessment of Research Needs of Women in the Rural United States: Literature Review and Annotated Bibliography." AE&RS 127. Pennsylvania State University, University Park. Mimeo.

Lane, Laura. 1984. "O Promise Me . . . But Put It In Writing." Paper presented at the American Farm Women in Historical Perspective Conference, at the New Mexico State University, Las Cruces, N. Mex., February 2-4.

Rosenfeld, Rachel Ann. 1985. *Farm Women: Work, Farm and Family in the U.S.* Chapel Hill, N.C.: University of North Carolina Press.

Ryan, Mary P. 1975. *Womanhood in America: From Colonial Times to the Present.* New York: New Viewpoints.

Sachs, Carolyn. 1984. *The Invisible Farmers: Women in Agricultural Production.* Totowa, N.J.: Rowman & Allanheld.

Smith, Dorothy. 1975-76. "Women, the Family and Corporate Capitalism." *Berkeley Journal of Sociology* 20: 55-90.

Starr, Karen. 1984. "Farm Women in the Nonpartisan League." Paper presented at the American Farm Women in Historical Perspective Conference, at the New Mexico State University, Las Cruces, N. Mex., February 2-4.

Tilly, Louise A., and Joan W. Scott. 1978. *Women, Work and Family.* New York: Holt, Rinehart Winston.

Weinbaum, Batya, and Amy Bridges. 1979. "The Other Side of the Paycheck: Monopoly Capital and the Structure of Consumption." In *Capitalist Patriarchy and the Case for Socialist Feminism*, ed. Zillah R. Eisenstein, 190-205. New York: Monthly Review Press.

Wagner, MaryJo. 1984. "A Question of Party Allegiance: The Political Ideology of Women Populists." Paper presented at the American Farm Women in Historical Perspective Conference, at the New Mexico State University, Las Cruces, N. Mex., February 2-4.

Wertheimer, Barbara Mayer. 1977. *We Were There: The Story of Working Women in America.* New York: Pantheon Books.

THE IMPACT OF SOCIAL
AND ECONOMIC CHANGE
ON FARM WOMEN

1

"TORE UP AND A-MOVIN'": PERSPECTIVES ON THE WORK OF BLACK AND POOR WHITE WOMEN IN THE RURAL SOUTH, 1865-1940

Jacqueline Jones

Sarah Easton, an eastern North Carolina tenant farm wife, had spent her long life working "early and late." Still, she noted in the late 1930s, "we ain't never had nothing and we won't never have nothing." Echoed Gracie Turner, a member of another North Carolina tenant household, "It's been nothin' but hard work . . . , and de boss man gettin' it all." Such was the common plight of tenant women in the South: their unremitting toil yielded only life-long poverty and life-long ironies. Sarah Easton and Gracie Turner had planted, chopped, and picked their share of cotton over the years, but they had both stopped going to church because they had no cotton dress "fittin' to wear." Although they labored within an agricultural economy, they and their families often went "without half enough to eat."[1]

Interviewed separately by different Federal Writers Project (FWP) workers, the two women nevertheless articulated strikingly similar themes related to their house and field responsibilities, standard of living, and family life. Each day they performed the constant and repetitive tasks that were the chief lot of poor women throughout the region: cooking, cleaning, and nurturing of household members without the benefit of cash or conveniences. (Gracie tended a garden and managed to make twelve dollars "do all it will" for eight people each month.) During the busy season they toiled alongside their children in the tobacco or cotton crop as directed by their husbands, and considered themselves fortunate if they were not "rush[ed] . . . to the field" after childbirth. Their families perpetually in debt to one landlord or another, they barely had time to hang threadbare curtains in a dilapidated cabin before they were once again "tore up and a-movin.'"[2]

Economic deprivation and insecurity profoundly influenced family relationships. Gracie Turner and Sarah Easton understood all too well the toll exacted from their menfolk by this bitter, rootless life. Sarah's husband would "raise hell" and abuse her and their six children whenever he drank. One of Gracie's daughters had also "married a drinkin' man" who "scrapped so bad she couldn't stay wid him." Still, both of these women expressed a firm commitment to the integrity of family life. They were illiterate ("all I learnt was to work in de field," noted Gracie), yet they had definite ideas about their children's

15

education, both formal and informal. "I's tried to raise my chil'en to be trusty and mannerable, to mind dey mama and papa, to be honest," said Gracie of her nine offspring. Remarked Sarah, "I wanted them to be educated, kind, polite, and humblesome. . . . I'm just sorry we couldn't give them a better start."[3]

These two housewives occupied a similar position within the southern staple-crop economy, and fulfilled similar kinds of obligations as farm women on a daily and seasonal basis. But Sarah Easton was white, and Gracie Turner was black. This simple fact poses problems for the historian, for an analysis of southern society on the basis of gender challenges the conventional means of defining social order in that region. Indeed, attention to women's experiences *qua* women can reveal the relative value of the concepts of class, caste, and race in illuminating relationships among Southerners.[4]

The purpose of this essay is to examine the work of black and poor white women who lived in the tobacco and cotton-growing regions of the South between 1865 and 1940. This includes the wives of tenants (sharecroppers and share tenants); wage laborers; cash renters; and the owners of small, "one-mule" farms, many of whom cultivated "land so doggone thin . . . 'it won't sprout unknown peas.'"[5] Similarities in the rhythm of their everyday lives, and in their lowly material condition, suggest that poor women of both races were members of the same economic group within southern society. However, this collective portrait, with its emphasis on class status as it affected gender roles, provides only a narrow and incomplete analysis of women's work – work which must be examined as part of a larger historical process. Indeed, careful examination of this process reveals quite clearly the divergent political meanings embedded in the daily labor of black women as opposed to their white neighbors. Stated simply, persistent attacks on black families – attacks that were by turns subtle and violent, initiated by individuals and by groups – heightened the political significance of black wives' and mothers' domestic obligations, carried out in the house and in the field.

A systematic exploration of these issues may enable us to move beyond one-dimensional approaches to southern history, and understand more clearly the interweaving of racial, sexual, class, and cultural factors in southern society. In sum, the recounting of poor women's experiences in the rural South from the Civil War to World War II consists of several different stories. One story focuses on their membership in households of a single economic class, and stresses the lot shared by black and white women and men. A second story emphasizes the obligations common to wives and mothers of the two races. And a final story explores the historical significance of the labor of black women within their own communities. We need to explore each of these stories in turn.

A CLASS PERSPECTIVE

Black and poor white women in the postbellum South belonged to the same class in the sense that their households were financially dependent on landowners, creditors, and merchants; and were nonlandowning in an economy based on large-scale crop production. Together these families of field workers provided the unskilled labor needed to fuel the technologically backward southern agricultural system, and together they shouldered the burdens caused by the collapse of that system in the 1930s.

Sharecropping – the most common form of tenancy in the South – did not emerge as a system of agricultural production until the late 1860s. An "almost unprecedented" form of family enterprise, it effected a "compromise" of sorts between, on the one hand, labor-hungry planters and, on the other, freed people who sought to weld work and family relationships into a unit of economic welfare. In addition, white up-country yeomen farmers were gradually drawn away from livestock and food production and into the commercial economy after the Civil War. In the process they lost their economic independence to a burgeoning system of financial credit.[6]

Thus, between 1865 and 1940, virtually all rural black women belonged to families which just barely subsisted within the South's commercial agricultural economy, while the number of white women in a similar position rose at a steady rate. The proportion of white farmers who worked someone else's land increased gradually after the Civil War, from no more than 20 percent in the 1850s to 63 percent in the mid-1930s. By that time a majority of tenant families in the Cotton Belt were white (1 million) and the rest (700,000) were black, accounting for about 9 million Southerners altogether. Regardless of race, these tenants found themselves trapped in a state of near peonage; they could move around within the plantation economy, but they could not escape from it. As one woman put it, "We seem to move around in circles like the mule that pulls the syrup mill. We are never still, but we never get anywhere."[7] Beholden to a landlord for equipment, supplies, clothing, housing, and often even food, sharecroppers ended each year relieved if they were free from debt and able to push on to another plantation that offered change, if not always brighter possibilities. Booker T. Washington told the story of the sharecropping household whose chickens "regularly presented themselves in the dooryard at Christmastime with their legs crossed for tying up before the next moving."[8]

A statistical analysis of household structure in twenty-seven cotton-belt counties for the years 1870, 1880, and 1900 indicates that local and regional economic forces had a profound impact on the way all poor black and white people organized their family lives. Households of the two racial groups exhibited similar characteristics in terms of the prevalence of two-parent families, the sex of the household head, the wife's age relative to her husband's, fertility rates, and the proximity of kin with the same surname. In sum, the South's peculiar land tenure system affected the ages at which these poor men and women married, the number of children they "chose" to bear, and their inclination to remain within kin clusters in a particular locale.[9]

And finally, during the Great Depression, the contraction of credit resources, combined with natural disasters and New Deal agricultural policies that hastened the displacement of rural tenants, led to a mass exodus of black and white farmers from the land, some into nearby towns and northern cities, and others to Far West valleys owned by vegetable and fruit growers. Southern landlords had few incentives to "furnish" families, especially those with large numbers of children, once the federal government encouraged them to reduce crop production. The stock market crash initiated a series of chain reactions (as revealed by the tenant mother who could not clothe her children, once fertilizer prices increased and burlap bags were harder to come by)[10] and the color of one's skin afforded little protection from larger economic transformations.

It is clear, then, that the concept of class helps us to locate sharecroppers of both races within the regional economy. After the Civil War, freed people and poor whites travelled different historical paths that intersected at the point of rural poverty and dependency. Black households struggled to achieve the true freedom that had been denied them for so long, while white households slipped from self-sufficiency into the quagmire of debt. Consequently black and white women shared certain liabilities as the South embarked on a "Prussian road" of economic development characterized by coercive and authoritarian labor arrangements.[11] Indeed, a class perspective seems to reinforce the notion that women of the two races had much in common.

A GENDER PERSPECTIVE

Yet we can refine our analysis if we focus on the concept of gender, and view tenant wives and mothers as a subgroup within this larger class of rural households, juxtaposing their labor patterns with those of their menfolk. In the process we will find that rural women possessed a distinctive set of obligations and a distinctive form of powerlessness compared to their husbands. Men of both races participated in the larger commercial economy and dominated positions of authority within local social and religious institutions.[12] And yet, although white male tenants followed the same work routine as black male farmers down the road, it is more difficult to consider these men together (in contrast to their wives) as a group, because white men took part in the South's *Herrenvolk* democracy from which rural black men (as well as women of both races) were excluded.

Of Alabama cotton tenants James Agee wrote: "The woman is the servant of the day, and of immediate life, and the man is the servant of the year, and of the basis and boundaries of life and is their ruler; and the children are the servants of their parents. . . ." Demands of the staple-crop economy, together with traditional assumptions regarding the role of women, produced a sexual division of labor characteristic of poor rural households throughout the South. Tenant farm wives of both races formed an identifiable social category by virtue of their status as producers of marketable goods and domestic services. Their experiences were marked by a high degree of historical continuity in terms of the labor they did and the way in which they did it.[13]

When the University of North Carolina sociologist Margaret J. Hagood noted in 1939 that tenant farm women produced ("at a ruinous cost to both the land and themselves") the South's cotton, tobacco, and children, she highlighted what feminist scholars term women's productive and reproductive functions. These wives performed a "double duty, a man's share in the field and a woman's part at home."[14] Their husbands, on the other hand (like men in most other times and cultures), only rarely accepted responsibility for child care or other domestic tasks. The household sexual division of labor revealed the complementary nature of each spouse's contribution to the family's welfare, yet it also institutionalized male supremacy inside and outside the home.

Wives identified with the class and racial interests of their husbands, but women of both races contended with male domination on the public, political and private, domestic levels. One young wife, "tired enough to die" as she tried to balance the nursing of a baby with stringing tobacco and cooking meals, told an FWP interviewer that "if he [her husband] wants to beat me or the children, he does, and that's all there is to it. He ain't got no mercy on nothing but mules and dogs." These women "never had no noon" (the midday rest period enjoyed by their husbands and children), yet formal authority in their households resided in an able-bodied male, if not the husband then an eldest son. Rural husbands and wives were "equal" in the sense that they had equally little in the way of material possessions. But men maintained control over the productive energies of household members, disciplined their wives and offspring, and at times prevented women from exercising their legal rights. Sarah Easton described her relationship with her husband this way: "I ain't never voted, but John's a Democrat. He ain't never let me vote but he thinks it's a woman's place to cut wood and stay all night in a mean neighborhood by herself." She thus pinpointed the discrepancy between the physical labor she performed and her relative lack of decision-making power at home and within the larger political process.[15]

Despite the rapid development of a national industrial economy, the work of rural southern black and white women did not change dramatically over the years. In urban areas, and in the more prosperous agricultural regions of the Northeast and Midwest, technological innovations had revolutionized the roles of middle-class homemakers and female wage earners by the 1930s, but tenant farm wives of the Great Depression lived lives similar to those of their grandmothers in the 1880s. This continuity had both a material and a cultural base. The sharecropper's cabin remained a permanent fixture on the southern landscape, and the succession of families who inhabited it continued to organize themselves and their work in a manner that defied the passage of time.[16]

The division of labor within these households was determined first by gender and second by age. The husband represented family interests outside the home and conducted transactions with the appropriate authorities. It was he who ventured to the "Big House" or the local country store to offer his household's services to a landlord for the coming year and to negotiate terms of a labor contract regarding land use, supplies, form of payment, and the leasing or borrowing of mules and horses. The father bought food staples during periodic visits to town and pocketed the small amount of cash earned by youngsters who had been "hired out" to work on nearby farms. In December he settled the family's financial affairs, a process which usually amounted to little more than certifying the landlord's account of his debts. In her sensitive study of white tenant farmers' wives in the Virginia and North Carolina Piedmont, Hagood found it be "almost univeral" practice that "the wife doesn't 'tote the pocketbook' and neither she nor her husband thinks it right for a woman to do so." This "absolute control of

money matters by the husband" was at times a prerogative more symbolic than
real, for many sharecroppers had very little cash to manage at all.[17]

However, the father did exercise meaningful authority when he orchestrated
the participation of household members in the several stages of tobacco or cotton
cultivation. Wives and children were "put to work" in the field at various times
of the year on the general assumption that the crop – the mainstay of the family's existence – took precedence over other kinds of work. The wives of black
Alabama sharecropper Hayes Shaw (he married three times) were hired out or
sent to the fields like children, while he spent his days in a characteristically
masculine fashion – alone, away from the farm, hunting. According to Shaw's
son Nate, his "daddy'd have his gun on his shoulder and be off on Sitimachas
Creek swamps, huntin," after commanding his wife to "Take that plow! Hoe!"
For the rest of his life Nate remembered with bitterness that his stepmother, who
had borne his father thirteen children, "put part of a day's work in the field" before she died one night.[18]

Several decades after this incident an FWP interviewer recorded a scene between white North Carolina tobacco farmer Ransome Carson and his wife
Frances. She was stringing tobacco with other women when her husband walked
into the barn and "white-faced, she shrunk back. 'If you don't git a move on I'll
git a "backer stick,"' he muttered,holding her tightly by the collar. Her eyes di-
lated and her lips quivered. Then he let go of her and walked hurriedly back towards the field. Frances said nothing but rushed more and more. . . ."[19] No
doubt Hayes Shaw and Ransome Carson were extreme examples of husbands determined to keep their wives hard at work. Still, it was the responsibility of all
household heads to see that crops were planted, hoed, and harvested on time; for
men who had so little control over other areas of their lives, family-farm management provided opportunities to exercise a limited form of personal power.

The type and extent of field work performed by women depended on their
age, the size and composition of the household, and the quality of land they
farmed. (One approving white husband noted that his wife was "hard-workin',
willin' to do anything that come to hand, in the house or in the field.") After the
Civil War, freedwoman Lettice Boyer and her husband scraped together enough
money to buy a small plot of land in North Carolina. She recalled, "It was hard
to make a livin', for de land was pore, but we scuffled along and got th'ugh
somehow." She continued, "Hard work? Lord, honey, I's done some hard work!
Don't ask me what I *has* done, but what I *ain't*. I's plowed, dug stumps,
chopped, broke steers, ginned cotton. . . ." Later, as a widow, she "tended to de
farm de best I could, plowed my co'n and cotton, and lived by myself part o' de
time." Her nephew helped her when she "gin to git old." Lettice Boyer spent her
last days in the household of her granddaughter's husband. At the age of 110 she
no longer worked in the field but she could still contribute to the family's welfare by sweeping the yard and washing and mending clothes.[20]

A woman's physical strength and expertise in the field served as a source of
pride and self-respect. On the Sea Islands in the early twentieth century, elderly
Aunt Adelaide introduced herself to a neighborhood school teacher this way: "I
ben strong ooman, I work fo' meself wid me han'. I ben ma[r]sh-cuttin' ooman.

I go in de ma[r]sh and cut an carry fo' myself." Hagood found that the white women she studied boasted of their "ability to work like a man," whether that meant plowing furrows, chopping wood, or grading tobacco.[21]

For many women the most difficult task was not picking cotton or worming tobacco plants, but combining this kind of labor with child-rearing. Because they had an average of six to eight children each (families of fifteen were not unheard-of among members of either race), chances were good that childbirth would sooner or later coincide with a hectic season of field work. In 1918, a Children's Bureau report noted that, "to some extent, the amount of rest a mother can have before and after confinement is determined by the time of year or by the stage of the cotton crop upon which depends the livelihood of the family." The birth of a child represented the promise of better times in terms of augmenting the household's labor supply, but for the time being it increased the workload of the other family members.[22]

When all the children were old enough to help out in the field, the family had achieved its peak productive capacity, and if there were a sufficient number of hands the mother would let "the house take her" (that is, devote full time to domestic chores). Until that time, a woman had to make some provision for the care of her youngest offspring while she worked on the crop. She might take an infant to the field with her, or leave it at home alone or under the care of an older sibling. All three of these solutions presented potential hazards. Some women managed to hoe and keep an eye on a baby at the same time. But others – like the South Carolina mother who laid her child to sleep on a nearby fence rail, only to return and discover "a great snake crawling over" him – found it difficult to divide their attention between the two tasks. Left to their own devices in the backyard, children would eat anything they could get their hands on, including, according to the first-hand observations of one mother, "sand, chicken manure, and strings." Baby-sitters who were little more than babies themselves posed additional dangers. When she was growing up in Mississippi, Anne Moody's little cousin set the cabin ablaze while he was supposed to be "minding" her and her sister.[23]

Regardless of her duties in the field, a farm wife's domestic obligations remained constant throughout the year. As Hagood noted, "Farm work varies with the seasons from almost full time to none at all, the burden of childbearing and caring shifts with time, but housekeeping – cooking, cleaning, washing, serving – goes on forever." To appreciate the arduousness of this labor it is necessary to examine the physical conditions that either aided or impeded the work process. The basic outline of chores changed little over the generations, but even more striking was the continuity in methods and equipment. Not until the late 1930s did southern tenant households benefit from electricity and even those could not afford modern appliances like vacuum cleaners, electric irons, refrigerators, and freezers readily available to middle-class cityfolk. Descriptions of sharecroppers' cabins provided by New Deal relief agents show that most did not have running water or indoor sanitary facilities. When tenants of both races lived on the same plantation, whites were inevitably assigned relatively better housing. Still, that did not necessarily mean that they always enjoyed a higher standard of living;

high annual rates of geographical mobility among sharecroppers in general meant that many cabins were never reserved exclusively for households of one color or the other. In his study of black and white sharecroppers in the Georgia cotton belt, Arthur Raper reported that "the dwellings occupied by whites make little better showing than those occupied by Negroes."[24]

Obviously, the completion of certain "homemaking" chores depended as much upon a woman's available time and equipment as upon her inclination for such work. For example, doing the laundry and preparing meals were carried out with limited resources. Whether women scrubbed clothes in the nearby creek, in a large kettle over a roaring fire, or in a metal tub with a scrub board, clothes washing was an arduous task that involved soaking, sudsing, scrubbing, rinsing, and eventually pressing with a heavy iron. Cooking equipment improved somewhat over the years – from the simple hearth of the freedman's cabin to the large wood cookstove of the twentieth century – but the basic diet of most sharecroppers did not. Women of both races continued to make biscuits or cornbread and to fry saltpork or sowbelly in lard. A mother usually rose before the rest of the family to make breakfast and if she worked in the field that day she hurried home an hour before the rest of her family to prepare the midday meal. Toting water and carrying firewood were among the worst forms of domestic drudgery.[25]

To offset the protein deficiencies in a diet of meal, meat, and molasses, some farm women assumed livestock and gardening responsibilities. Milking the cow, gathering eggs, and tending a vegetable patch were considered "women's work" among blacks and whites. (However, some landlords made it a condition of employment that their tenants not divert their energies from the cotton fields. According to Mary Matthews, "'Bout all I could raise widout creatin' a fuss was my flowers.'") In this way wives could supplement the family diet and earn a little money if they produced enough eggs, milk, sweet potatoes, and collards to sell. For some families, the mother's "patch money" provided the only cash for emergencies like burial expenses and for necessary, regular expenses like food staples and clothing.[26]

Depression conditions (characteristic of the South's overall economy from the early 1920s until World War II) only intensified the need for many women, married and unmarried, black and white, to supplement the family income. Black female household heads near Macon, Georgia, grew vegetables and caught fish which they then bartered for used clothing. They also took in boarders, did odd jobs, and shared stoves and wash buckets with each other. At times white women too would have to "go to the neighbors' house and wash for them for a piece of meat."[27]

A survey conducted by the Federal Emergency Relief Administration in 1934 revealed that about one-fifth of the Alabama black and white tenant families investigated received cash contributions from some source other than crop profits, most often from the wife's labors. Although modest in terms of financial reward, these activities were significant for several reasons. They yielded modest amounts of cash for families that relied chiefly on credit. Mothers could grow vegetables or produce goods at home and keep an eye on their children at the same time. Moreover, dairying and gardening provided women with an opportunity to engage in commercial exchange on a limited basis and in the process gain a measure of self-esteem through the shrewd use of trading skills. This form of work contrasted with their husbands' responsibilities for crop production, which included monthly and annual dealings with landlord-merchants. Men's income-producing activities took place within the regional staple-crop market, while women worked exclusively within the household and a localized foodstuff and domestic-service economy.[28]

Thus the tenant woman's "sphere" included not only the house but also the area immediately surrounding it. The tendency of sharecroppers annually to exchange one rundown cabin for another added yet another dimension to women's work. For example, when tenant families in Georgia's Black Belt moved at the end of the year, a mother "puts up new clothes lines and clears the path to the spring or well and chops the weeds from the back door." More generally, farmers' wives had little in the way of time, money, or incentives to make permanent improvements in or around a cabin the family did not own and hoped to leave within a few months anyway. One Alabama rural housewife summed up her frustration by noting, "I have done dug holes in de ya[r]d by moonlight mo' dan o[n]ce so dat whah I stay at might hab a rose-bush, but I nebber could be sho' whose ya[r]d it would be de nex' year." Nevertheless, many women remained sensitive to their domestic environment; if they could not always find time to clean up the mud tracked in from outside, black women still rearranged the house "very nice to meet the great Easter morning," white-washed it for a Christmas celebration, dug up flowers in the woods to plant in the yard, or attached brightly colored pictures to the inside walls. Margaret Hagood admired one white woman's "ingenuity with flour sacks," hand-embroidered to make attractive curtains.[29]

Most homemaking chores were repetitive and tedious but discrete tasks. Child care was a different matter. It began with the arrival of the first baby and ended only when the youngest left home – often, many years later. During that period, which typically spanned thirty-five or forty years for tenant farm wives, the nurturing of children could never be confined to one time of day, nor could it ever be far from a mother's mind. Recent demographic studies indicate that the crucial factor influencing high rates of fertility among these women was their rural environment, not their race. Few "mothers of the South" had knowledge of or access to artificial means of birth control. Those who relied on folk remedy abortifacients were often sadly disappointed, although Sarah Easton claimed that she once drank the cotton root tea prescribed by an "old granny" with the desired results. By the third decade of the twentieth century, some poor women in that region of the country were still marrying at age fifteen and having twelve children before they were thirty-six or sixteen before age forty.[30]

If, as the old saying went, "children is shore nuff riches," sharecropping families were wealthy indeed.[31] Although it is difficult to document the attitudes of nineteenth-century tenant wives toward childbearing, black and white women interviewed in the 1930s spoke eloquently about their offspring as their main source of both sorrow and joy. The experience of motherhood transcended racial differences, and it seems reasonable to assume that their perceptions resembled

those of earlier generations. These women frequently made the distinction between their love for their children already born and their dread of having any more
in the future. For example, Mary Matthews had so many children (fifteen) she
hardly knew how she found "enough names to go round 'mongst" them. She
observed, "I never had a child or a grandchild I felt I could do widout," but added,
"Course sometimes 'for dey got here I felt like I didn't want to own no more,
but when dey come dey was welcome. I ain't never had nary one I was willin' to
spare." Hagood found a similar attitude among the white tenant wives she visited; "There is pride in having borne the number they have, yet almost never is
there expressed a desire for more."[32]

The sociologist marveled that these women approached this most difficult of
tasks "with unbelievable calm and unconcern." She speculated that, the poorer
the family, the more prized large numbers of children because in such cases "they
represent about all a man and his wife can call their very own." The value of
children transcended their economic potential as field workers, or even the "great
help and comfort" they provided their mothers; to raise a family "right" gave a
woman the sense of competence and accomplishment that material aspects of her
life could not. "'Eleven, I done my share, didn't I?'" Hagood quoted one woman
as saying, and noted that this mother's "words and intonation" revealed the "ever-
present suggestion of self-esteem."[33]

A RACIAL-CULTURAL PERSPECTIVE

Thus far we have concentrated on those class and gender considerations that
seem to unify the experiences of black and poor white women in the rural South
– experiences shaped by the structure of the southern economy as well as by the
demands of everyday life. Yet such an analysis is at best partial, for the weight
of historical evidence tells us that southern blacks had a very different history
compared to whites, no matter how poor or downtrodden. This simple fact masks
a complex reality, one that we may profitably explore by examining first, the
peculiar legal and political liabilities imposed upon black women and men by
the racial caste system, and second, the significance of Afro-American culture as
both a product of prejudice and a means of resisting it. Here it is necessary to
keep in mind that, as Barbara J. Fields has suggested, the category of race derives
not from skin color or physiology, but from ideology; race is, therefore, a form
of social classification, determined by the peculiar exigencies of a certain time
and place.[34] Consequently, the distinction between "racial" and "cultural" influences on the lives of southern women is somewhat problematic.

If black and poor white women shared a great deal in terms of physical deprivation, backbreaking work, and constant childbearing, there is little evidence
that they were conscious of these similar patterns of womanhood. Victims of
history and circumstance, they remained in separate worlds, living parallel lives
that rarely intersected. Certainly black women as a group shouldered heavier burdens than did their white counterparts. Black women had higher rates of illiteracy
and worked as wage earners to a greater extent compared to poor white women in
the rural South during this period. Furthermore, the work of black and whte

women took place within radically different cultural contexts. For while family life defined the obligations of all poor rural women, its social importance differed for women of the two races, despite similarities in the routine of their daily chores or the demographic structure of their households. In essence, the climate of racism and violence that permeated the South invested black women's simple acts of nurturance with political and economic significance; as wives and mothers, they defied conventional (white) notions about the proper role of black women in southern society, and sought to preserve families continually under siege.[35]

Despite their common sorrows and joys, obligations and routines, blacks and whites failed to acknowledge these bonds of womanhood, for women of the two races rarely talked to one another. They co-existed but did not live together or even consider themselves neighbors. Unlike rural women in most other places and times, they lacked ties sustained by gossip, kinship, and mutual solace. Travelling along the back roads of Virginia and North Carolina in the 1930s, Margaret Hagood learned that when she asked a white person for directions, a reply of "'third house on the left' meant the third'white' house." One woman, a lifelong area resident, insisted that Hagood was mistaken in believing that there was a school in the neighborhood. "When the location was carefully specified, she [the woman] laughed and said, 'Oh, that's a nigger school – I knew there wasn't any school on that road.'" The rapidly deteriorating economic condition of landless whites, combined with historic animosities between poor people of the two races, exacerbated racial prejudice and rendered black folk nearly invisible to the whites who lived nearby.[36]

Men and well-to-do white women had more opportunities for interracial contact than did poor white and black women. Husbands and fathers of both races and all classes observed the ritualized etiquette of southern race relations in the public arena – hunting, or in town, at the post office, court house, or supply store.[37] Their wives were largely excluded from these encounters. Middle-class white women acted out their own presumptions of racial superiority in their dealings with black servants and laundresses. Tenant farm wives of course could not afford to employ black women for any length of time or exploit them in a direct way. A few women of the two races did come together in situations that held the promise of enhancing mutual respect and appreciation – for example, when they participated in the Southern Farmers Alliance (in the 1880s and 1890s) or the Southern Tenant Farmers' Union (1930s), or when black "grannies" attended white women during childbirth. Yet these opportunities were rare, and probably only a few women derived from them an awareness of shared oppression across racial lines.[38] Therefore we must question whether without this collective consciousness black and poor white housewives together constituted a "class" at all.

Although both groups of women adhered to the values of a rural Southern folk culture, the roots and branches of that culture intertwined at some points and diverged at many others. For example, black and white women often professed a devotion to fundamentalist Christianity, yet the Afro-American church offered its people a distinctive message of redemption through a fervently held faith in ultimate, divine justice, while white denominations and sects were built upon the rock of personal guilt provoked by original sin. To cite another example, tenant wives of both races were steeped in a pre-modern folklore that sought to explain the inexplicable workings of nature, but it is unlikely that black and white women in the same area at the same time agreed on the medicinal qualities of catnip tea, the significance of a female visitor on the sixth of February, or the prenatal habits that would harm an unborn child.[39]

We might take this discussion one step further and suggest that Afro-American culture combined elements of tradition and belief that were intended to combat the menace posed by whites and at the same time to preserve the integrity of black community life. Thus a black nationalist perspective would emphasize the component of political resistance (against whites) embedded in the Afro-American belief system. This was not simply a case of whites and blacks following two different, say, musical, culinary, or religious traditions, but rather a case of the subordinate group self-consciously shoring up its resources in the face of persistent assaults on its dignity and physical well-being. According to the folklorist and civil rights activist Bernice Johnson Reagon, black women played a vital part in this process:

> The problem of our people then was to turn around this dying recipe of slavery so that there would be a Black people. To take on that job is to be a nationalist, to be about the formation and continuance and survival of a nation. Black women as mothers have been the heart of that battle.
> We are, at the base of our identities, nationalists. We are people builders, carriers of cultural traditions, key to the formation and continuance of culture. We are the ones who touch the children first and most consistently.[40]

No doubt poverty helped to foster communalism and group solidarity among southern blacks; individualism was a luxury they just could not afford. Yet that "ethos of mutuality"[41] implicitly carried within it a political, as well as economic, purpose.

Family life affords a particularly vivid example of the ways in which black and white women's seemingly identical responsibilities could take place within strikingly different contexts. Although poor rural households of both races demonstrated similar patterns of organization and configuration, they derived their distinctive social meanings from history and from the political realities of the postbellum South. For instance, black mothers inculcated certain values in their children that prepared them for life in their own community as well as in the hostile white society. They taught their children to "put a handle" to white persons' names, and "never to lie except to white people."[42]

But even more significant were the larger social ramifications of black women's family duties, for they labored on behalf of households under siege; as wives and mothers they defied New South neo-slaveholders who believed that all black people should be submissive agricultural laborers first and family members only incidentally. North Carolina Governor James S. Jarvis stated the matter succinctly in 1883 when he told a group of black citizens: "Your work is the tilling of the ground. . . . Address yourselves to the work, men and women alike."[43]

The function of black family life as a means of resistance against racism reflected the legacy of slavery on the one hand and contemporary necessity on the other. The sexual division of labor within black households diverted the energies of women from the staple crop economy (that is, work that profited white men) to the family domestic economy (that is, work on behalf of their own families). Whites terrorized black wives and mothers in an effort to extract as much labor as possible from the adult female population. Thus violence against black women revealed that the economic interests of whites and black people's commitment to family continued to be competing, mutually exclusive priorities, just as they were under slavery. American history gave new meaning to black women's response to the age-old imperatives of human sustenance.

Slave women had fulfilled community obligations and in the process challenged the slaveholders' ideology that decreed that they should labor only as "human hoeing machines" or as reproducers of the captive work force.[44] The persistent, widespread physical abuse of black women under slavery represented a direct attack on family life, as did the forcible separation of parents from children and husbands from wives. During the post-emancipation period the form of these attacks changed, but not their purpose. In the mid to late 1860s, coupled with white planters' complaints about the inefficiency of free black (wage) labor, came reports from all over the South that freedwomen had "retired from the field." The withdrawal of black females from field work – a major theme in both contemporary and secondary accounts of the Reconstruction – occurred primarily among the wives and daughters of able-bodied men. Women who served as the sole support of their families had to take work wherever they could find it. White landowners made little effort to hide their contempt for these women who, as they put it, "played the lady" and refused to join gangs of workers in the field. In their haste to declare free labor a success, even northern Freedmen's Bureau agents and foreign visitors to the South ridiculed "lazy" freedwomen who labored within the confines of their own homes. Attending to the needs of their families, these women exemplified the "evil of female loaferism" which had such a dramatic effect on post-bellum crop production.[45]

An Alabama planter suggested in 1868 that it was "a matter of pride with the men, to allow all exemption from labor to their wives." He told only part of the story. Accounts provided by disgruntled whites suggest that husbands did often take full responsibility for deciding which members of the family would work and for whom: "Gilbert will stay on his old terms, but withdraws Fanny and puts Harry and Little Abram in her place and puts his son Gilbert out to a trade," reported a Georgia plantation mistress after the war. However, there is good reason to suspect that wives willingly devoted more time to child care and other domestic matters, rather than merely acquiescing in their husbands' demands. A married freedwoman, the mother of eleven children, reminded a northern journalist that she had had "to nus' my chil'n four times a day and pick two hundred pounds cotton besides" under slavery. She expressed at least relative satisfaction with her current situation: "I've a heap better time now'n I had when I was in bondage."[46]

When it became clear that black people would resist working in gangs, planters acceded to the sharecropping system. Under this arrangement, black families gained at least some control over the way a wife and mother balanced her domestic duties with field work. But between 1865 and 1940, black women paid dearly for their commitment to kin and community over slave-like labor as it became clear that white men would use force against women who appeared to shirk their duties. In Athens, Georgia, Margaret Martin left her place of work to visit her niece one day in the spring of 1868 and was "badly beaten and choked" by her employer when she returned. A few years later Lucretia Adams of Yorkville, South Carolina, endured a night of horror initiated by eight drunken white men (she recognized all her assailants). They "just talked as anybody would" and told her, "we heard you wouldn't work. We were sent for . . . to come here and whip you, to make the damned niggers work."[47]

In the 1930s, whites were still forcing black women to labor for them to the detriment of black families' welfare. Hattie Mae Lindsay of Philadelphia, Mississippi, wrote to President Franklin D. Roosevelt in 1933 and reported that she was made to "wash and iron for [the landlord's] wife without a penny of money." She knew that her family would be cheated out of their share of the year's crop. One night the white man had entered their cabin "to take me out and whip me, and he said if I repeated this we all would be kill [sic] in a pile." She concluded her letter, "I am treated like a slave . . . I can't leave. We work a crop with him and we have five children hungry and without clothes to wear. If I only could get pay for this year work what I done for him, I could get them clothes." From Millen, Georgia, came the plea of the widow Mosel Brinson, living on her own land with seven children, "plenty of help." She wanted to farm by herself but "these poor white people that lives around me wants the colored people to work for them for nothing. . . ." To white employers, these women represented nothing more or less than exploitable labor. Family ties and obligations, then, only served to thwart the financial interests of landlords.[48]

That a black tenant farm wife deprived a white person of her labor when she attended to the details of family life did not necessarily imply that she was aware of the political implications inherent in her daily activities. She labored for her own household, rather than against the interests of white planters. Still, her defiance was no less powerful because it was inarticulate and unconscious, and the cumulative effect of such defiance over the generations profoundly affected the size and shape of the South's labor supply. The social context of rural southern society reveals how black and poor white women could engage in the same household chores while not sharing the experiences of family life in precisely the same way. For a black woman, to labor for one's family was to labor for one's race, and in opposition to white hegemony.

In sum, the history of women in the rural South casts new light on issues related to work, class, gender, and culture. In a strict sense, poor black and white households constituted a single economic class, based on their material circumstances and their fixed relation to wealth-holders in southern society. Women of the two races paid obeisance to the patriarchal imperative, manifested in the public, economic activities of men and an explicit sexual division of labor and authority at home. Yet the legacy of slavery and the persistent exploitation of blacks as agricultural laborers produced histories of black and white women that were as separate as they were unequal. Efforts on the part of black women and men to control their family lives represented the nexus between racial oppression and political resistance – efforts that are most clearly understood as part of a historical process, and not a manifestation of static social relationships.

Gracie Turner and Sarah Easton could describe in great detail their grievances against individual greedy landlords and tyrannical male kinfolk without realizing that the two of them suffered in concert, at least to some degree.[49] For these Southerners, the sameness of their work lives was insignificant compared with the difference in their consciousness of skin color. It was, after all, Gracie Turner who remained trapped in the crosscurrents of the South's dual caste system. On the day of her interview in 1939, the FWP worker found her "downcast in spirit." Nevertheless, she revealed in no uncertain terms that she had managed to preserve her dignity in spite of poverty and injustice. Landlords, she noted proudly, regarded her as "defussin'est women [they] ever saw" when she refused to accept their reckoning on the crop settlement. At the age of forty-nine, her priorities were still clear; she wanted shoes for the family because "the chil'len's feet is on de ground," and she wanted "a place I could settle down on and nobody could tell me I had to move no more." She already knew that, despite the hard work of her family, "dey wouldn't be nothin' for us this year, not to look for it," but she still prayed each night for death to pass her by until she could "get out'n dis shape," or at least until she got some decent clothes in which to be buried. Now that the Turner family burial insurance had lapsed, she said that her greatest fear was that white county officials would "have to put me away."[50]

NOTES

[1]Federal Writers' Project, *These Are Our Lives As Told By the People and Written by Members of the Federal Writers' Project of the Works Progress Administration in North Carolina, Tennessee, and Georgia* (New York: W.W. Norton, 1975; orig. pub. in 1939), pp. 5, 4, 25, 17.

[2]*Ibid.*, pp. 24, 6, 21.

[3]*Ibid.*, pp. 6, 18, 20, 19, 16.

[4]See the excellent case study of black and poor white female tobacco workers in North Carolina, by Dolores Elizabeth Janiewski, "From Field to Factory: Race, Class, Sex and The Woman Worker in Durham, 1880-1940" (Unpub. Ph.D. dissertation, Duke University, 1979).

[5]Theodore Rosengarten, *All God's Dangers: The Life of Nate Shaw* (New York: Avon Books, 1974), pp. 109-110.

[6]Roger L. Ransom and Richard Sutch, *One Kind of Freedom: The Economic Consequences of Emancipation* (New York: Cambridge University Press, 1977), 88; Forrest McDonald and Grady McWhiney, "The South From Self-Sufficiency to Peonage: An Interpretation," *American Historical Review*, 85 (Dec.1980):1095-1118; David Eugene Conrad, *The Forgotten Farmers: The Story of Sharecroppers in the New Deal* (Urbana: University of Illinois Press, 1965), pp. 1-14. See also Jay R. Mandle, *The Roots of Black Poverty: The Southern Plantation Economy After the Civil War* (Durham, N. C.: Duke University Press,. 1978); Joseph D. Reid, Jr., "White Land, Black Labor, and Agricultural Stagnation: The Causes and Effects of Sharecropping in the Postbellum South," *Explorations in Economic History*, 16 (Jan. 1979):31-55; United States Department of Commerce, Bureau of the Census, *Plantation Farming in the United States* (Washington, D. C.: Government Printing Office, 1916); Rupert B.Vance, *Human Factors in Cotton Culture: A Study in the Social Geography of the American South* (Chapel Hill: University of North Carolina Press, 1929), pp. 53-79; Charles S. Johnson, Edwin R. Embree, and W.W. Alexander, *The Collapse of Cotton Tenancy: Summary of Field Studies and Statistical Surveys, 1933-35* (Chapel Hill: University of North Carolina Press, 1935).

[7]Tom E. Terrill and Jerold Hirsch, eds., *Such As Us: Southern Voices of the Thirties* (New York: W. W. Norton, 1978), pp. 41-3, 59.

[8]Pitt Dillingham, "Black Belt Settlement Work. Part II: The Community," *Southern Workman*, 31 (Aug. 1902): 441.

[9]Jacqueline Jones, *Labor of Love, Labor of Sorrow: Black Women, Work, and The Family From Slavery to the Present* (New York: Basic Books, 1985), pp. 333-42.

[10]Jean Collier Brown, "The Negro Woman Worker," United States Department of Labor, Women's Bureau *Bulletin* No. 165 (1938):7.

[11]Jonathan Wiener, "Class Structure and Economic Development in the American South, 1865-1955," *American Historical Review*, 84 (Oct. 1979):970-92; and *Social Origins of the New South: Alabama, 1860-1885* (Baton Rouge: Louisiana State University Press, 1978).

[12]Jones, *Labor of Love, Labor of Sorrow*, pp. 79-109.

[13]James Agee and Walker Evans, *Let Us Now Praise Famous Men: Three Tenant Families* (Boston: Houghton Mifflin, 1939), p. 325. Janiewski examines rural women of both races in "From Field to Factory," pp. 7-62. Arthur F. Raper, in *Preface to Peasantry: A Tale of Two Black Belt Counties* (Chapel Hill: University of North Carolina Press, 1936); Thomas J. Woofter, in *Landlord and Tenant on the Cotton Plantation*, Works Progress Administration, Division of Social Research, Monograph V (Washington, D.C.: Government Printing Office, 1936); and Vance, *Human Factors in Cotton Culture*, all describe similarities between the experiences of black and white tenant farm women.

[14]Margaret Jarmon Hagood, *Mothers of the South: Portraiture of the White Tenant Farm Woman* (New York: W.W. Norton, 1977; orig. pub. in 1939), p. 4; Frances Harper, "Coloured Women of America," *Englishwoman's Review* (Jan. 1878):10-15. See also Joan Kelley, "The Doubled Vision of Feminist Theory: A Postscript to the 'Women and Power' Conference," *Feminist Studies*, 5 (Spring 1979): 216-27.

[15]Terrill and Hirsch, eds., *Such As Us*, pp. 97-8; Hagood, *Mothers of the South*, p. 57; FWP, *These Are Our Lives*, p.9.

[16]See for example the description of homemaking in a small midwestern town (Muncie, Indiana) in the 1920s provided by Robert S. Lynd and Helen Merrill Lynd in *Middletown: A Study in Modern American Culture* (New York: Harcourt, Brace, and World, 1929), pp. 153-78.

[17]Hagood, *Mothers of the South*, pp. 160, 84.

[18]Rosengarten, *All God's Dangers*, pp. 5, 23-5, 13. For other descriptions of the sexual division of field labor, see Robert Preston Brooks, *The Agrarian Revolution in Georgia* (Madison: University of Wisconsin Press, 1914), pp. 46-7; Clyde Vernon Kiser, *Sea Island to City: A Study of St. Helena Islanders in Harlem and Other Urban Centers* (New York: Columbia University Press, 1932), p. 71.

[19]Terrill and Hirsch, eds., *Such As Us*, p. 96.

[20]*Ibid.*, pp. 110, 34-37.

[21]Rossa B. Cooley, *Homes of the Freed* (New York: New Republic, 1926), p. 76; Hagood, *Mothers of the South*, p. 89. Photographs of Aunt Adelaide are included in Edith M. Dabbs, *Face of an Island: Leigh Richmond Miner's Photographs of St. Helena's Island* (New York: Grossman Publishers, 1971).

[22]Frances Sage Bradley and M. A. Williamson, *Rural Children in Selected Counties of North Carolina*, U.S. Department of Labor Children's Bureau, Rural Child Welfare Series no. 2 (Publication no. 33) (Washington: Government Printing Office, 1918), p. 34.

For fertility rates of white and black women in the rural South, see Herman Lantz and Lewellyn Hendrix, "Black Fertility and the Black Family in the Nineteenth Century: A Re-Examination of the Past," *Journal of Family History*, 3 (Fall 1978):251-61; Stanley L. Engerman, "Black Fertility and Family Structure in the U. S., 1880-1940," *Journal of Family History*, 2 (June 1977):117-38; Bernice Milburn Moore, "Present Status and Future Trends in the Southern White Family," *Social Forces*, 16 (March 1938):406-10.

[23]Terrill and Hirsch, eds., *Such As Us*, pp. 91, 95; Kiser, *From Sea Island to City*, p. 253; Anne Moody, *Coming of An Age in Mississippi* (New York: Dell, 1968), pp. 14-17.

[24]Hagood, *Mothers of the South*, p. 92; Raper, *Preface to Peasantry*, p.65. For examples of relief agents' and researchers' reports on tenant housing, see the Research Bulletins of the Federal Emergency Relief Administration, Division of Research and Statistics, Record Group 69, National Archives, Washington, D.C. See also W. E. Burghardt DuBois, ed., "The Negro American Family," Atlanta

University Publication No. 13 (Atlanta University, 1908), pp. 52-3; Terrill and Hirsch, eds., *Such As Us*, p. 79; W. E. Burghardt DuBois, "The Problem of Housing the Negro. Part III: The Home of the Country Freedman," *Southern Workman*, 30 (Oct. 1901): 535-42; Carl Kelsey, *The Negro Farmer* (Chicago: Jennings and Pre, 1903), p.45; Raper, *Preface to Peasantry*, opposite p. 61 (a photo of a sharecropper's cabin that had been inhabited by black and white families successively); Vance, *Human Factors in Cotton Culture*, pp. 249-51; Woofter, *Landlord and Tenant on the Cotton Plantation*, pp. 91-106.

[25]David C. Barrow, "A Georgia Plantation," *Scribner's Monthly*, 21 (April 1881):832; Kelsey, *Negro Farmer*, p. 74; Hagood, *Mothers of the South*, pp. 92-107; Georgia Washington, "Condition of the Women in the Rural Districts of Alabama," *Proceedings of the Hampton Negro Conference*, 6 (July 1902):73-8. For descriptions of sharecroppers' diet, see Vance, *Human Factors in Cotton Culture*, pp. 243-9; Wilbur O. Atwater and Charles D. Woods, *Dietary Studies With Reference to the Food of the Negro in Alabama in 1895 and 1896* (Washington,1897). McDonald and McWhiney suggest that "Atwater and Woods studied only blacks, but their observations were equally applicable to white sharecroppers as the twentieth century wore on" ("The South from Self-Sufficiency to Peonage," p. 1117).

[26]Terrill and Hirsch, eds., *Such As Us*, p. 91; Hagood, *Mothers of the South*, pp. 16, 27; Cooley, *Homes of the Freed*, pp. 79-80.

[27]Federal Emergency Relief Administration (FERA) Division of Research, Statistics, and Finance, "Survey of Cases Removed from Relief Rolls in Macon, Georgia, for Administrative Reasons in May, 1935," Research Bulletin #6648, Sept. 24, 1935, p. 1, Record Group (RG) 69, National Archives, Washington, D.C. (NA); FWP, *These Are Our Lives*, p.35.

[28]FERA, Division of Research and Statistics, "Landlord-Tenant Relations and Relief in Alabama," Research Bulletin #2738, July 10, 1934, p. 4, RG 69, NA. White women picked or chopped cotton to earn extra money; black women performed this type of work and also cooked and washed.

[29]Raper, *Preface to Peasantry*, p. 74. Housewives quoted in Dillingham, "Black Belt Settlement Work," p. 442; Cooley, *Homes of the Freed*, pp. 64-5, 43; Hagood, *Mothers of the South*, pp. 42.

[30]Lantz and Hendrix, "Black Fertility and the Black Family in the Nineteenth Century," p. 255; Moore, "Present Status and Future Trends in the Southern White Family"; Hagood, *Mothers of the South*, pp. 64, 123-7, 148, 243-44, 109-110, 238; FWP, *These Are Our Lives*, p. 6.

[31]Terrill and Hirsch, eds., *Such As Us*, p. 61. Jessie Jeffcoat, wife of a white Durham County, North Carolina, tobacco farmer, said, "They say children is shore nuff riches. We's got five of them. But if you mean money and things, we ain't got 'em."

[32]*Ibid.*, p. 87; Hagood, *Mothers of the South*, p. 120.

[33]Hagood, *Mothers of the South*, pp.155, 121; FWP, *These Are Our Lives*, p. 60.

[34]Barbara J. Fields, "Ideology and Race in American History," in *Region, Race, and Reconstruction: Essays in Honor of C.Vann Woodward*, eds. J. Morgan Kousser and James M. McPherson (New York, 1982), pp. 143-178.

[35]Jones, *Labor of Love, Labor of Sorrow*, pp. 79-109, 196-231.

[36]Hagood, *Mothers of the South*, p. 178.

[37]Jack Temple Kirby, "Black and White in the Rural South, 1915-1954," *Agricultural History*, 58 (July 1984): 416-18.

[38]Raper, *Preface to Peasantry*, pp. 275-83; David M.Katzman, *Seven Days a Week: Domestic Service in Industrializing America* (New York: Oxford University Press, 1978), pp.184-222; Julie Roy Jeffrey, "Women in the Southern Farmers' Alliance: A Reconsideration of the Role and Status of Women in the Late Nineteenth Century South," *Feminist Studies*, 3 (Fall 1975); W.O. Brown, "Role of the Poor White in Race Contacts of the South," *Journal of Social Forces*, 19 (Dec. 1940):258-68; Donald H. Grubbs, *Cry from the Cotton: The Southern Tenant Farmers' Union and the New Deal* (Chapel Hill: University of North Carolina Press, 1971), pp. 66-69. On black midwives attending white women, see Hagood, *Mothers of the South*, pp. 63, 113.

[39]On Afro-American religion and culture see for example Eugene D. Genovese, *Roll, Jordan, Roll: The World the Slaves Made* (New York: Vintage, 1974), pp. 159-284; Lawrence Levine, *Black Culture and Black Consciousness: Afro-American Folk Thought From Slavery to Freedom* (Oxford: Oxford University Press, 1977). On white Protestantism in the South, see H. Shelton Smith, *In His Image, But...: Racism in Southern Religion, 1780-1920* (Durham: Duke University Press, 1972).

Sam Bowers' mother, a black woman, "made medicines out of herbs, shrubs, roots, sassafras tea, mullein tea, an' catnip tea" (FWP, *These Are Our Lives*, p.71). Aaron and Mary Matthews believed that, "If a woman comes de six' day o' Feb'uary, you won't have no poultry dat year" (Terrill and Hirsch, eds., *Such As Us*, p.93). Hagood describes Piedmont white women's "common superstitions about prenatal influences" in *Mothers of the South*, p.117.

[40]Bernice Johnson Reagon, "My Black Mothers and Sisters, or on Beginning A Cultural Autobiography," *Feminist Studies* 8 (Spring 1982):81-96.

[41]Edward Magdol, *A Right to the Land: Essays in the Freedmen's Community* (Westport, Conn.: Greenwood Press, 1977), p.11.

[42]Janiewski, "From Field to Factory," pp. 39, 206; Hortense Powdermaker, *After Freedom: A Cultural Study of the Deep South* (New York: Atheneum, 1968; orig. pub. in 1939), pp. 215-17.

[43]James S. Jarvis quoted (from a speech he made at the opening of the Colored Industrial Fair in Raleigh in 1883) in Frenise A. Logan, *The Negro in North Carolina, 1876-1894* (Chapel Hill: University of North Carolina Press, 1964), p. 75.

[44]Fanny Kemble, *Journal of a Residence on a Georgian Plantation in 1838-1839* (London: Longman, Green, 1863), p. 121. On the significance of the black family as a form of resistance to slavery, see Gutman, *The Black Family in*

Slavery and Freedom; Angela Davis, "Reflections on the Black Woman's Role in the Community of Slaves," *The Black Scholar*, 3 (December1971): 3-15.

[45]Francis W. Loring and C. F. Atkinson, *Cotton Culture and the South Considered With Reference to Emigration* (Boston: A.Williams, 1869), pp. 4, 15; Leon F. Litwack, *Been in the Storm So Long: The Aftermath of Slavery* (New York: Knopf, 1979), pp. 244-45; Joe M. Richardson, *The Negro in the Reconstruction of Florida, 1865-1877* (Tallahassee: Florida State University Press, 1965), p. 63; John W. De Forest, *A Union Officer in the Reconstruction* (New Haven: Yale University Press, 1948), p. 94.

Secondary accounts that mention the withdrawal of female labor in the postbellum period include Peter Kolchin, *First Freedom: The Responses of Alabama's Blacks to Emancipation and Reconstruction* (Westport, Conn.: Greenwood Press, 1972), pp. 62-3; Joe Gray Taylor, *Louisiana Reconstructed: 1863-1887* (Baton Rouge: Louisiana State University Press, 1974), pp. 326-27; Wiener, *Social Origins of the New South*, p. 47; Litwack, *Been in the Storm So Long*, pp. 244-45, 341, 393, 434; Gutman, *Black Family in Slavery and Freedom*, pp. 167-68.

[46]Loring and Atkinson, *Cotton Culture*, p. 13; Robert Myers, ed. *The Children of Pride: A True Story of Georgia and the Civil War* (New Haven: Yale University Press, 1972), p. 1370; John Townsend Trowbridge, *The South: A Tour of Its Battlefields and Ruined Cities, A Journey Through the Desolated States, and Talks With the People* (Hartford, CT: L. Stebbins, 1866), p. 394.

[47]A survey of contracts contained in the archives of the United States Bureau of Refugees, Freedmen, and Abandoned Lands, Record Group 105, National Archives, Washington, D.C. (hereinafter BRFAL) indicates that fathers and husbands usually signed labor agreements with landowners on behalf of entire families. Athens, Wilkes County Georgia, October 31, 1868, Reports Relating to Murders and Outrages, Letters Received, Georgia Assistant Commissioner, BRFAL; Senate Testimony of Lucretia Adams taken by the *Joint Select Committee to Inquire Into the Condition of Affairs in the Late Insurrectionary States*, Report 41, Pt. 5 (South Carolina), V. 3, pp. 1577-78.

[48]Hattie Mae Lindsay to Mr. Franklin D. Roosevelt, Aug. 18, 1934, Box 119-1 and Mosel Brinson to Dear Friends, Feb. 4, 1935, Box 119-2, Works Progress Administration Files, Howard University, Washington, D.C.

[49]Janiewski ("From Field to Factory," p. 50) notes, "Although black and white women criticized individual men, I have found no evidence of criticism of the relative place of men and women. The sharing of work and support in a complementary way within the context of the family economy did not engender sexual antagonism."

[50]FWP, *These Are Our Lives*, pp. 30, 22, 23, 21, 23-4, 30.

2

MAKING WOMEN INTO FARMERS' WIVES: THE NATIVE AMERICAN EXPERIENCE IN THE INLAND NORTHWEST

Dolores Janiewski

INTRODUCTION

To the heirs of an agricultural transition that occurred at some remote time, the role of a farmer's wife no longer represents a startling innovation. Instead it appears to be a timeworn choice, one that women may embrace or reject, but one that is a familiar part of women's possible roles. The implications of that status for women may be hard to see with fresh eyes. The five or eight millenia since agriculture began in some Native American, Asian, and African traditions makes the experience difficult to reconstruct. Fortunately, the Native American women of the Inland Northwest – members of the complex of Plateau cultures – experienced the arrival of agriculture within the last century. By observing their response to the imposition of the role of farmer's wife, we may see the meaning of that role for the women to which it was customary as well as to these women for whom it would require major changes in their work and their lives.

The process by which agriculture emerged in the Inland Northwest must be seen in the context of a long and turbulent history of Native American-Euroamerican conflict over alternative ways of supporting human existence. Different visions of correct economic relationships – redistribution vs. accumulation – were at stake in the conflict between peoples who organized their economies around communal exchange and those who produced for a market based upon profit-maximazation. In one society the path to power lay in giving away the most goods and providing services to the rest of the group; in the other, the most successful accumulator of great wealth acquired the greatest power over others in his society. Just as acutely, the struggle took place between two ethnic groups who came to be defined in opposition to each other – "red men" and "white men." But sexual politics were also implicated. Accompanying the model of agriculture that white officials, missionaries and settlers sought to implant in the Inland Northwest – now the states of Idaho and Washington – was a set of assumptions about correct gender relationships. These included men's primary role as breadwinner, citizen, household head, property-owner, manager, and public representative of the family. True women worked within the private household, depended economically upon their husbands, and obeyed the male head. Such practices were enforced through legal and governmental structures. In short, the arrival of commercial agriculture brought with it an assault on prexisting patterns of gender, ethnic and economic activities in the region.[1]

GENDER RELATIONS IN ABORIGINAL PLATEAU CULTURES

Economically, sexually, and politically, the Native Americans of the Inland Northwest had evolved patterns of behavior and beliefs that contrasted markedly with those accepted by the whites who migrated into the area. Belonging to the language groups called Interior Salish and Sahaptian, these peoples bear names in their own tongue – the Skitswash, the Scheulpi, the Nespelems, the Sinkaietk, the Palouse, the Wenatchees, the Nimipu, the Yakima, and the Cayuse. For purposes of simplicity and familiarity to English speakers, the European names given to three of these closely allied groups – the Coeur d'Alenes (Skitswash), the Colvilles (Scheulpi), and the Nez Perces (Nimipu) – will predominate in this text. These peoples participated in the Plateau cultural complex, experienced the impact of settler, federal, and military intrusions, and serve as examples of the process endured by all the peoples of the Plateau.

Women's work as gatherers supplied a major share of the food supply among their respective peoples. In addition to gathering roots and berries, hunting small animals, and participating in the salmon catch, women often accompanied the buffalo hunters eastward across the Rockies. The best gatherers of roots and fruits received respect for their skills and spiritual power. The gathering of the "first roots" and "first fruits" received ceremonial recognition as it signified the end to the privations of wintertime. Women dispensed the proceeds of their labor, controlled the household, and passed their possessions on to their kin. They engaged in trade at the various tribal and intertribal gathering places. They celebrated their own feasts and built their own sweatlodges.

Sometimes women became religious leaders and prophets. Although they rarely achieved formal political office a few women became chiefs. But band leaders exerted little authority in any case because decisions were reached by consensus. Kinship groups, not the conjugal couple, remained the source of women's and men's identity while marital bonds were relatively easily dissolved. Sexuality, especially in contrast to the emphasis on female chastity among nineteenth century Euroamericans, was relatively unregulated.[2] As analysed by anthropologist Alice Fletcher,

> Under the old tribal regime women's industries were essential to the very life of the people and their value was publicly recognized. . . . Her influence in the growth and development of tribal government, tribal ceremonies, and tribal power shows that her position has always been one of honor rather than one of slavery and degradation.[3]

As Fletcher's statement made clear, women in the Plateau cultures gained respect for their skills, exercised control over important resources, and enjoyed significant social freedoms.

MISSIONARIES PREACH
THE GOSPEL OF TRUE WOMANHOOD

The two cultures first came into contact when missionaries began to arrive in the area, then called the Oregon Territory, in the mid-1830s. Believing that a "settled community was basic to any systematic work," Presbyterian, Congregationalist, and Methodist missionaries under the auspices of the American Board for Foreign Missions preached the Gospel of the plow to male converts and the Gospel of domesticity to women.[4] As one scholar has explained, they simultaneously preached an ideological amalgamation of Christianity, 19th century capitalism, and republicanism.[5] Their message explicitly contained a sexual division of labor and space at variance with that already familiar to the people they encountered.[6]

The recorded traditions of the Nez Perces and the Presbyterians who sought to convert them reveal the conflict over gender issues that arose in the initial encounter. According to the oral tradition of the Nez Perces, "The missionaries very much wanted the Nez Perce to take up farming and leave their old ways. But we were not inclined to change our old way of life. . . . It seemed to us that the white man was asking us to become like women when they wanted us to garden."[7] Kate McBeth, a successor to Henry Spalding, described his methods, "He felt he was as much a missionary when planting or hoeing his corn and potatoes, as when translating the book of Matthew into the native tongue."[8] Eliza Spalding, his wife, taught reading, writing, and the domestic arts. She wrote in 1842, "Delia, Jane, and Sarah (names she'd given three converts), with my assistance having made twenty-four yards of good substantial woolen cloth. . . . They look to me much more comfortable and respectable in these dresses than any others I have ever seen them wear."[9] Later Kate would resume Eliza Spalding's duties in teaching Nez Perce women to become domestic caretakers.

Like the Protestants, Catholic priests and nuns preached agriculture and domesticity to their converts among the Colvilles, Coeur d'Alenes, and Nez Perces. Women must concern themselves with the "care and ordering of the house," the "duties of a good wife and mother...till then unknown to the Indians."[10] In the eyes of both groups of missionaries, Christianity meant a settled agricultural economy where the wife would become "industrious within doors. . . . The fences (would be) . . . up. The fields . . . planted." A good convert would praise the missionary influence by saying, as did one Nez Perce, that the missionaries had "stop all time lazy and make them all time work."[11]

As the contrast between Native American and missionary accounts attested, the efforts to change "the age-old living habits of a tribe" met with a mixed response.[12] After initial success, the Spaldings increasingly faced resistance and eventually open hostility once their presence appeared to pave the way for the encroachment of settlers, disease, and new ways of life upon the local peoples. After the nearby Cayuses killed the missionaries Marcus and Narcissa Whitman, the Spaldings left the mission field. When the Jesuit fathers in the 1870s urged the Coeur d'Alenes to move to land better suited to farming, one of their leaders responded:

We are not like you. You need bread. We have camas. You require
good clothing; we are satisfied with deer skins and buffalo hides. We
can live comfortably on what you would think poor and wretched.[13]

His words referred to the products of women's labor – camas root dug from the
soil of the high prairies and tanned skins – as concrete examples of profound
ethnic differences. Yet many Coeur d'Alenes heeded the words of the "black
robes" and moved away from their traditional homelands near the lake and forests
to the more open grasslands to the South.

In the 1870s Spalding returned after more than twenty years' absence. He
was joined, and, after his death in 1874, replaced by Susan McBeth, who carried
on his campaign to change religious and cultural habits. After Kate McBeth arrived in 1879, the two sisters found much to lament in sexual, domestic, and
work practices. Sue and Kate McBeth expressed horror that the Nez Perce tongue
contained no proper word for "husband" thus leading women to "think it nothing
more than fun to steal a man, or husband, from another woman." They noted
that their female converts listened reluctantly to "the doctrine that man is the
head of the woman."[14] Husbands, encouraged by the McBeths to expect wifely
submission, complained about wives who refused to remain at home in their
"proper place."[15] The McBeths and ultimately their niece, Mary Crawford, re-
doubled their efforts to convert the heathen Nez Perces while searching for allies
from the federal government.

FEDERAL POLICY AND GENDER TRANSFORMATION

Beginning in the 1840s the missionaries gained allies from the U.S. military, and, after its creation in 1849, the Indian Office or Bureau of Indian Affairs.
In 1842 the first Indian agent reinforced the efforts of the Spaldings by passing a
code of laws that punished transgressions against the rules of the new civilization. He also appointed a head chief.[16] A decade later Governor Isaac Stevens of
Washington Territory came to remove local Native Americans from the path of
future railroads and the overland emmigrants then passing through the area. The
treaty he urged their leaders to sign contained the same sexual and economic
agenda already undertaken by the missionaries. Stevens told the male representatives of various Plateau peoples gathered at Walla Walla in 1855 that the Great
Father wanted:

Each man who will work to have his own land, his own horses, his
own cattle, and his own home for himself and his children. . . . We
want your women to spin and weave and to make clothes. . . and all
the work of the house and lodges. . . . We also want to provide you
with tools for your farms, with ploughs and hoes, and shovels. . .
and all the implements the white man has; we want in your houses
plates and cups and brass and tin kettles, frying pans to cook your
meat and bake ovens to bake your bread, like white people.[17]

Later negotiations, like the 1863 treaty with the Nez Perces, reinforced the gender specific nature of the program. In that treaty, for example, each Nez Perces man received twenty acres of land but women gained nothing. At the same time some Nez Perces, led by Chief Lawyer, ceded the lands traditionally occupied by bands whose leaders refused to sign the new treaty. Significantly the Presbyterian Nez Perces signed, while the traditionalists, including Chief Joseph of the Wallowa Valley band, refused to yield their homelands to intruding white miners and settlers.[18]

NATIVE AMERICAN RESISTANCE

Responding to the combined pressure from Indian agents and missionaries, Native American men defended their traditions in their accustomed ways. The Coeur d'Alenes fought while the Nez Perces aided the U.S. in the late 1850s and, in the 1877 Nez Perce uprising against the terms of the 1863 treaty, the Nez Perces themselves were split into warring factions and neutrals. Some, like the famous Nez Perce leader, Joseph, "held to his heathenism with all the tenancity with which he has clung to his beloved Wallowa Valley," the valley whose loss forced him into a gallant attempt to escape the power of the U.S. through an 1500 mile campaign that brought the Nez Perces close to the Canadian border in 1877.[19] But the male pattern of resistance was forced to yield before superior military force and modern technology. Railroads and telegraphs led to the Nez Perces' defeat in 1877 and Joseph's famous surrender speech in which he pledged to "fight no more forever."[20] One of the last episodes in the history of Native American armed resistance had ended.

Those, who clung to the old ways, listened to prophets like Smohalla whose words gave spiritual support to their traditional gender and subsistence practices. Smohalla condemned the signers of treaties. "Those who cut up the lands or sign papers for lands will be defrauded of their rights and will be punished by God's anger."[21] He warned his followers, "Men who work cannot dream, and wisdom comes in dreams."[22] Voicing the outrage of those committed to the old ways, he responded to the preachers of the Gospel of the plow:

> You ask me to plow the ground. Shall I take a knife and tear my mother's bosom? . . . You ask me to cut grass and make hay and sell it and be rich like white men. But how dare I cut off my mother's hair?[23]

Wiskaynatonmay, a Nez Perce prophet, told her followers of her dream of a place in the clouds where "there weren't any White people." She criticized those who were miserly while preaching a creative synthesis of Christian and traditional beliefs. Her followers sang the song she brought back from the dead as they symbolically restored their own culture to life.[24] By heeding their prophetic fathers and mothers, some Nez Perces gave renewed dignity to their own traditions while rejecting the doctrines brought by the preachers of a new sexual and political economy. Despite military defeat, political subjugation, acculturating pressures, and the loss of traditional resources, some members of the Colvilles, the Coeur d'Alenes, and the Nez Perces would continue to practice ancient traditions that sustained a familiar pattern of gender relationships.

ALLOTTING LAND AND GENDER ROLES

No longer fearing the "Indian threat," reformers, Western politicians, and land-hungry settlers pushed for the Indian Allotment Act of 1887, popularly known as the Dawes Act for one of its chief supporters, Senator Henry Dawes of Massachusetts. Forswearing the reservation system, the act intended to break "up the tribal mass" by giving each "Indian a title to his allotment" so that communal property became individual possession to be bought and sold after an initial twenty-five years of guardianship by federal authorities.[25]

Senator Henry Dawes, chairman of the Senate Committee on Indian Affairs, explained the intentions behind the new policy shift in an 1884 speech to supporters of Indian "emancipation." Referring to the object of their solicitude, Dawes said, "We must take him by the hand and set him upon his feet, and teach him to stand alone first to walk, then to dig, then to plant, then to hoe, then to gather, and then to keep."[26] Merrill Gates, another active reformer and member of the Board of Indian Commissioners, spoke ten years after the passage of the Dawes Act to a similar group of reformers. He appealed to them to complete the unfinished business of leading Native Americans "out of savagery into citizenship" by "getting him out of the blanket and into trousers and trousers with a pocket in them, and with *pocket aches to be filled with dollars!*"[27]

Like Dawes and Gates, most advocates of the new policy concentrated on the goal of transforming male gender identity while grammatically emphasizing the "red man" as "he." Still, as believers in the notion of the "squaw drudge" under tribal customs, they also saw their program as one that would liberate Native American women from a benighted tradition.[28] In an 1892 speech to the American Missionary Association, Dawes concluded, "When the last Indian upon the prairie shall have put off his blanket . . . and the last teepee . . . shall have given place to the home . . . with manhood at the threshold and womanhood at the fireside, then there will be time enough for the church to say we will withdraw."[29] The Women's National Indian Association particularly devoted itself to teaching women "to make and properly keep comfortable homes." This was no easy task according to one agent who reported, "The question of ever elevating them is one that tries faith, for I have striven by all the arts I possess to have them see the contrast between uncleaness and cleanliness. . . ." Combining secular activities such as lobbying for legislation and sacred missions, reformers sought to teach the "clean, healthful Gospel of Christian home-life" to Native American men, women, and children.[30] Like the missionary Kate McBeth, they were "trying to break the old custom of the women doing most of the heavy work" while seeking to clothe them in "white women's dresses, cared for and worked for by their husbands."[31] Few doubted that women would be benefitted by the eradication of cultural traditions in the name of "progress," "civilization," or "citizenship."

Even a woman who found something to appreciate about women's position in aboriginal societies became actively involved in destroying the culture that gave women the honored place she recognized. Alice Fletcher journeyed to the Omahas in the early 1880s with the "intent to study the life of Indian women."[32] She also visited other reservations to recruit children for attendance at special boarding schools in the East. On one such visit, she recorded the words of Sitting Bull, the famous Oglala leader, on the woman question. As she recalled his words, he implored her:

> You are a woman, take pity on my women for they have no future. The young men can be like the white men, can till the soil, supply the food and clothing. They will take the work out of the hands of the women. And the women, to whom we have owed everything in the past, they will be stripped of all which gave them power and position among the people. Give my women a future![33]

Fletcher evidently took his impassioned pleas to heart. As she assured her audiences, she was determined to help Indian women.

But her solution lay in ardent support for the very forces that were undercutting women's position. Fletcher initiated the passage of a special allotment act for the Omahas in 1882. After lobbying for the bill, she accepted an unpaid position as allotment agent. The irony of her attempt to help women was made clear as she sought to persuade the Omahas that progress meant "the absorbing of the wife's right to land in that of her husband's."[34] Aware that the people upon whom she imposed the provisions of the Dawes Act might raise "their small moccasined feet to kick against the iron shod inevitable" she never wavered in her single-minded dedication to the imposition of the new order. While civilization might cost the Indian woman "her independence," a fact that Fletcher and her companion, E. Jane Gay, acknowledged, she saw no preferable alternative.[35] Fletcher, like those less sympathetic to the virtues of aboriginal culture, participated in a process that simultaneously aimed at producing farmers and farmwives while opening land to those already imbued with the values of an expansionist, market-oriented, agricultural society.

Even as its enthusiasts pushed to implement allotment, there were signs that the policy was rent with contradictions between its supporters' efforts to satisfy the demands of potential white settlers and their goal of bringing "manhood" and "true womanhood" to Native Americans. Some of the most sensitive to these portents were the Native Americans whose resources were at stake. The Indian agent on the Coeur d'Alene reservation in the 1880s described their "rapid progress in their farm work" but also noted their "dread...that their lands will be taken from them." Successful farming, they feared, would only incite whites to envy and encroachment. The Coeur d'Alenes issued an impassioned plea to federal authorities. Declaring that they were neither "squirrels" nor "fish," they insisted, "We say that we are men as any whites are. From the land that they would take away, we get our food, raise our clothing, and whatever we are in need of."[36] Twenty years later their fears became reality as they experienced forced allotment and their reservation thrown open to white settlement without their consent.[37]

When Fletcher arrived in 1889 to allot the land on the Nez Perce reservation, she found a sceptical, and sometimes, openly rebellious response to her activities. E. Jane Gay accompanied Fletcher as cook, photographer, and companion. Gay's letters to reform journals and friends in the East conveyed something of the irony in Fletcher's mission. She reported that Fletcher announced to the assembled Nez Perce men that she had "come to bring them manhood that they may stand up beside the white man in equality before the law." As Gay explained their stony silence, "All they know about the law is, that it is some contrivance to get ponies and cattle and land out of the red man's possession into that of the white man; it is a one-sided machine." She left unstated the incongruity represented by Fletcher, the image of the Victorian lady, offering to give manhood to those willing to submit to her plans. Repeatedly, Gay conveyed her admiration for the "unsubjugated" Indians like Chief Joseph who came to debate "monogamy" with the two unmarried women and for the other "superb old colossals who stand upon their treaty" like the mountains even as she joked about the "survival of the fittest."[38]

Still, bent on success and determined to "leave our Indian friends to work out their own salvation," Fletcher and Gay called "progressive" those who seized the opportunity to take private possession of the land. They especially favored those who had been good students of the "white man's civilization" at the hands of the McBeths or at eastern schools. By defining their opponents as obscurantists, tewats (sorcerers), and autocratic chiefs, Fletcher, Gay, and the McBeth sisters prevented their perceptions of the potential risks of allotment from interfering with their mission "to make the individual strong" at the expense of tribal unity.[39]

"Perhaps," Gay reflected, "the miscarriage of many of our efforts in behalf of the race comes from our ignorance of its own ideals." While Fletcher was still involved in the process of allotment, Gay reported that the "Government has given the N.P.R.R. (Northern Pacific Railroad) a right of way" across a farm. She wrote:

> One can forsee that before many years, under the pressure of the encroaching white man's civilization, all the little valley gardens of the Nez Perce will be destroyed by the railroad lines and the Indians driven back from their water courses; and it is not difficult to conceive of the suffering which will follow this sort of opening up of the reservation.[40]

Nor could she totally swallow the evolutionary optimism that depicted allotment as a necessary, albeit coercive, uplifiting of a people from "barbarism" to "civilization." As she concluded in an optimism tinged with cynicism, "The day must come when the strong will be just to the weak – if there be any weak left in that day. . . . The Lion will lie down with the Lamb inside of him – when the Millenium comes upon a Reservation." In the meantime she cooked and kept company with the woman who was putting into motion the "mechanism" whose bleak product she foretold so acutely.[41]

Neither sensitive observers nor resisting Native Americans halted the process that transferred communal resources into the hands of individual property-holders. Indeed, the allotment process accelerated as subsequent modifications of the Dawes Act made it easier to open the reservation for settlement, mineral exploitation, railroad rights of way, or the leasing and sale of allotted lands to white tenants or purchasers.[42]

While Fletcher among other reformers pressed for women's right to land, govenment policy did nothing to enhance Native American women's ability to farm. Defining women as domestic creatures, policy makers sought to transform gender relations by turning those Native Americans most familiar with the culture of plants into tenders only of flowerbeds and, at best, garden plots. Rather than utilize the skills of successful gatherers, the Bureau of Indian Affairs and the Department of Agriculture acted as though men were the only appropriate farmers.[43] Instead of working with the cultural and gender assumptions of Native Americans, reformers and officials dedicated themselves to making Indian men and women into replicas of their idealized models of femininity and masculinity.

In the schools the curriculum followed strict gender lines. At the Colville School in the 1870s, boys were taught "manual labor. . . . The girls are instructed in housework and to cut and make their own clothes and clothing for the boys."[44] The Catholic school on the Coeur d'Alene reservation placed the "larger girls . . . in the care of the matron, seamstress, cook, and launderess" so that they might become like the "'pale-faced maidens'" who attended the same school.[45] Instructions from Commissioner Thomas J. Morgan to the school superintendant on the Nez Perce reservation directed that the boys be taught "the care of cows and other stock" and the girls, the "manufacture of butter and possibly cheese," as well as attention to "neatness, cleanliness, and order."[46] Successfully educated female students would never learn the necessary skills to cultivate the land Fletcher and others managed to bestow upon them.[47]

Similar policies addressed adults. Each agency employed farmers and matrons to advise residents on the correct duties and skills allocated to each sex by governmental decree. Beginning in the 1910s Indian agricultural fairs provided occasions where agricultural extension and home economics agents lectured Native Americans while awarding prizes for those who excelled in the agricultural and domestic arts.[48] Such activities systematically excluded Native American women, as they also did white women, from access to agricultural education even though women owned a significant portion of Indian land. (See Table 2.1)

At the same time that policies of the Bureau of Indian Affairs favored the leasing of Indian land to whites, its interpretation of its own regulations also contributed to women's inability to farm their land. A pamphlet, written by the Superintendant at Fort Lapwai Agency, then the official name for the Nez Perce reservation, explained that Indians suffering from disabilities would be allowed to lease or sell their allotments. His definition of disabilities, however, began first by invoking sex and martial status. Widows, single women, and married women, whose husbands were unable to cultivate their wives' land, were defined as disabled in his interpretation of the regulations.[49] Repeatedly the forms filled out by agents on the Coeur d'Alene, Colville, and the Nez Perce reservations cited a woman's sex or manless status as the sole justification for granting her permission to sell or rent her land.[50] The epitome of self-fulfilling prophets, Bureau agents transformed an ideological assumption into a social fact. Femininity became an official disability that was, in part, responsible for the results described in Table 2.1.

The culmination of these contradictory policies that simultaneously placed land in women's hands while doing nothing to aid them in farming it was the formation of Indian Home and Farm Associations in the 1920s. The 1923 declaration of purpose for the Nez Perce Indian Home and Farm Association began with a quotation from Edward Everett, the nineteenth century orator and Harvard president:

> The man who stands upon his own soil,who feels that by the laws of the country in which he lives, he is the rightful and exclusive owner of the land which he tills, feels more strongly than another the character of a man as the lord of the animate world.[51]

Two years later the preamble to the Coeur d'Alene Indian Home and Farm Association paraphrased a still more familiar source of inspiration:

> When in the course of the advance of civilization, the members of a tribe . . . find . . . their lands passing from their ownership . . . and desire to reform their ways and to assume among the people of the dominant race equal station in life and to acquire the economic competence and independence to which the laws of God and nature entitle them.[52]

The two organizations sought to encourage men to take up farming, establish "independent homes," and get the "women interested in home improvement . . . poultry and garden activities . . . and *Good Housekeeping*."[53] As the Everett quote suggested, policymakers were still trying to instill nineteenth century yeoman ideals into twentieth century men and women in the face of already accumulating signs of the failures of the allotment act to turn Native American men into farmers or even to keep the land they had been allotted.[54]

Had Native Americans been consulted about the reasons for their loss of land, they might all have responded as the Colvilles had already done in a 1915 petition against the opening of the southern half of their reservation. The petitioners asked for a delay because the "older people . . . cannot be made over. They remain as the Great Spirit made us and cannot change." Even the younger people, they added, "are not yet fully educated in the ways of white men."[55] Five

Table 2.1 *Percentage of Women among Native American Allottees, Lessors, and Potential Sellers of Their Land for Sampled Years[56]*

	Allottees	Lessors	Given Patents in Fee*
Coeur d'Alene	37.5%	59%	46.9%
Colville	46.6%	51.8%	56.3%
Nez Perce	38.9%	64.8%	56.5%**

*Patents in fee allowed the individual to dispose of the land through sale or mortage leading to its more likely loss

**Actual sales records

years later, after crop failures, they asked a Congressional committee, "Did we give away all our inherited rights when we signed the treaties? Our field crops failed; we are left to starve! Is this what the white man calls the 'square deal'?"[57] Such arguments fell on deaf ears. Their only answer was the insistence that the Colvilles and others continue to pursue the elusive yeomen dream that was failing so many of their white contemporaries in the 1920s.

But the evidence of failure could not be overlooked completely. By the mid-1920s, a team of investigators began to examine the "problem of Indian administration." Led by Lewis Meriam, the investigators' assumptions marked them as heirs to the supporters of the Dawes Act even as they sought to modify policy to come to terms with the realities of Native American land loss, limited involvement in farming, and the maintenance of traditional customs. The authors of the Meriam report suggested that the Bureau of Indian Affairs should shift its emphasis from commercial agriculture to "subsistence farming for the support of Indian families" while insisting that the "Indians must either be adjusted to a new economic basis or go through the slow, painful process of vanishing" using words that echoed the late nineteenth century. Administrators must work to achieve the "ideal" arrangement of a "permanent home for every Indian family," supported, in the main, by the earnings of the husband in order to restore "the balance in the division of labor between men and women" upset by the man's loss of his warrior and hunter role. Agents must prevent women from "becoming the sole or chief dependence of the family." Traditional subsistence practices such as "quests for vegetable foods" and the "care-free camp life existence" must give way to stable, settled family life. Women must devote themselves to domestic cares while men supported the family. While modifying the goal to fit the more limited possibilities they saw for Indian farmers in the 1920s, these investigators still prescribed the same changes in gender relations and economic roles favored by the past generations of policymakers and reformers.[58]

The sexual implications of the report were clear. In seeking a solution to the problem of the "Indian brave" whose occupation had been "destroyed by the advent of Caucasian civilization," it proposed to destroy the occupations that women had retained despite white intrusion. Rather than supporting the resourcefulness of women in continuing to extract subsistence from nature, it sought to curtail the "quests" even while reassuring its readers that "women's work goes on forever."[59] Focusing only on the changes forced upon men, the report's authors ignored the implications of their own recommendations for changing the nature and the social significance of women's work.

THE INDIAN NEW DEAL

Finally, in 1933, John Collier, Roosevelt's Commissioner of Indian Affairs, launched the "Indian New Deal." Inspired by his own previous service with the American Indian Defense Association and his respect for Native American cultures in the Southwest, Collier shifted policy from the goal of assimilation to "preserving Indian civilization" and restoring Indian rights to "religious and social freedom."[60] He actively solicited Native American ideas and sought to hire agents and administrators from the people served by his agency. He sent out his agents to investigate conditions and gain support for new legislation he wished to pass – a reversal of the Dawes Act – that would become known as the Wheeler-Howard Act or the Indian Reorganization Act when it was enacted in 1934.

Archie Phinney of Nez Perce and white ancestry was one of the new shapers of Indian policy. Trained by anthropologist Franz Boas of Columbia University, Phinney first sought to influence federal policy in a 1932 paper sent to Collier's predecessor. Advising the Bureau that it had often operated beyond the "pale of the Nez Perce mind and heart," Phinney asked the Bureau to develop policies that would draw upon the "survivals of certain positive forces of ancient culture." "Native, traditional associations, beliefs and customs" should be combined with "the elements of civilized life."[61] In 1937, after several years spent studying Soviet minority policy, Phinney was able to secure a position as special agent for the Bureau. Finally, in the early 1940s, he became the first Nez Perce to run the Northern Idaho Agency. Here he could seek to establish self-government and economic self-determination for the Nez Perces and the Coeur d'Alenes who were now placed within his agency.[62]

Despite the arrival of Collier and likeminded associates, the "Indian New Deal" did not mark a total break with the past. Its agricultural policy, in particular, resembled those that had already been tried and found wanting. Unable to secure sufficient funding from Congress to buy back lost Native American lands, the new policy operated within the constraints bequeathed by the failed policy of the past. One of Collier's special agents visited the Nez Perce Business Committee, the heir to the Nez Perce Home and Farm Association. He asked the secretary of the Committee "whether it might not be better if the Indians operated their own land, living on their farms instead of in the little villages and homes along the creeks." As he reported the Nez Perce response:

> I am not sure whether he was having fun with me or not but he
> closed the conversation by saying that the white man occupied the
> Indian land, worked hard on it all summer, and at the end of the year,
> had nothing; the Indian leased the white man the land, did nothing,
> but at the end of the summer, apparently had as much as the white
> man.[63]

Having seen the near-collapse of the vaunted white man's civilization, Nez
Perces apparently felt sufficiently confident to mock the persistent attachment to
a policy that equally benefitted those who "worked hard" and to those who "did
nothing."

Perhaps the joke also arose from Native American perceptions of the gap
between Collier's hopes for the Wheeler-Howard Act and the hard political realities. Collier's underfunded administration could not reverse the "very bad
checkerboarding" or bring back "the wild life and other resources" destroyed by
"white hunters, fishermen, and commercialists" on the Colville reservation as
one of his advisors pointed out.[64] Furthermore, Collier used nontraditional
methods – constitutions, elections, official governing bodies – to restore tribal
autonomy instead of traditional practices. His reform could, therefore, not offer
enough to satisfy traditionalists among the Nez Perces, the Coeur d'Alenes, and
the Colvilles who wished to return to traditional ways of obtaining subsistence
and self-government.

Conversely, Collier's reform threatened too much change to those who had
been inculcated with the assimilationist goal. The "progressive" Indians responded with anger at a policy that repudiated their own efforts to assimilate.
The Nez Perce Business Committee informed Collier in February 1934:

> We object to the plan. . . . We want our people to be kept on safe
> ground and our children's future to be preserved. We do not want
> them to be turned back forty years to take up the old communal life
> which never made for progress. After forty years of progress, we ob-
> ject to going back to the status of the Navajos and Pueblos which
> you mention in your letter.[65]

This odd coalition, composed, in the words of missionary Mary Crawford, of
"some of our old heathen men with their good sense and love of justice and fairness lined up with the Christians," frustrated Collier's and Phinney's attempts to
reorganize tribal affairs.[66] The same alliance held strong among the other peoples of the Plateau. Although Christine Galler of the Colvilles urged her people
to "try a new deal," the Colvilles and the Coeur d'Alenes also declined to
participate as traditionalists and progressives joined together in an alliance
against the Indian New Deal.[67]

In an unpublished history of the Numipu, another variation in the spelling
of "Nez Perces" in their own tongue, Phinney described the prevalent attitude as
the outgrowth of a "negative 'reservation' personality" and the transference of

hostility "once shown toward local settlers . . . now directed towards the Indian agency."[68] But the negative response to the Indian New Deal may have had greater validity than Collier or Phinney was willing to concede. One of the flaws in Collier's scheme may well have been his tendency to see all Indians in the guise of the Pueblos. Certainly neither his administration nor the IRA itself effectively restored political autonomy or economic self-determination. Indeed, Collier seems to have accomodated himself to the building of dams along the Columbia that flooded Native American lands and further curtailed the salmon, their traditional mainstay. As Archie Phinney, then a special agent, observed in 1942, the tribal councils actually remained "instrumentalities of the Indian Service . . . which has kept community participation in tribal affairs at a minimum."[69] Certainly, the "new deal" could not fundamentally overcome the "raw deal" which had already deprived the Nez Perces, the Coeur d'Alenes and the Colvilles of so much, nor could positing an essential unity to the Indian experience comprehend their differences.

Insofar as the gender question was concerned, neither the Collier administration, the progressives, nor the traditionalists altered the practice of excluding women from leadership roles. At a conference held in April 1934 to discuss the implications of the Wheeler-Howard Act for the Pacific Northwestern peoples, Christine Galler of the Colville Confederated Tribes was the only woman actively participating. She began her remarks by saying, "I am a woman and you might think it funny that the Colvilles elect a woman for a delegate" and concluded, "I hope you don't think I am like Emma Goldman or any other woman but as an Indian, my heart is with the Indians."[70] It was not until the mid-1940s, when Collier himself had resigned, that a woman's name appeared on the list of tribal leaders, as secretary for the Coeur d'Alene Tribal Council, and not until the late 1950s that a Nez Perce woman achieved a similar position. At approximately the same time Lucy Covington, a grand-daughter of Chief Moses of the Columbias, one of the groups on the Colville reservation, led her people's fight against termination, the next major shift in federal Indian policy.[71] Only after the Indian New Deal had ended did women participate directly in the official decision-making process.

Economically, during the Collier years, women appeared in the plans and programs of the agricultural extension agents as farmers' wives, not farmers. The reports filed by the Extension Agents spoke repeatedly of jars of canned fruit, of quilts, of pattern making, and other tasks that Kate McBeth had once tried to instill among Nez Perce women in the late nineteenth and early twentieth centuries. Agricultural extension agents targeted men while home economics workers reached out to women. The 4-H clubs for the Coeur d'Alenes, according to the 1934 report, included corn and hogs for boys, and cooking for the girls. Women did not appear in the plans established by the tribal business councils for enterprises in the 1930s and 1940s. If they farmed, like many other women, they remained "invisible farmers" insofar as the makers and deliverers of agricultural training and services were concerned.[72] The Indian New Deal failed to recognize the needs of Native American women to fill any other position than that of the dutiful housewife.

CONCLUSION

But Native American women did not depend upon government policy for guidance. The available evidence suggests that many women continued to practice their traditional skills. They helped their families survive the depression by digging "quantities of nourishing roots" even as they enlarged gardens and canned their produce.[73] To the best of their ability, within the environmental constraints imposed by white intrusions in the form of dams, game laws, no trespassing signs, and commercial exploitation of natural resources, men and women continued the seasonal movements for roots, berries, fish, and game. The frequent laments of agricultural extension agents attest to that practice because roaming, in their eyes, meant the neglect of stock, garden, and fields. Women testified repeatedly to the importance of the old ways as their communities sought to reclaim their accustomed resource base.[74] Women continued to trade traditional goods and pass on ancient skills to newer generations.[75] Discouraged from becoming farmers by policies that refused to recognize their right to economic self-determination, these women refused to accept the model of dependent womanhood.

What can these women's story tell us about farm women? If we can look at farmwomen's situation through their eyes, we can learn a great deal. Why was it unappealing? Certainly their fathers', husbands', and sons' reluctance to bear the burdens and take the risks of farming in the twentieth century shaped their decision. But what other reasons entered into their decision? They may well have preferred a situation in which they controlled economic resources, shaped their own work rhythms, and practiced and passed on their own skills rather than turn themselves into someone else's ideal of femininity. Rather than risk the invisibility that is the frequent lot of farmwomen, they perpetuated a culture in which their work received tangible rewards and ceremonial honor. We may well learn important lessons from these women's efforts to remain self-determining agents in the face of persistent efforts to turn them into dependent, domestic creatures.

Perhaps our own root-digging expedition has turned up some sources of the present plight faced by farm women that renders them "invisible farmers." An analysis of a century and more of policy, designed and implemented as though only men could farm, reveals how deeply rooted is our definition of the farmer as the *man* who takes a wife. Women, in effect, have been defined as objects, rather than subjects in the long agricultural tradition to which we are heir. Policy based upon that male-defined agricultural pattern can never give women the consideration or the resources they need. The history of Native American women in the Inland Northwest can tell us, therefore, what we must uproot before we can create policies that would meet the needs of rural women.

NOTES

[1] For useful examples of literature examining this process globally, see Barbara Rogers, *The Domestication of Women: Discrimination in Developing Societies* (New York: St. Martin's Press, 1979); Eleanor Leacock and Helen I. Safa, eds., *Women's Work: Development and the Division of Labor by Gender* (South Hadley, Ma.: Bergen and Garvey, 1986); Margot I. Duley and May I. Edwards, *The Cross-Cultural Study of Women: A Comprehensive Guide* (New York: The Feminist Press, 1986), and Ester Boserup, *Women's Role in Economic Development* (London: Allen and Unwin, 1970); for literature more specifically addressing this issue in relation to Native American women, see Joan M. Jensen, "Native American Women and Agriculture: A Seneca Case Study," *Sex Roles* 3:5 (1977) 423-441; Theda Purdue, "Southern Indians and the Cult of True Womanhood," in Walter J. Fraser, Jr., R. Frank Saunders, Jr., and Jon L. Wakelyn, eds., *The Web of Southern Social Relations: Women, Family and Education* (Athens, Ga.: University of Georgia Press, 1985); and Patricia Albers and Beatrice Medicine, eds., *The Hidden Half: Studies of Plain Indian Women* (Washington, D.C.: University Press of America, 1983).

[2] The ethnographic account above is based upon the following: Robert H. Ruby and John A. Brown, A *Guide to the Indian Tribes of the Pacific Northwest* (Norman: University of Oklahoma Press, 1986); Deward E. Walker, Jr., "Mutual Cross-Utilization of Economic Resources in the Plateau: An Example from Aboriginal Nez Perce Fishery Practices," Washington State University Laboratory of Anthropology, *Report of Investigation* No. 41, Pullman, Wn., 1967; Verne F. Ray, "Cultural Relations in the Plateau of Northwestern America," *Publications of the Frederick Webb Hodge Anniversary Publication Fund*, 3, Southwest Museum, Los Angeles, Ca., 1939; Angelo Anastasio, "The Southern Plateau: An Ecological Analysis of Intergroup Relations," University of Idaho Laboratory of Anthropology, Moscow, Idaho 1975; Judith Giniger, "Aboriginal Female Status and Autonomy on the Columbia Plateau," M.A. Thesis, Washington State University, 1977; Alan Gould Marshall, "Nez Perce Social Groups: An Ecological Interpretation," Ph.D. Dissertation, Washington State University, 1977; and David Haydn Chance, "Influences of the Hudson's Bay Company on the Native Cultures of the Colvile District," M.A. Thesis, University of Idaho, 1973.

[3] Alice Fletcher, "The Indian Woman and Her Problems," unpublished lecture, Alice C. Fletcher and Francis LaFlesche papers, National Anthropological Archives, Smithsonian Institution, Washington, D.C.; hereafter, ACF/DC.

[4] Clifford Drury, *First White Women over the Rockies*, Vol. 1 (Glendale, Calif: Arthur H. Clark, 1963), 214.

[5] Francis Paul Prucha, "The New Christian Reformers," in Francis Paul Prucha, *American Indian Policy in Crisis: Christian Reformers and the Indian, 1865-1900* (Norman: University of Oklahoma Press, 1976), 132-168.

[6]As discussed in a perceptive analysis, Michael C. Coleman, *Presbyterian Missionary Attitudes toward American Indians, 1837-1893* (Jackson: University Press of Mississippi, 1985).

[7]Allen P. Slickpoo and Deward E. Walker, Jr., *Noon-Nee-Me-Poo: (We, The Nez Perces): Culture and History of the Nez Perces*, vol. 1 (Lewiston, Idaho: the Nez Perce Tribe, 1973), 72.

[8]Kate McBeth, *The Nez Perces Since Lewis and Clark* (New York: Fleming H. Revell, 1908), 46.

[9]Eliza Spalding to Mrs. Smith, February 14, 1842, Henry H. Spalding papers, Washington State University, Pullman, Wash. (hereafter, HHS/WSU.)

[10]Reverend Peter (Pierre) DeSmet, "Louise Sighouin," *Coeur d'Alene Teepee*, April 1938.

[11]General O. A. Howard, *Chicago Advance*, June 14, 1877, quoted in N.W. Durham, *History of the City of Spokane and Spokane County Washington from Its Earliest Settlement to the Present Time* (Spokane: The S.J. Clarke Publishing, Co., 1912), 105.

[12]Drury, *First White Women over the Rockies* Vol. I, 213.

[13]*Coeur d'Alene Teepee*, March 1938.

[14]McBeth, *The Nez Perces* which includes an introduction written by Alice C. Fletcher, 76, 120, 102-104.

[15]Coleman, *Presbyterian Missionary Attitudes*, 94-96.

[16]McBeth, *The Nez Perces*, 50-52.

[17]Slickpoo and Walker, *Noon Nee-Me-Poo*, 92, 94.

[18]For a discussion of the 1863 treaty and its repercussions for Nez Perce unity, see Alvin M. Josephy, Jr., *The Nez Perce Indians and the Opening of the Northwest* (Lincoln: University of Nebraska Press, 1979), 377-433.

[19]McBeth, *The Nez Perces*, 98.

[20]Josephy, *The Nez Perce Indians*, 609. For his account of the campaign, see 538-613.

[21]Josephy, *The Nez Perces*, 425.

[22]Quoted in Herbert J. Spinden, "The Nez Perce Indians," *Memoirs of the American Anthropological Association* 2, pt. 3, November 1908, 260. Later anthropologists dispute Spinden's claims that the Nez Perces depended "on prophets from other tribes" but heeded similar prophecies from spiritual leaders among themselves. See Deward E. Walker, Jr., *Conflict and Schism in Nez Perce Acculturation: A Study of Religion and Politics* (Moscow, Idaho: University Press of Idaho, 1985), 49-52.

[23]Josephy, *The Nez Perces*, 426.

[24]Walker, *Conflict and Schism*, 40-51.

[25]For discussions of the Dawes Act, see Loring Benson Priest, *Uncle Sam's Stepchildren: The Reformation of United States Indian Policy, 1865-1887* (New Brunswick, N.J.: Rutgers University Press, 1942); Henry E. Fritz, *The Movement for Indian Assimilation, 1860-1890* (Philadelphia: University of

Pennsylvania Press, 1964); Francis Paul Prucha, ed., *Americanizing the American Indians: Writings by the "Friends of the Indian," 1880-1900* (Lincoln: University of Nebraska Press, 1978); and Francis Paul Prucha, *The Great Father: The United States Government and the American Indians*, Vol. 2 (Lincoln: University of Nebraska Press, 1984).

[26]Dawes quoted in Prucha, *Americanizing the American Indians*, 29.

[27]Gates quoted in Prucha, *Americanizing the American Indians*, 334.

[28]David B. Smits, "The 'Squaw Drudge': An Index of Savagism," *Ethnohistory* 9:4 1982, 281-306.

[29]Henry Dawes, "Past and Present Indian Policy," Hartford, Conn., 1892, in Henry L. Dawes papers, Library of Congress, hereafter Dawes/LC.

[30]Women's National Indian Asociation, Missionary Committee, "Missionary Work of the Women's National Indian Association and Letters of Missionairies," Philadelphia, November 17, 1885, 1, 5, 18.

[31]Mary Crawford, *The Nez Perces Since Spalding* (Berkeley, Ca.: The Professional Press, 1936), 55; Coleman, *Presbyterian Missionary Attitudes*, 85.

[32]Fletcher, "The American Indian Woman," ACF/DC.

[33]Fletcher, "The Indian Woman and Her Problems," ACF/DC.

[34]Alice Fletcher to the Hon. Commissioner of Indian Affairs, June 1884, ACF/DC.

[35]E. Jane Gay to B. May 11, 1890; E. Jane Gay, Squirrel Camp, July 15, 1889, contained in E. Jane Gay, "Choup-nit-ki, With the Nez Perces," illustrated with photographs by the Author and with Decorations by Emma J. Gay, unpublished, in two volumes, Jane Gay Dodge Papers, Schlesinger Library; hereafter Dodge/SL.

[36]U.S. Senate, 50th Congress, 1st Session, Ex. Doc. No. 77, "Letter from the Secretary of the Interior, transmitting, in response to Senate resolution of January 25, 1888, information about the Coeur d'Alene reservation, in Idaho," 5-6; Andrew Seltis, et al., to Honorable John J. Simms, U.S. Indian Agent, Coeur d'Alene Agency, October 21, 1883, Coeur d'Alene Agency, Letters Received, Bureau of Indian Affairs, Record Group 75, Seattle Branch, National Archives; hereafter RG75/NA/Seattle.

[37]Ross R. Cotroneo and Jack Dozier, "A Time of Disintegration: The Coeur d'Alenes and the Dawes Act," *The Western Historical Quarterly*, 5:4 (October 1974), 405-420.

[38]E. Jane Gay, Kamiah, June 24, 1890; E. Jane Gay to J., Lapwai, October 28, 1890, in "Choup-nit-ki," Dodge/SL.

[39]Alice C. Fletcher, introduction, McBeth, *The Nez Perces*, 12; McBeth, 17.

[40]E. Jane Gay, Kamiah, August 17, 1889; Camp Kinkaid, September 10, 1889; Kamiah, June 24, 1890; in "Choup-nit-ki."

[41]E. Jane Gay, Lapwai, May 30, 1891, *Ibid.*

[42]Prucha, *The Great Father*, Vol. 2, 864-88.

[43] According to ethnohistorian Richard White, camas gatherers, for example, were practicing horticulture because the plant needed cultivation and the separation of its bulbs in order to continue to produce. See Richard White, *Land Use, Environment & Social Change: The Shaping of Island County, Washington* (Seattle: University of Washington Press, 1980), 19-23.

[44] John A. Sims to Honorable J. L. Smith, August 26, 1876, Colville Agency, Archives & Manuscripts, Washington State University, Pullman, Wn.; hereafter, Colville/WSU.

[45] Sister Amadeé, Superintendant, Providence of Mary Imaculetta, Coeur d'Alene Reservation, Idaho Territory, to S. D. Waters, U.S. Indian Agent, Colville Agency, July 23, 1884, RG75/NA/Seattle.

[46] Commissioner Thomas J. Morgan to D. W. Eaves, Superintendant, Ft. Lapwai School, January 9, 1890, RG75/NA/Seattle.

[47] Robert A. Trennert, "Educating Indian Girls at Nonreservation Boarding Schools, 1878-1920," *The American Indian: Past and Present*, Roger L. Nichols, ed. (New York: Alfred A. Knopf, 1986), 218-231.

[48] Central Classified Files, Coeur d'Alene, Colville, and Fort Lapwai Agencies, Bureau of Indian Affairs, Record Group 75, National Archives; hereafter, RG75/NA/DC.

[49] Oscar H. Lipps, "Laws and Regulations relating to Indians and Their Lands," (Lewiston, Idaho: 1913).

[50] Based upon my reading of the lease, sales, and patent in fee files, Central Classified Files, RG75/NA/DC.

[51] Nez Perce Home and Farm Association, "Declaration of Purpose and program," Slickpoo and Walker, *Noon Nee-me-poo*, 243-251.

[52] Coeur d'Alene Indian Home and Farm Association, "Constitution," 1925, in Central Classified Files, RG75/NA/DC.

[53] *Ibid.*

[54] Leonard A. Carlson, *Indians, Bureaucrats and Land: the Dawes Act and the Decline in Indian Farming* (Westport, Conn: Greenwood Publishing Co., 1981), 138; Prucha, *The Great Father*, 883-86.

[55] The Petition of the Colville Indians of Washington State to the Honorable Secretary of the Interior and the Honorable Commissioner of Indian Affairs, January 19, 1915, Central Classified Files, RG75/NA/DC.

[56] Based upon my reading of the lease, sales and patent in fee files, Central Classified Files, for the Colville, Coeur d'Alene and Nez Perce agencies, 1907-1918.

[57] James Bernard, et al., to the Honorable Committee on Indian Affairs of the United States Congress now in session at Washington, D.C. (marked received April 18, 1921), Central Classified Files, RG75/NA/DC.

[58] Lewis Meriam, et al., *The Problem of Indian Administration* (Baltimore: The Johns Hopkins Press, 1928), 488-491, 499.

[59] *Ibid.*,523-524.

[60]Kenneth R. Philp, *John Collier's Crusade for Indian Reform: 1920-1954* (Tucson: The University of Arizona Press, 1981), 46-47.

[61]Archie Phinney, "The Nez Perces of Idaho," February 26, 1932, submitted to the Honorable Charles J. Rhoads, Commissioner of Indian Affairs, Central Classified Files, RG75/NA/DC.

[62]Archie Phinney papers, Northern Idaho Agency, RG75/NA/Seattle.

[63]W. A. Lloyd, Special Advisor, to John Collier, Commissioner of Indian Affairs, Memorandum, October 29, 1934.

[64]Louis Balsam to J. M. Steward, November 23, 1938, Central Classified Files, RG75/NA/DC.

[65]Enclosed in a letter from Mary Crawford, missionary to the Nez Perces and niece of the McBeth sisters, to Senator William J. Borah, March 16, 1934, was a copy of a letter from the Nez Perce Tribal Business Committee, dated February 8, 1934 to John Collier, William J. Borah papers, Library of Congress; hereafter, Borah/LC.

[66]Mary Crawford to Floyd O. Brunett, November 22, 1934, Borah/LC.

[67]Proceedings of the Conference at Chemawa, Oregon, April 8 and 9, 1934, to discuss with the Indians the Wheeler-Howard Act," Borah/LC.

[68]Archie Phinney, "Numipu among the White Settlers," Archie Phinney papers, RG75/NA/Seattle. Internal evidence suggests that this history was written in 1936 and 1937 while Phinney was still in the Soviet Union. As a linguist he chose the spelling of his people's name which is variously spelled as other sources indicate.

[69]Donald L. Parman, "Inconstant Advocacy: The Erosion of Indian Fishing Rights in the Pacific Northwest, 1933-1956," in *The American Indian*, 256-271; Lawrence C. Kelly, "The Indian Reorganization Act: The Dream and Reality," in *The American Indian*, 254.

[70]"Proceedings of the Conference at Chemawa," Borah/LC.

[71]Main Classified Files, Northern Idaho and Colville Agencies; Peter Maurice Well, "Political Modernization on the Nez Perce Indian Reservation, 1940-1963," M.A. Thesis, University of Oregon, 1965, 34, 51, 57; film, "Lucy Covington: Native American."

[72]Main Classified Files, Northern Idaho Agency, Colville Agency, RG75/NA/DC; Carolyn Sachs, *Invisible Farmers: Women and Agricultural Production* (Totowa, N.J.: Rowan & Allanheld, 1983).

[73]Crawford, *The Nez Perces*, 48.

[74]Main Classified Files, Northern Idaho Agency, RG75/NA/DC.

[75]According to the testimony of Leah Slaney, whose grandmother is teaching her the arts of root-gathering.

3

SIDELINES AND MORAL CAPITAL:
WOMEN ON NEBRASKA FARMS IN THE 1930s

Deborah Fink[1]

On May 1, 1931, a rural community club in Boone County, Nebraska, held a program in their schoolhouse. The highlight of the evening program was a debate between two teams of women. The topic: "Resolved: That the farm is the most pleasant place for a woman to live." The negative side won (Norskov 1986, 258).

While the family farm has always needed women, women have had their own sensibilities and reactions. Life has never been easy for women in rural Nebraska, from the early days of white settlement in the late nineteenth century, through the hardships of the 1930s and up to the present economic crisis. Most of Nebraska's settlers had migrated through the central corridor of the country – through the humid prairies of Ohio, Indiana, Illinois, Wisconsin, Minnesota, and Iowa – and their backgrounds were in cornbelt farming. They were prepared to grow corn and other humid-area crops and raise livestock in a relatively hospitable prairie climate. What they met in the plains of Nebraska radically changed their way of life.

Both scholars and popular writers have explored the problems of plains farming, but women have been largely absent from the discussions (Baltensperger 1985; Kraenzel 1955; Malin 1984; *Nebraska Farmer*; Olson 1966). This absence weakens such accounts, as women have been central to the farm economy. Indeed, one might argue that the magnitude of women's input and its centrality to farm production have not been carefully assessed precisely because such an analysis would reveal fundamental contradictions in a system that has used women so fully but evaluated and rewarded them so meagerly.

Using an analytical structure that I developed to conceptualize labor in rural Iowa, I find that in Nebraska in the 1930s, just as in Iowa, much of farm women's energy was devoted to the reproduction of the farm work force, while men concentrated on farm commodity production (Fink 1986b, 31-39). Just as in Iowa, women's sidelines – particularly their weekly egg and cream trade – were crucial in maintaining most homes at a time when men made very little income.

In addition to the material contribution, women added an element that I call "moral capital," which was especially critical in the extreme trials of the 1930s. A woman's position as wife and mother in the farm family gave her primary responsibility for nurture. Women were to supply the emotional strength for everyone to keep going; women nursed people, listened to troubles, cheered people up. A woman who fulfilled this role was uncomplaining and thought more of others' needs than of her own. Through her strengths, such a woman would neutralize the shocks of the cruel world and keep a family on the farm – not just in terms of physical needs, but also in terms of the emotional climate. Religious, commercial, governmental, and popular messages prescribed a nurturing role for women. But women's personal experiences of rural life also shaped the way they constructed their roles. Poverty, isolation, and hard work could frustrate a woman's desire to follow the prescribed patterns. Although the provision of moral capital remained as part of women's prescribed role, their own experiences were leading some of them to question, and ultimately reject, an agrarian life.

The 1930s was indeed a time of testing of the agrarian pattern that political and economic interests had promoted on the plains. In the western Cornbelt, the 1930s separated the period of erratic expansion of the farm population from the extended out-migration that continues to the present day in spite of efforts to stem it. Agrarianism and manifest destiny may be blinders leading us to see the earlier historical movement to the plains area as somehow natural or inevitable. By focusing on the experiences of rural women in the western Cornbelt fringe in rural Nebraska, I point to a long-standing pattern of distress and disaccommodation with farm life. By the 1930s, suffering was acute, and women such as those in the debate could persuade their friends and neighbors that farm life in rural Nebraska was not all one might wish. With special reference to Boone County in east central Nebraska, I will discuss farm women and their evolving responsibilities for the maintenance of the family farming operations.

Data for this paper derive from a variety of sources. These include women's manuscripts, articles written by women in the *Nebraska Farmer*, records of deeds, and published census and statistical reports. My great grandparents homesteaded in this area in 1883 and I lived there from 1946 to 1961. Thus, this work draws on my own family stories and observations. In 1986 and 1987 I spent seven months living in Boone and nearby Madison Counties doing participant observation, archival work, and intensive interviews. I have drawn on transcripts of taped interviews done with thirty women and two men, all born between 1892 and 1922, and all having lived in this area in the 1930s.[2]

THEORETICAL CONSIDERATIONS

In her analysis of housework in the antebellum industrialization of America, Jeanne Boydston (1986) establishes that the unpaid work of women and children provided the surplus that made it possible for employers to pay workers wages that were less than the cost of the reproduction of the workforce. Women's work, which was not quantified or acknowledged, was important precisely because its invisibility enabled industrialists to discount it: being invisible, it was free.

What made women's work invisible and removed it from accounting as a factor of production was the separation of the domestic and political/legal domains. As Anna Tsing and Sylvia Yanagisako (1983, 511-12) point out, this separation does not result from natural, biological characteristics of women; it is a product of particular historical circumstances. In America and Europe two hundred years ago, such economic operations as bakeries, farms, and craft manufacturing were located in the home. Membership in the household entailed shared responsibility for the household business. When businesses were enlarged and removed from the home, the majority of women and children were defined as nonworkers.

While farms remained household operations, statisticians and economists began to consider the farm work force as consisting of the adult males on the farm and to consider work done by other household members as not being farm work. Although the farm continued to draw on the labor of the farm household in a more direct manner than did large urban businesses, the concept of separate spheres appeared in the farm setting just as it had in the city. When the U.S. Department of Agriculture established the Extension Service in 1914, a separate home economics section dealt with the problems of farm women, which were assumed to be restricted to food preparation and home management. The women's pages of the *Nebraska Farmer* were called "Home Circle" (1932a, 1932b), thereby placing women's sphere in the home. Even when they managed poultry operations, cooked, or did various livestock chores, women were apt to report that they did not do farm work. When farmers quantified their production inputs (as directed by the Extension Service), they did not factor in the labor contributed by women; this was separate. This separation arose from the qualitatively different value assigned to family as a sphere in which relations were positive and nonquantified.

With farming in Nebraska, just as with eastern antebellum industrialization, a full accounting of production costs – including the value of women's labor – would not support the developing production system of family farms. Nebraska farming was labor intensive. There were few trees to break the wind or to provide wood for fuel, fenceposts, houses, and barns. Although pioneers learned to build temporary sod buildings, wood and other building materials had to be imported, necessitating increased outputs of labor and capital. Plains dwellers used buffalo and cow chips as fuel, but this also entailed added labor inputs. Rainfall was less than optimal for corn farming, and locating water was frequently a problem. The necessity of finding and carrying water presented an unexpected challenge to those from the East. The soil was of marginal quality for corn production. Compared to the eastern cornbelt regions, more acres of Nebraska land had to be plowed, planted, and cultivated to produce a given crop.

In spite of intensive labor on Nebraska land, crop failures could wipe out the slender margin of surplus needed for continued farming. Subsistence was precarious under normal conditions; during the Depression and drought of the 1930s the situation was desperate. During this time women extended themselves to the fullest to continue the daily reproduction of the farm work force. Following the analyses of Boydston (1986), and Tsing and Yanagisako (1983), we can go beyond describing the horrors of the Depression in terms of low farm income to examine the unpaid labor and emotional resources exacted from women.[3] The family was the institution that mediated the contradiction of highly valued, but unremunerated, labor.

GEOGRAPHIC AND HISTORIC BACKGROUND

The ninety-eighth meridian, roughly the transition between the cornbelt and the drier, less hospitable farming environment to the West, divides the eastern, more populous third of Nebraska from the western region of the state. Even eastern Nebraska is marginal as a corn-producing area, yet the state was settled with the same optimism as the earlier frontier to the east. Samuel Aughey, a professor at the University of Nebraska, theorized that plowing the soil increased evaporation and produced rainfall. He put forth his hypothesis that "rain follows the plow" in 1880 (Creigh 1977, 174). C. D. Wilber popularized the hypothesis in 1881 in a tract widely used by the railroads. Those who disagreed were unpopular. Wilber and Aughey later declared that those who disputed the claim that cultivation increases rainfall were in league with cattlemen to monopolize the West and keep farmers out (Olson 1966, 167). Railroads, which had received substantial land grants in exchange for laying tracks, put out glowing promotional literature to attract buyers for their land and business for their trains. The U.S. government also promoted westward migration with a number of measures. Since women's fertility was the key to populating the region on a permanent basis, women were encouraged to go West as wives (Fink 1986a).

But optimism was not enough. The rain did not follow the plow, although there were several encouraging years in the 1880s. Women were faced with the responsibility of bearing and rearing children, clothing and feeding the farm labor force, and nursing people through illness and discouragement without the medical or social services or household amenities to which they had been accustomed. Mari Sandoz's (1970, 17) description of the young bride's arrival in western Nebraska is accurately bleak:

> Usually she had grown up in a settled region, perhaps with Victorian sheltering, and was shocked by her new home, isolated, at the best a frame or log shack with cracks for the blizzard winds, or only a soddy or dugout into some bank, with a dirt floor and the possibility of wandering stock falling through the roof.
>
> The long distance to the stagecoach or the railroad, with walking not good, kept many a woman to her bargain. There are, however, stories of desperate measures used to hold the wife – ropes or chains or locked leg hobbles, but the more common and efficacious expedient was early pregnancy.

Luna Kellie, who arrived in central Nebraska in 1876, did not get to town for eighteen months after her arrival. Besides losing two babies in the early years, she and her husband experienced crop failure, poverty, and hunger before losing their first homestead (Kellie, date unknown). Agnes Suiter Freeman, the wife of the famous first homesteader, Daniel Freeman, never managed to feel at home and, according to her great grandson, always hated Nebraska. Both Agnes and Daniel Freeman were physicians, and although they achieved substantial wealth and eminence, Agnes Freeman's heart remained in Le Claire, Iowa, which had been her earlier home. According to her daughter, she often visited there and wished to be buried with her relatives in Iowa. Significantly, her body lies at her husband's side in Nebraska ("The First Homesteader" 1935, 19).[4]

Grace Snyder, who moved from Missouri to a homestead in central Nebraska as a young girl, claimed that life in rural Nebraska was hardest on her mother, who had never wanted to make the move. Continuing, she wrote:

> [Mama] had grown up among the green fields and woods of Missouri where she lived in a big white house. She liked nice things, good food, pretty clothes, handsome furniture. I wonder, now, how she stood the hard life we lived, those first years in Nebraska. I know she must have been nearly crushed by the unexpected bigness of the prairie, the endless blue of the sky, our rough, homemade furniture, and the almost total lack of neighbors (Snyder 1963, 15).

Still, her mother, although a frail woman of less than one hundred pounds, planted a garden, sold eggs and homemade butter for her income, sewed the children's clothing, and had a baby every other year for over twenty years. Even for those women who coped well, life on the pioneer Nebraska farm was difficult at best. There are many stories of suicide, insanity, and deep depression.

My reading of Nebraska pioneer history confirms Carl Kraenzel's (1955, 4) claim that a civilization such as that in the eastern United States which was based on a humid climate, cannot thrive in the Great Plains without subsidy or without the impoverishment of the residents. Although settlers continued to homestead the 160-acre plots that had been ample as farms in neighboring Iowa, fewer than half of the Nebraska homesteaders lasted the five years necessary to receive land patents. The land records of Boone County show numerous instances in which a series of five or more homesteaders in succession would stake a claim on a given quarter section, make improvements on it, and try unsuccessfully to live on it for five years before relinquishing the claim to the next optimist. Life on the plains entailed a painful and continuing adaptation of agricultural practices and basic cultural assumptions. Rural Nebraska taught its own lessons and made its own demands of those who lived there.

Cattlemen of the West, who had been using the unassigned range as free grazing for their cattle, sneered at the lifeways of the homesteaders who staked claims and put up fences. The cattlemen stood to lose their livelihoods, and they resisted the migration of eastern settlers. Mari Sandoz (1935, 1937), the daughter of a western Nebraska homesteader, wrote of violent confrontations in the closing years of the nineteenth century in which cattlemen murdered farm settlers, burned buildings, and stole livestock. Farmers fought back by arming themselves, but their most important ally was the government. The ranchers also appealed to the government for grazing rights. They hoped that President Theodore Roosevelt, having been a rancher himself, would support their cause. But the federal government had consistently seen its interest in populating the middle of the country with farmers. Farmers' settlement was denser and more stable than that of ranchers, and farms produced more market goods and tax revenue than did ranches. In 1904 Congress passed the Kinkaid Act, which provided for homesteading of 640-acre plots in thirty-seven counties of western

Nebraska. These plots were too small for ranches, and they encouraged farm settlement in areas that were clearly unsuitable for the smaller farms of the original Homestead Act. Thus, the dominant interests in the state were committed to an economy of family farms. Family farms, unlike cattle operations, involved extensive exploitation of the labor of women and children.

THE 1930s

The conditions of the 1930s presented Nebraska farming with the greatest threat to its survival since settlement. The post-World War I period of the 1920s had brought a drastic deflation of farm prices, which forced many farms and rural banks into insolvency. Between 1921 and 1923 one-quarter of Nebraska's farms had failed; 650 Nebraska banks had closed in the 1920s (Creigh 1977, 185). But other farmers took over the bankrupt farms, and the system as a whole continued. In spite of the stock market crash of 1929, Nebraska farmers entered the 1930s with the optimism they had to have to stay in business. In the 1930s, however, Nebraska's marginal rainfall failed. Year after year the state was blistered by searing mid-summer winds that killed whatever was not already dead from the drought. Winds whipped up the soil that had been plowed on the fragile hills of the West and carried it in dark clouds for hundreds of miles. Fences and machinery were buried in drifts of dust, cars stalled, and people and animals choked to death. The farm commodity economy failed completely; it netted nothing. The critical challenge was the survival of the farm population, and it was this challenge, the reproduction of the farm population, that had been women's traditional sphere of responsibility on the farm.

Farm women's reports of the Depression fall into two broad patterns: some women were able to maintain a farming life with some semblance of normalcy, while others saw their lives overtly disintegrating into confusion and desperation. While the accounts of the two groups differ markedly, I have not been able to find a concrete material basis for the difference in terms of farm tenure, farm enterprise, family size, or family history. The line separating the two groups was thin. The very uncertainty and indefiniteness of this line may have led those women on the ordered side to exaggerate their security and position in order to effect some separation between their conditions and what they feared and knew might happen to them.

Women who stayed on the farms assumed new responsibilities in providing for their families during this period. Farm women's letters appearing in the *Nebraska Farmer* in the early 1930s told about their lives and described how their hard work was bringing their families through the hard spell. Women interviewed in 1986 and 1987 recalled extraordinary measures that they and other women took to provide for their families.

The first line of defense against the hard times was increased subsistence production. One woman told of how, when the rain failed, her mother put a barrel of water on runners and dragged it out to the garden so that they could water. Women planted large potato patches both on top of hills and in ravines so that they had a greater likelihood of harvesting at least one planting. They made clothing with flour sacks. A woman wrote to the *Nebraska Farmer* detailing her strategy for managing: in addition to grinding their own grains for flour, breakfast cereal, and cornmeal, she had raised 100 pounds of pinto beans; she canned 22 quarts of stringbeans, 40 quarts of tomatoes, 200 quarts of cherries, 50 quarts of apples and 40 quarts of beef and pork; she cured 6 hams and rendered 70 pounds of lard. By cutting out tea and coffee and substituting her labor for money, she had reduced her grocery bill, which was $700 in 1929, to $249 in 1932 ("How One Family Managed" 1934, 12).

Many women would stress the satisfaction they received from doing their jobs well and being thrifty. One woman wrote to the *Nebraska Farmer* to say:

> We do our own butchering, raise as much food as the grasshoppers will allow, make our own soap, can all we can and utilize everything possible to add to our means and fill that gap science calls the stomach.
>
> We always bought bread but now I bake and oh, what satisfaction it is to turn flour, lard, salt and yeast into crusty, brown loaves or to magically mix eggs, sugar, flour, etc. into a cake or pie!
>
> There is so much pleasure for us if we but open our eyes and see it ("Home Circle" 1932b, 10).

In reports such as these, Depression difficulties seem bearable.

Small scale production for local exchange intensified during the Depression, as farm people sought new ways to make their household economies function. Articles in the *Nebraska Farmer* detailed reports of women selling garden plants, baby ducks, canned goods, cottage cheese, butter, canaries, hooked rugs, and yeast cakes (Home Circle 1932a, 8; "How We Earn Extra Money" 1932, 10). In addition to cash exchanges, home produce could be traded for services that normally necessitated money. Karen, whose daughter was born in 1932, related that after the birth she dressed chickens each week and took them to the doctor until the bill was paid.[5] As before the 1930s, many farm women made approximately twenty dollars per month by keeping country schoolteachers in their homes. Since most of what the schoolteachers consumed would have been produced by women on the farm, this boarding enterprise was another way to transfer home production into the exchange economy.[6]

Women also continued important poultry and cream enterprises, which had been their traditional source of money for household items. In most instances men helped milk, produced the feed for the cows, moved them, and cleaned the stalls, but women usually did some milking, separated the cream, stored it, and carried the skimmed milk to the pigs; women were always responsible for the tedious chore of washing the cream separator. Women and children produced the butter that some farm people sold or traded. Ona, born in 1908 and married in 1927, was one of many who stressed the centrality of eggs and cream in the household economy of the 1930s when she related, "Most of the income in the thirties was from eggs and cream. You didn't raise crops to sell."

A 1935 *Nebraska Farmer* article on poultry made the point that, while farm women could not control market conditions, they could manage their laying enterprises to get their families through. According to the article, "Flocks of 200 hens have paid for their own feed and the grocery bill of a family of eight, with a little over to buy gas" (McKenney 1935, 6). In the 1930s, on a farm that produced much of its own food, a woman who could earn several hundred dollars a year with small enterprises might support a household.

It was small enterprises, carried on in the margins, that provided cash for the households when major crops and livestock enterprises failed. A 1935 article in *Nebraska Farmer* stated,

> Sidelines have saved many a trying situation during the last few years. Often it is the wife and mother who finds pleasure in doing something profitable to help her family. Some women have turned to chicken raising, others to baking, needle work, painting or various other lines of endeavor (Baier 1935:60).

Even when a woman marketed her products, she was viewed as a wife and mother finding pleasure in helping her family. The *Nebraska Farmer* article went on to tell of a housewife and mother who raised sheep as "an interesting and enjoyable sideline." In seven years she had purchased stock and equipment to build up a flock of ninety-nine sheep and earned nine hundred dollars for her home. The definition of these enterprises as sidelines was significant in that they were held separate from the mainstream of the economy, which was reserved for men's activities.

When women contributed wages or salaries to the farm family it was more often as daughters than as mothers or wives. Married women lost their teaching jobs during the 1930s, but a daughter's income from teaching country school was a common source of cash for a household. One Boone County woman recalled that seventy-one students graduated with her high school class of 1932 and about thirty-five of them took a normal course, which allowed them to teach in a rural school. Although there were over ninety rural schools in the county, there were many applicants for each job. A young woman was lucky and respected if she could get a job. If she could live with her parents while she taught, her fifty-dollar monthly check might pull her parents through.

Jane told of helping her family when she was teaching from 1932 to 1939:

> During the time that I taught . . . I didn't make big wages, but teachers did get paid. . . . I loaned my dad money to buy a tractor to continue farming, bought my brother-in-law a car that he thought he had to have, and then, of course, I had to save enough to go to summer school to renew my certificates, too. . . . On top of that, I saved up enough to furnish my house when I got married. All the furniture and dishes and linens. That much in seven years.

She was, of course, forced to give up her teaching job when she was married.

Edith, born in Boone County in 1917, lived with her parents and taught school from 1935 to 1940. She recalled:

> After I started teaching I bought the groceries every Saturday, because it was hard times. And when we got a catalog I'd always send for things for my sisters. . . . I helped out. I suppose they would have made it okay, but his made it much better.

While reports such as these would lead us to believe that the Depression was manageable, other farm women of this area had less rosy memories. Like the more fortunate young women who could go to high school and get teaching certificates, these women also contributed to their families, but in harsher and more isolated settings. Lenora, born on a farm in 1916, was unable to go to high school as she had no support for either the six-mile round-trip commute or for getting a room in town. She stayed on the family farm and struggled. Her narrative described a long life of work with precious little relief. It started in 1930 when she was fourteen:

> You know, that's hard work when you go out and do a man's work. See, when my brother got married I had to go out and be Dad's hired man. I milked the cows at night. We had a few sheep and I took care of the sheep, manured the barns, did the calf pens and things like that. That's man's work, but I went out and done it. . . .
> No wonder I'm so tired and wore out. People say, "Well, Lenora, you're not old." I'm not old, but I've worked down 'til I am old. I can't go no more like I should.

Valerie, born in 1922, said she came "from the wrong side of the tracks," although her family (like Lenora's) owned their farm and had the same production lines that others did. Valerie quit school in the tenth grade in order to earn money and not be a burden to her family. One of eight children, she started to help with milking when she was six. In 1934 her family packed up and left for Oregon, where she picked fruit, worked in cafes, and did housekeeping. In 1938 the family returned, having been unable to establish themselves in truck gardening on the west coast. They were able to rent their old farm:

> I'll never forget it. We were desperately poor. We had nothing to eat. We came back in the winter. We had our canned goods with us. We had no meat, no milk, no eggs, no money to buy any chickens. So my dad hunted. I know people find this hard to believe. . . . Dad hunted rabbits and I tell you we ate rabbits and pheasants just about any way that you could fix them.

She noted that in Oregon there were canning factories, and this meant that a woman could always find a job of some kind, while in Nebraska most women did not work outside the home. Valerie's family was unusual in that they came back to Nebraska. She said that not one of the friends she knew in Nebraska in the 1930s is living in Nebraska now.

As the drought and Depression continued, more and more farm operations disintegrated. In Boone County, where average annual rainfall is 25.48 inches, rainfall dropped from 25.28 inches in 1930 to a low of 12.63 inches in 1936, and it did not reach a normal level again until 1941 (USDA 1930-1941). Wind and grasshoppers, which thrive in dry weather, completed the devastation. In 1937 Boone County pastures and crops were reduced to five percent of normal production, gardens dried up, horses were unable to work, and farmers were forced to sell or slaughter starving livestock. Only one-fourth of the farm families were receiving direct government grants. Farmers, who had held themselves to be independent and disdainful of government assistance, petitioned for immediate drought aid (*Albion News* 1937). The local newspaper carried notices of thirty-eight sheriff's sales in 1938, and there were scores of other farm families who voluntarily liquidated their assets (*Albion News* 1938).

For the state as a whole, between 1935 and 1940 over 60,000 persons migrated to the west coast, and over 40,000 moved to contiguous states (USDC 1946, 106, 134). There were 87,534 fewer farm people in 1940 than in 1930 – a drop of fifteen percent. Among farm people between the ages of fifteen and forty-four, there was an eighteen percent drop in population (computed from USDC 1943, 590). Although the fertility rate was high by national standards, the 1930s showed a marked decline in the number of births on Nebraska farms: in 1930 there were 506 farm children under age five for every 1000 women aged fifteen to forty-four; in 1940 there were 424 (USDC 1943:590).

For Boone County, an assessment of the number of births and the declining population reveals that the county's net migration loss during the 1930s was twenty-nine percent (computed from USDC 1932, 1934-43, 1943). This was a demographic response to the diminishing returns of labor applied to a poor farming environment, and it represented a defeat of the vision of prosperity through intensive farming. Unlike the situation in neighboring Iowa, where farms offered subsistence and refuge from Depression hardship (Fink and Schwieder 1984), rural Nebraska was shaken to its roots. As the 1930s developed from a time of economic crisis to a time of crisis of spirit as well, women's moral resources became critical.

The *Nebraska Farmer* and the local newspapers frequently predicted an early end to the Depression, but people were becoming more and more discouraged as the years passed with no relief. Psychological as well as economic depression became a major problem. Carrie, a Boone County woman who was married in 1934, explained that she had swept up mounds of dirt every day and struggled with her gardens and chickens, besides giving birth to three daughters. She said:

> I was just so busy. . . . The heat was what I thought was the worst.
> Day after day it was so awful hot, and the southwest winds would
> just clip things on the southwest side of our house.

Margaret, born in 1892, saw her children growing up on the farm as the family was losing it. She said that the thirties were "terrible, heartbreaking years." Margaret and her husband had originally hoped and planned that their three children would stay in the area and farm, but they finally came to believe that leaving the farm was the best thing for the children. The children left; then Margaret and her husband also left to be sheltered by relatives in rural Iowa.

Many people lost heart. In 1938 a farm woman wrote to the *Nebraska Farmer* of her deep disappointment that her daughter, who had graduated from high school and was working in town, was now preparing to marry a farmer:

> They will start farming with a load of debt. When I think of the struggle ahead for her, I actually ache. I didn't plan this kind of life for her, but what can I do? Has some mother had a similar experience? ("Let's Talk it Over" 1938, 6)

Women's replies to this mother concerned ways that she could come to terms with her daughter's life and with Nebraska farming. No one suggested a way that either the mother or daughter might change her lot as a farm woman. For these *Nebraska Farmer* readers, the challenge was to learn to like farm life and support others in staying on the farm.

By the time the Depression and drought had run for nearly ten years, farm leaders turned from prescriptions for making it through the hard times to exhortations not to leave. The *Nebraska Farmer*'s editorials became increasingly critical of those who sought relief and those who left. The editor of the local newspaper in Boone County defended the publication of the names of persons on relief by stating,

> No one wishes to embarrass those who through no fault of their own find themselves dependent on relief funds for the necessities of life, nor do those who are compelled to dig deep into their jeans for money with which to meet the relief load feel that they should contribute to the support of professional reliefers (*Albion News* 1938).

In the spring of 1940, at the annual state convention of the women's extension project clubs, Clayton Watkins, the state extension forester addressed the gathered women with a plea to stay on the farm and fight the good fight:

> A city job may mean a greater income but I wonder if it always means contentment and a satisfactory way of life. Material things can be bought at a price but you can't buy satisfaction at any price (Weaver 1940, 8).

A woman might have asked him if life on a Nebraska farm always meant contentment and a satisfactory way of life. His speech, besides being a call for women to commit their moral resources to the agrarian way of life, was a farewell address as he left for a city job in Colorado.

Nebraska farm leaders tended to see farm problems in terms of federal government policies that channeled people out of farming. Toward the end of the 1930s, the *Nebraska Farmer*, never a supporter of President Franklin Roosevelt or the New Deal, became increasingly critical of the federal attempts to discourage corn farming in Nebraska. Editorials argued that the farm program, under the direction of Secretary of Agriculture Henry A. Wallace, an Iowan, favored Iowa and penalized Nebraska. Iowa was a major producer of corn,

Nebraskans were trying to buy feed for their livestock, and the aim of supporting corn prices by curbing production made little sense to Nebraskans. Indeed, carloads of starving cattle had been shipped to Iowa from Nebraska, and Iowa farmers bought them cheap and fed them from their ample supply of hay and grain. Wallace was reducing corn acreage allotments in Nebraska in order to relieve the corn surplus and to take fragile soil out of row-crop production. The *Nebraska Farmer* charged that the farm program was tailored to meet the needs of Iowa and that Iowa, rather than Nebraska, was responsible for the corn surplus (*Nebraska Farmer* 1939B, 8). The journal protested vigorously when the U.S. Department of Agriculture tried to encourage range and grass rather than wheat farming in western Nebraska (Cargill 1939, 18). This reaffirmed the vision of Nebraska as a farm state.

Accordingly, by the late 1930s, *Nebraska Farmer*'s articles addressed to women no longer told of ingenious and enjoyable ways they could bring their families through. The later messages were oriented toward convincing women that their lives on Nebraska farms were noble and that they were superior to those who had left farming.

From 1938 to 1940 Blanche Pease, the wife of a tenant farmer in central Nebraska, wrote a series of features called "Daughter of Nebraska," in which she examined farm life in Nebraska and decided that it was beautiful and that farm people were strong and honest. One of her first features read:

> Prairie Haven is a rented house, and ours is a happiness made up of the singing drums of nature, good neighbors and good books. . . .
> Like a mother I may recognize [Nebraska's] shortcomings but her good points overcome them.
> Nebraska, how your charms enchant me! You are the song that sings within my heart! (Pease 1938, 11).

Readers wrote to praise Pease for her uplifting portrayals of farm life. One letter stated:

> I admire Mrs. Pease for her intense loyalty to our state. Citizens of California have popularized their state through good salesmanship. Are we to stand idly by, and let other states entice our young folks away from Nebraska? Why not convince them through salesmanship that Nebraska has much to offer? Mrs. Pease has truly launched a very worthy campaign (*Nebraska Farmer* 1939a, 22).

Blanche Pease continued to write descriptive and encouraging essays for the *Nebraska Farmer* in the latter 1930s, but increasingly her columns turned to an outpouring of sadness at the hard work and futility of farm women's lives in the margins of the farm belt. "Moving Time" told of her feelings at her move on March 1, the day when all shifting tenant farmers across the state took up their new homes:

Moving time is a heartbreaking time for farm wives. . . .

March first is so often a stormy, unpleasant day, and that makes moving time all the harder. . . .

Arriving at the new home, the farm wife goes into the cold and chilly interior and watches while they set up the stoves and bring in the piles of boxes, the beds and mattresses and the many odds and ends, setting them down in incongruous piles in the shabby, ill-smelling rooms.

Somehow or other they get the beds set up, and she finds some sort of food to feed her huddled brood. She makes a great pot of coffee, her husband drinks of it and keeps trying to tell her with glances and clumsy words that things won't be so bad when they get things straightened out and arranged.

But what does a man know of the desolated heart of a woman in a strange house, among forbidding walls and with their belongings piled so strangely they cannot recognize them?

At times like this the farm woman feels like crying her heart out, but she seldom does. It does so little good (Pease 1940, 10).

But true to the continuing theme of the publication, Pease ended with an optimistic assessment of life on the Nebraska farm:

For the heart of a woman is an elastic thing. And none is stronger and sturdier and more filled with courage than the farm wife's, for she knows how to sift the bitter from the sweet, and savor it. She knows that it is not such a bad world after all (Pease 1940, 10).

This was one of the last "Daughter of Nebraska" essays printed in *Nebraska Farmer*.

CONCLUSION

The nature of women's contribution to the Nebraska farming operation shifted in the course of the Depression and drought of the 1930s. When the hard times were perceived as a short-term phenomenon women were urged to simply produce more, consume less, and be more thrifty. By the end of the Depression, however, women's most important job was to generate the satisfaction that could not be bought at any price. All through the ordeal the family was the idiom in which women's labor was defined, and their production was circumscribed within the limits of the family. As such, this production remained outside the farm economy as this economy was defined in public debates by those who contributed to the formation of farm policy. Its invisibility made impossible accurate assessment of the costs of Nebraska farming. It may have been that women's input was so vital that assessing it was a threat to the structure of Nebraska farming.

There were strong pressures on women to be heroic, self- sacrificing individuals, but this ideal of rural Nebraska women seems to have come more from those who were prescribing behavior than from women who were describing their own experiences. The daughters who taught school and the other women who managed to hold the farms together did enable the survival of Nebraska farming. On the other hand, Lenora had this message for an urban relative who saw her family's Nebraska farm as a comfortable haven in the Depression years:

> She hollered she had it hard in the city. Well, boy, you come out in the country if you thought you had it hard. You'd learn something. You could wade in the mud. If there was shit you could wade in it and *like it*. Aach! I don't care much about the farm (emphasis added).

Liking it was a critical contribution, but as the Depression wore on women like Lenora were less and less inclined to provide the optimism and encouragement that were so necessary for farm life on the Great Plains. Lenora was running low on moral capital. Like the women in the rural school debate who succeeded in making the point that the farm was not the most pleasant place for a woman, Lenora could resist the pressures of prescribed values.

Contradictory tensions, including economic depression, drought, the advantages of farm life, the difficultires of farm life, and the admonitions of farm leaders, all impinged on Nebraska farm women. Some left the area; some stayed on farms; some stayed in rural Nebraska but left the farms. Few were unaffected. As the Nebraska farm production outlook deteriorated in the 1930s, farm women's production role shifted. Of equal significance was the shift in the way women viewed their lives on the farm, a shift which ultimately could not be totally prevented by the efforts of farm leaders to convince them that farm life was good for them and their families.

NOTES

[1] My sister, Kate Hansen, a farm woman living in Madison County, Nebraska, has provided insight and support throughout the period of research and writing. Jane Knowles made helpful comments on an earlier draft of this paper.

[2] Being an anthropologist, I have followed the accepted practice within this discipline of protecting the anonymity of my informants. At each interview I promised the interviewee that, while I anticipated using the interview transcript and quoting from it in my writing, I would not identify her or him by name or include details that would lead others to easily do so. Like the notes containing my other field data, the complete interview transcripts are not available to the public. When I quote from interview transcripts I use pseudonyms consisting of a single given name.

[3] Although the issue is beyond the scope of this paper, a considerable amount of free labor was also extracted from children during the Depression. The debates on the child labor law and several reports of children's contributions

to the household make clear the economic advantage of children (see, for example, "The Children's Part With Poultry" 1939; "Farmers Oppose Child Labor Amendment" 1935; Hampsten 1986; Leadley 1935).

[4]In addition to information taken from the cited *Nebraska Farmer* article, I learned more about Agnes Suiter Freeman from her great grandson, Berne Miller, of Altadena, California.

[5]Karen, Jane, Edith, Lenora, Valerie, Carrie, and Margaret are pseudonyms of Boone County women interviewed in 1986 and 1987.

[6]In fairness to men (but beyond the scope of this paper), I note that I have recorded several reports in which farm men appear to have increased their efforts in helping with women's traditional work such as gardening and poultry. As one woman explained, "Time was the one thing we had plenty of." Unable to harvest their crops and forced to drastically reduce their livestock holdings, farm men had unaccustomed leisure. Some of them turned their time to helping their wives.

BIBLIOGRAPHY

Albion News. 1937. Sept. 2.

_____. 1938. Feb. 24.

Baier, Hazel. 1935. "Sheep Are Her Hobby." *Nebraska Farmer* 77 (Apr. 27): 6.

Baltensperger, Bradley H. 1985. *Nebraska: A Geography*. Boulder, Colo.: Westview Press.

Boydston, Jeanne. 1986. "To Earn Her Daily Bread: Housework and Antebellum Working-Class Subsistence." *Radical History Review* 35: 7-25.

Cargill, Mary. 1939. "Protests Wheat Goals." *Nebraska Farmer* 81 (Aug. 26): 18.

"The Children's Part with Poultry." 1939. *Nebraska Farmer* 81 (Feb. 11): 6, 23.

Creigh, Dorothy Weyer. 1977. *Nebraska: A Bicentennial History*. New York: W.W. Norton.

"Farmers Oppose Child Labor Amendment." 1935. *Nebraska Farmer* 77 (Feb. 16): 36.

Fink, Deborah. 1986a. "Constructing Rural Culture: Family and Land in Iowa." *Agriculture and Human Values* 3: 43-53.

_____. 1986b. *Open Country, Iowa: Rural Women, Tradition, and Change*. Albany: State University of New York Press.

Fink, Deborah, and Dorothy Schwieder. 1984. "Iowa Farm Women in the 1930s — A Reassessment." Paper presented at the American Farm Women in Historical Perspective Conference, 2-4 Feb., Las Cruces, N. Mex.

"First Homesteader." 1935. *Nebraska Farmer* 77 (Sept. 14): 1, 19.

Hampsten, Elizabeth. 1986. "Child Care on the Homestead Frontier." Paper presented at The Second National American Farm Women in Historical Perspective Conference, 16-18 Oct., Madison, Wis.

"Home Circle." 1932a. *Nebraska Farmer* 74 (Apr. 30): 8.

_____. 1932b. *Nebraska Farmer* 74 (July 23): 10.

"How One Family Managed." 1934. *Nebraska Farmer* 76 (Mar. 17): 12.

"How We Earn Extra Money." 1932. *Nebraska Farmer* 74 (Apr. 2): 10.

Kellie, Luna. Date unknown. Memoirs. Nebraska State Historical Society. Manuscript 3914.

Kraenzel, Carl Frederick. 1955. *The Great Plains in Transition.* Norman: University of Oklahoma Press.

Leadley, Thomas A. 1935. "Shall Congress Control Our Children?" *Nebraska Farmer* 77 (Feb. 2): 1-24.

"Let's Talk it Over." 1938. *Nebraska Farmer* 80 (Mar. 26): 6.

Malin, James. 1984. *History and Ecology: Studies of the Grassland.* ed. Robert P. Swierenga. Lincoln: University of Nebraska Press.

McKenney, Ellen. 1935. "Outlook and Inlook." *Nebraska Farmer* 77(Feb. 16): 6.

Nebraska Farmer. 1939A. Letter. Vol. 81 (Apr. 8): 22.

_____. 1939B Editorial. Volume 81 (Aug. 12): 8.

Norskov, Arnold L. 1986. "Dennison Community Club." In *History of Boone County, Nebraska 1871-1986,* Boone County Historical Society, Inc., 258-59. Dallas, Tex.: Curtis Media.

Olson, James C. 1966. *History of Nebraska.* Reprint. Lincoln: University of Nebraska Press.

Pease, Blanche. 1938. "Daughter of Nebraska." *Nebraska Farmer* 80 (Sept. 24): 11.

_____. 1940. "Moving Time." *Nebraska Farmer* 82 (Mar.23): 10.

Sandoz, Mari. [1935] 1962. *Old Jules.* Boston: Little, Brown; reprint Lincoln: University of Nebraska Press.

_____. [1937] 1981. *Slogum House.* Boston: Little, Brown; reprint Lincoln: University of Nebraska Press.

_____. 1970 *Sandhill Sundays and Other Recollections.* Lincoln: University of Nebraska Press.

Snyder, Grace (As told to Nellie Snyder Yost). 1963. *No Time on My Hands.* Caldwell, Idaho: Caxton Printers.

Tsing, Anna Lowenhaupt, and Sylvia Junko Yanagisako. 1983. "Feminism and Kinship Theory." *Current Anthropology* 24: 511-516.

USDA (U.S. Department of Agriculture), Weather Bureau. 1930-41. *Climatological Data for the United States by Sections. Nebraska Section.* Lincoln.

USDC (U.S. Department of Commerce), Bureau of the Census. 1932. *Fifteenth Census of the United States: 1930. Population.* Vol. 3, Pt. 2: *Montana-Wyoming.* Washington, D.C.: U.S. Government Printing Office.

_____. 1943. *Sixteenth Census of the United States: 1940. Population.* Vol. 2, *Characteristics of the Population.* Pt. 4: *Minnesta-New Mexico.* Washington, D.C.: U.S. Government Printing Office.

_____. 1946. *Sixteenth Census of the United States. Population. Internal Migration 1935 to 1940. Social Characteristics of Migrants.* Washington, DC: U.S. Government Printing Office.

Weaver, Anna Dee. 1940. "Project Club Women Meet." *Nebraska Farmer* 82 (June 29): 8

PORTRAITS
OF FARM WOMEN'S LIVES

4

LAND, IDENTITY, AND AGENCY IN THE ORAL AUTOBIOGRAPHIES OF FARM WOMEN

Nancy Grey Osterud

The most eloquent statement I know of a woman's relationship to the land comes from a Russian immigrant who farmed in upstate New York for more than thirty years. Nadya Stastyshyn, born into a poor peasant family in 1890, emigrated to the United States at the age of sixteen. After working in factories in New England and Binghamton, New York, Nadya and her husband Simon Fenson bought a farm in the Nanticoke Valley. As Nadya recalled the event nearly sixty years later:

> From 1920 we came on this farm. We were poor; it was a hard life; we had a dilapidated farm. My husband was working in the factory, but there wasn't much work so he quit. We decided we would farm. He didn't know anything about farming and I didn't understand farming, but we were young, so we figured we would get along.... I was in town occasionally and saw, every once in a while, a farmer would come into town with his horse and wagon and bring in different things to sell. I thought, I too will try, will take the horse and wagon downtown and sell something. We owned three cows, so I made cheese and butter and took it with me. Many customers bought these from me.[1]

Before long, Nadya had established a regular stand at the Farmers' Market in Johnson City. In addition to butter and cheese, she sold chickens and vegetables. "But vegetables very little profit; too much work and not much good of it," Nadya explained. So, on the advice of another market woman, she decided to begin selling flowers.

> My customers were pleased. I had such a beautiful assortment of flowers; I had asters, zinnias, gladiolas. I sure found success with my flower sales. Many people did not believe me, that I could earn more money at the market than the lady who works in a factory. I found if you have the will, strength, you can do very well.

73

At the end of her interview, Nadya affirmed that:

> even with all of life's tribulations, if I had to relive my life, honest
> to God, I would relive it the same way. If God told me to relive what
> I have been through, I would! Only give me back my strength. I just
> love to work in the fields, in the garden. That was my love, the
> outside, to work. When we were younger, we were able to work the
> fields, the garden, milk cows, tend to the chickens. I liked planting
> new things. When I saw different interesting plants or vegetables, I
> always wanted to have them, too. I feel if I wanted to take the trouble
> to plant, take care of it, why not? I had everything! I loved to work.

Nadya and her husband had to stop farming in 1953, when the public market
closed and ill health made it impossible for Nadya's husband to continue
working outdoors. Then Nadya herself became disabled by arthritis and could no
longer tend a garden.

> We sold everything with the farm but two acres, where we built a
> small house. The land is idle. I can't work it anymore. There it lies
> dormant. When I was able to work I had everything, raspberries,
> vegetables, even flowers. Now, I look at the idle land and it hurts; it
> pains me to know I have the land but I can't work.

Nadya identified with the farm so intimately that she thought of both the land
and herself as "idle" in old age; the pain she felt came from seeing the land lie
dormant, as much as from the arthritis that prevented her from cultivating it.

Nadya's statement epitomizes the way that farm women can develop a sense
of identity through their relationship with the land. For Nadya, living and
working on the farm were central to her self-definition; making things grow was
a source of joy, and making money was a source of self-respect. Indeed, moving
to the farm transformed Nadya's sense of herself. In the earlier sections of her
oral autobiography, Nadya described herself as controlled by necessity and the
will of others. When she arrived in Rhode Island, "they took me to the factory,
so I work in the cotton mill"; when she first came to New York, "my husband
bought a house, so I had to stay at home." After the move to the farm, however,
Nadya became an active agent in her own life history. She described making
decisions herself and controlling her own work. Even her relationship with her
husband changed, as Nadya discovered the value of her labor and her business
acumen.

Most farm women's sense of identity has been shaped by their relationship
to the land. That relationship is not always so positive as Nadya's, and not all
farm women develop so strong a sense of being in control of their own destiny.
But land, identity, and agency – women's sense of their ability to shape their
lives – are nonetheless closely and complexly intertwined in their life histories.
This chapter examines these dimensions of the lives of farm women by looking
closely at their oral autobiographies. Nadya Stastyshyn Fenson was
exceptionally articulate about what the land meant to her; most farm women

speak more indirectly. But the language they use to describe themselves, their families, and their farms expresses their sense of identity. The way they present critical events in their lives – as things that "happened to" them, or that they actively chose – expresses their sense of agency. In oral autobiographies, women articulate their own perceptions of their place in the world.

The oral autobiographies I will draw upon are those of women born before 1920 who lived in the Nanticoke Valley, a dairy farming community in south-central New York State, before World War II. As part of a research project on relations among women and men in the community since its settlement in the late eighteenth century, I interviewed more than three dozen women, including members of poor and socially marginal families as well as more comfortable and well-connected descendants of the "old settlers."[2] The interviews had a simple life-historical framework; I asked each woman to tell me about her life, beginning with childhood and continuing into the present. Because I wanted these women to tell me their stories in their own ways, I tried to avoid imposing an order on the interviews through the questions I asked. The loosely structured interview format allowed the women to shape their own autobiographies.[3]

Most women told their stories from the view of the life-historical self, placing themselves at the center of their narratives and describing events as they experienced them at the time. They spoke of other people primarily in relation to themselves. The interviews contain relatively little self-conscious retrospection, explaining present situations in terms of the more distant past. They also contain little explicit interpretation, explaining past situations through present understandings. Rather, the women describe situations as they occurred and explain them in terms of their immediate antecedents. The connections between events are primarily historical – as a series linked temporally and causally to one another – or autobiographical – as the distinct experiences of an integral and continuous self.[4]

The modes of narration adopted by Nanticoke Valley women express various ways of conceiving of the self and its relation to experience. Two dimensions are especially salient: the relationship between the self and others, and the relationship of the self to critical life events. At the same time that these women described the past from a subjective perspective, they defined the self as constituted in relationship to others. In most instances, the self was neither independent of nor dependent upon others, but rather interdependent with them. This shaped women's consciousness; the awareness of the narrator was not simply personal, but included her perceptions of and concern about the welfare and feelings of others. Women conceived of relationships in interactive terms. They recognized that not all relationships are symmetrical; children grew from dependence to independence, and husbands had sufficient legitimate social power to try to dominate their wives if they chose. But women themselves espoused an ideal of mutuality.

Nanticoke Valley women expressed two distinct views of the relationship between themselves and the critical events in their life histories. One regards the self as engaged in decision-making, while the other regards the self as engaged primarily in meaning-making. Some women felt that they had shaped their lives by making choices and taking action; although their alternatives may have been limited, their decisions were nonetheless consequential. Other women felt that they were not active agents in their life histories, but rather responsive subjects. They shaped their own life experience through the attitudes they assumed toward external events; although they did not control what happened, their subjective feelings and personal beliefs determined the significance of those events. Both views of the relationship between the self and critical life events see the self as shaping experience rather than simply being shaped by it, but they differ in the degree of agency attributed to the self.[5]

Few women regarded themselves as passive objects, victims of circumstance who had been unable to create meaning in their lives. Women who regarded themselves as powerless and felt that their life histories were without significance either declined to be interviewed or refused to release the interviews they had initially consented to give, so the selection of subjects had a definite bias. These silent women remind us that neither a sense of self-worth nor the possibility of self-determination are givens in many women's lives. Most women felt themselves to be victims of circumstance in some aspects of their lives; they had to struggle for whatever measure of agency they did attain. Nanticoke Valley women, then, experienced a structural and sometimes conscious tension between the forces that would keep them powerless and their desire to shape their own lives. While some women were able to see themselves as active agents in their life histories, most saw themselves as responsive subjects. Telling their stories became another way to create meaning in their lives.

The self-conceptions of Nanticoke Valley women reflect their families' relationship to the land. I will describe five types of relationships women have with the land: as inheriting daughters, wives of inheriting farmers, daughters of marginal farmers, farm partners, and daughters of displaced farmers.[6] Each type will be illustrated by a representative woman whose sense of identity and agency typifies those developed among women with similar relationships to the land.[7] For women whose families had been established on the land for several generations, and who by some lucky accident became the inheritors of their families' farms, there was no separation between autobiography and family history; the self was defined by her position in the line of generational succession and by her family's location in the community. Women who married into established farm families had a somewhat different experience. By marrying inheriting sons, they became absorbed into their husbands' lineages. Their ties to the land came through marital rather than filial relationships and involved the assumption of a new identity.

Women whose parents were struggling to found farms developed a very different sense of self. European immigrants who bought abandoned farms in the early twentieth century shared the goals of the initial settlers of the Nanticoke Valley: to establish their families securely on the land and to pass their farms on to the next generation. But their children did not necessarily internalize those aspirations. Cultural differences between immigrant parents and American-born children exacerbated the tensions inherent in intergenerational relationships in farm families. The daughters of immigrants express an ambivalence toward family and farm expressed by few daughters of long-time residents.

Women who committed themselves to establishing a farm with their husbands shared the identification of self with family and farm that characterizes the descendants of the initial settlers, but did not express the same sense of perpetuity; without an integral connection to the past, these women did not project the existence of the family farm into the future. For some women, finally, relationships to the land were no longer central. Growing up in rural families that were too poor or peripatetic to own land, or that lost their farms as a result of death or the Depression, these women never aspired to found farm families, although some continued to live in the country.

Women's sense of agency, like their sense of identity, is connected with their families' relationship to the land. Inheriting daughters of long-established farm families took for granted their ability to actively shape the course of their lives. Because their individual identity was founded upon their place in the line of generational succession, it did not occur to them to define personal goals in opposition to familial ones. Their families provided them with both security and ample means to attain the ends they sought. Women who married inheriting farmers had a clearer sense of the demands of interdependence. Aware that it limited their autonomy, they chose to make the aspirations of their husbands' families their own and attained a sense of agency by maintaining harmonious family relationships and facilitating farm succession.

Daughters of marginal farmers developed a very different sense of the meaning of interdependence and the possibility of agency; in their experience, both were powerful but problematic. The daughters of immigrants valued family solidarity and romanticized their parents' struggle to get established on the land. At the same time, their families could offer them neither the security nor the resources that long-established farm families provided for their daughters. These women's relationships with their parents were often strained by cultural differences; those who sought to find another path for themselves could expect neither guidance nor support in the effort. Immigrants' daughters were simultaneously compelled to make their own choices and inhibited from doing so. Ultimately, many doubted their ability to direct their own lives.

Farm partners developed a strong sense of interdependence, especially between husbands and wives. While they took pride in having achieved the goal they set early in their married lives, these women did not aspire to autonomy. In some cases, they simply did not conceive of themselves separately from the farm family; in others, the dream of founding a farm was not their own. Farm partners thought of themselves not as having shaped their situation, but rather as having fulfilled its demands. They were meaning-makers rather than decision-makers, and found significance in the very interdependence that inhibited their sense of autonomy. Like the wives of inheriting farmers, farm partners valued family closeness and attained a sense of agency through their familial role.

Women who neither came from nor founded farm families, finally, conceived of themselves as victims of circumstances or as coping with conditions beyond their control much more often than did women from families with more substantial ties to the land. Those who saw their parents lose the family farm felt that people were powerless to determine the course of their own lives; the very notion of agency was beyond these women's experience. A few women from poor, rural non-farm families struggled to improve their situation, asserting their right to a future different from the one that lay before them. While these women were more acutely aware than any others of the institutional and cultural barriers women faced in their struggle for self-determination, they also had the clearest vision of the possibility of autonomy. For them, however, autonomy was a necessity; they had never belonged to a farm family. Most women in the Nanticoke Valley sought fulfillment through their relationships with others and attained whatever sense of agency they did within the limits set by interdependence.

Sarah Briggs Brookdale exemplifies the fusion of autobiography with family history that characterizes inheriting daughters of long-established farm families. As Sarah often pointed out, her ancestors were among the earliest settlers of the Nanticoke Valley, and the land they cleared has remained in the family for five generations. Her paternal grandfather built the house in which Sarah grew up; he shared the house with her parents, and his presence was a central fact of Sarah's childhood. In old age, Sarah identified with him as the inheritor of the land and the narrator of the family history. She told stories she had heard from her grandfather in the same way he had told them, adopting his perspectives as her own. Sarah also told stories she had heard from her father. These too she repeated much as she had heard them; sometimes she used her father's kin terms, referring to her grandfather as "Father," for example. Sarah told two different versions of some stories, one from her grandfather's point of view and the other from her father's. Her father interpreted the past differently than her grandfather did and often implicitly criticized his father's conduct, although not his character. Sarah told both versions at different times without any sense of contradiction, for the fixed and encapsulated form of these narratives allowed her to believe them both without having to reconcile them or decide upon one "truth."[8]

Sarah was also familiar with the history of her mother's family, the Davenports, for her mother's maternal grandmother had lived with her mother's family and told the children of her life in New England and her family's migration to the Nanticoke Valley. Sarah repeated these stories as she had heard them from her mother. She also adopted her mother's ambivalent attitude toward the Davenports. While taking pride in the family's distinguished past and carrying on the women's traditional skill in fine needlework, Sarah's mother maintained a certain distance from her immediate family, first by leaving home and then by joining the Briggs family in their ancestral home when she married. Sarah's mother was always bitter about the fact that she did not inherit a share of her father's land. Sarah internalized the separation from the Davenport family that her mother had initiated. Sarah always referred to her father's father, rather than her mother's father, as her grandfather; when this was pointed out, she replied, "I divorced my mother's family." The intergenerational distance in the Davenport family, although not extreme by contemporary community standards, contrasted sharply with the close ties in the Briggs family. It was the Briggs family history, embodied in their house and land, that was still alive in Sarah's memory.

Sarah Briggs Brookdale found meaning in the continuity between past and present, the ties of descent and inheritance that linked her with previous generations. The family was fundamental, defining the self, locating her on the land, and placing her within the community. For women like Sarah, historical time gave extension and significance to individual lives; the self merged with the family and farm to form a collective and enduring subject. This sense of self nurtured a strong sense of agency in inheriting daughters. Secure in her position within her family of origin, Sarah enjoyed an independent career as a teacher and remained single long past the normal marriage age. Her close relationship with her parents supported rather than restricted her individual achievements. Sarah knew she did not have to marry in order to have a home. She avoided men whom she suspected of "looking for a wife" and waited until she found a man who was willing to assume the obligations of a son in her family. Her position as an inheriting daughter strengthened her position within marriage as well. Sarah chose to maintain close ties with her parents throughout her life. While she was aware of the alternative possibilities she was foreclosing, she never seriously entertained them herself, and never felt pressured by her parents as she made decisions. Sarah appreciated her parents' acceptance of the fact that the demands of her husband's career required Sarah and her children to spend the winters away from the farm. Both parents and daughter accommodated one another's needs, strengthening the ties between generations. Interdependence and agency supported and enhanced one another in the lives of inheriting daughters of long-established farm families.

Women who married into long-established farm families had somewhat different experiences from women who were born into them. Those who married inheriting sons and went to live on their husbands' farms developed new identities as members of their husbands' families. Hattie Bieber Smith and Ruth Woods Brown both came from farm families whose resources were limited; neither was in a position to inherit land. Like Sarah Briggs Brookdale's mother, both married into families whose land had been passed down from one generation to the next since the initial settlement of the Nanticoke Valley. As Ruth Woods Brown put it, the farm on which she lives "has been in this family always." Ruth and Hattie both began their autobiographies with histories of their husbands' family farms and ended with the transmission of the farms to their children, placing themselves with their husbands in the middle of the line of succession. They described their individual lives as if they were tributaries flowing into a larger stream, with a separate origin but losing their distinct historical identity at the moment of marriage. Yet these women's identification with their husbands' families involved an expansion rather than an extinguishing of the self; participation in their husbands' family farms gave them scope for action and enhanced the significance of their lives.

Hattie Bieber Smith and Ruth Woods Brown both told their stories as joint autobiographies, including their husbands' experiences as well as their own and interpreting events from a perspective the couple shared. Hattie Bieber and Edmund Smith gave joint interviews. They took turns as narrator, one completing a story the other hand begun or supplying more details on the topic under discussion. Each spoke of the other's experience with the assurance that comes from a common understanding. Both used "we" much more often than "I," "he," or "she." Ruth Woods Brown was recently widowed when I interviewed her, but her late husband Douglas remained a vital presence in her autobiography. Occasionally she quoted things he had said. These women's identification with their husbands' families, then, was based not only upon their position in the line of succession, but also upon the quality of their marriages. Both women conceived of marriage as a partnership and placed a high value on mutuality. The couples' shared labor in the farm enterprise and their planning for farm succession provided, in these women's eyes, the foundation for those characteristics of their marriages.[9]

To women who married inheriting farmers, interdependence was central. Both Douglas Brown and Edmund Smith worked with male relatives in relatively large-scale and capital-intensive farm operations, Douglas with his brother Hugh and Edmund with his father William. Ruth and Hattie were aware of the possibility of conflict within farm families and of the serious consequences interpersonal conflict can have in joint farm enterprises. Both Ruth and Hattie assumed responsibility for the management of relationships not only within their conjugal families, but also with their husbands' families; they sustained the delicate balance of cooperation and autonomy that made these partnerships work.

Ruth and Hattie described themselves as working within a situation they did not create, but whose meaning they had power to shape. Their power was not simply subjective, but actually consequential, for they could affect the situation's outcome for themselves and their families. Ruth Woods Brown took pride in the fact that the farm was passed on to her two sons, who work in partnership as her husband and his brother did. The Smiths passed their farm on to their son, who works in partnership with several of his children. For Hattie Bieber Smith, family solidarity lay not only in interpersonal relationships, but also in shared values. The Smiths felt free to express their "unorthodox" values – chiefly a commitment to the intellectual examination of religious beliefs – because the farm provided them with a certain independence of other people. To Hattie, these distinctive values were the essence of both family solidarity and personal agency.

All of these families occupied relatively secure positions at the upper end of the community's socioeconomic scale. They owned adequate land and had enough capital to conduct commercial dairy, poultry, and fruit operations. The Watson family was at the other end of the scale, for they were as poor as a family could possibly be and still hold onto their land. Yet the Watsons' self-conception was strikingly similar to that of their more fortunate neighbors. They recounted the history of their ancestors who came to the Nanticoke Valley during the late nineteenth century and identified their family with the land they shared. Most of the Watsons lived on land purchased by their grandfather and his three sons around World War I; during the 1920s there were eighteen cousins growing up together in the neighborhood. The Watsons valued close ties within the extended family and incorporated those who married into the family rather than losing those who married out. Although they were given little credit for it in the community, the Watsons still practiced the virtues that local residents attributed to farm families in the past. The Watsons' sense of family identity, in fact, was so strong that they must be described as a corporate kin group rather than simply an extended-family network.[10]

Hazel Watson Bullis' parents were full-time farmers, although they lacked the capital necessary to make their land yield a stable income. Hazel's husband's family was as poor as her own; Sam had no prospects of inheriting land. Soon after their marriage, Hazel and Sam moved in with her parents. Eventually they renovated a garage on her parents' land into their own home, where they formed a vital part of the extended-family residential group. Hazel's family affiliations have been essentially continuous throughout her life; marriage did not disrupt her primary family ties but rather augmented them. Hazel placed a high value on family solidarity. In much the same way that Sarah Briggs Brookdale proudly displayed the Bible and fine furniture that have been passed down in her family, Hazel showed me the stoneware buckwheat-pancake-batter pitcher and hand-cranked wringer washing machine she inherited from her parents. Both the difference in these women's economic positions and the similarity of their self-conceptions are expressed by the fact that they still used these objects; to neither woman was their value merely symbolic.

Hazel Watson Bullis' relationship with her family supported her sense of agency, although in a very different way than Sarah Briggs Brookdale's did. Hazel saw herself as integral to her multigenerational extended family: working with her parents on the farm and in the household, caring for her younger siblings and cousins when she was only a child herself; supporting her disabled husband and their daughter by "working out" for wages and helping on her parents' farm; and taking care of her parents in their old age. Her self-image was of a strong, capable, hard-working, and reliable woman, the mainstay of her family. For Hazel, interdependence was expressed primarily in labor and took the form of providing direct physical care and subsistence for others. Hazel had no sense of making choices among alternatives, but rather of responding to her family's immediate needs and doing what had to be done. Indeed, Hazel thought of herself as an active agent only within her family. Helping others kept her from feeling helpless herself; caregiving was a source of self-confidence. The story Hazel told about her daughter and husband exemplifies this perspective.

> I always felt bad about my daughter having to work so hard. Because I know I had to work hard, and I didn't want her to do it. But she did – it was nothing to her to mop and scrub and clean and take care of her father. That's where the Welfare got me stuck; they said it wasn't good for to bring up a child in a home like that. Because she had to be with her father being sick, and like that. I don't think that hurts; I would rather my kid be with somebody that was sick than to think that they couldn't help a person that was sick.

For Hazel, affirming the value of "helping" was a way of creating meaning in a life she could not control.

Eastern and Southern European immigrants who purchased farms in the Nanticoke Valley during the early twentieth century hoped to establish their families securely on the land and to pass on their farms to the next generation. They held those goals all the more intensely because many had lost their land in Europe and their relationships with their own parents had been disrupted by emigration. Most women of the immigrant generation identified strongly with the farms they and their husbands struggled to establish. Nadya Stastyshyn Fenson was among the most fortunate. She and her husband established a successful mix of dairying and market gardening; although none of their children carried on the farm, parents and children continued to live in close proximity on the land.

Josie Sulich Kuzma was less fortunate, although ultimately perhaps just as successful. Her entire life was spent struggling to get a foothold on the land. Josie's parents emigrated from the Ukraine to Pennsylvania, where she was born, and then homesteaded in Alberta, Canada. Conditions there were too harsh, so they migrated to the Nanticoke Valley in 1916, when Josie was nine. Their farm never provided much more than a minimal subsistence, so Josie's father and then Josie herself left home to work for the Endicott-Johnson Company. When Josie married, "I married very poor family, very poor. More so than my own. So that was very hard." At first Josie and her husband Alex lived with his father, but the two generations could not agree on the division of the farm income, so Alex gave up his hopes of inheriting the land and bought a farm in the Nanticoke Valley. He built a barn and began to build up a herd of dairy cattle. But Alex's death from pneumonia put an end to farming; Josie was pregnant with her seventh child, and the older children were still too young to carry on the work. Josie held onto the land, however. Selling the cows to pay off the mortgage, she eked out a living for her family by cleaning houses in the village. One son eventually became a farmer and established a substantial dairy operation. Josie took pride in the fact that she was able to keep the land for him.[11]

A few immigrant women, like Nadya, came into their own after they moved to farms. But most, like Josie, always felt powerless to determine their fate. Josie's life seems entirely defined by her roles as daughter, wife, and mother. She resented the ill-treatment she received as a daughter and daughter-in-law from parents who neglected to consider her welfare. But she did not demand that those situations be changed until she had the support of other family members – or, more accurately, until her father and her husband were ready to change those situations for their own reasons. Josie had little conscious awareness of the limitations placed upon her choices because the possibility of self-determination had seldom occurred to her. Poverty and isolation intensified interdependence and undermined agency. While Hazel Watson Bullis developed a sense of agency by acting as family caregiver, Josie Sulich Kuzma did not. Relationships in her family did not counteract, but rather succumbed to, economic deprivation and cultural marginality. Josie's sense of strength came from having coped with the constraints and losses inherent in family life.

The children of immigrants shared their parents' struggle to get established, but did not always share their aspirations. Most did not take over the farms their parents had sacrificed so much to purchase, but rather returned to the urban manufacturing jobs their parents had tried to escape. Their ethnic identity distinguished them from the dominant rural culture and linked them to the urban subcultures created by other immigrants and their children. Cultural differences between the children of immigrants and those of native-born families were not the only reason that young people did not remain on the farm, however; tensions within their families were equally important. Relationships were often strained by cultural differences between immigrant parents and their American-born children. Even in long-established farm families, the process of generational succession was always a delicate one; in immigrant families, cultural conflicts between parents and children might disrupt it entirely.

The daughters of immigrants expressed considerable ambivalence toward farm and family, and their life histories suggest unresolved tensions in their sense of identity. The narratives of immigrants' daughters focused upon their parents rather than upon themselves. They portrayed the immigrant generation in heroic terms, describing the difficulties their parents surmounted and the hardships they endured in order to become farmers in America. Immigrants' daughters were more reticent about their own adult lives, perhaps because they had left the farms upon which they grew up and/or married outside of their ethnic group. In contrast to the daughters of long-established farm families, who identified with their mothers and drew parallels between the lives of the two generations, the daughters of immigrants discussed the complex relationship between the two generations and stressed the differences in their life experiences.

Rosa Socher Malone, whose parents emigrated to Endicott from the Austro-Hungarian Empire shortly before World War I, articulated experiences that many daughters shared. Rosa focused her narrative upon her parents' lives and her own childhood. She spoke sympathetically of her father's attempts to escape the Endicott-Johnson tannery. Her parents first bought a large abandoned farm, but they lacked the capital to establish a commercial dairy, so they moved to a small farm and her father returned to the tannery. "It was very hard," Rosa commented; "they came here and had it harder than they did in Europe." Their problems were not simply economic. The neighborhood into which they moved was composed primarily of native-born families, although Rosa's mother's sister and her family lived on an adjacent farm. Rosa recalled that there was a good deal of prejudice against immigrants. "When we were growing up, we were always made to feel that we didn't belong." "And to tell you the truth," she continued, "we were always a little ashamed, because we always felt we were foreigners. . . . We always felt a little inferior to the old settlers." Rosa described her childhood as a special, somewhat isolated world. Within it there was warmth and security, as well as hard work and poverty. But the security her family provided did not offer her a place in the outside world. The daughters of immigrants had to negotiate between two worlds as they grew up. Rosa Socher Malone married a non-Slovak when she was fairly young and moved away. She recalled her childhood on the farm with a powerful fusion of pleasure and pain, as an encapsulated world that she was forced to leave behind.[12]

Not all immigrants' daughters chose to leave the world of their childhood. Many rejected the models their parents offered them for adulthood, but few rejected their responsibilities as daughters. Some rebelled "in my heart" and others "with my mouth," but few rebelled with their whole selves. Sally Seferis Clark was representative. Both her parents were born in Greece, and both lost their parents in the war. Her father and his brother made their way to upstate New York, where they worked as farm laborers and saved their wages for ten years until they could buy land together. Her mother, who was much younger, remained in an orphanage in Greece. Sally repeated the story of her parents' marriage as if she had heard it many times. First she described how her father had heard of her mother through mutual friends and went to Greece to bring her back as his bride; then she retold the story from her mother's point of view. Sally's accounts of her father's efforts to expand the farm and her mother's learning to keep house in the American way presented her parents as almost larger than life, in the heroic proportions parents often assume in the eyes of their children. Compared to her parents' lives, Sally's own life must have seemed insignificant to her.[13]

At the same time that Sally presented her parents through the uncritical eyes of her childhood self, she revealed her own ambivalence toward the identity her parents offered her. The family was not isolated from their native-born neighbors. They were readily accepted into the Congregational Church, for her father had converted to Protestantism. Her parents kept their distance from the Greek religious and political organizations in Binghamton. So cultural differences between herself and others were not much of a problem for Sally. Although she was proud of her Greek ancestry, she entered easily into the dominant rural culture. Intergenerational differences within her family posed more difficult problems. Sally was often caught between her respect for her parents and her desire for autonomous adulthood. After graduation from high school, she got a job in the city but continued to live at home. Her parents felt that their authority over her extended not only to her conduct within the family, but also to her social life. Sally was a good daughter. But she could not pattern her own life upon her parents' lives. She once had a Greek suitor, but "his parents broke it up" because she was not Orthodox. Sally remained single for a long time and then "had to get married" to an American; the marriage ended in divorce soon after the birth of her second child. Sally raised her sons on the land she inherited from her parents. Although Sally could not follow the path her parents set before her, she did not choose her own path either. Being a Greek daughter made it difficult for her to become an American adult.

Women who established farms with their husbands developed a strong sense of the unity of family and farm, but rarely passed on that identification to their children. None of the children of farm partners I interviewed took over their parents' farms. There is no evidence that intergenerational conflict prevented farm succession in these families. Rather, these couples do not seem to have aspired to pass on their farms to their children. In contrast to both long-established and immigrant families, native-born couples who established farms themselves did not adopt a multigenerational perspective towards their enterprises. Having chosen farming and gotten started independently from their parents, they did not expect their children to succeed them. While the maintenance of close ties was as important to these families as to the others, family continuity was not linked, in their minds, to the inheritance of land.

Farm partners regarded their families as the basis of their farms, rather than basing their families upon their farms. These couples had purchased land relatively early in their marriages; paying off the mortgage represented the fulfillment of a dream. Yet it was not the land itself so much as the shared labor and planning that mattered to these women. Farm partners often spent the early years of their marriages running the day-to-day farm operations while their husbands worked off the farm to earn money to invest in cattle. Some of the men were eventually able to quit their jobs and farm full-time, while others hired help, but by then the women had developed a strong sense of partnership in the farm enterprise.

Elizabeth Wheaton Graves was especially eloquent about the family values that lay at the basis of the farm. Kenneth Graves had not yet decided to be a farmer when he and Elizabeth were married; they lived in Maine village for seven years before buying their land. Since Kenneth continued to work off the farm, Elizabeth was actively involved in the farm operations. Still, she did not define herself as a "farm wife." Indeed, she once exclaimed: "I didn't marry a *farm!*" She had married Kenneth, and when he said he wanted to farm she made his dream her own. "I said, well, this is what my husband wants to do; if this is what will make him happy, this is what I'm going to do." Elizabeth described her entire life history in terms of her relationships with others and said that she "always tried to foster family feeling" among those with whom she came in contact. The farm that she and Kenneth established provided a secure home not only for their immediate family, but also for a variety of relatives, hired men, and tenants.[14]

Farm partners developed strong and mutually supportive senses of interdependence and agency. In this respect, they resemble daughters and daughters-in-law of long-established farm families, However, farm partners did not develop the same sense of shaping their own life course that inheriting daughters did; farm partners had a more acute awareness of the ways their family commitments limited their autonomy. Most were meaning-makers rather than decision-makers. In their espousal of the value of interdependence, they resemble women who married into farm families. Elizabeth Wheaton Graves, for example, never felt able to determine her own life course, but she did feel that she could give it meaning. Like Hattie Bieber Smith, Elizabeth held a distinctive set of values that she expressed in action; like Ruth Woods Brown, she valued human relationships above all else. Elizabeth consciously nurtured mutually supportive relationships among people with whom she came in contact. She was aware of the fragility of interpersonal relations, their vulnerability both to death and to internal disruption; she devoted much of her energy to the mediation of differences. While Elizabeth did not live vicariously through others, her sense of agency was expressed primarily in her relationships with family and friends.

Women whose parents had lost their farms rarely married into established farm families or founded new farms with their husbands. Women who were not from farm backgrounds often married inheriting farmers or became farm partners, but those who had lived through the collapse of their families' farms in childhood seldom aspired to belong to farm families themselves. Families adopted new ways of making a living and carried on, but their trust in the land was gone; most felt not that they had abandoned the land, but rather that the land had failed them. Daughters of displaced farmers spoke of family farms as part of the irretrievable past.

These women saw themselves as victims of circumstance, or as coping with conditions beyond their control, much more often than did women with more substantial and stable ties to the land. The only farm daughters who expressed a similar sense of helplessness were those whose families had been profoundly disrupted in childhood, for example by the death or desertion of their mothers. The sense of confronting life without a solid grounding was common among women who grew up in displaced farm families and meant that most had little sense of agency. A few women from poor families rejected passivity and strove for self-determination. It was these women, who asserted their right to shape their own lives, who had the clearest consciousness of the constraints placed upon women by their families and society. These women's strong desire for self-determination and their awareness of the limitations upon women's autonomy went together. They differed from most Nanticoke Valley women not only because they were aware of these contradictions in their own lives, but also because autonomy was an imperative for them. Without the base that a family farm provided, interdependence and agency were indeed contradictory in women's lives.

Still, the ideal of gender relations these women articulated was held by most women in the Nanticoke Valley. Women and men, they believed, should share in the necessary labor of farm and household and share in farm family decision-making. In the experience of most farm women, interdependence and agency were not opposed. Their identities had been formed by the fusion of land and family, and family farms provided the framework within which they sought to create meaning in their lives.

NOTES

[1] Nadya Stastyshyn Fenson, interviewed by Nettie Politylo, 25 April and 20 June 1978, for the Broome County Oral History Project. The tape and typescript are located in the Archives and Library of the Broome County Historical Society, Roberson Center, Binghamton, New York.

[2] Nancy Grey Osterud, "Strategies of Mutuality: Relations Among Women and Men in an Agricultural Community," unpublished Ph.D. dissertation, Brown University, 1984. See also Nancy Grey Osterud, "'She Helped Me Hay It as Good as a Man': Relations among Women and Men in an Agricultural Community," in *"To Toil the Livelong Day": America's Women at Work, 1780-1980*, ed. Carol Groneman and Mary Beth Norton (Ithaca: Cornell University Press, 1987), pp. 87-97.

[3] Tapes and transcripts of these interviews are in the archives of the Nanticoke Valley Historical Society, Maine, New York. All names have been changed to protect the privacy of informants.

[4] The fact that these oral autobiographies are presented from the perspective of the life-historical self does not mean that people do not revise their autobiographies as their understanding of themselves and their place in the world

changes over time. They do, but they rarely distinguish between what they felt at the time events occurred and what they now think about those events when telling stories about the past.

[5]The discussion of agency in this chapter pertains only to women's sense of the degree to which they controlled their own lives. It makes no judgment about whether women actually were active agents, but focuses instead upon their self-conceptions.

[6]This typology is ordered by class, as well as by kinship; while it describes women's relationship to property, it also reflects the amount of land to which they had access.

[7]Three dozen completed oral autobiographies have been analyzed within this framework; the patterns described here appear in the whole set of life histories. In this chapter, I have selected one or two women to illustrate each type. It should be noted that this analysis follows the methodological canons of qualitative research. The major concepts, including the five types of women's relationship to the land and the two types of agency women assume, were developed from the interviews themselves. The connections among these concepts, i.e., how women's relationship with the land affects their sense of agency, emerged through the analysis of the interviews as well. Accordingly, individual cases are used to exemplify these concepts and connections. However, in this type of research generalizations cannot be made beyond the original body of evidence. For further information about qualitative research methods, see Barney G. Glaser and Anselm L. Strauss, *The Discovery of Grounded Theory: Strategies for Qualitative Research* (New York: Aldine Publishing Company, 1967).

[8]Sarah Briggs Brookdale, interviews with author, Maine, New York, 20 March and 12 July 1981.

[9]Ruth Woods Brown, interview with author, West Chenango, New York, 18 July 1984. Hattie Bieber Smith, interviews with author, Maine, New York, 14 and 25 August 1982.

[10]Hazel Watson Bullis, interviews with author, Maine, New York, 12 August and 12 September 1982; the Watson family, interview with author, Maine, New York, 14 November 1982.

[11]Josie Sulich Kuzma, interviews with author, Maine, New York, 6, 10 and 14 August and 10 September 1982.

[12]Rosa Socher Malone, interview with author, Newark Valley, New York, 11 July 1982.

[13]Sally Seferis Clark, interview with author, Maine, New York, 10 August 1982.

[14]Elizabeth Wheaton Graves, interviews with author, Maine, New York, 7 May and 14 August 1981, 20 April 1982, and 6 July 1983.

5

IMAGE AND BEHAVIOR: WOMEN'S PARTICIPATION IN NORTH AMERICAN FAMILY AGRICULTURAL ENTERPRISES

Seena B. Kohl

THE IMAGE OF WOMEN IN THE HISTORY OF WESTERN SETTLEMENT

Within the past decade, the roles women played on the frontier and in western settlement have been reexamined. The writing about women in the history of the West ranges from works concerned with ensuring women's recognition to works challenging accepted generalizations regarding the settlement process itself and the impact the frontier had on gender ideology (Armitage 1985; Faragher 1981; Jackel 1982; Jeffrey 1979; Jensen and Miller 1980; Kolodny 1984; Myres 1982; Schlissel 1982; Silverman 1984; Stratton 1981).

Implicitly or explicitly, all these writers are concerned with understanding the impact of gender and ideology on the writing of history. While it is beyond the scope of this paper to review the full historiography of women on the frontier, the questions and issues raised by the feminist revision of the history of western settlement provide a framework within which I compare the image of women presented *by* the participants or their descendants in their reminiscences with the images of women presented in more formal, academic analyses of western settlement.

The reminiscences of frontier women and their descendants are located in community sponsored local history books – books that were organized by committee, collectively written, and locally produced – which serve as community and family histories of agricultural settlement.[1] These books represent a unique resource for an examination of women's roles in frontier settlement. As collectively written material they can be considered cultural artifacts reflecting a shared ideology about the past and the expectations held for women.

The community history books begin with the entrance of homestead settlers into what for the writers of the books was an "empty frontier." The history of the local community begins with the experience of individual settlers and their kin. When transmitted across generations, these experiences develop a generalized and shared character. History becomes a collective consciousness of the past, continuously modified by national and mass cultural understandings of this same past. It is in this sense that the collectively or committee-written history books

can be considered a cultural construction through which a particular characterization of a pioneer community and its people is presented, created, or "invented."[2]

The data for this paper come from an analysis of material written within the
past decade regarding the role of women in western settlement and of a selected
sample of community-written local histories.[3] Interviews with the editors of the
books done as part of a cultural history of the Canadian-American western
plains,[4] and field data collected during 1963-1983 as part of the longitudinal
Saskatchewan Cultural Ecology Research Project,[5] are also used.

THE STUDY REGION

The local histories are the accounts of the agricultural homestead populations that attempted settlement at the turn of the century. The area of the western
plains under examination – southwestern Saskatchewan, southeastern Alberta,
and the northern tier of Montana counties on the U.S.-Canadian border – has
been subject to continual failure of agricultural enterprises from the initial period
of settlement. The climate is variable and severe, subject to extremes of heat,
cold, and moisture. Intermittent droughts and economic difficulties led to considerable population turnover and decline before a reasonable degree of social and
economic stability was obtained. Out-migration was an option that a major portion of homesteaders eventually chose (Bicha 1968; Fowke 1947; Mackintosh
1934).

Prior to European colonization, this region provided a homeland for native
American hunting populations: the Cree, Nez Perce, Gros Ventre, and
Assiniboine, among others. The historical sequence of ranch and homestead settlement on both sides of the border follows a similar although not identical pattern at roughly the same period – 1895-1915.[6]

Rancher settlers moved into the region in the late 1870s in Montana and the
1880s on the Canadian side. Surveyed districts were established for homesteading
on both sides around 1900, with the majority of the farmer-settlers arriving
around 1910. As with Great Plains settlement elsewhere in the United States and
Canada, the initial optimism produced by the lure of cheap land was soon damp-
ened by the reality of the limited agricultural potential of the small, 160-acre
homestead tracts.

Today the livelihood of the people on both sides of the international border
is based on a mix of grain farming and cattle ranching, plus the services needed
to sustain this economy. The variability and uncertainty of climate, particularly
moisture, creates special hazards for agriculture. These uncertainties are accentu-
ated by the economic vulnerabilities associated with national and international
markets and banking practices; residents have little control over either.

The present-day residents of this region, especially the rural areas, are for the
most part descendants of the original homestead population. The struggles of the
pioneer generation on the frontier remain vivid and are exemplified in family
stories. There is shared agreement that the settlement of that part of the country

was an important and heroic act that should not be forgotten.[7] The residents' reminiscences celebrate survival of family, if not of the agricultural enterprise, and elevate their ancestors' experience of hardship and privation to moral worth creating personal triumph over systemic disaster (Kohl 1986).

HISTORY WITHOUT DISCORD:
THE COMMUNITY-SPONSORED LOCAL HISTORY

Within the past decade, there has been a vast proliferation of community-sponsored and -written local history books.[8] The committee members, overwhelmingly women, for the most part lack previous research, writing, editing, or publishing experience. They do, however, have a plethora of organizational skills, common to all rural areas, honed in previous work in community volunteer associations.

The organizers and editors of the books are the "stayers" – those who established economic enterprises and maintained communities and their descendants.[9] With few exceptions, they present a collective representation of a past with implicit comparisons to the present. The decrease in the sense of community, altruism, and independence is regretted. It is hard for the reader to escape the inference that the past life, although hard, was better and the struggles worth the effort. In this retrospective view, hardships were mitigated by neighbors and other wonderful people, or by the eventual success of building something from nothing.[10] In fact, it is this characterization that gives these books their similarity, despite differences in place, national origins, and economic adaptations.

Controversy is avoided.[11] The editors have been warned by their local printer or publisher's agent of the danger of libel, and they attempt to steer a middle line between "making things interesting" and "staying out of trouble." In "steering a middle course," the editors leave out virtually all conflict and disagreements among groups. With rare exceptions, the past is endowed with an *ex post facto* harmony.[12]

The books are intensely local in orientation, concerned with the individuals or their family members who actually lived the homestead settlement experience in the particular place. This emphasis on the particularistic and the local has in fact elicited criticism from academic historians whose ideas regarding settlement history differ (Bowsfield 1969; Oliver et al. 1984; Voisey 1985).

History as local experience is inevitably particularistic and personal. The recitations in the community histories are also inevitably nostalgic. As such, they are viewed with suspicion by the professional historian who is understandably wary of allowing nostalgia to pass for clarity of cause and effect. This is one reason, among others, that the community-written local history books have been ignored by historians. In this paper I use these books for their qualitative merit.

THE IMAGE OF WOMEN
IN THE COMMUNITY HISTORY BOOKS

In their review of historical and literary materials, Jensen and Miller (1980, 181) list stereotypes of women in the West. Their list includes the "gentle tamers" (civilizers, ladies, and suffragists), the "sunbonneted helpmates" (virtuous and strong women who "fulfill[ed] duties which enabled men to succeed"), the "hell-raisers" ("super cowgirls" and "Calamity Janes"), and the "bad women" (prostitutes and dance hall and gambling-saloon women).[13] Jensen and Miller (1980, 183) note:

> While these literary studies sharpen our perception about the context and limitation of these images, they do little to answer the question of how accurate these images are or to what extent they reflect the reality of women's lives. The studies which do attempt to test images against realities seem to conclude that congruence between image and reality is almost nonexistent.

With the exception of the "bad women," who are either ignored or transformed into unique personalities, all of these types are present in the community histories. However, they appear not as stereotypes, but as real people who belong to kin groups and particpate in family agricultural enterprises, who exhibit behaviors and attributes common to several of the categories. The following reminiscence (New Horizons Committee 1982, 310) illustrates how helpmates can be civilizers, super cowgirls and partners in building an economic enterprise:

> That Mabel was a determined and resourceful person is exemplified by the following. . . . [During a prairie fire] she resolutely hooked up four half broke horses and plowed a fire guard around the building and haystacks. . . . Mabel was an accomplished horsewoman, but every inch a lady. She rode side saddle, but always in dresses.[14]

What may be considered stereotypic in the sense of the "conventional, formulaic, and usually oversimplified"[15] is the context in which women (and men) are described in the community histories. Family lineage and connections provide the setting in which people are identified and placed. Since this is a region of depopulation with massive homestead abandonment, most accounts emphasize family survival, simply listing subsequent generations and their progeny rather than emphasizing settlement or the building of an enterprise. This pattern is illustrated in the following passage (Foremost Historical Society 1975, 418):

> Mr. and Mrs. Andrew Schile came to Harvey, North Dakota from Russia in the early spring of 1908, with two small children. . . .
>   They lived there for about two years, and one more child . . . was born. In the year 1910 they came to the Bow Island district and then

homesteaded about seven miles north and west of Foremost. Six more chldren were born. . . . These children all received their education in the rural school at Remainder, in the district north of Foremost.

Through the years, members of the family married and started homes of their own.

A list of the children's location and marriages and the parents' deaths follows. The account ends with the statement: "There are 28 grandchildren and 54 great-grandchildren in the family."

Women are embedded in a family unit in which their history is written as "we,"[16] as illustrated by the following short passage (Ravenscrag History Book Committee 1981, 293):

> We milked cows, raised pigs and chickens. We sold cream for eleven cents per pound, eggs at four cents per dozen and Grade 1 wheat for nineteen cents per bushel.

Local histories vary in how they identify family members: some list the first name of both husband and wife; some list only the married household name – for example, "The Eckford Family" – or use the more formal "Mr. and Mrs. William Nicoll." Although the woman's birth name is (with some exceptions) given in the family account, most commonly she has no independent listing. Some family accounts list only the man's name; however in twenty to forty percent of those cases, when one reads the account one finds that the women in these families are given recognition for their contributions to the family settlement. In a content analysis of gender citations,[17] between one-quarter and one-third of family history entries are listed in the man's name;[18] nevertheless, the experiences are phrased in terms of "we."

Although family history accounts vary widely in depth of information presented – some families are represented with a few lines whereas other families are represented with several pages[19] – women figure consistently as work partners.

Women made economic and cash contributions as cooks, boarding-house operators, postmistresses, storekeepers, housekeepers, seamstresses, school teachers, midwives, and the like.

The family histories make clear that women's work outside the household economy was an economic necessity and part of the maintenance of an enterprise and survival of a family. There is no indication in these accounts of a hope of getting rich or of self-fulfillment (although women were proud of their work and their ability to survive). Statements of work are matter-of-fact, part of the family record and history of what needed to be done (Ravenscrag History Book Committee 1982, 266, 338, 420):

> Mother served as Secretary-Treasurer of the Farwell Creek School Board during the depression years of the 1930's. In place of receiving

any salary, what she would have received was applied to land taxes. This helped to prevent the building up of "back taxes" on our land.

My mother and us three kids moved into Ravenscrag in 1935 where my Mother ran a restaurant. [Dad remained on the homestead]. . . . We left Ravenscrag in 1938 and settled in Shaunavon. Mother worked at various jobs.

Len and I were married in July 1924. His brother Roy and he farmed the home place, but the same year we were hailed out [crops were ruined by hail], so we decided to look for work. We spent the winter on the Kirkaldy ranch at Raymond, Alberta where Len was one of the riders. I cooked for the crew.

The family histories record baking bread for bachelors, serving as nurses and midwives, sewing, cooking for threshing crews, supplying neighbors with garden produce, and so on, but rarely make note of the amount of money exchanged. Some of these services were embedded in elaborate networks of mutual aid between kin and neighbors; however, others were cash exchanges, about which there is silence.[20]

It is interesting to contrast the retrospective presentation – or, more precisely, the lack of presentation – of women's cash work with letters written home. The letters make clear statements about economic opportunities for women as well as men. For example,

Verna Benson writes from the newly homesteaded area near Munson, Alberta, to her family in Duluth, Michigan, encouraging her sister-in-law, Anna, to take advantage of the economic opportunities (Benson n.d.). She writes to her father-in-law in 1910:

[I]f Anna cared to do it she could make pretty good money with a bakery out here in some of these new towns. There is so many bachelors out here I should think the baked goods would sell pretty good and there is lots of carpenter work in all these new towns.

She writes directly to Anna in 1911:

I will . . . tell you what a good chance there would be for you to make a little money out here if you wanted to do it. The blacksmith's wife . . . keep[s] boarders and baked bread to sell last year. And she says . . . she cleared about $300. Then one of our neighbors went into town last fall and ran a restaurant and they claim to of cleared about $500.

The silence about women's cash earnings is a consequence of at least two factors: (1) the overwhelming desire to emphasize mutual aid on the frontier, and (2) the taking for granted of women's contribution to the establishment and maintenance of the family enterprise.

What is not camouflaged in these community histories, however, is the recognition of the work, effort, fortitude, and above all the "doing what was necessary" on the part of all – men, women, and children – for the survival and continuity of the family. Acceptance of and ability for hard work and "doing what has to be done" defines the pioneer character and, for some, separates the generations, as is expressed in the following passage (Pollock n.d., 29-30):

> As a child, one of the happy memories was the good preserves that my mother used to make after we kids had picked pails of saskatoons. . . . Picking the wild berries seemed a pleasure. We could eat all we liked but when we were called to pick up the bushels of potatoes . . . it was far from interesting. It was back breaking, dusty, hot, heavy work. . . . Another job I failed to enjoy was milking cows, turning the separator and pail feeding the skim milk to 20 calves before walking two miles to school. . . . I can look back now and smile to myself on the joys of childhood. Why the poor kids today have nothing to do but play and many of them can't do that without leadership. I wonder what their childhood memories will be.

Throughout the local community histories are many anecdotes recalling the way women expanded their work arena to include a number of activities not considered "women's work" – like this brief description from *Robsart Pioneers Review the Years* (1955, 80):

> Mrs. Morrison, like many women of that day, was a woman of resourcefulness. She could take a hammer and nails, make a screen door, a go-cart for a baby, pen for the pigs or anything.

At the same time, traditional expectations for women continued. Accounts in the history books note women's prowess as cooks, mothers, seamstresses, and as household managers, all crucial facets of family survival and enterprise continuity (Kohl 1976, 1977).

It is only when those writing the family history tell an anecdote or mention a characteristic considered unique to women in general by the women's children or the writers themselves, that other facets of women's lives emerge. These unique characteristics include lack of fear of snakes, Indians, and being alone; ability as a sharp shooter; and special skills in art, poetry, and musicianship – all characteristics commonly considered unusual for women.

Accounts such as the following, (New Horizons Commitee 1982, 202) make clear that the blurring of gender roles occurred through necessity, not ideology:

> Those first few years were very hard on all of us with the breaking and clearing the land with horses. After a long while we got it broke. By then Dad was not too well and ended up with heart trouble, so mom and I [his daughter] did most of the field work and the chores. Dad . . . loved to garden so he spent most of the time gardening. . . .

In her diary, kept during the first year of homestead settlement (1907-08),[21] Sarah Roberts (1971, 226) describes her reluctant participation in cattle branding:

> I stayed with my job until it was done, and I am glad that I never had to do it again. I think that it is not a woman's work except that it is everyone's work to do the things he needs to do.

In contrast with Sarah Roberts, other women enjoyed work commonly considered the domain of men, as the following account reveals (New Horizons Committee 1982, 235):

> My mother broke the land to prove up on the homestead while my father was freighting supplies for ranchers in the area. . . .
> Mother often said these early summers on the homestead were among the best of her lifetime. . . . Many times she laughed about how the children and the milk cow would follow along behind the walking plough as she was turning the sod.

Whether they enjoyed the work or not, however, women "did what had to be done." The point is not that women worked in "male" jobs on the enterprise but that they did what was necessary, a system that continues today.

The scarcity of labor meant that men also crossed gender roles to "do what was necessary." Roy Benson (Benson n.d.) writes to his father in March 1911:

> [Y]ou are not alone on the trouble question for one thing I have a son Fred Benson Jr. that's as it should be but I can get no one to stay here and take care of the folks and I wasn't cut out for a nurse cook and baby tender. They say you never know what you can do until you are up against it Well! I am up against it. . . . everyone is doing well but me. . . . Got to wash and dress the baby get dinner do the washing melt some snow and a few other things. . . .

Doing what was necessary required that both women and men give up rigid gender expectations. The diaries, letters, and reminiscences are filled with these experiences, highlighting the fact that the frontier, like other crisis situations, demanded a loosening of sex-role expectations (Lipman-Blumen 1973).

Homesteading required both men and women to learn new skills and to put aside, or hold in abeyance, traditional concepts of "feminine" and "masculine" behavior. What is important to remember is that variation in gender expectations was as prevalent at the time of homesteading as it is today.

A comparison of two recollections of being lost at night on the prairie is instructive. Both recollections emphasize values of frontier hospitality; both also illustrate differences among the settlers about appropriate behavior between men and women. In the first recollection, the man in-need is permited to stay at the home of a lone young women. In the second case, the visitors are turned away. In the first instance, the writer (Foremost Historical Society 1985, 74) recalls:

> I was still miles from the stopping place when night came on. . . .
> At length a lone light appeared in the distance. . . . I approached . . .
> hoping I had arrived at my destination only to be told . . . I was on
> the wrong trail. . . . To attempt to find it in the darkness was hope-
> less so I asked for shelter. Although her husband was away and she
> was alone in the house the young woman quite matter-of-factly re-
> ceived the wayfarer. Where I slept I do not remember, quite probably
> on the kitchen floor. In the morning I was given breakfast and a
> friendly send-off.

In the second recollection (Ravenscrag History Book Committee 1982, 424)
two lost young women are directed elsewhere because the man is alone at home.

> Another time [we] . . . went out to look for our brands on range cat-
> tle. She, I am sure was not over 18 years of age [the writer was about
> 12 years]. . . . darkness overtook us and we were lost. . . . Eventually
> we saw a light and found a house. The man told us he was alone and
> that we couldn't stay there but his sister and family were some dis-
> tance away and for us to follow the fence as they might take us in for
> the night. . . . It was well after midnight when we found the right
> place. . . . The next morning the kind family gave us our breakfast
> and home we started.

THE IMAGE OF WOMEN IN FRONTIER HISTORY

The history of women in the West has been characterized by concern with
the preponderance of men in frontier regions, the consequent exclusion of women
from frontier settlement history, and the stereotyping of women when they are
included (Jensen and Miller 1980). This history has also centered on the
contributions women made in settlement of the frontier and the impact the frontier and/or homestead experience had on women's life chances and on gender ideology and expectations. The past five years has seen a plethora of publications
questioning the masculinity of the frontier and identifying women's experiences
and contributions.[22] In part, this revision emerges from a recognition of the
confusion surrounding conceptions of what is a "frontier" (Jensen and Miller
1980). In part, the revision has been a natural extension of the inclusion of
women in the writing of all history.

As a concomitant of the inclusion of women in western settlement history,
frontier families have received new recognition, revising the traditional frontier
image of the lone male adventurer.

In fact, all the books referred to here focus on women as part of families,
recognizing agricultural settlement as one particular dimension of the "frontier."
They leave for others the examination of women's roles on other frontiers: in fur
trapping and mining camps, and among specific populations such as army
wives, wives of fur trappers, teachers, prostitutes, and servants.[23]

Schlissel (1982, 31) makes clear the survival advantage of family on the journey:[24]

> Whenever possible, families moved west within a kinship network. It seemed to matter very little whether one traveled in matrilinear or patrilinear families. Once the decison was made, families drew together from neighboring counties and states so that the extended family with all its households might be transplanted. On the Trail, families were the natural unit of social order. Single men attached themselves to family groups, engaging to serve as extra hands rather than outfitting a wagon alone. Wherever there was a woman, there was the nucleus of a home.

At the same time, Schlissel notes women's reluctance to make the trip, reinforcing the stereotype of women as "reluctant pioneers." Schlissel (1982, 28) writes: "Women understood the decision to cross the continent as a man's decision. Diaries are eloquent records that leave-taking was a painful and agonizing time."

Men's desire to emigrate West to explore, conquer, and transform the wilderness has traditionally been contrasted with women's primary concern with maintenance of family and home (Kolodny 1984).[25] A selection from Stratton (1981, 44-5) epitomizes this view:

> "My memory," wrote Mrs. W.B. Caton, "goes back almost fifty years to a humble home with the library table strewn with literature extolling the wonderful advantages of the new haven for immigrants – Kansas. To me it spelled destruction, desperadoes, and cyclones. I could not agree with my husband that any good could come out of such a country, but the characteristic disposition of the male prevailed, and October 1, 1879, saw us – a wagon, three horses and our humble household necessities – bound for the 'Promised Land.'
>
> "To say I wept bitterly would but faintly express the ocean of tears I shed on leaving my beloved home and state to take up residence in the 'wild and woolly West.'"

Although Stratton (1981, 45) and Schlissel (1982, 99-102) include material from women who see emigration as adventure or opportunity, the dominant image they present is woman as a reluctant migrant. They ignore that men as well as women felt pain upon leaving their families and that men were also filled with doubts about the move West to an unknown, albeit hopeful, economic opportunity (Myres 1982, 101).

Reluctance to emigrate West need not be considered as an essential part of women's character but rather as one response to situational and life-cycle factors. Simply put, women responsible for children have quite different demands placed upon them than do women without children.[26]

Schlissel (1982, 155) makes clear that women's reluctance to move West or their pain upon leaving home and family need not be considered as a negation of their participation and contribution to western settlement:

> [T]he period of the Overland Trail migration (1840-60) produces overwhelming evidence that women did not greet the idea of going West with enthusiasm, but rather that they worked out a painful negotiation with historical imperatives and personal necessity. . . . The West to them meant the challenge of rearing a family and maintaining domestic order against the disordered life on the frontier. Once embarked on the journey, they were determined and energetic in their efforts to make the move a success.
>
> If any idea joined the women to their men, if any expectation made the strenuous journey bearable, it was the idea that the move would bring them and their children a better life. . . .

There is no evidence that men and women did not share similar views regarding homestead settlement as a way to ensure a future for themselves and their children. Towards that goal, there is no disagreement among historians of western settlement regarding the expectations for women (and children) to "do what was needed" for the survival of the family and their homestead enterprise, a consistent theme in the community history books as well. There are no disagreements that, with few exceptions, women crossed over into traditionally male work arenas to ensure family survival and enterprise establishment. Controversy persists among historians over the evaluation of women's workloads, the relative power and autonomy women held in the family household, and the social consequences of these household economic changes, issues ignored by the writers of the community histories.

Discussions of workloads confuse the degree of hardship, the type and activity of the work, with exploitation and power relationships within the household. Hardship is relative to experience, time, and place, and difficult to evaluate from a more distant perspective even when the memories are one's own. Thus, memories of hardship are mitigated in retrospect from positions of survival and relative success (Myres 1982, 145; Schlissel 1982, 155; Silverman 1984, 73).

Women's participation in "male" areas of work can be viewed as both liberating and exploitive: liberating from the rigid confines of gender roles with concomitant expansion of opportunity (Harris 1987; Jackel 1982). At the same time, participation in "male" spheres can be exploitive without either a reciprocal exchange on the part of men in the necessary "female" work in household activities or without shared economic and social rewards.

Generalizations about women's workloads tend to cast frontier women either as objects of pity, overworked and overburdened, an image of women rejected by the community history book writers, or as the sturdy, forward-looking "sunbonneted helpmate" in partnership with her husband, the image projected by the community history books and challenged directly by some historians (Faragher 1979, 1981; Stansell 1976) and indirectly by others (Jeffrey 1979; Stratton 1981).

Stratton (1981, 75) reinforces the view of women as overworked and overburdened:

> For these women, life was far from easy. The endless hours of back-breaking toil left little time for rest and leisure. Day in and day out, they worked in the house and in the fields to produce the basic necessities of life and to build a future for their children. At first, the heavy work load seemed almost unbearable; it was physically exhausting and emotionally draining. Over the years, however, most women learned to abide the drudgery and monotony which filled their lives. They developed a certain fortitude and reliance which enabled them to withstand the privations and overcome the hardships.

In response to interpretations of women's homestead experience as unrelieved drudgery, Silverman (1984, 73) writes:

> I think that the reality of women's work on the rural and urban frontier was more complicated. . . . Women worked hard. . . .
>   Their days often seemed to go on endlessly, leaving them, at certain times of the year, nothing for themselves – not time, not leisure, not energy, not inner resources. . . . The routine may have seemed like hell to observers; I would suggest that the women themselves did not perceive it in that way. Instead, the often inordinate amounts of work that frontier women did seemed to them simply something they had to do.

Myres (1982, 164-65) does not deny the hard work in frontier settlement, but takes issue with those (Faragher 1979, 1981; Stansell 1976) who see women's work in terms of exploitation:

> It is clear from women's diaries that in many families women's work was respected; their role in the family's fortunes, and therefore in the decision-making process, was an important one. . . . Many women considered theirs a cooperative rather than a competitive enterprise, and they certainly did not view their position as 'second class'. . . .

The discussions regarding women's work are concerned with work within the household, the "intimate economies," in which personalties mitigate the formal legal codes giving men economic and political control over their children and wives. It is from this view that Stratton (1981, 57) writes:

> Men and women worked together as partners, combining their strengths and talent to provide food and clothing for themselves and their children. As a result, women found themselves on a far more equal footing with their spouses.

Jeffrey (1979, 62) also suggests that the formal ideology of appropriate family and gender roles changes with change in women's economic contribution:

> One might expect . . . that women's economic importance to the family enterprise might result in a reordering of family relationships and the reallocation of power within the family.
>
> Ideology of course, characterized the nineteenth-century family as a patriarchy, with men making decisions and women obediently accepting them. Actually, all American women probably had considerably more power that this model implied. . . . Ideology never tells all.

However, as Faragher (1981, 550) emphasizes, although women's work was valued, the legal code and (for some), religious ideology favored the control of labor and family resources by men.

CONCLUSION

For both, the community history participants and the historians interested in documenting women's experience, the value of women's work is clear. The evaluation of the workload of women and rewards of their work, in dispute among historians, is not an issue for the participants, the writers of the reminiscences. Their image of women is epitomized by the "partner model" of women's contribution to homestead settlement with shared social and economic rewards.

As they ignore other national and political issues, all the community history books ignore the legal/juridical structures that prevented formal acknowlegment of women's contributions. As summary statements about the past, these books are reflections of people who today have gained a modicum of economic security and urban amenities: paved roads, telephones, electricity, water, and indoor plumbing. It is from this vantage point of relative economic well-being they remember the past. The books celebrate survival – if not of enterprise, then of family – and the stories they tell are of cooperation and shared goals.

Just as community values of consensus set parameters for what is included or excluded from the community history books so do the differing feminist views. Myres and Silverman emphasize women's participation in economic production playing down the image of woman as victim and drudge. Jeffrey, Stratton, and Schlissel emphasize those events that demonstrate the particular valor and special character of women's experience. It is ironic that in their desire to depict the heroism of women in frontier settlement, they portray women as victims, an image rejected by the writers of the family accounts in the community histories. Both genres leave out the daily processes of negotiation required on the part of all household members in which the context of the particular household relationships and the associated cultural expectations of that kin and ethnic group become relevant in an evaluation of status.[27] In community book reminiscences, household conflicts and dissension is smoothed over. The community history book writers leave no doubt about the way they want women to be remembered. Pride in work is clear, exploitation and the lack of autonomy is unmentioned. The image may not apply to all and the lack of exploitation may be "invented" but it sets a useful model for future generations.

NOTES

[1]Paul Voisey (1985) uses the term "community sponsored local history book" to clearly identify and distinguish this type of history from other types written by single authors, professional historians, or amateurs, based on their own or others' experience or memories.

[2]Clyde Milner (1985) has used this concept from Hobsbawm (1983,4) to look at the history of Montana.

[3]The books represent the central geographical areas of the Northern Plains Culture History Project: Hill County, Montana; the maple Creek region of southeastern Saskatchewan, and the Foremost-Manyberries area of southwestern Alberta.

[4]The Northern Plains Culture History Project, a three year study, funded by the National Endowment for the Humanities.

[5]See Bennett and Kohl (1981) for a summary of this project.

[6]On both sides of the border there was an important presence of early mercantile traders like the A.B. Baker Company based in Fort Benton, Montana. One major difference between the United States and Canada was the appearance, prior to settlement, of the Royal Northwest Mounted Police which acted as a frontier constabulary and symbol of political and moral order. There was nothing comparable in the United States: law enforcement and social order were late, indigenous, casual, and often ineffective.

[7]The dedication page in the community history of the southwestern corner of Alberta (Forgotten Corner History Book Committee 1982, iii) exemplifies this shared value. The committee writes: "In deciding to prepare this book, the committee determined that the history of this corner would not be forgotten; that the people, their labours, their perseverance and their achievements should not go unrecognized and unremembered."

[8]These community histories are present in virtually every hamlet and village throughout the northern plains. By 1983, there were more than 800 accounts for the Province of Alberta alone. These accounts range in size from a short pamphlet to 500-600 page books (Krotki 1983). Similar proliferation is found in Saskatchewan and Montana. The Regina Saskatchewan Public Library's Prairie History Room has printed a bibliographic and location aid to local and district histories that lists more than 700 volumes (Regina Public Library 1986). Walter (1978) locates 878 pamphlets and volumes in Montana.

The common organizational procedure for the initiating the club or individuals was to place an announcement of an organizational meeting in the local newspaper. School districts formed at the time of homestead settlement commonly formed the basis for committees, each school district selecting a representative who then became responsible for contacting the families in that dis trict. Where the initial homestead family was not found, the usual practice was to have some old-timer write a short bit about that individual.

[9]In a prior paper Bennett and Kohl (1975) have described these peoples as "survivors"; by that we emphasize the ability to cope with social and economic hardships through a wide variety of behavioral strategies concerned with continuity and maintenance of the family enterprise.

[10]Oliver et al. (1984, 18) write:

> When the settlers recollect their past life in the community, the memories they submit to the local histories usually reflect the positive aspects of life. . . . Few people remembered tragedies, unless it was the misfortune of others, where the compassion and mutual concern that was valued in the community was revealed in the memory related by the writer/contributor. . . . Overall, the histories contain optimistic viewpoints, memories of the good times, and they thereby reveal a sentimental preference for the "good old days" of the past, whether the present is better or not.

[11]Not surprisingly, accounts that are self-written are self-censored to avoid controversy both within the family and among community members. Where items were submitted that editors and their committee members felt would "hurt someone," they exercised their editorial judgment and edited these specifics out, sometimes after consultation with other family members, sometimes not.

[12]Those individuals in conflict with (or outside) the larger group become the community's "local characters," that is, they are cleaned up and repackaged as special or unique or even mythical characters. This repackaging glosses over past schisms and past conflicts, permitting the community to be presented as a harmonious whole. For example, the Ravenscrag community book (Ravenscrag History Book Committee 1982, 276) includes an account of a Mrs. Dale.

> Mrs. Dale was remembered as one of the most colourful people to pass this way. She was most charming to meet and intelligent to talk to. However, if she had a point to make or an argument to win she did not hesitate to let her opponent know she was armed and ready! Many are the stories of her home . . . often referred to as "Robbers' Roost", probably rightfully named as it was general knowledge that she was the brains behind a gang of horse and cattle thieves for which she put in "time."

A "Ballad of Robber's Roost" is included as part of this account of "colour," as well as a listing of Mrs. Dale's family connections and the members of the community who rented her ranch. The prosaic is linked to the unique, and the social outcast (the cattle thief) is transformed into a historical figure, a character of the West. Similar transformations of outsiders occur in virtually all the books.

[13]Jensen and Miller (1980) are clear in their intention to move beyond stereotyping and typology . They see stereotypes of women as products of a confusion of time and space in the use of the terms "frontier" and the "West," the unquestioned assumption that the West was the frontier of men, and the consequent failure to include women as active agents in settlement and development. Also see Faragher (1981, 541) regarding the futility of sterotypes.

[14]The concern with "lady-like" behavior was a continual refrain in interviews I conducted during 1963-1965. Ranchwomen raised on the frontier avowed that they disliked "town" and what they perceived as the boredom and pettiness of town life. However, these women also were concerned with appearing in town as they perceived a "lady" should. In my book *Working Together: Women and Family in Southwestern Saskatchewan* (Kohl 1976, 34-35). I discuss this characteristic in terms of the duality of expectations held for women.

[15]This definition is from *The American Heritage Dictionary of the English Language* (Morris 1969, 1264).

[16]The use of "we" among contemporary agriculturalists to describe family enterprise development and activities is common, a reflection of the merged character of farm family and economic enterprise (Kohl 1983).

[17]This is a pilot project to examine the relative frequency of the recording of men's and women's contributions to the family enterprise and to the local community. Quantitative analysis from school districts in three selected community history books (Ravenscrag History Book Committee 1982; New Horizons Commitee 1982; Foremost Historical Society 1975) have been used.

[18]The use of the men's names to record the lives of women has begun to be redressed. For example, the genealogical society of Havre, Montana, prepared an extensive index to the community history book *Grit, Guts and Gusto* (Hill County Bicentennial Commission 1976) and archivists are now publishing special bibliographies (e.g., Dryden 1980).

[19]The family history accounts vary widely in depth and degree of information presented since they are written by family members. Inevitably there is differential response: some families are represented with a few lines, others with several pages. The amount of print devoted to a particular family depended more on idiosyncrasies of the respondent than on the respondent's social standing or contribution to the community.

[20]In their content analysis of thirty-four local community histories, Oliver et. al. (1984, 16) note common "silences" about social facts whose features are undesirable. . . . For example, the harsh years of the depression are documented yet there is very little mention of the number of occurences of suicide or the problem of abandoned land. . . . [S]ome ethnic groups are rarely mentioned. . . . Although certain racist organizations existed like the Ku Klux Klan their presence is not acknowledged. . . .

[21]Sara Roberts's diary differs from the reminiscences in the local community-sponsored history books. A diary or a letter is a first-hand account, written at the time of the experience, in contrast to retrospective accounts. Although all writing involves some retrospection, the reminiscence tends to feature special or

unique events or to sum up a life, rather than a recounting of mundane experiences or an immediate response to a specific situation.

[22]Faragher (1979) and Schlissel (1982) analyse diaries of an extreme event over a short time period – the duration of the journey West. Jeffrey (1979) and Myres (1982) examine letters, diaries, and early interpretations of women's experience on the frontier. Silverman (1984) and Stratton (1981) use retrospective materials: Silverman conducted oral interviews with aging homesteaders in Alberta, Stratton analyses retrospective questionnaires initiated in the 1920s to preserve the experiences of women homesteaders in Kansas.

[23]Armitrage (1985, 389-91) reviews some of this recent literature. Both Myres (1982, 181-184 and Jeffrey (1979, 89-94) note opportunities for women as teachers.

[24]See Faragher (1979).

[25]In her summary of migration studies, Walsh (1981, 64) writes that "migration – at least to agricultural and urban frontiers – was as much a family affair as a single person's prerogative."

[26]Schlissel notes how the diary accounts of the two single women differ from those written by the majority of women, who were married with children, with regard to the hardships of the trip. In her study of Colorado settlers, Harris (1987, 174) finds that "Unreserved enthusiasm for homesteading was almost always associated with youth."

[27]There were (and remain) important differences in household concepts of patriarchal power and control. See, for example the reminiscence of Mary E. Weeks, *Forgotten Pioneers* (Weeks, n.d.). This is a history of a Belgian Catholic family living near Chinook, Montana, a family in which there were particularly oppressive patriarchal controls on children and women. Harris (1987, 175) makes a similar point about family variation affecting power sharing in households.

BIBLIOGRAPHY

Armitage, Susan. 1985. "Women and Men in Western History: A Stereoptical Vision." *Western Historical Quarterly* 16: 391-95.

Bennett, John W., and Seena B. Kohl. 1975. "Characterological, Institutional, and Strategic Interpretations of Prairie Settlement." In *Western Canada Past and Present*, ed. A.W. Rasporich, 14-27. Calgary: McClelland & Stuart West and the University of Calgary.

_____. 1981 "Longitudinal Research in Rural North America: the Saskatchewan Cultural Ecology Research Program, 1960-1973." In *Anthropologists at Home in North America: Methods and Issues in the Study of One's Own Society*, ed. D. Messerschmidt, 91-105. New York: Cambridge University Press.

Benson, Roy. n.d. "Letters from an American Homesteader." Glenbow Archives, Calgary, Canada.

Bicha, Karel D. 1968. *The American Farmer and the Canadian West*. Lawrence Kans.: Coronade Press.

Bowsfield, Hartwell. 1969. "Writing Local History," *Alberta Historical Review* 17: 10-19.

Dryden, Jean E. 1980. *Some Sources for Women's History at the Provincial Archives of Alberta*. Edmonton, Alb.: Alberta Culture Historical Resources Division.

Faragher, John Mack. 1979. *Women and Men on the Overland Trail*. New Haven: Yale University Press.

_____. 1981. "History from the Inside-Out: Writing the History of Women in Rural America." *American Quarterly* 33: 537-57.

Foremost Historical Society. 1975. *Shortgrass Country: A History of Foremost and Nemiskam*. Editor-in chief Alyce Butterwick. Foremost, Alb.: Foremost Historical Society, D. W. Friesen and Sons.

Fowke, Vernon C. 1947. *An Introduction to Canadian Agricultural History*. Toronto: University of Toronto Press.

Harris, Katherine. 1987. "Homesteading in Northeastern Colorado, 1873-1920: Sex Roles and Women's Experience." In *The Women's West*. eds. Susan Armitrage and Elizabeth Jameson, Norman: University of Oklahoma Press.

Hobsbawm, Eric. 1983. *The Invention of Tradition*. Cambridge: Cambridge University Press.

Hill County Bicentennial Commission. 1976. *Grit, Guts and Gusto: A History of Hill County*. Ed. Signe Sedlacek. Havre, Mont.: Bear Paw Printers.

Jackel, Susan, ed. 1982. *A Flannel Shirt and Liberty: British Emigrant Gentlewomen in the Canadian West, 1880-1914*. Vancouver: University of British Columbia Press.

Jeffrey, Julie Roy. 1979. *Frontier Women: The Trans-Mississippi West, 1840-1880*. New York: Hill & Wang.

Jenson, Joan M., and Darlis A. Miller. 1980. "The Gentle Tamers Revisited: New Approaches to the History of Women in the American West." *Pacific Historical Review* 49: 173-213.

Kohl , Seena B. 1976. *Working Together: Women and Family in Southwestern Saskatchewan*. Toronto: Holt, Rinehart & Winston of Canada.

_____. 1977. "Women's Participation in the North American Family Farm." *Women's Studies International Quarterly* 1: 47-54.

_____. 1983. "Working Together: Husbands and Wives in the Small-Scale Family Agricultural Enterprise." In *The Canadian Family*, ed. K. Ishwaran, 234-243. Toronto, Canada: Gage Publishing.

_____. 1986. "Writing Local History: The Creation of A Shared Past." Paper presented at the Palliser Triangle Conference, 15-17 May, at Medicine Hat College, Medicine Hat, Alberta, Canada.

Kohl. Seena B., and John W. Bennett. 1985. "Culture, History and Personal Experience In the Canadian American West: The Generational Rhythm of Historical Interpretation." Paper presented at the Social Science History Meeting, 23 October, Chicago, Ill.

Kolodny, Annette. 1984. *The Land Before Her*. Chapel Hill, N.C.: University of North Carolina Press.

Krotki, Joanna E. 1983. *An Annotated Bibliography of Local Histories in Alberta*. Calgary: Department of Slavic and East European Studies, University of Alberta.

Lipman-Blumen, Jean. 1973. "Role De-differentiation as a System Response to Crisis: Occupational and Political Roles of Women." *Sociological Inquiry* 43:105-29.

Mackintosh, W.A. 1934. Prairie Settlement: The Geographic Background. Vol.1 of *Canadian Frontiers of Settlement*. Toronto: Macmillan.

Milner, Clyde. 1985. "Inventing Montana: Pioneer Memoirs as Cultural History." Paper presented to the Montana Historical Society Conference, 8 November, Helena.

Morris, William, ed. 1969. *The American Heritage Dictionary of the English Language*. Boston: Houghton Mifflin; New York First American Heritage.

Myres, Sandra L. 1982. *Westering Women and the Frontier Experience 1800-1915*. Albuquerque: University of New Mexico Press.

New Horizons Commitee. 1982. *The Forgotten Corner: A History of the Communities of Comrey, Catchem, Hooper-Pendland, Onefour, Wild Horse (also including the Range Land), Townships One to Four, Ranges One to Six*. Eds. Olive Lanz and Beatrice Kusler. Medicine Hat, Alb.: The New Horizons Committee.

Oliver, Barbara, Mark Vigrass, Wendy Whelan, and Michele Young. 1984. *Regional Heritage Project: A Content Analysis of Selected Local Histories in Saskatchewan*. Regina, Saskatchewan: Canadian Plains Research Center, University of Regina.

Pollock, Grace. comp. n.d. *Our Pioneers*. Maple Creek, Saskatchewan: Cypress Hills Pioneer Association.

Ravenscrag History Book Committee. 1982. *Between and Beyond the Benches: Ravenscrag*. Ann Saville, ed. Ravenscrag, Saskatchewan: Ravenscrag History Book Commmitee.

Regional Public Library. 1986. *The Saskatchewan Local History Directory: A Locality Finding Aid to the Collections of the Prairie History Room of the Regina Public Library*. Compiled by the staff of the Prairie History Room. Regina, Saskatchewan. Mimeo.

Roberts, Sarah E. 1971. *Alberta Homestead: Chronicle of a Pioneer Family*. Ed. Lathrop E. Roberts. Austin, Tex.: University of Texas Press.

Robsart Committee. 1955. *Robsart Pioneers Review the Years*. Maple Creek, Saskatchewan: The Committee.

Schlissel, Lillian. 1982. *Women's Diaries of the Westward Journey*. New York: Schocken Books.

Silverman, Eliane Leslau. 1984. *The Last Best West: Women on the Alberta Frontier 1880-1930*. Montreal, Canada: Eden Press.

Stansell, Christine. 1976. "Women on the Great Plains, 1865-1890." *Women's Studies* 4: 86-98.

Stratton, Joanna L. 1981. *Pioneer Women: Voices from the Kansas Frontier*. New York: Simon & Schuster.

Voisey, Paul. 1985. "Rural Local History and the Prairie West." *Prairie Forum* 10: 327-38.

Walsh, Margaret. 1981. *The American Frontier Revisited*. Atlantic Highlands, N. J.: Humanities Press.

Walter , D.A. 1978. "Guide to Montana Local History Materials." *Montana Historian* 8: 24-56.

Weeks, Mary E. n.d. *Forgotten Pioneers*. No. 978.6k5/W4kf, Montana Historical Society Archives, Helena.

6

"THIS COUNTRY'S HARD ON WOMEN AND OXEN": A STUDY OF THE IMAGES OF FARM WOMEN IN AMERICAN FICTION

Julia Hornbostel

The many new publications on women's history, on women in the economy, and especially on women's work, strikingly document the tremendous number of working women in our society and the variety of jobs they perform. If one reads only the popular press, it is easy to assume that the number of contemporary women working outside the home is a recent phenomenon and that the image of the "angel in the house" (the protected woman with delicate hands and complexion, the guardian of morals, gracing her home and enlightening her family and community) is an accurate reflection of the lives of most women in the past. The reality is quite different, however, for most women have always worked, combining outside employment with family and housework, as over fifty percent of us do today. How then can we explain the difference between assumption and fact?

If the source of one's impression of the past is fiction, the discrepancy may be attributable to the fact that American fiction poorly represents the reality of working women's lives. In fact, my lengthy search of over one hundred mid-nineteenth-to-mid-twentieth century American novels and short stories by both men and women has turned up very few examples of women doing the jobs we know they have done. For example, there are very few novels about women teachers although we know many, many women were employed as teachers from the early 1800s on (when public education became required). The same is true of nurses or the many female textile mill workers; very few of them appear as fictional heroines. My intent here is not to consider why working women are so poorly represented in American fiction. Rather, I would like to explore the one working role we do see accurately portrayed in fiction: women farming, both with their husbands and alone.

Many novels and short stories vividly portrayed women as farm, ranch, or plantation workers or managers. Why is this role so well represented? There are three main reasons: (1) farming is a job women do at home, within the family unit; (2) it has been a job for which women usually have not been paid, thus supporting a general societal attitude concerning what is suitable for women to do; and (3) farm work is compatible with the traditional female nurturing role of planting, tending, and bringing to harvest. So, in spite of the fact that farm work is extremely hard and dirty, it has been considered appropriate for women to do – and as a fictional topic, has offered much opportunity for praise, admiration, or warning for readers.

As one reads American novels and short stories about farm women in many different settings and periods, a number of characteristics emerge quite clearly. Whether these women live and work in Appalachia, New England, the midwest, or on the Great Plains, recently or in the past, their reactions and experiences are similar. There are frequent statements of mood (particularly of loneliness) and expressions of feeling about the land and scene, the hard work farm women do, and their perseverance. Also, the portrayals of single women farmers and those of farm wives are interestingly different.

Fictional pioneer women and farm wives often express loneliness. They are usually separated from their kin, especially if they moved west with their husbands to claim new land (a decision often made by the man alone). But even if they have not moved far, they are often isolated because of bad roads, lack of ability or time to correspond, and lack of other means of communication. Many have no neighbors (or no compatible ones), and most have little long-term emotional support from their husbands. For example, in the 1923 novel *Weeds* by Edith Summers Kelley (a friend and contemporary of Upton Sinclair and Sinclair Lewis), the protagonist Judy Blackford marries and lives within a few miles of her family. Yet she has an appreciation of beauty and a yearning to satisfy her aesthetic nature that sets her apart from both family and neighbors. She has very little in common with them except hard work. In Bess Streeter Aldrich's *A Lantern in Her Hand* (1928), Abbie Deal moves to the Nebraska frontier with her husband and first child. In a sod house on the far-reaching prairie, she yearns for the sight of her mother's face and for family closeness. There are no neighbors and her one female friend is miles away. In Willa Cather's *O Pioneers!* (1913), Alexandra longs for companionship – male or female – that will give meaning to her life and accomplishments. Even though she becomes a successful farmer, her life looms empty before her without that support. In Susan Glaspell's short story "A Jury of Her Peers" (1917), two women realize how their friendship might have helped a neighbor cope with loneliness and an abusive husband.

The land itself can increase the sense of isolation. Women in western frontier stories remark over and over how the wind and vast treeless expanse intensify their loneliness. Rain, heat, and snow also increase the sense of distance from neighbors, especially sustaining female friends.

Although at first many pioneer women hate the empty expanse of their rural settings, most farm women soon come to love the land. A short interchange between two characters in Rose Wilder Lane's *Free Land* exemplifies these reactions. Nettie, a young woman who has been on the prairie for a time says, "I like it where there aren't any people, where it's big and new and – fresh." However, her new friend Mary who is a newlywed far from home is getting a rough initiation to frontier life. Mary replies "I hate it!...the bareness, the emptiness, the winds. . . . the grass swishing at [my] skirts" (Lane 1938, 92). One feels openness and independence, the other, oppressive isolation. Over and over in these stories, women remark how they have come to love the land with its delicate colors and seasonal changes of the prairie grass and wild flowers, the mountain hues, the vistas. From being barren and overwhelming scenes that depress, the natural settings become what refreshes and supports. Nell Connor in Josephine Donovan's 1930 novel, *Black Soil*, is a good example of this changing female relationship with the prairie. At first, Nell is negative, lamenting that her husband has selected land so far from any signs of life. She feels that the prairie stretches endlessly, with no direction, to the ends of the world. As they drive toward their land for the first time, she muses "Why had Tim selected land so far from any signs of life? It was hours, days, since the railroad terminal – the last connections with civilization – had been swallowed in those palpitating grasses" (Donovan 1930, 1). But soon she comes to love the prairie's fruitfulness. She envisions how their love and sacrifice will cause it to blossom and takes real pleasure in the whispering of the wind, the bird and insect sounds, and the "subdued murmurs of moving grass; voices of children – a prairie diapason" (Donovan 1930, 22). Even as a young girl, Alexandra Bergstrom in *O Pioneers!* is inspired by the land's beauty and promise: "It [the land of the Great Divide] seemed beautiful to her, rich, and strong and glorious" (Cather 1913, 65). A woman's appreciation of the prairie's irreplaceable beauty is also clearly expressed in Margaret Lynn's *A Stepdaughter of the Prairie* (1914, 280-81):

> Soon long brown [plowed] lines would divide its wonderful surface into parallel sections, and the lines would broaden and the sections narrow until there was nothing of them left. And next year an uneven . . .yellowish crop of sod corn would take the place of this full, rich, pleasant growth. The grass under my feet would never reach its promised winter rosiness and would never turn again in its rare spring green. And no other would ever come to take its place. . . . There was a kind of worth in my feeling now which raised it almost to the level of great emotion. . . . one was not lonely on the prairie.

The farm women who do not move west but stay in familiar surroundings also express a sensitive and enriching closeness to the land. Gertie Nevels in Harriette Arnow's *The Dollmaker* (1954) feels completely at home and capable in the potato or corn fields, cutting wood in her farm's forest, and planning the development of land she intends to buy with her carefully saved money. Cather's Alexandra and Antonia, Judy in *Weeds*, and many other fictional heroines turn to the land for a feeling of independence and spiritual support. As Margret says in Josephine Johnson's *Now in November* (1934, 34-35):

> To us [the land] was a thing loved for its own sake, giving a sort of ecstasy and healing . . . and we felt a nameless, not wholly understood love. . . . There was the hill quiet and the stony pastures, and sometimes they made me ashamed of being what I was . . . more often they were like hands to heal.

As Annette Kolodny (1984) observes in *The Land Before Her*, the typical fictional response of women to the land is not a desire to conquer or possess it but to preserve its beauty and to change it only as much as necessary – to create

a garden and an area of community. Although fictional farm women rarely have
the opportunity to move about freely and explore the land unless they do so as
children, they see its beauty. They also create beauty in it by planting flowers,
gardens, and (if they are single women), by planting crops and admiring their
fruition. These women see acts of creation and nurturance as acts of strength.[1]

The women certainly see the power of the land and the difficulty of making
and keeping it useful farm land. But primarily they see it as compatible and
beautiful, not hostile. They have a strong sense of mutuality with it, a sense of
its potential for crops and as something beautiful in its own right. In addition,
their relationship with nature gives them a sense of renewal and spiritual uplift.
Thus, after a particularly awful period when Judy in *Weeds* discovers she is
pregnant *again* and feels ill with work and worry, she runs off into the woods for
some peace and comfort. She looks away from the top of a ridge to the horizon
(Kelley 1923, 240):

> It seemed endless . . . out of its calm and magnitude a sense of peace
> welled up and gradually enfolded her. . . . She half forgot the things
> that she had fled from and . . . felt almost happy with the happiness
> that comes of peace and solitude and wide spaces. It was more than
> three years since she had been by herself in the open country.

The beauty of the natural world gives her peace and joy.

Another characteristic of fictional farm women is that they all work very
hard. They have to, for their work is extremely important for family survival.
They tend gardens, cook, wash, care for their children, even teach the children if
no school exists; they work in the fields, even in some cases substituting for
horses by pulling the plow as in *Kit Brandon* by Sherwood Anderson (1936);
they nurse family and neighbors, prepare the dead, and so on. Often the sale of
the women's poultry or garden produce provides the only cash income the family
has. If they do not sell the products to individual buyers, they offer the goods to
local stores for cash or credit. Care of children and young animals and the
gardening are usually exclusively women's jobs, for in farm novels there is a
clear sexual division of labor except in extreme emergencies. When grasshoppers
attack, when a hail storm strikes, or simply at the outset when establishing a
farm, the women join in the heavy field work. Men, however, very rarely pitch
in to do housework except when the wives are ill or in childbirth. Their strength
eroded by hard physical labor and childbearing, many of the women die before
they are thirty as does Mary in *Zury* by Josephine Kirkland (1887). As a character in *Free Land* says, "This country's hard on women and oxen" (Lane 1938,
82).

Although most of the women seem resigned to their early aging, inwardly
many rebel and question why their desires must be postponed or suppressed. In
Hamlin Garland's story "Lucretia Burns," Lucretia avoids her insensitive farmer
husband for days, essentially going on strike because she is angry that she is expected to do so much, yet gets no thanks. But eventually she realizes there is
nothing to do but go on; there is no hope their lives can be any better. Judy in
Weeds rebels too. Fed up with the demands of housekeeping and childcare, she

escapes into the woods and fields in search of a restoring, beautiful scene that she longs to capture in painting. But without time or instruction, she cannot. Her desires remain dreams. Abbie Deal (*A Lantern in Her Hand*) wants to learn how to paint what she sees and how to develop her lovely voice, but there is too much work to be done and no money for such things. In Zora Neale Hurston's beautiful novel *Their Eyes Were Watching God* (1927), Janie works as a field laborer on Okeechobee, Florida, truck farms. She, too, works very hard and regrets lost opportunities to be herself, but when she is in the company of friends and her loving (third) husband, she never regrets the exhausting labor. However, she is a rarity in this fictional world in that she has no children. Most of the farm women in these stories have many, and it is on the children that they focus their hope. What the mothers have not had, they hope their children will, and this hope enables them to go on.

Despite their physical and emotional hardships, the women stay, in part because of their lack of money, but more importantly because of their sense of responsibility and love for their children. One of the few exceptions appears in Fielding Burke's *Call Home the Heart* (1932), where Ishma cannot bear the constant pregnancies and extreme poverty of her life in the Kentucky hills and so runs away to a mill town where she hopes to find a better life. Judy in *Weeds* works happily and hard with her husband in the fields until she has a child, then she feels so housebound with small babies coming one after another that she hungers for solitude, even for the ability to hibernate as animals do through the winter. "She wished she had a hole to crawl into…where there were no meals to cook, no fire to keep going, no fretful child…a nice quiet hole where nobody came and where she could curl up and be at peace" (Kelley 1923, 208). But, as is typical of most of these women, Judy stays.

Although the married women are often more educated than their husbands, they are rarely the "culture bearers." Only occasionally do the men or women have time or energy to be culturally refining forces on the frontier. Much Victorian romantic fiction and didactic literature perpetuates the myth of women as the ones who instruct, who urge interest in music, art, religion, and reading. The desire to do so does appear in the minds and hearts of fictional rural women as they dream for their children's futures, but primarily they concentrate on surviving. Whatever it takes to survive – innovation, hard work, guts, companionship, or prayer – is what they seek. Only if they become financially comfortable and have hired help can the rural women turn to these other interests or encourage their young people to do so. Even then, however, the interest rarely produces sustained satisfaction, as is evident at several points in *O Pioneers!* A person with "refined" interests may even be ridiculed in a rural setting as is Annie Sparrow in *Zury*. A young school teacher from Boston, she is jeered: her speech, clothing, and bearing ridiculed, and her room set on fire. She and many people in the community feel she is out of place.

Nevertheless, there is a persistent sentimental image in some of the popular novels such as *A Lantern in Her Hand*, showing the ideal mother as the one who sacrifices so her children can have music lessons, schooling, church teaching, and opportunities to read. The more romantic the novel, the more one sees this theme; it is certainly in keeping with the nineteenth-century ideal of female behavior and our ideal of the family farm as the bastion of morality and individualism.

Another strong characteristic of farm women in fiction is that they usually see themselves as work partners, not just workers on the family farm.[2] Until the farm is established, the women work hard in the fields as well as indoors. They help to clear the land, pick rocks, plant, cultivate, and harvest. Like Judy in *Weeds* and Gertie in *The Dollmaker*, they are physically capable of the outdoor work and often clearly prefer it. However, as the farm prospers, the women (even single women farmers) leave field work to the men or hired hands. This change is an indication of the farmer's success, but not always of the woman's desire. Fictional married women farmers also often consult with their husbands about the business of the farm. They may actually be the business decision makers or the impetus behind the decision to plant many of the farm's crops as in Martha Ostenso's *O River Remember!* (1943) or in Cather's *My Antonia* (1918) where Antonia has much to do with the planting and nurture of her beautiful orchard. Thus, whether working on the land or inside the more "feminine" boundaries of garden and house, women in fiction are usually clear partners in the creation and development of the farm.

Although the great majority of women farmers in fiction are married, there are a number of outstanding examples of women farming alone – that is, without a husband or father to direct or aid them. These women are often innovators, have considerable input into community affairs, and gain hard won recognition. They are frequently concerned with their community's production: how others are doing and how others' farm production can be improved. They are also interested in what social improvements need to be made and how. If these unmarried women farmers become successful, they are often generous benefactors of the community.

These fictional female sole proprietors tend to experiment far more than men do. They take chances such as buying up more and more land as ruined neighbors leave or experimenting with new inventions. Dorinda in Ellen Glasgow's *Barren Ground* (1925) is the first in her area to plant alfalfa; Alexandra in Cather's *O Pioneers!* risks community criticism by erecting the first silo in her community; Selina in Edna Ferber's *So Big*, by growing unusual vegetable crops. Beret in Ole Rolvaag's *Giants in the Earth* and *Peder Victorious* (1927 & 1929) is also an innovator and she, not her sons, is begrudgingly described by her neighbors as the ablest farmer in the area. All of these women are extremely practical, even to the point of wearing men's clothes for farm work. Although ridiculed for these innovations or unusual behaviors, they are, in the end, imitated and greatly respected for their farsightedness and success. Finally, there is a particularly strong sense of the "earth mother" about the single woman farmer. She is enriched by her relationship with the soil and enriches it in return.

In fiction as in real life, women who farm alone usually inherit their land from fathers and husbands. In *O Pioneers!* Mr. Bergstrom leaves his daughter Alexandra in charge of the farm rather than one of his sons, for he knows Alexandra is the most capable, and he has faith in her ability and vision. In her, he recognizes a:

strength of will, and the simple direct way of thinking things out. . .
He would much rather . . . have seen this . . . in one of his sons, but
it was not a question of choice. He had . . . to be thankful that there
was one among his children to whom he could entrust the future of
his family and the possibilities of his hard-won land. (Cather 1913,
24).

Dorinda in *Barren Ground* also inherits her farm from her father, Selina in *So
Big*, from her husband. They too take over and continue to develop the farms.
These women are capable managers and caring people. Often by the time they
inherit the land, their children are grown, or they have no children; thus they can
concentrate their energy and thought on the land. But in some cases, a child
gives the widowed mother the impetus to break from a traditional female role.
For example, when a farmer criticizes Selina for selling vegetables at Chicago's
Haymarket amid men, she replies, "Don't talk to me like that, you great stupid!
What good does it do a woman to stay home in her kitchen if she's going to
starve there, and her boy with her!" (Ferber 1924, 178).

Although we have few fictional portrayals of single women as farmers, there
is considerable historical evidence that many women operated farms alone. After
the Homestead Act of 1862, many women claimed land, which they could do if
they were single, over twenty-one, or heads of households. As much as one-third
of the land in some states (the Dakotas, for example) was owned by women, and
they were more likely than men to make the final claim to this land (thirty-seven
percent of the men did, forty-two percent of the women did). But well into the
nineteenth century, a woman had no right to own land in most states unless she
was single. When she married, her husband alone had legal title to their land.
However, by the end of the nineteenth century, nearly one-quarter of a million
women ran farms of their own (Smuts 1971, 10). Whereas we have few novels
about single women farming, there seem to be none about women homesteading
alone. One reason may be that many single women who own land are older and
widowed and the life of an older woman who has outlived her husband is not the
usual stuff of a novel. Another reason may be that our usual concept of the farm
is that of the stereotypical family farm, worked primarily by a married couple
and their children; this then becomes the common subject matter of fiction.

Loneliness, hard work, frustration over sublimation of desires or talents, and
awareness of nature's vastness, beauty, and spiritual sustenance are frequent
themes in stories of farm women in the past. It is interesting that recent sociological studies of contemporary farm women seem to support the portrayal of
women found in fiction. For example, in a brief summary of their study on the
causes of anxiety, depression, and hostility in rural women, Hettsgaard and Light
(1984, 673-74) acknowledge that these characteristics are problems for rural
women. The authors report that the two main factors that increased farm
women's levels of anxiety, depression, and hostility were having a husband with
less than a high school education and more than two children under fourteen.

Factors that reduced these emotions were regular church attendance, involvement in decision making on the operation of the farm, regular visits with
friends, and a husband with more than a high school education.

There is also a great deal of nonfictional evidence to support the argument that farm women worked hard; fictional portrayals of this characteristic seem quite realistic. In both types of sources, it is clear that women labor endlessly and also contribute significantly to the family's economic position. In *With These Hands*, Joan Jensen (1981, 44) quotes this autobiographical reminiscence:

> To bear two children in two and a half years from my marriage day, to make thousands of pounds of butter every year, cook for workers, visitors, and family, sew, wash, iron, bake, clean, in short, to be a pioneer drudge with never a penny of my own, was not pleasant for an ex school teacher whose salary then had not gone for groceries, taxes, or farm equipment.

We know that the farm women's work contributed greatly to both the family health and economy. In areas where a market was available, the sale of her eggs, butter, chickens, and other produce often provided eighty percent of the household's living expenses (Rosenfeld 1985, 20). Nearly every novel or short story in which farm women figure portrays them as involved in this kind of production, although often in a very modest way.

Through surveys, nonfiction also provides considerable evidence that farm women often do what is considered "men's work," but men rarely do "women's work." Farm jobs seem to remain largely sex stereotyped (Rosenfeld 1985, 11).

It appears that the portraits we see of farm women in fiction are with few exceptions, realistic. The characteristics of their fictional lives are certainly supported by available diaries, letters, and surveys.[3] Much of the authenticity may be due to the fact that most authors of novels and short stories about farm women spent a great part of their own lives in the settings they describe. Willa Cather lived on the Nebraska prairie; Bess Streeter Aldrich and Josephine Donovan created their characters from their mothers' experiences and reminiscences; Edith Kelley and her husband lived and worked on a Kentucky tobacco farm; Rose Wilder Lane lived on farms in Wisconsin, Iowa, and the Dakotas. They were writing from experience or very recent memories.

Women have left a more substantial record of their life and work experiences than we may think from reading the usual histories of America. But because women in the past were seldom professional historians, their accounts were rarely in the form of traditional histories. Instead, they were in genres more familiar to them, such as letters, diaries, autobiographies, novels, and poetry. We need to examine these materials for records of experience, social history, and reactions.

At the same time we must remember that literature is not necessarily history. We need to be careful not to make that automatic leap. Fiction can tell us much about the past, but it can also romanticize and cloud reality as one suspects is the case in Aldrich's *A Lantern in Her Hand,* for Abbie Deal is such an endlessly perfect mother. Readers and editors may seem to demand softened reality as the editor of *The Farmer's Wife* did in 1935, rejecting Zona Gale's story "Flying Acres" as too depressing and true in its description of women as victims of frontier life (Fairbanks 1986, 108). Some writers bow to that desire for happy stories or may exaggerate hardships, thus skewing reality. Nevertheless, although literature is not history, it can be a good source of knowledge and companion to history. By surveying an extensive body of fiction on a particular topic, one becomes aware of the feelings, actions, and interactions of people in a particular world. Both history and literature begin with selected facts and are shaped by their recorders. Both are important sources of knowledge.

Close to ninety percent of Americans lived on farms in the mid-nineteenth century; sixty percent still lived there in 1900. The ideal of an agriculturally based society has been a cornerstone of American ideology, and certainly what farmers produce has always been of great importance to us all. Thus it seems appropriate that of all women's work roles, the agricultural is the one most frequently portrayed in fiction. Though their work is neglected in formal histories, American farm women's lives *are* described in our fiction. Whether "accurately" portrayed or mixed with the author's – or society's – desires and expectations, the representation is valuable. Indeed, fiction may well be one of the most important sources of information on women's work in U.S. agriculture.

NOTES

[1] In her book, *In a Different Voice*, Carol Gilligan (1982) suggests that this is a generally female attribute, whereas men believe being powerful means being assertive.

[2] In her study of American farm women, *The Invisible Farmers*, Carolyn Sachs (1983) argues that on the frontier, married women had independence in their own sphere of work but not in the fields. In the fields, she says, they were workers, not partners. Fictional images belie this.

[3] See for example, Joanne Stratton's *Pioneer Women* (1981), the material in Joan Jensen's collection *With These Hands* (1981), and in Linda Brent's *Incidents in the Life of a Slave Girl* (1861).

BIBLIOGRAPHY

Aldrich, Bess Streeter. 1928. *A Lantern in Her Hand.* New York: D. Appleton.

Anderson, Sherwood. 1936. *Kit Brandon.* New York: Arbor House.

Arnow, Harriette. 1954. *The Dollmaker.* New York: The MacMillan Co.

Brent, Linda. 1861. *Incidents in the Life of a Slave Girl.* Reprint: New York: Harcourt Brace, 1972.

Burke, Fielding. 1932. *Call Home the Heart.* New York: Longmans, Green. Reprint: The Feminist Press, 1983.

Cather, Willa. 1913. *O Pioneers!* Boston: Houghton Mifflin.

_____. 1918. *My Antonia.* Boston: Houghton Mifflin.

Chase, Joan. 1983. *During the Reign of the Queen of Persia.* New York: Harper & Row.

Chestnut, Mary B. 1949. *A Diary from Dixie.* Boston: Houghton Mifflin Co.

Donovan, Josephine. 1930. *Black Soil.* Boston: Stratford.

Fairbanks, Carol. 1986. *Prairie Women: Images in American and Canadian Fiction.* New Haven: Yale University Press.

Faragher, John M. 1981. "History from the Inside Cut: Writing the History of Women in Rural America." *American Quarterly* 33: 537-57.

Ferber, Edna. 1924. *So Big.* Garden City: Doubleday, Page.

Garland, Hamlin. 1899. "Lucretia Burns." In *Prairie Folks.* Reprint: New York: AMS Press, Inc., 1969.

Gilligan, Carol. 1982. *In a Different Voice: Psychological Theory & Women's Development.* Cambridge, Mass: Harvard University Press.

Glasgow, Ellen. 1925. *Barren Ground.* New York: Harcourt Brace & Co., Inc.

Glaspell, Susan. 1917. "A Jury of Her Peers," in *The Best Stories of 1917.* Ed. E.U. O'Brien. Boston: Small, Maynard, 1918.

Hertsgaard, Doris, & Harriett Light. 1984. "Anxiety, Depression & Hostility in Rural Women." *Psychological Reports* 55: 673-74.

Hudson, Lois P. 1957. *Reapers of the Dust: A Prairie Chronicle.* Boston: Little, Brown.

Hurston, Zora Neale. 1937. *Their Eyes Were Watching God.* New York: J.B. Lippincott Co. Reprint: Urbana, Illinois: University of Illinois Press, 1978.

Jensen, Joan. 1981. *With These Hands: Women Working on the Land.* Old Westbury, N.Y.: The Feminist Press.

Johnson, Josephine. 1934. *Now in November.* Reprint: New York: Carroll & Graf Publishers, 1962.

Kelley, Edith Summers. 1923. *Weeds.* New York: Harcourt, Brace & Co., Inc.

Kirkland, Joseph. 1887. *Zury, The Meanest Man in Spring County.* Reprint: Urbana, Illinois: University of Illinois Press, 1956.

Kolodny, Annette. 1984. *The Land Before Her: Fantasy & Experience of the American Frontiers, 1630-1860.* Chapel Hill: University of North Carolina Press.

Lane, Rose Wilder. 1933. *Let the Hurricanes Roar.* New York: Longmans, Green.

_____. 1938. *Free Land.* New York: Longmans, Green.

Lumpkin, Grace. 1932. *To Make My Bread.* New York: The MacCaulay Co.

Lynn, Margaret. 1914. *A Stepdaughter of the Prairie.* New York: MacMillan.

Morris, Wright. 1980. *Plains Song – for Female Voices.* New York: Harper & Row.

Ostenso, Martha. 1943. *O River, Remember!* New York: Dodd, Mead & Co.

Rolvaag, O.E. 1927. *Giants in the Earth: A Saga of the Prairie.* Trans. Lincoln Colcord & O.E. Rolvaag. Reprint: New York: Perennial Library, 1955.

_____. 1929. *Peder Victorious.* Trans. Nora O. Solum & O.E. Rolvaag. New York: Harper.

Rosenfeld, Rachel. 1986. *Farm Women: Work, Farm, and Family in the United States.* Chapel Hill: University of North Carolina Press.

Sachs, Carolyn. 1983. *The Invisible Farmers: Women in Agricultural Production*. Totoma, New Jersey: Rowman & Allanheld.

Schliesel, Lillian. 1982. *Women's Diaries of the Westward Journey*. New York: Schocken Books.

Smedley, Agnes. 1929. *Daughter of Earth*. Reprint: Westbury, New York: Feminist Press, 1973.

Stratton, Joanna. 1981. *Pioneer Women: Voices from the Kansas Frontier*. New York: Simon & Schuster.

Smuts, Robert. 1971. *Women & Work in America*. New York: Schocken Books.

Suckow, Ruth. 1924. *Country People*. New York: Alfred A. Knopf.

_____. 1926. *Iowa Interiors*. New York: Alfred A. Knopf.

Walker, Alice. 1982. *The Color Purple*. New York: Washington Square Press.

_____. 1983. *In Search of Our Mothers' Gardens: Womanist Prose*. New York: Harcourt Brace Jovanovich.

Walker, Margaret. 1966. *Jubilee*. New York: Houghton Mifflin.

Wilder, Laura Ingalls. 1935. *Little House on the Prairie*. Reprint: New York: Harper & Row.

_____. 1937. *On the Banks of Plum Creek*. Reprint: New York: Harper & Row.

_____. 1939. *By the Shores of Silver Lake*. Reprint: New York: Harper & Row.

FARM WOMEN'S ECONOMIC ROLES

7

THE PARTICIPATION OF WOMEN AND GIRLS IN MARKET AND NON-MARKET ACTIVITIES ON PENNSYLVANIA FARMS

Carolyn E. Sachs

The extent of women's work on farms has been increasingly documented in recent years. Utilizing the categories of several theoretical perspectives, researchers have attempted to increase the visibility of farm women's work both in the past and in the present. The purpose of research on farm women has been to clearly understand the contributions of women to farm enterprises, to comprehend the lives of women on farms, and to gain information useful for the formulation of public policy. As Harding (1986) and other scholars of women's activities have suggested, feminist theory and research initially "began by trying to extend and reinterpret the categories of various theoretical discourses so that women's activities and social relations could become analytically visible within the traditions of intellectual discourse" (Harding 1986, 645). Through our work, we have come to find that the interpretation of theories and the addition of new categories in an attempt to understand women's lives and gender relations have often distorted the original theories. At the same time, the revised theories often fail to fully explain the complexity of women's activities. As Rosenfeld (1985) has observed in her book on American farm women, the difficulty in predicting what a farm woman does may be due to the fact that women's roles are fluid, especially in periods of transition. Given the major changes in agriculture occurring at the present time, periods of transition are almost a constant for many farm families. Thus, the major purpose of this chapter is to critique the applicability of categories borrowed from three theoretical perspectives to a comprehensive understanding of women's work on farms. Drawing on a case study of Pennsylvania farm women and girls, the chapter will describe the complexity of women's work and illustrate the problems with using categories derived from traditional theoretical perspectives for understanding women's work.

THEORETICAL APPROACHES TO WOMEN'S WORK

Perhaps the greatest difficulty in documenting women's work in general and farm women's work in particular involves development of appropriate categories for analysis. Several theoretical frameworks have been used to explain women's work and the sexual division of labor. Reinterpretation of the categories of Marxist, neoclassical economist, and structural-functionalist theories of work have provided the background for understanding women's work. In attempts to describe women's work, Marxists have distinguished between productive and reproductive labor, economists have distinguished between market production and subsistence production and wage and non-wage labor, and sociologists have distinguished between work in the home and work outside the home. On U.S. farms, where households are generally the units of production and production is directed primarily towards the market, these theoretical categories are both helpful and distorting. In their daily lives, women often cross the boundaries of these categories. The invisibility and undervaluing of women's work in all three paradigms have created a need to develop new categories for understanding women's work.

The Marxist tradition

Productive and reproductive labor are categories developed from the Marxist theoretical tradition to explain women's work. With the development of industrial capitalism, production increasingly moved outside the home and the role of the family became limited to the reproduction of the labor force. Prior to a feminist critique, Marxist analyses had focused primarily on productive labor; thus, women's reproductive labor was undervalued. In the past fifteen years, a number of scholars have attempted to assess the value of women's reproductive labor (Vogel 1973; Fee 1976; Macintosh 1979). Reproductive labor, primarily women's work, includes childbearing, child care, household work, and subsistence production within the household. The connection between productive and reproductive labor is that both serve the interests of capital accumulation. Women's work involves both productive and reproductive labor, and, as Safa points out, women's lives involve "a constant attempt to reconcile the dialectic between the two" (1983, 95).

In analyzing work on farms, the focus on productive labor at the expense of reproductive labor has emphasized work associated with the production of agricultural commodities. Theorists of the structure of agriculture have emphasized that farm households are involved in simple commodity production. Production on farms in the United States often occurs outside of the capitalist organization of labor with labor organized within the farm household. The work of women on farms differs from women's work in the nonfarm labor force because agricultural production is organized differently from other types of production. Unlike many other types of production in advanced industrial society, agricultural production is based on cycles of nature and therefore is sequential and seasonal rather than continuous (Flora 1985). Also, the family farm is a last vestige of the organization of labor through the household. Because much of agricultural production is organized with the household as the unit of production, the sexual division of labor assumes a different form on farms than it does in other sectors of the economy and in nonfarm households (Sachs 1986).

Buttel (1980) has led the way in pointing out how family production allows the use and often the exploitation of unpaid family labor. Nevertheless, because production and reproduction both occur on the farm, the distinction between productive and reproductive labor is muddy and does not provide clear categories for analyzing women's work. Jensen's (1986) recent study of Mid-Atlantic farm women from 1750 to 1850 includes an insightful analysis of women's involvement in reproducing the family farm. Her analysis reveals the connections between women's reproductive labor and farm production and provides a model for scholars doing research on contemporary farm women.

The Neoclassical economic tradition

The neoclassical economic tradition has analyzed work primarily as labor market activities. As a result, women's work outside the labor market has often been overlooked and excluded from economic analyses. Recently, economists interested in women's work have noted the importance of examining both labor market activities and nonmarket activities. In a review of recent economic research on women's work, Ferber (1982) points out that there is an increasing awareness of the interrelations between women's work in the labor market and women's non-labor market activities. Nevertheless, most studies of women's work emphasize either labor market or non-labor market activities. As Ferber (1982) notes, economists have been reluctant to assign value to nonmarket activities performed in the household. However, a recent estimate of the value of home production is at 60 percent of the value of family income before taxes (Gronau 1980). It might be assumed that the value of home production is even greater for farm families. The distinction between labor market and non-labor market activities presents problems for analyzing the work of farm women. Both farm women and farm men perform work on the family farm that does not conveniently fit the categories of labor market or non-labor market activities. Off-farm employment of the farm woman or man fits into the category of labor market activities, but work on the farm in the production of commodities for the market is performed outside the wage-labor market. When the household is the unit of production, non-labor market activities are quite complex and tied to the market. Gladwin (1982) has led the way in examining the connections between women's off-farm employment and production on the farm.

The Structural-Functionalist tradition

Finally, the structural-functionalist approach of sociologists and anthropologists has largely followed the distinctions of the neoclassical economic tradition. Following Parsons (1949), men's roles have been seen as being in the public sphere, whereas women's activities have been assumed to occur in the home. During the 1950s and 1960s, studies of the division of labor on farms focused on the husband's achievements with the farm operation and the wife's supportive behavior (Straus 1958; Blood 1958). Recent studies of farm women's work have sought to determine women's involvement in specifically defined tasks (Rosenfeld 1985; Wilkening 1981). By asking women the extent of their involvement in specific tasks, researchers have gained detailed and useful documentation of women's participation.

All of these efforts have attempted to find appropriate categories to explain women's work on farms. Perhaps all three approaches have succeeded in illuminating the fact that women contribute substantially to the farm operation.

Nevertheless, the complexity of women's work and the interconnections between different types of work have not been adequately addressed. The balance of this chapter will draw on a study of Pennsylvania farm women to illustrate how women describe their work activities and resulting problems with using the categories discussed above to distinguish between types of women's work.

THE PENNSYLVANIA FARM WOMEN'S STUDY

Methodology

The study reported on here involved in-depth interviews with husbands and wives on twenty-four farms in one county in central Pennsylvania. The sample was randomly drawn from a list of farm households in the county provided by the Cooperative Extension Service. Because the list did not include all farm households in the county and underrepresented smaller farms, it was supplemented with a mailing list for small farmers in the county provided by the Cooperative Extension Service.

Interviews were conducted separately with the wife and husband in the farm households. Questionnaires were used to obtain information on labor activity in farm households. Each interview was tape-recorded. Information was collected on the farming operation, involvement of family members in farm operations, off-farm employment, participation in subsistence activities, and demographic characteristics of the farm household.

Structure of farms

The farms in the sample were primarily dairy and livestock farms (Table 7.1). Of the twenty-four farms, sixteen were dairy enterprises, three were beef cattle enterprises, three were both dairy and beef enterprises, one was a diversified livestock and vegetable enterprise, one was a hog enterprise, and one was a crop and strawberry enterprise. The farms ranged in size from 6 to 823 acres. Thirteen of the farms were between 101 and 250 acres (Table 7.1). The number of milking cows varied from twenty-five to one hundred. The herd size for beef cattle ranged from three to forty. All of the livestock farms raised the majority of feed for their livestock. All of the farms were family operated. In five cases, more than one nuclear family was involved in the farm operation. All of the families owned at least some of the land being farmed. Eleven households rented acreage in addition to the land that they owned.

Work Activities of Farm Women

The women were asked to describe their involvement in the farm operation. The majority of the women reported that they were either regularly or occasionally involved in the farm operation. Table 7.2 presents the extent of farm women's involvement. Due to the nature of farming, labor demands vary from day to day, month to month, and season to season, and in describing their involvement in particular tasks, almost all of the women mentioned that the extent of their involvement varied by day, week, season, or year. In contrast, men often stated that they work a constant number of hours on the farm per day.

Table 7.1 *Type and Size of Farms*

Type of Farm	
Enterprise	*Number*
Dairy	16
Beef cattle	3
Dairy and beef cattle	3
Diversified livestock and vegetable	1
Hogs	1
Crops and strawberries	1
Size of Farm	
Acreage	*Number*
0-100	2
101-250	13
251-500	7
500+	2

Dairying provides the most regular hours on a daily, weekly, and seasonal basis. On most dairy farms, milking is performed twice a day. Women performing milking in the dairy barns were most likely to report a fairly steady amount of time per day or week that they spent on farming activities. However, even women involved in dairying reported wide variation in their work schedules. For example, a woman who lived on a 240-acre dairy farm milking sixty-three cows reported her participation as follows:

> I milk every day except on weekends. Every now and then, I get the weekends off since the boys are home. In the summertime, I don't have to milk every night. During school, I milk every morning except weekends, and then in the evenings, if they have track meets, I fill in; or in the fall when they have field work that they're doing, I work then. It's just kind of a part-time thing in the evenings. It's not a definite that I have to be there every night.

Although she milked regularly on weekday mornings, her participation at other times varied according to the schedules of her husband and her sons. She was available for evening milking when necessary, allowing her husband's and sons' schedules to be flexible.

Women who reported that they were involved only occasionally in farm tasks often explained that they helped when needed. Despite their claims that they were only minimally involved, the women often listed a number of tasks that they performed. For example, a woman on a 180-acre dairy farm with seventeen milking cows stated:

Table 7.2 *Involvement of Women in Farm Operation*

Farm Women	
Regularly	15
Occasionally	5
Rarely	4
Never	0
Daughters/Daughters-in-Law of Farm Operators	
Regularly	6
Occasionally	2
Rarely	1
Never	3
No daughters at home	12

I don't help a lot. I care for the calves and bottle-feed them. Every day, I carry the milk out. Also, I drive the tractor when he [her husband] needs me. I shovel corn at harvest time. During haymaking, I'm out there every day. And sometimes I work in the fields.

Another woman who resided on a beef farm and whose husband worked full-time off the farm described her involvement:

I only work when I'm needed. Not a lot. During the harvest, when it takes two, I drive the tractor, and they do the heavy work. And when they get up in the morning and go to work, I do the barn work. I take care of feeding the cows.

Participation in farm activities changes over time for most farm women. The presence of children, changes in the farm operation, movement in and out of the labor force, and age are factors that contribute to changes in women's involvement. A fifty-eight-year-old woman, who was working full-time as a nurse at the time of the interview, described the changing nature of her involvement in the farm operation:

I did milk cows, and there was a rare load of manure that went out of here that I didn't help to fork it. I'm not saying that as bragging; it's the truth. Cleaned chicken coops and at that time we had pigs and I cleaned the pig pens and so on like that. So, after 1954, I rode and drove tractor and those things and I've done all kinds of things. Of course, when I'm not inside the house, I'm outside working, but I mean I haven't been hauling manure since 1954. But as far as going out and rolling bales off occasionally, or I go out and drive tractor. But, I gave up forking manure after my daughter was born.

Thus, this woman had less involvement in the farm as a result of her children, changes in the farm, and her off-farm employment. Another woman who resided on a 230-acre beef cattle farm that was previously a dairy and chicken farm reported the changes in her work over time.

> I used to take care of everything with the dairy cows because my husband taught. We decided to sell the dairy cows after the war, but I kept on with the chickens. I had around 300 chickens and we also had some cows. We had sheep and hogs. My mother helped take care of the children and with the cooking so that I could farm. When mother passed away, we got rid of the chickens, sheep, and hogs.

The work that she performed was altered with changes in the type of livestock. Also, as a result of her husband's employment and the death of her mother, she was unable to perform all of the work with the animals.

The presence of children often affects women's involvement with farming. Young children place a demand on women's time that competes with their availability to perform tasks in the fields or in the barn. Nevertheless, many women reported taking their infants and young children to the barn while they performed the milking or livestock feeding. As the children became older, they often substituted for their mother in the performance of various tasks. As one women with eleven children explained:

> I help very little at the barn. Once in awhile if they are short of help, I go out and wash the udders. But I don't very often run the milkers. I used to when the children were small and sometimes when he was busy in the fields with hay, I would help with the milking. But as the children got older, I didn't need to because we had eleven children, and so we always had lots of help at the barn. Then, when the children got old enough to help, I didn't, so I never really helped in the barn like a lot of farm wives do.

Non-market Activities of Farm Women

All of the women reported that they had primary responsibility for cooking, shopping, laundering, cleaning and child care, although some women reported that their husbands helped with child care. The women moved back and forth from one activity to another and the activities frequently overlapped. For example, one thirty-five-year-old woman with three children reported that housework took a large part of her time, but she explained that "housework would be my kids, too." She did not draw a distinction between housework and child care. When asked whether barn work, housework, or child care took most of her time, she replied: "I don't know. They all seem to come right in there. It don't much matter." Another woman explained that she was able to care for her young children while working in the barn. She described that when her children were infants she "would put them in a box and take them to the barn and sit them in the cow stable." Another woman on a dairy farm explained:

Those kids went to the barn with us when they was little. When they came home from the hospital, I wrapped them up and took them to the barn. They laid right there in a stroller while we did the milking. In fact, I did the milking the day one of them was born.

A major activity mentioned by many of the women was gardening. All of the farm households raised gardens. The percentage of the family food supply produced on the farms varied from twenty-five percent to approximately one hundred percent. Eighteen of the twenty-four households produced over forty percent of the family food supply on their farms (Table 7.3). Women reported that they had the major responsibility for the garden in twenty-two of the twenty-four households. In the other two households, the wife and husband shared the responsibility. Six of the women with major responsibility for the garden reported that their husbands or sons were involved in tilling the garden, but the women assumed the responsibility for all of the other gardening tasks.

The division of labor in the garden often involved men in preparing the soil or doing work with the tractor. For example, one woman explained that both she and her husband worked in the garden: "Bill gets the ground ready, and he plants the corn and beans with the planter. But setting the tomatoes out and stuff, I do. He doesn't help with harvesting because he doesn't like doing that sort of thing." The man did the work that utilized the tractor while the women did the work performed by hand. As one man described the typical division of labor, "we men, we don't do very much, other than get it ready. The women take care of it after that." He claimed that "I try to get my fields looking according to what her garden looks. It don't always quite come up to it."

In some families, women from several households shared the gardening and preserving work. As one woman explained:

I work with Grandma's garden. We all plant a garden together. We put things in the freezer, and we make jellies and jams. Grandma and Aunt Grace do that. I pick the berries. I freeze about 120 quarts of corn a year. I can peaches and pears, if we have them, and I can tomatoes. I make vegetable soup, grape juice. We have a grape arbor.

All of the women reported that they preserved food, including products from the garden and livestock. The woman from the farm that produced virtually one hundred percent of the food consumed by the household explained:

We raise all our meat, and of course we have our own milk and eggs and vegetables. What we buy mostly are those extra goodies you could do without, except for flour and sugar.

Many of the families raise livestock for home consumption. On some of the farms, the livestock was both marketed and used for the family food supply. One woman explained the connections between production for use and production for market:

Table 7.3 *Percent of Family Food Produced on Farm*

Percent	Number
0-20	0
21-40	6
41-60	6
61-80	7
81-100	5

I market pigs that we raise. I do the marketing, make sure they get butchered and distributed. It's not a big thing; it really pays for what we raise, and I get it for nothing really. We usually buy extra steers or whatever and raise them and sell them. We don't make extra, but it pays for what we got. It pays for our steer, or it pays for our pork.

Labor market activities

Off-farm employment contributed to the income of thirteen of the twenty-four households. Women worked off the farm on ten of the farms, and men worked off the farm on ten of the farms. Examining husband's and wife's employment together, neither the husband nor the wife was employed on eleven farms, both were employed on seven farms, only the husband was employed on three farms, and only the wife was employed on three farms (Table 7.4). Many of the women explained that they sought employment as the farm enterprise changed or as other family members assumed more responsibility for certain farm activities. The type of work that women performed on the farms varied with their own movement and that of their husbands in and out of the labor force.

Employment opportunities for women in the county were fairly limited. The majority of the women were employed in the service sector. Some of the women's jobs were bookkeeper, secretary, cafeteria worker, housecleaner, school bus driver, and postmistress. The one professional woman was a nurse in a local school. The jobs were generally low-wage positions with little opportunity for advancement.

Contribution of Daughters and Daughters-in-Law to Farm

Daughters or daughters-in-law were present on only twelve of the farms. Daughters contributed to farm work on nine of the twelve farms, although the extent of their involvement varied (Table 7.2). On some farms, the daughters were extensively involved with the farm operation. On a fifty-seven cow dairy farm, two daughters aged twenty and twenty-four helped with the milking for four hours every day. One man proudly described his daughter's contribution:

Debbie is a very good worker. I put a lot on Debbie, but she didn't mind. It didn't matter what I said, Debbie would do it. If I told her to

Table 7.4 *Labor Force Participation of Husband and Wife*

Employment	*Number*
Neither husband nor wife employed	11
Both husband and wife employed	7
Only husband employed	3
Only wife employed	3

try to lift the end of that barn, she'd lift it. Many, many a load of hay we baled. She'd be up on the wagon and she could load it as good as I could. She started helping before she went to high school, when she was in grade school. Like delivering calves and that, she was awful good, very good.

On farms where the daughters were not extensively involved in farm activities, they often had other responsibilities in the household. One woman explained that one of her daughters helped now and then with the milking: "Milking is a good change for her when she gets tired of washing dishes." On another farm where the fourteen-year-old daughter did not work on farm tasks, two older brothers worked on the farm. The mother, who was employed full-time as a secretary, paid her daughter to do the housework.

CONCLUSIONS

Farm women's descriptions of their work consistently revealed the complexity and diversity of their activities. In the study reported here, women's descriptions of their work raised questions as to the utility of theoretical categories in understanding the day-to-day realities of the women's lives. The Marxist categories of productive and reproductive labor must not be examined as separate activities but must be viewed in terms of their interconnectedness. The neoclassical distinction between market and nonmarket activities is also problematic in understanding farm women's work. The distinction between market activities and nonmarket activities was not always clear in the women's description of their work. For example, women reported raising hogs and chickens for both the market and home consumption. In reporting the relation between farm work and home work, many women described their movements back and forth between the two throughout the day. Also, many of the activities overlapped in time. For example, women often cared for children at the same time as they were milking cows.

Demands on farm women change from day to day, month to month, season to season, and year to year. Although time allocation in particular activities could be measured on a daily basis, variation from one day to another was extreme. Thus, the amount of time women devote to market versus subsistence activities, production versus reproduction, or farm work versus home work is difficult if not impossible to measure accurately.

Yet, in our efforts to explain the importance of farm women's contributions, we need to go even further, beyond the theoretical frameworks we have been utilizing to describe women's activities. Women's work is diverse, flexible, and difficult to quantify. In addition to quantitative measures of women's work, qualitative measures must also be used. As scholarship proceeds on women's invovlement in agriculture, we must explore at a deeper level the contributions of women.

BIBLIOGRAPHY

Blood, Robert O., Jr. 1958. "The Division of Labor in City and Farm Families." *Journal of Marriage and the Family* 10: 170-74.

Buttel, Frederick H. 1980. "The Political Economy of Agriculture in Advanced Industrial Societies." Paper presented at the Canadian Sociology and Anthropology Association Meetings, June, at Montreal, Canada.

Fee, Terry. 1976. "Domestic Labour: An Analysis of Housework and Its Relation to the Production Process." *Review of Radical Political Economy* 8: 1-8.

Ferber, Marianne A. 1982. "Women and Work: Issues of the 1980s." *Signs: Journal of Women in Culture and Society* 8: 273-95.

Flora, Cornelia. 1985. "Women and Agriculture." *Agriculture and Human Values* 2: 5-12.

Gladwin, Christina. 1982. "Off-Farm Work and Its Effect on Florida Farm Wives' Contribution to the Family Farm." Paper presented at the Conference on Rural Women in the United States, at Blacksburg, Virginia.

Gronau, Reuben. 1980. "Home Production-A Forgotten Industry." *Review of Economics and Statistics* 62: 408-16.

Harding, Sandra. 1986. "The Instability of the Analytical Categories of Feminist Theory." *Signs Journal of Women in Culture and Society* 11: 645-66.

Jensen, Joan M. 1986. *Loosening the Bonds: Mid-Atlantic Farm Women 1750-1850*. New Haven, Conn.: Yale University Press.

Macintosh, Maureen. 1979. "Domestic Labor and the Household." In *Fit Work for Women*, ed. Sandra Burman, 173-91. Canberra: Australian National University Press.

Parsons, Talcott. 1949. "The Structure of the Family." In *The Family: Its Function and Destiny*, ed. Ruth Nanda Anshen. New York: Harper & Row.

Rosenfeld, Rachel Ann. 1985. *Farm Women: Work, Farm, and Family in the United States*. Chapel Hill: University of North Carolina Press.

Sachs, Carolyn. 1986. "American Farm Women." *Women and Work* 2: 233-49.

Safa, Helen I. 1983. "Women, Production, and Reproduction in Industrial Capitalism: A Comparison of Brazilian and U.S. Factory Workers." In

Women, Men, and the International Division of Labor, ed. June Nash and
Maria Patricia Fernandez-Kelly, 95-116. Albany: State University of New
York Press.

Straus, Murray A. 1958. "The Role of the Wife in the Settlement of the
Columbia Basin Project." *Marriage and Family Living* 20: 59-64.

Vogel, Lise. 1973. "The Earthly Family." *Radical America* 7: 9-50.

Wilkening, Eugene A. 1981. *Farm Husbands and Wives in Wisconsin: Work
Roles, Decision-Making and Satisfactions, 1962 and 1979.* Bulletin R3147.
Madison, Wis.: College of Agriculture and Life Sciences, University of
Wisconsin.

8

OFF-FARM LABOR ALLOCATION BY MARRIED FARM WOMEN: RESEARCH REVIEW AND NEW EVIDENCE FROM WISCONSIN

Mary R. McCarthy
Priscilla Salant
William E. Saupe[1]

INTRODUCTION

Adults in farm families must choose how they will allocate their time and effort among farm production, child rearing and other home production, off-farm employment, and leisure. These are complex decisions affected by factors such as the returns from farming, family life-cycle stage, the match between family members' employable skills and local employment opportunities, and family goals. For several decades, farm families in the Midwest and the nation have been choosing to allocate more time to off-farm employment.

Evidence from a variety of sources indicates that off-farm employment plays a major role in the well-being of farm families. Not only do off-farm earnings supplement low farm earnings in an absolute sense, they also appear to alter relative income distribution toward more equality within the farm population (Shaffer, Salant, and Saupe 1985). Since off-farm earnings fluctuate less than farm income, they may alter the risk environment in which families manage their farm operations (Deaton and Weber 1985).

Recent statistics show that while labor force participation by females who live in nonmetro counties is below that of their metropolitan counterparts (49 percent versus 54 percent in 1982), it has been growing at a faster rate in the last decade (Brown and O'Leary 1979).

The decision by married farm women to allocate more of their time to off-farm employment affects more than just the mix and level of total family income. Taken in aggregate, the allocation may affect the organization of farm businesses and thus the structure of agriculture, the physical and social development of children present in the households, the marital stability of farm couples, and the community environment in which they live. Thus, analysis of the decision by married farm women to allocate labor to off-farm employment is worthy of close examination and study.

Such examination and study is the objective of this chapter.

RESEARCH REVIEW

We first review and summarize the findings of other researchers and then present information from recent studies in southwestern Wisconsin.

Research issues

First, some background on research issues and methodology is necessary because of the statistical problems that early researchers had to overcome before their analyses of labor force participation could proceed. The root of the problem was in developing valid methods of estimating, first, the probability of taking a job, and second, the wage rate that would be received by persons for whom no data were available – for example, persons who had never worked out of the home (or off the farm) before.

The literature on married female labor supply has expanded at a rapid rate since the initial stimulus provided by Mincer (1962) and theoretical consolidation by Becker (1965). Early studies (Kalachek and Raines 1970; Boskin 1973; Schultz 1980; Hall 1973; Liebowitz 1974) were subject to criticism for statistical problems. The methodological issue that the decision to work and how much to work were made simultaneously was raised by Ben-Porath (1973) and Lewis (1974), while Hanoch (1980) considered the distinction between hours and weeks supplied.

A second methodological problem is that we can observe wages only for women who have jobs. If we want to generalize the results of our analysis to all women (not just those who work), we must overcome the limitation of our "censored" or partial sample, a problem called sample selection bias. The presence of sample selection bias was discussed by Gronau (1974), and the appropriate method of analysis under such circumstances was described in seminal contributions by Heckman (1974, 1976, 1979). For the most part subsequent studies have utilized the Heckman correction. Exceptions include Schultz (1980) and Cogan (1980a), while another method of dealing with sample selection bias is provided by Chiswick (1982).

Labor force participation

The decision to seek work outside the home (that is, to participate in the labor force) has usually been modeled in terms of the family or household production model (Mincer 1962; Becker 1965; Cain 1966; Kosters 1966; Muth 1966; Gronau 1973). Such analyses have generally evaluated the effect of the wife's wages or earnings, the husband's earnings, the family's nonemployment income, and other explanatory variables including personal characteristics of the participant. These analyses were all designed to capture the availability of time and money in the family, the wife's productivity at home, and her personal tastes.

Consistent with theory, the likelihood that a woman would seek a job outside her home was found to be higher if her potential wage was high, and lower if her husband's wage was high. Income from interest, rent, and transfers was not found to affect her labor market participation (Bowen and Finegan 1969; Schultz 1980; Cogan 1980a). Schultz (1980) suggested that the wife's responsiveness to wage differences was highest for the youngest and oldest age cohorts, and exhibited less variance over the life cycle of black women. Heckman (1979) found that the wife's past labor market experience had a positive effect on present participation. The presence of preschool children apparently restricted the decision to participate (Heckman 1979; Cogan 1980b). Schultz (1980) argued that it is the age of children that is the crucial factor in the participation decision. Schultz also reported a negative effect for living on farms on married women's labor force participation.

Wages

Analyses of market wages usually consider education, work experience, age, number of children, health, and distance from work as explanatory variables. Studies by Cogan (1980), Hanoch (1980) and Heckman (1979) suggest that the problem of not having data on the market wage rate of women who do not work (again, sample selection bias) leads to overestimation of their potential wage. The problem also leads to a slight underestimation of the effect of education on wages and a serious underestimation of the effect of work experience on wages. Hanoch (1980) found a negative relationship between the number of children in the home and the wage rate. He suggests that this finding may indicate the adverse effect of children on a women's past labor market experience.

Labor Supply

Studies of the number of hours or weeks that women work outside the home (that is, women's "labor supply") exhibit a large diversity, partly from the use of different structural models and partly from the presence of statistical problems in the estimation process.

Some researchers have found that the number of hours that a woman works outside the home is not affected by market wage rates over a certain range of wages. Cogan (1980b) and Hanoch (1980) attribute this phenomenon, which is referred to as a discontinuity in the labor supply, to fixed costs of participation. After a certain number of hours worked (for example, over two hours per day), the family may need to purchase labor-saving appliances. To cover these costs, the woman must seek a substantially higher wage rate. Heckman (1979) attributes the discontinuity to the lack of low-cost substitutes for the wife's time – again, after a certain number of hours worked. She may, for example, face higher hourly day care costs when she switches from part-time to full-time work.

Fringe Benefits

Cash payments as a proportion of total compensation to the worker have fallen over time as the use of fringe benefits has increased. The most important fringe benefits include health insurance, paid leave, social security, worker's compensation, unemployment insurance, and private pensions. Freeman (1981) found the growth of fringe benefits to be significantly related to the presence of unions, whereas Woodbury (1983) explained the phenomenon in terms of tax-rate increases. Ehrenberg and Smith (1982) and Woodbury (1983) found evidence of a high degree of substitution between wages and fringe benefits on the part of the worker – a willingness to accept less of one in exchange for more of the other. Whatever the reasons for their growth, the availability of fringe benefits is likely to be an important factor in comparing the returns from a market job to those from a farm job. This issue was discussed by Jensen and Salant (1985), who found the presence of fringe benefits was associated with more off-farm work by farm operators.

Farm Women

As early as 1955, Bishop documented the significant contribution of women to farm family income through off-farm employment. However, although empirical research on nonmetro female labor force participation has increased since the mid -seventies, it is only recently that attention has been given to the labor force activity of farm women.[2] Brown and O'Leary (1979) used 1960 and 1970 Census of Population data to describe the labor force activity of metro and nonmetro women. They emphasized the occupational and industrial structure of jobs in an area as playing a major role in the participation decision. It is difficult to draw any conclusions from the results of this study since the direction of causation is unclear. That is, was it the presence of a pool of low-skilled, low-wage female labor that attracted a particular industrial structure into the area or did the existing industrial structure condition women's pattern of participation? Adjacency to a Standard Metropolitan Statistical Area (SMSA) or metro area did not appear to be a significant factor in explaining the participation decision.

In a study comparing labor force participation rates for metro, nonmetro, and farm women, Bokemeier, Sachs, and Keith (1983) used a linear probability model and found that higher education and higher household income were associated with increased probability of wage work outside the home, whereas age, marriage, and having higher gross farm sales decreased the probability. Metro proximity had no effect on participation.

Locational variables, however, did appear to be important in a study of female participation in three rural counties in North Carolina by Pendleton (1985). A recent study by Leistritz, Ekstrom, Vreugdenhil, and Leholm (1986), using a sample of 933 farm operators and their spouses in North Dakota, found that the following variables significantly influenced the likelihood of the spouse working off-farm (in order of entry): education of the spouse of the worker (+); age (-); presence of children aged five to eighteen (-); adjacency of the county to an SMSA (-); and employment of the worker's spouse off the farm (+).

Other Wisconsin Studies

Kada (1978) surveyed 193 farm families engaged in part-time farming in five counties in central Wisconsin. The survey was limited to (a) farms that produced at least $250 from the sale of farm products and/or contained at least ten acres in 1975, and (b) farm families where at least one member worked off-farm at least thirty days in 1975. Kada's analysis of simple correlations between the variables showed that farm size was not a relevant factor in the farm wife's decision to seek work off the farm, whereas personal factors such as education level, skills, and/or some particular interest in working off the farm were important.

Moore (1986) studied the differential allocation of labor by members of farm-based households, especially spouses. Using discriminant analysis, Moore found that size of holding and recent entry into farming were statistically significant factors influencing the wife's decision to work off the farm. Farm and family characteristics correlated with the wife's off- farm employment included dairying (-), total farm horsepower (-), husband's age (-), presence of a son aged eighteen or over (-), presence of a daughter aged 18 or over (-), husband's education (+), and wife's education (+).

Although studies by both Moore and Kada yield interesting insights into the pattern of the farm wife's off-farm employment in Wisconsin, there is scope for further analysis. In both studies the results relating to farm wives' off-farm labor force participation decisions are based on simple correlations between variables. This technique does not provide any information on which individual variables explain off-farm labor force participation when the effect of other variables is held constant. We remedy this latter problem by using regression analysis.

SOUTHWESTERN WISCONSIN STUDY

The Sample

The data used in this analysis are from the 1983 Wisconsin Family Farm Survey. The survey, which yielded 529 usable questionnaires, was based on a random sample of all farm households in eight southwestern Wisconsin counties.[3] Households were included in the survey if they reported farm sales of at least $1,000 in 1982. The survey site was chosen, in part, because of its similarity to some 200 additional counties in the Midwest and New England in matters of (relatively small) farm size, dependence on dairying as a major source of farm receipts, and use of family labor. The data presented in this report refer to the eight-county farm household population, which numbered approximately 12,240 at the time of the survey (March 1983).

Description

Thirty-nine percent of the married farm women in the sample reported off-farm employment in 1982. The typical married farm woman who worked off-farm or was looking for off-farm work in 1982 (that is, who was a labor force participant) was forty-four years old, had almost one year of education beyond high school, and had at least four years of off-farm work experience (Table 8.1). Significant differences between labor force participants and nonparticipants are noted among women age sixty-five and older, those with less than nine years or more than fourteen years of education and with off- farm work history.[4]

We expected that the presence of young children in the household would reduce opportunities for off-farm work, as has been found in other studies. In examining characteristics of participants and nonparticipants, we found no statistically significant differences between the proportion of women who had children in various age categories (Table 8.2).

The amount of off-farm work varied widely (Table 8.3). Forty-five percent of the employed married women in the sample reported less than the equivalent of four days per week for thirty-six weeks (less than 1,153 hours per year). Twenty-eight percent reported at least the equivalent of five days per week for forty-two weeks (over 1,680 hours per year).

Table 8.1 *Selected Demographic Characteristics of Married Farm Women, by Labor Force Status, Southwestern Wisconsin, 1982*

			Labor Force Status[a]	
Item	Unit	Total[b]	Participant	Nonparticipant
All married farm women	Number	10,595	4,140	6,455
	Percent	100	39	61
By age:				
16 to 24 years	Percent	3	5	2
25 to 34 years	Percent	21	19	22
35 to 44 years	Percent	24	28	21
45 to 54 years	Percent	26	26	26
55 to 64 years	Percent	20	19	21
65 years and over	Percent	6	3*	8*
Mean age	Years	45.2	43.9	46.1
By years of school completed:				
Less than 9 years	Percent	13	8*	16*
9 to 12 years	Percent	59	56	61
13 to 14 years	Percent	16	18	15
15 years and over	Percent	12	18*	8*
Mean years of school completed	Years	12.1	12.7*	11.7*
By off-farm work history:				
Employed in 1981	Percent	38	89*	6*
Employed in 1980	Percent	37	80*	9*
Employed in 1979	Percent	37	74*	13*
Employed in 1978	Percent	38	72*	16*

Source: 1983 Wisconsin Family Farm Survey.
* Indicates a significant difference (at the .05 level) between means and proportions, using the t-statistic and the Z-statistic, respectively.
a Participants were employed off-farm or looking for work in 1982.
b Excludes 1,645 households without a female spouse.

For those employed off-farm, the average number of hours worked was 1,119 hours, or roughly four days per week for thirty-five weeks. Ninety percent of married women working off-farm in 1982 worked for wages or salaries; 10 percent were self-employed.

In Tables 8.4-8.6, we examine off-farm work by industry, occupation, and fringe benefits and explore the differences between jobs held by married farm women working full-time and those working part-time.

Almost half of the women employed for wages or salary worked in the service industry (for example, in schools and hospitals) (Table 8.4). Seventeen percent worked in trade, (for example, in grocery and clothing stores). Jobs in thes ervice industry (specifically, education) were more likely to be part-time, whereas jobs in durable manufacturing were likely to be full-time.

TABLE 8.2 *Presence and Age of Children in Families of Married Farm Women, by Women's Employment Status, Southwestern Wisconsin, 1982*

| Item | Total[b] | Labor Force Status[a] | |
		Participant	Nonparticipant
		Number	
All married farm women	10,595	4,140	6,455
		Percent	
By age of children present:			
1 to 5 years of age	22	20	23
6 to 12 years of age	33	36	32
13 to 17 years of age	33	37	31
18 years and over	33	34	33
(None present)	27	26	28

Source: 1983 Wisconsin Family Farm Survey.
a Participants were employed off-farm or looking for work in 1982.
b Excludes 1,645 households without a female spouse.

Self-employment of married farm women was concentrated in the trade industry (for example, sales of household products) and in services (most often home-based child care).

Thirty percent of the women employed for wages or salary had marketing, sales, or clerical occupations (Table 8.5). Roughly one-fourth had administrative, professional, or technical jobs (for example, as teachers, nurses, or counselors), and one-fourth had service occupations (as waitresses, nurses aides, and hair dressers). One-tenth had production jobs (as, for example, assemblers in factories) and were most likely to be full- time.

Health insurance and paid sick leave and vacation were the most common fringe benefits reported by women working off-farm (Table 8.6). For each of the five kinds of fringe benefits, women were much more likely to receive benefits if they worked full-time.

Forty-eight percent of married farm women working part-time and 85 percent of those working full-time received health insurance from their employers. Health insurance is a particularly important fringe benefit for farm families and appears to be an important consideration in the decision to work off-farm (Jensen and Salant 1985). It is often costly because farming is a high-risk occupation and self-employed farmers may not be eligible for large group, lower-cost plans. In addition, premiums are most often paid from after-income-tax dollars unlike the tax-free benefits provided for wage earners by their employers. On average, farmfamilies have less health insurance protection than full-time wage workers (Jensen 1982).

In Table 8.7, we examine how characteristics of farm households and farm businesses differ when farm wives join the off-farm labor force. As expected, participants tended to live in households in which net farm income was lower and off-farm earnings were higher. On average, however, total income from all

TABLE 8.3 *Selected Off-Farm Employment Characteristics of Married Farm Women, Southwestern Wisconsin, 1982*

Item	Unit	Married Farm Women
All married farm women		
employed off-farm	Number	3,980[a]
Part-time or part-year:[b]		
Under 1,153 hours/year	Percent	45
1,153 to 1,440 hours/year	Percent	15
1,441 to 1,680 hours/year	Percent	12
Full-time or full-year:[b]		
1,681 to 2,080 hours/year	Percent	24
2,081 or more hours/year	Percent	4
Mean hours employed off-farm	Hours	1,119
Wage and salary employment	Percent	90
Self-employment	Percent	10

Source: 1983 Wisconsin Family Farm Survey.
a Excludes those labor force participants who were looking for work in 1982.
b This classification system accommodated the wide variety of off-farm work schedules reported by respondents. The data were summarized in terms of total hours worked off-farm during the year. Based on a standard work week of 40 hours, 2,080 hours constituted 52 standard work weeks, 1,680 hours constituted 42 standard work weeks, and 1,440 hours constituted 36 standard work weeks. The last category, 1,152 hours, represents 32 hours per week for 36 weeks.

sources was not significantly different between households of participants and nonparticipants.

Our data clearly indicate that farm wives who participate in the labor force tend to live on smaller farms. Their household assets (farm and nonfarm) and net worth were lower, as were total and cultivated acreage. Participants were less likely than nonparticipants to live on dairy farms.

Descriptive analyses such as the ones presented above enable us to build a profile of women's off-farm work. However, simple cross tabulations do not allow us to isolate the independent effect of the factors associated with labor force participation. For example, we cannot determine whether it is education or, alternatively, the presence of small children that has an effect on participation among women of the same age.

To solve this problem, we used data from our random sample to estimate a model of off-farm labor supply that would control for the effects of different variables. The model of the labor allocation decision included determination of (a) the likelihood of a married farm woman's off-farm labor market participation, (b) the level of her off-farm market wage rate, (c) the likelihood of her receiving

TABLE 8.4 *Industry of Employment Among Married Farm Women, by Part-Time and Full-Time Off-Farm Work, Southwestern Wisconsin, 1982*

Item	Unit	Total	Part-Time[a]	Full-Time
All married farm women employed off-farm for wages or salary				
	Number	3,585	2,520	1,065
Agriculture	Percent	3	4	0
Manufacturing				
Durable	Percent	7	4*	16*
Nondurable	Percent	7	5	12
TCPU, FIRE[b]	Percent	8	6*	15*
Services				
Education	Percent	21	29*	2*
Other	Percent	28	25	35
Trade, wholesale				
and retail	Percent	17	16	17
Other	Percent	9	11	3
All married farm women self-employed off-farm				
	Number	395	350	45
Manufacturing	Percent	12	13	0
Trade	Percent	59	60	50
Services	Percent	29	27	50

Source: 1983 Wisconsin Family Farm Survey.
* Indicates significant difference (at .05 level) between proportions, using Z-statistic.
a Part-time workers reported 1,680 hours or less of off-farm work in 1982; full-time workers reported more than 1,680 hours in 1982.
b Transportation, Communication, and Public Utilities (TCPU); Finance, Insurance, and Real Estate (FIRE).

fringe benefits, and (d) her hours of off-farm market work. (The model is described more fully in McCarthy and Salant 1986). The theoretical model underlying our analysis is based on the assumption that farm households behave as if they were trying to maximize well-being (utility). The model is outlined in Summer (1982) and described in Jensen and Salant (1985).

Model Results

The model used in this analysis encompasses both labor force participation and labor supply decisions made by farm wives in the context of the off-farm labor market. The results from the participation model indicate that the decision to seek off-farm employment is influenced by variables representing personal, farm, financial, and area characteristics.

TABLE 8.5 *Occupations of Married Farm Women, by Part-Time and Full-Time Off-Farm Work, Southwestern Wisconsin, 1982*

Item	Unit	Total	Part-time[a]	Full-time
All married farm women employed off-farm for wages or salary	Number	3,585	2,520	1,065
Administrative,professional, and technical	Percent	26	29	17
Marketing, sales and clerical	Percent	30	27	37
Service	Percent	26	28	22
Production work	Percent	10	6*	20*
Other	Percent	8	10	4

Source: 1983 Wisconsin Family Farm Survey.
*   Indicates significant difference (at .05 level) between proportions, using Z-statistic.
a   Part-time workers reported 1,680 hours or less of off-farm work in 1982; full-time workers reported more than 1,680 hours in 1982.

Specifically, years of schooling and nonfarm job training (representing general and specific human capital, respectively) significantly increase the likelihood that a married farm woman will participate in the labor force. Women who live on dairy farms and farms with higher net farm income are less likely to participate in the off-farm labor force.

We expected that distance from an employment center would act as a deterrent to labor force participation. In our analysis, however, the distance from the township of residence to the nearest town of at least three thousand population had no affect on whether a married farm woman participated in the labor force. Infact, the analysis suggests that if the distance variable could be measured more accurately than our data allowed, then the deterrent effect might diminish with distance traveled.

We found that years of formal education was the only significant variable explaining variation in the wage rate. We estimate that an additional year of education increased the mean wage rate by $.84 per hour. The wage rate was not affected by age, nonfarm job training, health problem, or distance from an employment center.

Years of formal education again had a positive effect on the likelihood of receiving health insurance as a fringe benefit, whereas having a health condition that interferes with productivity had a negative effect.

Finally, we turn to the supply equation for hours of off-farm work in 1982. The presence of a health problem and the presence of preschool children in the

TABLE 8.6 *Fringe Benefits Received by Married Farm Women, by Part-Time and Full-Time Off-Farm Employment, Southwestern Wisconsin, 1982*

Item	Unit	Total	Part-Time[a]	Full-Time
All married farm women employed off-farm for wages or salary	Number	3,585	2,520	1,065
Fringe benefits received:				
Health insurance	Percent	59	48*	85*
Paid vacation	Percent	44	28*	83*
Pension or retirement plan	Percent	32	24*	50*
Life insurance	Percent	31	19*	59*
Paid sick leave	Percent	45	39*	61*

Source: 1983 Wisconsin Family Farm Survey.
* Indicates significant difference (at .05 level) between proportions, using Z-statistic.
a Part-time workers reported 1,680 hours or less of off-farm work in 1982; full-time workers reported more than 1,680 hours in 1982.

home significantly reduced the number of hours worked off- farm. The effect of the wage rate variable is positive – higher wages increase off-farm labor supply. The results indicate, however, that a change in the wage rate results in a less than proportionate change in hours worked – that is, the labor supply response is relatively inelastic with respect to the wage.

CONCLUSIONS

The results of this study of southwestern Wisconsin farm women offer interesting insights into the off-farm work decisions of farm wives, decisions that are important both to individual women as they view their options and to public policymakers and program managers. In particular, our analysis of the Wisconsin data indicates that education plays an important role in both supply and demand aspects of off-farm labor. Higher levels of formal education result in a greater likelihood of labor force participation, as well as in higher wage rates. These results are consistent with many other studies of women's off-farm labor force participation (Buttel and Gillespie 1984; Wilkening 1981). These results imply a positive financial return to farm wives' investments in general human capital, investments that may have involved decisions made years earlier (e.g., to drop out of high school, to acquire post-high school vocational training or a college or professional education, etc.. These decisions are shaped by parents and other family members, high school advisors and teachers, and other adults influential with teen-age women.

TABLE 8.7 *Selected Farm Household and Business Characteristics by Off-Farm Labor Force Participation of Female Spouse, 1982*

Item	Unit	Labor Force Status	
		Participants	Nonparticipants
Households	Number	4,140	6,455
Farm family income			
Net cash farm operating income			
	Dollars	9,617*	19,882*
Off-farm earned	Dollars	13,088*	4,328*
Other (transfers, interest, etc.)			
	Dollars	3,755	4,749
Total	Dollars	26,461	28,959
Family assets	Dollars	281,604*	382,823*
Total debts	Dollars	71,747	82,727
Net worth	Dollars	209,857*	300,096*
Farm business			
Acres operated	Acres	250*	316*
Acres cultivated	Acres	133*	170*
Dairy farms	Percent	57	75

Source: 1983 Wisconsin Family Farm Survey.
* Indicates a significant difference (at the .05 level) between the means and proportions using the t-statistic and the Z-statistic, respectively.

Age was not a significant factor in explaining participation, wage rates, or labor supply. It is possible that an analysis of farm women by age cohort would reveal significantly different results (Bowen and Finegan 1969; Schultz 1980).

Of the married farm women working off the farm in 1982, 11 percent "broke into" the off-farm labor market that year. That is, 89 percent had worked off the farm the preceding year, and 72 percent did so four years earlier. This suggests that once the initial entry is made, off-farm work tends to be continued. If off-farm work is seen as desirable, then public sector assistance in making that initial entry should be considered. This might involve employment internships and vocational counseling for high school seniors, expansion of the counseling and job-search training functions of the Job Service, or training and placement programs in the vocational schools and institutes.

The presence of young children of various ages in the farm household did not differ for labor force participants and nonparticipants. The presence of preschool children at home significantly reduced the number of hours worked off the farm, which is consistent with prior research. Our data indicate that in 1982 there were slightly over one hundred farm women providing child care services as a self-employed business in our eight county study area, while as a potential market there were about one thousand five hnundred married farm women with children age five or younger who were not working off the farm and about eight hundred who were. This suggests opportunities may exist for private entrepreneurs (other married farm women, perhaps) to provide child care services so mothers can take, or increase, off-farm work. If the net effect of off-farm work by married farm women is considered to be desirable by the farm family and the community, then there may be reason for public sector action to augment the supply of child care services in the community through, for example, incentives to employers for place-of-work care, local government programs, and the like.

We found no evidence that the presence of older children who might substitute for the farm wife in nonmarket work (that is, do more farm work) influenced the off-farm work decision. Older children may be constrained by their own farm work responsibilities.

We examined the effects of three sources of income on off-farm labor decisions. Only net farm income had a significant (negative) effect on participation. We conclude that current financial stress (and declining net farm income) may result in increased off-farm participation by farm wives.

Holding net farm income constant, we found that dairy farming had the same negative effect on farm wives' participation as it did on operators' participation (Jensen and Salant 1985).

While our estimated fringe benefits variable was not significant in the labor supply equation, our results do shed light on the factors affecting the likelihood of receiving benefits. We found that farm wives with health problems are less likely to receive insurance and that public administration jobs (for example, in local government) are more generous with such benefits.

RECENT CHANGES IN OFF-FARM WORK
BY MARRIED FARM WOMEN

During the last few years the farming sector has experienced unexpected financial reversals to an extent not seen since the Depression some fifty years ago. Few farm families have been untouched, and some have found themselves in severe financial stress. Farm families have responded in many ways, one of which has been to increase off-farm employment. We have some preliminary evidence to document this change.

Early in 1987 we returned to the same 529 families we had interviewed in the 1983 Wisconsin Family Farm Survey. About three-fourths continued to farm in 1987, and in that group we interviewed 294 families in which the female spouse of the farm operator was present in both 1982 and 1986. The proportion of farms on which a female spouse worked off-farm increased from 39 percent during 1982 to 46 percent during 1986. The percentage that worked from 1 to 399 hours per year off the farm decreased. Among the larger dairy farms (with gross sales of over $65,000 in 1986), the greatest percentage point increase was in the number of spouses working from 400 to 1599 hours, in contrast to the smaller dairy farms where the largest increase was in spouses working full-time off the farm.

Until we complete a more detailed analysis, we cannot identify how much of the increased employment among these female farm spouses was caused by farm financial stress. At this stage, it would be misleading to assign all of the increase to financial stress. First, there had been a long-term trend toward increased off-farm work for many years before the recent farm financial stress began, and some part of the recent increase should be attributed to those (unidentified) influences. Second, each of the farm spouses, as well as their children, were four years older in 1986 than in 1982. Considering the age distribution of spouses, relatively few new infants and small children would be present in 1986. This would reduce the need for child supervision and care in most households and provide the family with options for shifting adult labor from home production to increased involvement in farm production or off-farm work.

NOTES

[1]Support for this research was received from the Research Division, College of Agricultural and Life Sciences, University of Wisconsin-Madison and the Cooperative Extension Service, University of Wisconsin-Extension, in cooperation with ERS, USDA.

[2]In the case of the farm operator, the theory and evidence of off-farm labor supply has greatly expanded (Lange 1979; Huffman 1980; Rosenzweig 1980; Sumner 1982) and is summarized in Huffman (1986).

[3]The eight counties included in the survey were Buffalo, Crawford, Jackson, LaCrosse, Monroe, Richland, Trempealeau, and Vernon.

[4]Statistical tests of significant differences between group means (and proportions) were made on all data presented in this report. As used here, "significant difference" indicates that chances are 95 out of 100 that the two groups could not have been drawn at random from the same population and still display such divergence.

BIBLIOGRAPHY

Becker, Gary. 1965. "A Theory of the Allocation of Time." *Economic Journal* 75: 493-517.

Belknap, John, and William E. Saupe. 1986. "Estimation of Farm Production Functions and Off-Farm Labor Supply." Research in progress, Dept. of Agricultural Economics, University of Wisconsin- Madison, 1986.

Ben-Porath, Yoram. 1973. "Labor Force Participation Rates and the Supply of Labor." *Journal of Political Economy* 81: 697-704.

Bishop, Charles E. 1955. "Part-Time Farming and the Low Income Problem." *Journal of Farm Economics* 37: 1438-45.

Bokemeier, Jan L., Carolyn E. Sachs, and Verna Keith. 1983. "Labor Force

Participation of Metropolitan, Nonmetropolitan, and Farm Women: A Comparative Study." *Rural Sociology* 48: 515-39.

Boskin, Michael J. 1973. "The Economics of Labor Supply." In *Income Maintenance and Labor Supply*, ed. Glen G. Cain and Harold W. Watts, 163-81. Chicago: Markham Press.

Bowen, William G., and T. Aldrich Finegan. 1969. *The Economics of Labor Force Participation*. Princeton, N.J.: Princeton University Press.

Brown, David L., and Jeanne M. O'Leary. 1979. "Labor Force Activity of Women in Metropolitan and Nonmetropolitan America." Economics, Statistics, and Cooperatives Service Rural Development Research Report No. 15. Washington, D.C.: U.S. Department of Agriculture.

Buttel, Frederick H., and Gilbert W. Gillespie, Jr. 1984. "The Sexual Division of Farm Household Labor: An Exploratory Study of the Structure of On-Farm and Off-Farm Labor Allocation Among Farm Men and Women." *Rural Sociology* 49: 183-209.

Cain, Glen G. 1966. *Labor Force Participation of Married Women*. Chicago: University of Chicago Press.

Chiswick, Carmel U. 1982. "The Value of a Housewife's Time." *Journal of Human Resources*, 17: 413-25.

Cogan, John. 1980a. "Married Women's Labor Supply: A Comparison of Alternative Estimation Procedures." In *Female Labor Supply: Theory and Estimation*, ed. James P. Smith, 90-118. Princeton, N.J.: Princeton University Press.

_____. 1980b. "Labor Supply with Costs of Labor Market Entry." In *Female Labor Supply: Theory and Estimation*, ed. James P. Smith, 327-64. Princeton, N.J.: Princeton University Press.

Deaton, Brady, and Bruce Weber. 1985. "Economics of Rural Areas." Paper presented at the Annual Meetings of the American Agricultural Economics Association, 4-7 August, at Iowa State University, Ames, Iowa.

Ehrenberg, Ronald G., and Robert S. Smith. 1982. *Modern Labor Economics: Theory and Public Policy*. Glenview, Ill.: Scott, Foresman, and Co.

Freeman, Richard B. 1981. "The Effect of Unionism on Fringe Benefits." *Industrial and Labor Relations Review* 34: 489-509.

Greene, William H. 1981. "On the Asymptotic Bias of the OLS Estimator of the Tobit Model." *Econometrica* 49: 505-13.

Gronau, Reuben. 1973. "The Intrafamily Allocation of Time: The Value of the Housewife's Time." *American Economic Review* 63: 634-51.

_____. 1974. "Wage Comparisons: A Selectivity Bias." *Journal of Political Economy* 82: 1119-45.

Hall, Robert. 1973. "Wages, Income, and Hours of Work in the U.S. Labor Force." In *Income Maintenance and Labor Supply*, ed. Glen G. Cain and Harold W. Watts, 102-62. Chicago: Markham Press.

Hanoch, Giora. 1980. "Hours and Weeks in the Theory of Labor Supply." In *Female Labor Supply: Theory and Estimation*, ed. James P. Smith, 119-65. Princeton, N.J.: Princeton University Press.

Heckman, James J. 1974. "Shadow Prices, Market Wages, and Labor Supply." *Econometrica* 42: 679-94.

_____. 1976. "The Common Structure of Statistical Models of Truncation, Sample Selection and Limited Dependent Variables and a Simple Estimator for Such Models." *Annals of Economic and Social Measurement* 5: 475-92.

_____. 1979. "Sample Selection Bias as a Specification Error." *Econometrica* 47: 153-61.

Huffman, Wallace E. 1980. "Farm and Off-Farm Work Decisions: The Role of Human Capital." *Review of Economics and Statistics* 62: 14-23.

_____. 1986. "Human Capital in Agriculture." Paper presented at a Dept. of Agricultural Economics Seminar, 30 Jan., at the University of Wisconsin-Madison, Madison, Wis.

Jensen, Helen H. 1982. "Analysis of Fringe Benefits for Nonmetropolitan versus Metropolitan Employee Compensation." *American Journal of Agricultural Economics* 64: 124-28.

Jensen, Helen J., and Priscilla Salant. 1985. "The Role of Fringe Benefits in Operator Off-Farm Labor Supply." Paper presented at the Annual Meetings of the American Agricultural Economics Association, 4-7 August, Iowa State University, Ames, Iowa.

Jensen, Helen H., and William E. Saupe. 1986. "Health Insurance on Family Farms: A Study Based on the 1983 Wisconsin Family Farm Survey." Agricultural Economics Staff Paper, No. 247. Madison, Wis.: Dept. of Agricultural Economics, University of Wisconsin- Madison.

Kada, Ryohei. 1978. "Off-Farm Employment and Farm Adjustments: Microeconomic Study of the Part-Time Farm Family in the United States and Japan." Ph.D. diss., Dept. of Agricultural Economics, University of Wisconsin-Madison, Madison, Wis.

Kalachek, Edward, and Fredric Raines. 1970. "Labor Supply of Lower Income Workers and the Negative Income Tax." In *President's Commission on Income Maintenance Programs, Technical Studies*, ed. Alfred J. Tella, 159-86. Washington, D.C.: U.S. Government Printing Office.

Kosters, Marvin. 1966. "Income and Substitution Effects in a Family Labor Supply Model." P-3339. Santa Monica, Calif.: The Rand Corporation.

Lange, Mark D. 1979. "An Economic Analysis of Time Allocation and Capital-Labor Ratios in Household Production of Farm Families in Iowa." Ph.D. diss., Iowa State University, Ames, Iowa.

Leistritz, Larry L., Brenda L. Ekstrom, Harvey G. Vreugdenhil, and Arlen G. Leholm. 1986. "Effect of Farm Financial Stress on Off-Farm Work Behavior of Farm Operators and Spouses in North Dakota." Paper presented at the Annual Meetings of the American Agricultural Economics Association 27-30 July, Reno, Nev.

Lewis, H. Gregg. 1974. "Comments on Selectivity Bias in Wage Comparisons." *Journal of Political Economy* 82: 1145-55.

Liebowitz, Arleen. 1974. "Home Investments in Children." *Journal of Political Economy*, 82: 111-31.

McCarthy, Mary, and Priscilla Salant. 1986. "The Off-Farm Labor Supply of Married Farm Women." Agricultural Economics Staff Paper No. 257. Madison, Wis.: Dept. of Agricultural Economics, University of Wisconsin-Madison.

Mincer, Jacob. 1962. "Labor Force Participation of Married Women." In *Aspects of Labor Economics*, ed. H. Gregg Lewis, 63-97. Princeton, N.J.: Princeton University Press.

Moore, Keith H. 1986. "The Household Labor Allocation of Farm-Based Families in Wisconsin." Ph.D. diss., Dept. of Sociology, University of Wisconsin-Madison, Madison, Wis.

Muth, Richard. 1966. "Household Production and Consumer Demand Functions." *Econometrica* 34: 699-708.

Pendleton, Shelley. 1985. "Labor Force Participation of Women in Rural Environments: A Case Study of North Carolina." Paper presented at the Annual Meetings of the American Sociological Association, 26-30 August, Washington, D.C.

Rosenzweig, Marc R. 1980. "Neoclassical Theory and the Optimizing Peasant: An Econometric Analysis of Market Family Labor Supply in a Developing Country." *Quarterly Journal of Economics* 94: 31-56.

Schultz, T. Paul. 1980. "Estimating Labor Supply Functions for Married Women." In *Female Labor Supply: Theory and Estimation*, ed. James P. Smith, 25-89. Princeton, N.J.: Princeton University Press.

Shaffer, Ron, Priscilla Salant, and William Saupe. 1985. "Rural Economies and Farming: A Synergistic Link." Agricultural Economics Staff Paper No. 235. Madison, Wis.: Dept. of Agricultural Economics, University of Wisconsin-Madison.

Sumner, Daniel. 1982. "The Off-Farm Labor Supply of Farmers." *American Journal of Agricultural Economics* 64: 499-509.

Wilkening, Eugene A. 1981. "Farm Families and Family Farming." In *The Family in Rural Society*, ed. Raymond T. Coward and William M. Smith, Jr., 27-37. Boulder, Colo.: Westview Press.

Woodbury, Stephen. 1983. "Substitution Between Wage and Nonwage Benefits." *American Economic Review* 73: 166-82.

9

A CHARACTERIZATION
OF THE KENTUCKY FARM MOONLIGHTER

Mary Harmon

INTRODUCTION

Although the proportion of the total labor force holding a second job is only about one in twenty, this phenomenon is much more prevalent in the agricultural sector where the percentage of off-farm employment almost doubled between 1929 and 1969. In 1976, less than 5 percent of all farm families reported farming as their sole source of income (Deseran, Falk, and Jenkins 1984).

This trend toward off-farm employment is the result of structural changes in agriculture that have forced farm family members to seek alternative sources of income. Thus, many farmers, particularly small farmers, have become increasingly dependent on off-farm employment. While this was initially viewed as a characteristic of a transition into or out of farming, it is now considered a permanent fixture in United States agriculture. Off-farm employment, as a single job held by a member of the farm family, has become a strategy designed to insure that the farm operation can continue.

The farm family warrant particular attention because, though structural changes in agriculture have resulted in the concentration of production on a smaller number of farms, American agriculture has remained chiefly a family-operated activity.

This chapter presents a descriptive analysis of Kentucky farm families where one or both members of the farm couple hold at least one off-farm job. Such an analysis can aid in sorting out the basis of this trend and help develop an understanding of the importance of off-farm employment to the survival of the family farm.

LITERATURE REVIEW

Deseran, Falk, and Jenkins (1984) report that approximately one-half of farm husbands and over one-third of farm wives nationwide are employed off the farm. In recent studies, approximately 45 percent of farm families reported off-farm employment as their major source of income, with 63 percent of those reporting also having multiple off-farm earners in the family (Banks and Kalbacher 1981; Deseran, Falk, and Jenkins 1984).

The picture is not very different for Kentucky farm families. Coughenour, Swanson, and Stockham (1983) report that in 1981 less than 40 percent of farm families in Kentucky were full-time farmers. In two of every three farm households, one or more of the adults had employment off the farm. Of these, one-half of the men and one-third of the women worked off the farm in some capacity. Further, off-farm employment provided ninety cents of every farm family dollar on one-half of Kentucky farms (Bokemeier *et al.* 1981).

Why are the rates of dual jobholding so high in the agricultural sector? Researchers have hypothesized a number of explanations, most of which attribute the phenomenon to structural changes external to the farm household. As agriculture slipped into the debt crisis, and land values and produce prices dropped, off-farm employment may have been the only course for retaining the family farm for many farmers. Farmers may desire to keep farming as their primary occupation, yet the current situation necessitates additional income to meet the needs of farm families or pay farm debts. Fuguitt (1959) hypothesized that whereas the extent of off-farm employment is inversely related to employment opportunities in agriculture, the proportion of farm family members working off the farm is positively related to off-farm employment opportunities. Push-pull factors work together to create opportunities for the farm family to continue operating a farm without limiting income or restricting the individual interests of farm household members. Yet there comes a point when one must question whether the acquisition of off-farm jobs and the continuation of farm production reflect a level of desperation rather than aspiration.

DATA AND METHODS

Data for this research were collected in the spring of 1984 by a statewide mail survey of Kentucky farm women. The sampling frame included a list of all households of patrons of Southern States Agriculture Cooperatives (which represent 89 percent of all farm supply cooperative in Kentucky) and a stratified list of Kentucky farm landowners provided by the Agricultural Stabilization and Crop Service of the U.S. Department of Agriculture. Multiple lists were compiled because no single reliable list of Kentucky farm operators is available. A sample of 1,372 eligible respondents was developed. Of these, 880 returned usable questionnaires for a response rate of 64.1 percent.

Respondents were asked if they or their husbands were currently employed outside the home and off the farm and if they or their spouses held a second job off the farm in addition to the first. The following typology of farm families was developed using the off-farm employment status of both the farm husband and wife:

> *Traditional Family*: Husband and wife both work on the farm; neither is employed off the farm in any capacity.
> *Contemporary Farm Family*: Wife works off the farm; husband is a full-time farmer.
> *Part-Time Farming Family*: Husband works off the farm; wife is a full-time farm homemaker.

   Dual Career Farm Family: Both husband and wife are involved in
farm work, and both work off-farm in some capacity.

   This typology was chosen not only because it permits an analysis of the divisions of labor off the farm among farm household members, but also because
of the light it might shed on other studies that have shown a pattern of interrela-
tionships between men's and women's off-farm employment. This type of
grouping takes into consideration the relationship of joint work roles and the effect one family member's work role may have on the work roles of other household members (Buttel and Gillespie 1984; Lodwick and Fassinger 1979).
   Additional measures employed in the analysis are mainly interval scale variables. Age, education, number of children, hours and years worked off the farm,
years lived on the farm, and farm size and ownership are all original values provided by interviewees. Variables regarding family income and gross farm sales
are categorical variables. Respondents were asked to estimate the percentage of
total family income produced by the wife's employment, the husband's employment, and farm sales, and to indicate the primary type of farm operation
(crop, livestock, both or other). The 1980 Census Job Classification code was
used to code respondents' answers to the questions regarding husbands' and
wives' main occupations and primary off-farm occupations.
   The analysis was performed in four steps: 1) calculation of the distribution
of farm families into the four family types (according to the family typology); 2)
a description of these family types; 3) a statistical examination of differences
among the family types; and 4) an examination of selected demographic and farm
characteristics of those families where at least one spouse held two jobs off the
farm.

FINDINGS

   Table 9.1 provides a proportional distribution of the four types of farm
families under consideration. As can be seen from the table, the traditional farm
family is the single dominant family type in Kentucky with almost 33 percent
of all families in the sample composed of husbands and wives who are full-time
farmers. However, we also see that two-thirds of Kentucky farm families have at
least one person working off the farm. Among those families with at least one
member working off the farm, the proportion of dual career families and part-
time families is almost the same, whereas the contemporary family, where only
the wife works off the farm, is clearly the least likely type of farm household to
be found in Kentucky.
   Also evident in this distribution are those families where at least one person
holds more than one job off the farm. The spouses in these families may be
considered multijobholders – holding two off-farm jobs in addition to their farm
and household responsibilities. These families make up less than 2 percent of the
contemporary and part-time farm families. Among dual-career farm families the
proportion with a multiple off-farm earner is greater: of the 206 families, almost
5 percent have at least one multijobholder.

Table 9.1 *Distribution of Kentucky Farm Families by Family Typology*

Type of Farm Family	Frequency	Percent
Traditional Farm Family	251	32.50
Husband Full-Time Farmer		
Wife Full-Time Farm Homemaker		
Contemporary Farm Family	127	16.40
Wife Works Off-Farm		
Husband Full-Time Farmer		
(Wife holds 1 off-farm job)	(121)	(0.00)
(Wife holds 2 off-farm jobs)	(6)	(0.78)
Part-Time Farming Family	189	24.50
Husband Works Off-Farm		
Wife Full-Time Farm Homemaker		
(Husband holds 1 off-farm job)	(183)	(0.00)
(Husband holds 2 off-farm jobs)	(6)	(0.78)
Dual Career Farm Family	206	26.60
Husband and Wife Both Work Off Farm		
(Both hold 1 off-farm job)	(169)	(0.00)
(Wife holds 2 off-farm jobs)	(17)	(0.00)
(Husband holds 2 off-farm jobs)	(15)	(0.00)
(Both hold 2 off-farm jobs)	(5)	(4.79)
	773	100.00

DUAL JOBHOLDERS

Demographic characteristics

As can be seen in Table 9.2, traditional families appear to be in the latter stages of the family life cycle. They are the oldest of the family types and have the smallest household population. In contrast, member of the dual career family are in their prime earning years. Their age, along with their higher levels of education – highest of all four family types – is mirrored in the median family income – $30,000-$34,900 – which is also highest among all households.

Contemporary and part-time farm families both have one person working off the farm, yet there are significant differences in their educational and farm income levels. In the contemporary family, the wife's educational level is significantly higher than the husband's, which may be one reason why she works off the farm instead of her spouse. There is also a significantly higher percentage of total family income from farming operations than that found in the part-time farm family – 41 percent as opposed to 22 percent – probably the result of the man's work role and contribution to on-farm labor (Huffman 1976; Coughenour and Swanson 1983). The part-time farm family also has a larger home popula-

Table 9.2 *Selected Characteristics of Spouses in Different Types of Farm Familes*

Selected Characteristics	Traditional	Family Typology Contemporary	Part-Time	Dual Career
Wife's Age (median)	56	46	42	42
Husband's Age (median)	60	52	44	45
Wife's Education (mean)	11.0	12.9	11.9	13.1
Husband's Education (mean)	10.4	11.2	11.6	12.5
Wife Raised on Farm	75.9%	70.2%	63.6%	57.6%
Husband Raised on Farm	91.1%	87.2%	73.9%	72.7%
Median Years Living on Present Farm	20	17	10	11
Number of Persons Living in Home (median)	2	3	4	3
Total Number of Children (median)	2	2	3	2
Number of Children at Home (median)	.5	1	2	1
Median Family Income (in thousands of dollars)	15-19.9	25-29.9	25-29.9	30-34.9
Family Income from Wife's Work (mean)	0	38.09%	0	32.84%
Family Income from Husband's Work (mean)	0	0	64.33%	48.19%
Family Income from Farm Operations (mean)	64.63%	41.01%	21.91%	16.35%

tion and greater number of children at home. In these families, as well as in the dual-career families when the husband works off the farm, the proportion of total family income from the husband's off-farm job is nearly twice that from the wife when she works off the farm

These differences are supported in the between-family type variations found in Table 9.3. Statistically significant differences were found among the age and educational levels of the family types, which may help explain the statistically significant differences found in family income. Differences in the percent of family income attributable to the wife's work, the husband's work, and the farmoperations were also significant. All were significant at the .0000 level. While the variables of home population and number of children at home were found to vary significantly across family types, the total number of children did not prove to be statistically significant.

Table 9.3 *Variance of Farm Family Types by Selected Characteristics*

Characteristic	F	F prob.
Demographic Characteristics		
Wife's Age	4.5963	.0000
Husband's Age	4.5684	.0000
Wife's Education	5.5067	.0000
Husband's Education	4.0616	.0000
Home Population	19.5818	.0000
Total Number of Children	1.6505	.0668
Number of Children at Home	10.5794	.0000
Family Income	12.9899	.0000
Family Income from Wife's Work (%)	2.9393	.0000
Family Income from Husband's Work (%)	13.2713	.0000
Family Income from Farm Operations (%)	4.4285	.0000
Farm Characteristics		
Total Acres	1.2407	.0218
Acres Rented	1.0175	.4379
Acres Owned	1.1794	.0628
Type of Farm Operation	.3081	.8195
Gross Farm Sales	4.8554	.0000

Employment characteristics

Comparison of the men's and women's primary occupations in Table 9.4 reveal some interesting findings. Men in the traditional and contemporary families who do not work off the farm identify farmer as their major occupation. However, women in the traditional and part-time farm families – those women not employed off the farm – identify themselves first as homemakers and secondly as farmers. In the part-time farm families, 83 percent of the wives view themselves as homemakers; in traditional families, only 58 percent of women identify themselves as primarily homemakers.

It is also interesting that a significant number of women who work off the farm continue to identify their primary occupation as homemaker whereas only a few identify themselves as farmers. In contrast, men who work off the farm continue to identify farming as their major primary occupation.

Women who are employed off the farm and who do not identify their primary occupation as farmer or homemaker are found in a wide range of jobs. However, they tend to be concentrated in the peripheral sector in traditionally "female" white-collar jobs as teachers, secretaries, clerks, and nurses, as well as in the industrial sector as machine operators. Although men with off-farm jobs are fairly equally divided between blue- and white-collar jobs, there is a signifi-

Table 9.4 *Selected Employment and Occupation Characteristics of Different Types of Farm Familes*

A. Wife

Selected Characteristics	Family Typology			
	Traditional	Contemporary	Part-Time	Dual Career
Primary Occupation				
Farmer	36.9	5.7	13.5	2.5
Homemaker	57.8	18.0	82.6	20.7
Teacher	-	18.0	-	14.1
Secretary	-	9.0	-	6.1
Bookkeeper, Acct. Clerk	-	4.9	-	7.1
Machine Operator (factory)	-	3.3	-	5.1
Registered Nurse	-	3.3	-	2.5
Primary Off-Farm Occupation				
Teacher	-	19.2	-	14.6
Secretary	-	10.4	-	7.5
Bookkeeper, Acct. Clerk	-	6.4	-	10.6
General Office Clerk	-	5.6	-	3.0
Machine Operator (factory)	-	4.8	-	5.0
Registered Nurse	-	3.2	-	3.5
Sales Occupation & Mgt.	-	0	-	3.5
Cashier – Grocery	-	.8	-	3.5
Off-Farm Industry				
Education	-	25.2	-	23.7
Medical	-	8.1	-	11.1
Finance	-	7.3	-	6.1
Manufacture – Nondurable Goods	-	11.4	-	9.1
Manufacture – Durable Goods	-	8.9	-	3.5
Retail Sales	-	3.3	-	10.1
Public Administration	-	4.1	-	5.1
Median Number of Years Employed Off-Farm	-	11.5	-	10.0
Median Number of Hours Worked Per Week Off-Farm	-	40.0	-	40.0

Table 9.4 *Selected Employment and Occupation Characteristics of Different Types of Farm Familes*

B. Husband

Selected Characteristics	Family Typology			
	Traditional	Contemporary	Part-Time	Dual Career
Primary Occupation				
Farmer	93.3	90.7	15.6	12.9
Sales Occupations – Mgt.	-	-	5.0	11.3
Machine Operator (factory)	-	-	5.0	6.7
Truck Driver	-	-	4.5	3.1
Supervisors (Prod. Occup.)	-	-	3.4	2.6
Teacher	-	-	2.2	3.6
Managers and Administration	-	-	2.2	5.2
Primary Off-Farm Occupation				
Sales Occupation – Mgt.	-	-	5.5	13.4
Truck Driver	-	-	6.1	4.0
Machine Operator (factory)	-	-	5.0	6.4
Managers and Administration	-	-	2.8	5.0
Logging	-	-	2.8	0.0
Electrician	-	-	2.8	1.0
Teacher	-	-	2.2	3.5
Off-Farm Industry				
Agriculture	-	-	6.1	6.1
Mining	-	-	7.3	3.1
Manufacture – Durable Goods	-	-	20.1	15.8
Manufacture – Non-Durable Goods	-	-	10.1	7.1
Transportation	-	-	6.1	5.6
Construction	-	-	12.3	5.1
Education	-	-		
Retail Sales	-	-	1.1	8.2
Median Number of Years Employed Off-Farm	-	-	15.0	15.0
Median Number of Hours Worked Per Week Off-Farm	-	-	40.0	40.0

Table 9.5 *Selected Farm Characteristics of Different Types of Farm Families*

	Family Typology			
Characteristics	Traditional	Contemporary	Part-Time	Dual Career
Total Acres in Farm (median)	160.0	143.0	91.5	90.0
Acres Rented (median)	0	2.0	0	0
Acres Owned (median)	110.0	100.0	62.5	70.0
Type of Farm Operation				
% Crop	23.3	35.5	37.2	37.2
% Livestock	13.4	7.4	7.8	11.7
% Both	61.2	55.4	53.9	50.5
% Other	2.2	1.7	1.1	.5
Median Gross Farm Sales (in thousands of dollars)	10-19.9	10-19.9	2.5-9.9	2.5-9.9

cantly greater proportion of men in the dual-career family employed in white-collar jobs. This most likely results from this group's higher educational level and contributes to higher family income.

For both men and women of all family types where at least one person works off the farm, the median number of years employed off the farm is between ten and fifteen years. The median number of hours worked off the farm each week indicates that most off-farm employees have full-time jobs.

Farm characteristics

Table 9.5 indicates that in traditional and contemporary families characterized by full-time male farmers the farms are larger and farm sales are higher than in those operated by part-time and dual-career families. Traditional and contemporary families own farms nearly twice the size, and have more than double the amount of farm sales, of farms where the man has an off-farm job.

In all four family types, farms typically combine livestock and crop production. On farms where a single farm enterprise is dominant, the production of crops is most prevalent. In the case of part-time and dual-career families, this is not surprising because crops are periodically labor intensive, in contrast to livestock and especially dairy production, which are continuous labor operations.

Between-family type variations (Table 9.3) indicate statistically significant differences in the size of farms and gross farm sales of the four family types. However, acres rented, acres owned, and type of farm operation showed no significant differences across family categories.

MULTIJOBHOLDERS

Table 9.6 provides demographic and farm characteristics of families where at least one member has a second off-farm job. As can be seen from the table, 3 percent of the men in part-time farm families have a second job off the farm

Table 9.6 *Selected Characteristics of Multijobholders in Different Types of Farm Families*

Selected Characteristics	Contemporary	Part-Time		Dual-Career	
	Wife holds more than 1 off-farm job (N=6)	Husband holds more than 1 off-farm job (N=6)	Wife holds 2, Husband holds 1 off-farm job (N=17)	Husband holds 2, Wife holds 1 off-farm job (N=15)	Both Husband and Wife hold 2 off-farm jobs (N=5)
% Working 2 Jobs Off-Farm	4.7%	3.2%	8.3%	7.3%	2.4%
Wife's Age (median)	41.0	48.0	44.0	41.0	40.0
Husband's Age (median)	44.5	50.5	49.0	41.0	41.0
Wife's Education (mean)	13.7	13.2	13.1	13.9	15.4
Husband's Education (mean)	11.2	13.2	11.4	14.2	14.4
Median Family Income	20-29.9K	35-39.9K	35-39.9K	35-39.9K	25-29.9K
% Family Income from Wife's Work (mean)	44.0%	0	38.5%	37.1%	*
% Family Income from Husband's Work (mean)	0	*	42.3%	50.7%	*
% Family Income from Farm Operations (mean)	34.1%	35.0%	19.5%	10.8%	*
Wife Raised on Farm	50.0%	66.7%	64.7%	60.0%	20.0%
Husband Raised on Farm	100.0%	66.7%	76.5%	80.0%	60.0%

*Insufficient Numbers
(*continued*)

Table 9.6 *(continued)*

Selected Characteristics	Contemporary — Wife holds more than 1 off-farm job (N=6)	Part-Time — Husband holds more than 1 off-farm job (N=6)	Dual-Career — Wife holds 2, Husband holds 1 off-farm job (N=17)	Dual-Career — Husband holds 2, Wife holds 1 off-farm job (N=15)	Dual-Career — Both Husband and Wife hold 2 off-farm jobs (N=5)
Median # Persons in Home	4	3	3	3	3
Median # Total Children	3	1	2	2	2
Median # Children at Home	2	1	1.5	2	1
Total Acres in Farm (median)	65.0	162.5	81.0	67.5	*
Acres Rented (median)	25.0	.5	1.5	0	*
Acres Owned (median)	27.0	162.5	67.5	67.5	*
Type of Operation					
% Crop	40.0%	33.3%	57.1%	20.0%	80.0%
% Livestock	0%	16.7%	7.1%	20.0%	0%
% Both	60.0%	50.0%	35.7%	60.0%	20.0%
% Other	0%	0%	0%	0%	0%
Median Gross Farm Sales	2.5-9.9K	10-19.9K	2.5-9.9K	2.5-9.9K	1-2.49K

* Insufficient Numbers

whereas nearly 4 percent of the women in contemporary families have a second off-farm job. The proportions for the dual-career families, where both spouses work off the farm and at least one holds a second job, is even higher: in 8 percent the wife is the multijobholder, in 7 percent the husband holds an additional job, and in 2 percent both spouses work two jobs off the farm. While the ages of men and women are significantly lower in the dual-career families where the husband works two jobs off the farm and where both spouses hold additional off-farm jobs, all groups are in their prime earning years. One interesting finding is the high educational level across the board, particularly for women, with the two exceptions of men in the contemporary and the dual-career/wife-multijobholder families. The reverse is seen in the case of the dual-career/husband-multijobholder family, where the man's level of education is higher than the woman's.

Of all multijobholding families, the part-time farm families and dual-career families of wife-multijobholders and husband-multijobholders appear to be the most affluent. Their high levels of education likely account for the high median family incomes, $35,000-39,900 in each case, highest of all family types under consideration. In the case of the dual-career families, the proportions of total family income from the husband and the wife are significantly different in each family subtype. When the wife holds two off-farm jobs and the husband holds one, the wife's contribution to total family income amounts to only about 39 percent whereas the husband's contribution is approximately 42 percent. When the husband is the multijobholder and the wife works one off-farm job, the latter's proportion of family income is 37 percent whereas the former's is nearly 51 percent. In this instance, the man's educational level is significantly higher than the wife's, yet their respective contributions to family income approach the same level as those in the dual-career/wife-multijobholder family.

Median family income in contemporary families where the wife holds two off-farm jobs is significantly less than median family income in part-time families where the husband is the multijobholder. The median home population, the number of children, and the number of children at home are highest for the contemporary family and lowest for the part-time family. The dual-career family where both spouses work two jobs off the farm is the youngest of all family types in the study, and the spouses have the highest educational levels both for their respective genders and as a family. Also, these dual-career farm families exhibit the lowest proportion of husbands and wives raised on a farm, with 60 percent of the men and only 20 percent of the women having grown up on a farm.

Among multijobholder families, the farms of contemporary and dual-career families are significantly smaller than those of part-time families, whose farms rival those of traditional and contemporary/singlejobholder families in size. The median gross farm sales of the multijobholder/part-time farm family also approach those of the traditional and part-time/singlejobholding farm families.

While the multijobholder/dual-career families and the part-time farm families own the majority of their land, multijobholder contemporary families rent a significant part of their land. This is interesting because only 31 percent of the total contemporary family income is from farm operations, yet the number of acres rented would indicate that farming should account for a larger share of the total family income. The median gross farm sales are only $2,500-9,900, derived mainly from the combination of livestock and crop production. As is the case with singlejobholders, the major operation of the part-time multijobholder family and the dual-career/husband-multijobholder family is a combination of crops and livestock. The pattern among dual-career families where the wife is the multiple earner and where both spouses work two off-farm jobs deviates from that found among single jobholders. These families are predominantly crop producers. This is not surprising because, as previously mentioned, crops are periodically labor intensive and do not require the continuous attention a livestock operation does.

CONCLUSIONS

This paper's principal objective has been to arrive at an overall portrait of the Kentucky moonlighting farm couple. By using the family as the unit of analysis, the distribution of family labor on and off the farm is recognized as being important to on-farm labor and farm production.

Some of the results found in this study correspond with those found by Coughenour and Swanson (1983). They reported 65 percent of farm households with at least one person working off the farm. The present study found approximately 68 percent of families reporting a member employed off the farm. This is most likely a reflection of the dominance of small-scale farming in Kentucky. The proportion of dual jobholders with a multiple off-farm earner was second only to the traditional farm family. This lends credibility to the belief that families where both spouses work off the farm tend to be "gentlemen" farmers or farm families.

Demographic characteristics

Traditional farm families are the oldest and have the lowest educational and income levels. As income had been linked to education both directly and via occupation (Sewell and Hauser 1975), the low median family income could partly be a reflection of the families' low levels of education. This factor may influence their decision or ability to work off the farm.

In contrast, the dual-career family's high income, high educational attainment, and low farm income may suggest that farming is a hobby rather than a way of life for this type of family. On the other hand, it may imply that the family wants the "country" style of living yet works off the farm as a means of maintaining a higher standard of living and greater purchasing power than farming alone could provide. In any case, when examining income from farm operations, it is important to keep in mind that this is a difficult concept to measure because of the problem of income-in-kind which may take the form of farm tenants or relatives who do not pay rent or production of food for home consumption. This type of income is usually not included in measured income and therefore may have distorting effects (Sweet 1972).

Women have higher educational levels than men in all family types. However, this is not reflected in their proportion of family earnings: when the woman works off the farm, her income is just under one-half that of her male counterpart. In spite of this, women's income earning ability appears to be limited by the structure of the local labor market. In the case of the part-time farm family, the lower wages paid to women may be a factor in determining who works off the farm: the husband may be forced to seek gainful employment instead of the wife as a result of inequality in nonfarm earnings (Bokemeier, Sachs, and Keith 1983; Coughenour and Swanson 1983; Haney 1983).

Employment

The issue of the value of women's work is also raised by the way that women identify their primary occupations. In all cases where women are employed off the farm, the majority continue to identify themselves first as homemakers. The majority of women in traditional farm families view themselves as homemakers, with a smaller proportion identifying themselves as farmers. However, the proportion of women identifying themselves as farmers is highest in traditional farm families. This may indicate that women in traditional families consider themselves more as partners in farming than do women in other family types. However, the high proportion of women identifying themselves as homemakers is most likely a manifestation of the socialization process whereby particular farm roles are socially defined as "men's" or "women's" roles enforced by religious and cultural values (Boulding 1980).

Not surprisingly, women are concentrated mainly in traditional, supportive, white-collar jobs, which is most likely part of the reason women's contribution to family income is significantly less than the men's. Also, men's lower educational level is reflected in their concentration in mainly blue-collar jobs, with the exception of men in the dual-career family, who not only have higher educational levels but also tend to be employed in white-collar jobs.

Farm characteristics

Those farms where the man is a full-time farmer are the largest and have the highest farm sale. This finding is consistent with those of Coughenour and Swanson (1983) and Coughenour, Swanson, and Stockham (1983). Further, it appears to support Buttel and Gillespie's (1984) argument that size of the farm is directly and strongly related to men's off-farm employment and inversely and weakly related to women's off-farm employment.

Multijobholders

Families with multijobholders are the youngest, the highest educated, and the most economically well off. Women's higher educational attainment in the contemporary multijobholding and dual-career wife-multijobholding families is significantly higher than the men's. This may be the reason the woman is the multiple earner and not her spouse.

The differences in median family income among the multijobholding families is additional evidence of inequality of earnings and the restricted structure of the rural labor market. Further, differences in home population and the number of children at home may indicate that for the part-time family the second off-farm job was acquired not necessarily to meet family needs but to raise the standard of living or increase purchasing power. This is also probably the case for the dual-career families with wife-multijobholders and husband -multijobholders where home population remained the same though the number of children at home was slightly higher.

The farm size and income from farm sales are also among the lowest among multijobholders; for the part-time farm family the median gross farm saleS are significantly higher than those of other multijobholding families. As the size of the part-time family farm is more than double the size of any other multijobholding farm, and most of the farm is owned, the husband may choose to work off the farm to enable the family to hire farm labor to work the large tract of land.

As more household members of farm families seek employment off the farm, multijobholding in U.S. agriculture will continue to rise, and farm families will increasingly become dependent on off-farm employment. A significant proportion of off-farm workers are women, and it appears that women's labor force participation is taking the places of men working two jobs off the farm. This situation is certainly preferable, and in many cases it may be the only strategy for hanging onto the family farm. The most obvious consequence of this trend is the stress felt by members of the farm household; yet more and more farm families will face the need to acquire off-farm employment because of economic pressures. Where a large portion of farm land is owned, off-farm employment may be the only course to retain the family farm to pass on to succeeding generations. However, as children see their parents juggling off-farm jobs and farm work, the result may be the loss of a significant portion of the nest generation of farmers.

BIBLIOGRAPHY

Banks, V.J., and J.Z. Kalbacher. 1981. *Farm Income Recipients and Their Families: A Socioeconomic Profile*. Rural Development Research Report No. 30. Department of Agriculture, Economic Research Service.

Bishop, C.E. 1955. "Part-Time Farming and the Low-Income Problem." *Journal of Farm Economics* 37:1438-45.

Bokemeier, Janet, and C. Milton Coughenour. 1980. "Men and Women in Four Types of Farm Families." Paper presented at the Annual Meeting of the Rural Sociological Society, August, Ithaca, NY.

Bokemeier, Janet L., Carolyn Sachs, and Verna Keith. 1983. "Labor Force Participation of Metropolitan, Nonmetropolitan, and Farm Women: A Comparative Study." *Rural Sociology* 48:515-39.

Bokemeier, Janet, Pamela Brooks, Verna Keith, and Carolyn Sachs. 1981. "The Employment of Farm, Rural Nonfarm, and Urban Women in Kentucky." *Community Issues* 3-4.

Boulding, Elise. 1980. "The Labor of U.S. Farm Women: A Knowledge Gap." *Sociology of Work and Occupation* 7:261-90.

Buttel, Frederick H., and Gilbert W. Gillespie, Jr. 1984. "The Sexual Division of Farm Household Labor: An Exploratory Study of the Structure of On-

Farm and Off-Farm Labor Allocation Among Farm Men and Women."
    Rural Sociology 49:183-209.
Coughenour, C. Milton, and Louis Swanson. 1983 "Work Statuses and
    Occupations of Men and Women in Farm Families and the Structure of
    Farms." *Rural Sociology* 48:23-43.
Coughenour, C. Milton, Ann Stockham, and James A. Christenson. 1980
    "Kentucky Farm Families." *Community Issues* 5.
Coughenour, C. Milton, Louis Swanson, and Ann Stockham. 1983. "Kentucky
    Farmers, 1982." *Community Issues* 2.
Deseran, Forrest A., William W. Falk, and Pamela Jenkins. 1984.
    "Determinants of Earnings of Farm Families in the U.S." *Rural Sociology*
    49:210-29.
Fuguitt, Glenn. 1959. "Part-Time Farming and the Push-Pull Hypothesis."
    American Journal of Sociology 64:375-79.
_____. 1961. "A Typology of the Part-Time Farmer." *Rural Sociology* 26:39-
    48.
Fuguitt, Glenn, Anthony Fuller, Heather Fuller, Ruth Gasson, and Gwyn Jones.
    1977. *Part-Time Farming: Its Nature and Implications.* Ashford, England:
    Wye College.
Haney, Wava Gillespie. 1983. "Farm Family and the Role of Women." In Gene
    F. Summers ed., *Technology and Social Change in Rural Areas: A
    Festschrift for Eugene A. Wilkening.* Boulder, Colo.: Westview Press.
Hill, Frances. 1981. "Farm Women: Challenge to Scholarship." *The Rural
    Sociologist* 1:370-82.
Huffman, W.E. 1976. "The Production Value of Human Time in U.S.
    Agriculture." *American Journal of Agricultural Economics* 58:672-83.
Kada, Ryohei. 1980. *Part-Time Family Farming: Off-Farm Employment and
    Farm Adjustments in the United States and Japan.* Tokyo, Japan: Center for
    Academic Publications.
Lodwick, Dora A., and Polly A. Fassinger. 1979. "Misconceptions of Part-Time
    Farming: Recognizing the Impact of Women and Children." Paper presented
    at the Annual Meeting of the Rural Sociological Society, Burlington, Vt.
Miller, Glenn W. 1972. "The Extent, Characteristics and Effects of
    Multijobholding in South Central Kansas." *Rocky Mountain Social Science
    Journal* 9:19-25.
Schertz, Lyle P. 1958. "A Dramatic Transformation." U.S. Dept. of Agriculture,
    Agricultural Economic Report No. 441. Washington, D.C.: U.S.
    Department of Agriculture.
Sekscenski, Edward S. 1980. "Women's Share of Moonlighting Nearly Doubles
    During 1969-1979." *Monthly Labor Review* 5:36-42.
Sewell, W., and R. Hauser. 1975. *Education, Occupation, and Earnings.* New
    York: Academic Press.
Sweet James A. 1972. "The Employment of Rural Farm Wives." *Rural
    Sociology* 37:553-77.
U.S. Dept. of Agriculture. *A Time to Choose: Summary Report on the
    Structure of Agriculture.* Washington, D.C.: U.S. Dept. of Agriculture.

Waldman, Elizabeth. 1970. "Changes in the Labor Force Activity of Women." *Monthly Labor Review* 93:10-18.

Whitener, LEslie, ed. 1985. "Farm Women's Contributions to Agriculture and Rural Economy." *Rural Development Perspectives* 1:20-26.

Wilkening, Eugene A. 1981. "Farm Families and Family Farming." In *The Family in Rural Society*, ed. R.T. Coward and W.M. Smith, Jr., 27-37. Boulder, Colo.: Westview Press.

10

MARITAL STATUS AND INDEPENDENT FARMING: THE IMPORTANCE OF FAMILY LABOR FLEXIBILITY TO FARM OUTCOMES

Rachel A. Rosenfeld
Leann M. Tigges[1]

INTRODUCTION

In outlining a theory of the family farm in advanced capitalism, Friedmann (1981) emphasizes the unity of labor and ownership within the farm enterprise, an enterprise subject to the general laws of the larger economy. This unity within the farm household provides the major defining characteristic of agriculture as a simple commodity form of production. The household is the unit of production and consumption, allowing greater flexibility in production than capitalist enterprises, which must separate wages, reinvestment, and profit. This flexibility has allowed the family labor farm to persist. Recognition of the importance of the farm household has led rural sociologists to increasingly focus on the farm family (Flora 1981) rather than on farmers per se and has brought new attention to the role of women in the farm family labor system (Haney 1983).

Research on women in agriculture often highlights the important role farmwives play in the survival and economic well-being of farm enterprises by helping a farmer husband on the farm (Maret and Copp 1982; Reimer 1986) and by contributing earnings from off-farm employment (Coughenour and Swanson 1983; Rosenfeld 1985). Not all farm women have husbands, however. Further, just as not all farmwives are involved in the day-to-day work of farming, neither are all farm husbands. Increasingly, farms depend on off-farm income (Mooney 1983). Although farmwives often provide this supplemental income, leaving farm tasks to their husbands, the reverse may also be true. When the husband takes one or more off-farm jobs, the woman may take over the daily farm management (Gladwin 1985).

Women without husbands doing daily farm work are often running the farm alone and are what we call in this paper "independent farm women." We present below some evidence that the relative number of independent women farmers has been increasing. Many women so classified, though, are probably doing what they have always done – helping out as needed. They are contributing their labor in whatever ways the farm family seems to require. We explore a variety of farm family labor arrangements by classifying farm operations by the absence of a woman's or man's on-farm labor. Using data from a 1980 national farm survey, we compare the family and farm characteristics of independent women farmers with those of other farm women. In addition, we compare the independent women farmers with a group of "independent male farmers" – men farming without a wife's regular farm labor. For each group of independent farmers, we examine the relationship of marital status to economic outcomes of independent farming to help gauge the importance of spouses' direct and indirect labor contributions. Family labor flexibility naturally will be greater where there are more family members available to offer labor on the farm, in the household, or to an outside employer. As we argue below, neglecting older or unmarried farmers, or focusing only on variations in off-farm employment by farm couples, leaves researchers with an incomplete understanding of the structure and range of family labor allocations and their importance to family income.

FAMILY FARM LABOR – WOMEN'S AND MEN'S

There is relatively little information available on women farmers, especially on those who operate farms without the assistance of a husband. What information we do have varies according to the definition of farmer used (see Table 10.1). Occupational data for men and women from the decennial population censuses provide the longest historical perspective on women's participation in agricultural operations. The population censuses identify farmers and farm managers by occupation in principal employment during the reference week, regardless of operator status. According to census data, the percent of farmers and farm managers who are women nearly doubled between 1970 and 1980, from 5.0 percent to 9.9 percent. These data are limited in that they neither include those secondarily employed in these occupations nor provide much detail about the farm or farm family.

Concerned primarily with gathering information about farms rather than persons, the Census of Agriculture allows for identification of one operator per farm, the operator being the person with the primary responsibility for running the farm. Unfortunately, prior to 1978 the Census of Agriculture did not ask the operator's sex, giving very little historical perspective on women's involvement as primary operators. According to this source, the relative number of farm operators who are female increased from 5.2 percent to 5.4 percent between 1978 and 1982. These data give us a national picture of the demographic and farm characteristics of farm women operators (e.g., Kalbacher 1985), but are limited in detail about the farm family. Further, they may underestimate the extent to which women are farming alone (Scholl 1983), especially when a husband not regularly active on the farm or ranch is named as the operator. Friedland (1987:4) argues that the faulty conceptualization of women's role in agriculture has "cheated" women "out of their direct, less direct, and indirect contributions to agriculture." At a minimum, he calls for a more objective methodology that would take into consideration the continuum of production and reproduction activities of farming.

Smaller studies provide some description of the range of women's involve ment on farms. Lodwick and Fassinger (1979), adapting a typology developed by Pearson (1979) to their study of farm women in two Michigan townships, find only 2 percent independent producers (the major laborer and manager) and 15 percent agricultural partners (coexecutor of labor and management). Their approach has the advantage of bringing in some information on the family labor structure, although the emphasis is on the woman's work. Another study, conducted by Sachs (1983), gathered indepth information from twenty-one women "who had major responsibility in a farming operation" (p. 76), nine of whom were married. While her book gives an insightful picture of these women, Sachs's sample (like Pearson's) is probably biased against married women who run their own operations, but whose husbands at least occasionally farm, given that she relied on informants to identify women farmers.

In addition to such studies focusing on women's labor are those that have tried to develop typologies of the couple's labor structure to predict farm outcomes. Many of these studies use variation in off-farm employment to define categories, which means that one does not get a true measure of whether the husband or wife has the regular help of a spouse in *farm work*. Coughenour and Swanson (1983) and Deseran, Falk, and Jenkins (1984), for example, develop typologies concerned with paid employment, which leave the actual performance of the day-to-day work of farming unknown and exclude couples in which the respondent is age sixty-five or older. (See also Moore and Wilkening 1982.)

While trying to characterize the farm family labor structure, researchers often miss the contributions of women actually running the farm on their own. This can be because the sample depends on a list of male farm operators or is limited to a particular geographic region with a particular commodity, in which independent women are underrepresented. Studies limited to farm couples exclude those women and men farming without any spouse present, even though other household members may be contributing to the farm enterprise. They neglect the true structure of and constraints on family labor by limiting the field of study. By studying couples rather than farmers, their goal is to bring in women's contributions. In doing so, however, they (perhaps unwittingly) restrict the range of women's activities to traditional roles as farmwives and assess only their direct economic contributions, contributions likely to be underestimated by the type of data available (Reimer 1986).

While we build on the valuable conceptual contributions other scholars have made to understanding family labor farms, our focus is a bit different from that of those who have studied farm couples or farm women. We create a typology of farm families based on variations in on-farm labor. We do not use off-farm labor to differentiate among farmers, but see it as a class characteristic of the farm household. We therefore do not need to restrict ourselves to young and middle-aged farmers or only those who are currently married. Unlike most studies telling us about farm labor allocations, our's uses national data with considerable detail about the farm and family. We directly examine independent farming by women and men and consider the direct and indirect contributions of spouses and, to some extent, other family members.

PREDICTIONS

On the basis of previous research on farming and women farmers, we can make some predictions about what we will find with our data. To the extent that a spouse's farm labor contributes to the economic success of a farm and family, one might expect to find that women and men who are independent farmers have farms that are less successful than others. Empirical evidence, however, suggests disadvantages exist only for independent women farmers. Kalbacher's (1985) analysis of the 1978 Census of Agriculture reveals that, compared with men, women operators have smaller operations and lower income. She acknowledges that at least part of this inequality can be explained by the older average age of women operators.

Coughenour and Swanson (1983) provide a technologically based reason for the lower profitability of women in farming. They conclude that "the man's involvement in farming is clearly the most important to farm business performance" because men operate more productive equipment than do women (p. 39).[2] Those farms with the husband having off-farm employment have fewer acres and smaller sales than those in which the man has no off-farm job. The authors assume that decisions for men to take off-farm employment affect farm scale, rather than farm resources (such as acreage) influencing family employment decisions. Kalbacher (1985) notes that the extent (hours per week and weeks per year) of men's off-farm work varies by farm size for women's and men's operations, "but farm size has little effect on the amount of time female operators spend working off their farms" (p. 12). More could be going on than men doing more productive labor, however. A man with a nonfarming wife still has the advantage of her household labor, whereas an independent married woman farmer probably does not benefit greatly from the husband's housework. In fact, she may be doing the inside work as well as the farm work (e.g., Pearson 1979; Sachs 1983).

Also, men – married or not – undoubtedly have an advantage in the predominately male occupation of farmer, with greater access to the networks, credit, help, and advice that add to a farm's success (Sachs 1983). Although indebtedness is often seen as evidence of diminishing owner control (or "proletarianization") in farming, Mooney (1983) argues that the very forces creating dependence on credit and other markets also contribute to the viability of the farm operation by expanding the scope of production. Kalbacher (1985) found women operators had lower debts-to-assets ratios than male operators, suggesting that they were at a disadvantage in being able to expand if one follows the logic above. What constitutes good farming practices in one period, however, may create weakness in another (Mooney 1986). In the 1980s, we have witnessed the dangers of the previous decade's farm overexpansion, so that women's lower relative debt may now be to their advantage.

A farm spouse contributes in ways other than providing farm labor and management. As mentioned, many farms now depend on the off-farm earnings of family members. Because men earn more on average than women, women who are running farms while their husbands are employed off-farm may have higher total family incomes than women who provide the only off-farm income

(Deseran, Falk, and Jenkins 1984). On the other hand, when independent farming represents a situation where there is not a spouse, family income probably will be lower still.

A final consideration is that independent farming may represent different life- and farm-cycle stages for women and men. Many women become "independent" through the death or incapacity of their husbands and are at a late farm- and life-cycle stage (Fink 1986; Pearson 1979). Kalbacher (1985) found that women operators were nearly ten years older on average than male operators, and Geisler, Waters, and Eadie (1985) point out that about 50 percent of the farmland owned by women in 1978 belonged to women sixty-five and older. For a man, being independent of a wife's farm labor could indicate that he is at a peak in the farm cycle and can afford to do without the wife's help on the farm (Kohl 1976). Buttel and Gillespie (1984) found the highest gross farm income in their New York sample on farms where only the man worked on the farm. Such men may still have children's labor available, but the independent woman farmer probably has fewer household members to contribute farm labor. Thus, we might find that at least part of any sex differences in outcomes for independent farmers represents differences in stage of the farm and family life-cycle.

In sum, we expect farms run by women to be less profitable, less in debt, and smaller than other farms, not because women are worse farmers, but because of barriers they face and their life-cycle stage. Married independent women farmers, though, might have family income at least as high as other farm women, and married independent men farmers could be better off than any other category of farmer. Unmarried independent farmers probably have the least favorable financial situation (at least in terms of farm and family income), partly because they lack a spouse's paid and unpaid labor and partly because many are widowed and at a late stage in the family and farm life-cycle.

DATA AND VARIABLES

The data used in this paper are from the 1980 Farm Women Survey, conducted by the National Opinion Research Center (NORC) under a cooperative agreement with the U.S. Department of Agriculture (USDA). The sampling frame, developed by USDA, was based on land use stratification in the forty-eight contiguous states. A woman was included if she was (1) the 1978 operator or (2) the wife (even if widowed or divorced) of a 1978 operator. A 25 percent subsample of eligible male operators was contacted as well. All designated respondents were screened as to whether they were still farming at the time of the survey. Thus, generalizations from this sample are limited to those who were farming in 1978 and still in business in 1980. Although this includes a majority of agricultural operations in 1980, the population to which we can generalize is likely to be older, more stable, and more successful than the total 1980 farm population. The sample was not designed to include only family farms, but 90 percent of the respondents reported owning at least some of their farm land.

NORC carried out telephone interviews with this sample in the summer of 1980. Men were asked a subset of the questions asked of women. The final response rate was 83 percent, with a final N of 2509 for women and 569 for men.

(See Jones and Rosenfeld 1981 and Rosenfeld 1985 for further description of the sample.)

The definition of independent operator we use has two components: labor and management. Labor is indicated by the absence of a spouse in farming, and management by operator status. Women without husbands were classified as independent operators. They lacked husbands' farm labor, and we assumed that in the absence of a husband the woman acted at least to some extent as an operator. Eighty percent of this group actually identified themselves as main operators in response to the question: "Do you consider yourself to be one of the main operators for your farm/ranch? (By main operator we mean a person who makes day-to-day decisions about running the whole operation.)"[3]

If a husband was present, we decided whether the woman was an independent operator on the basis of her responses to two questions. After listing household members, women were asked whether each member "was regularly involved in the day-to-day work on this farm/ranch," not counting helping out seasonally or for very short periods. If a married woman said her husband did not do this work, she was a candidate for independent operator. Because Sachs (1983) points out that when a husband is present he is usually managing, we added a further criterion for married women: self- identification as a main operator on the question described above. A married woman whose husband did not regularly do farm work and who considered herself a main operator was included in our analysis as an independent operator.

Slightly over 9 percent of the NORC women, married and unmarried, were categorized as independent farmers by these criteria. (See Table 10.1.) Our figure is nearly twice as large as the proportion female of primary operators given by the Census of Agriculture and is about the same as the proportion of farmers and farm managers who are women, suggesting that responses allowing this identification in the Census of Population could reflect women independently involved in their operations.

Men were not asked the question about main operator status. Sachs's (1983) observations and the nature of the NORC sampling frame make it probable that a large proportion of the men interviewed would have identified themselves as "main operators." Therefore, the criterion for whether they were farming on their own (i.e., were not just one of the main operators but also independent operators) was the absence of a wife or the presence of a wife who, the husband reported, "never" did any farm task listed in the survey (with the exception of gardening and running errands). Over 16 percent of the men were classified as independent farmers by this procedure.

Our analysis focuses on the differences among farm households with various types of operators: independent women and men (with unmarried and married subgroups), and other (nonindependent) women and men. We bring marital status (currently married or not) into our analysis to see whether lack of a spouse per se rather than lack of a spouse's farm labor is important. (The unmarried are too few in number to further differentiate marital status.) We are interested in the economic and psychic returns to farming for each type of operator. The major variables used to further describe groups of operators fall into four general cate gories: relationship to farm; class characteristics; farm characteristics; and family characteristics.

Economic Outcomes and Satisfaction

The economic outcomes on which we focus are the 1979 net farm income, family income, and debts-to-assets ratio. Net farm income is a good short- term indicator of how well the farm is doing.[4] Family income – here net farm income plus the couple's or unmarried individual's off-farm income – gives a sense of the economic position of the family. (We were not able to create this variable for men because for them we did not have wife's income.) The debts-to-assets ratio gives an impression of the long-term viability of the farm, although we know it is also a function of age (Tigges and Rosenfeld 1987), with older farmers more likely to have paid off their land and machinery. In addition to these economic outcomes, we have measures of psychic returns to farming: responses to questions about satisfaction with farming as a way of life and as a way to earn a living.

Relationship to Farm

For women and men, we know the proportion of various types of farm decisions in which they participated, alone or with someone else (a spouse if married, other person if not married). In addition, we have information on whether anyone besides the respondent or farm couple regularly helped with farm decision making, although we do not have much information about who such decision makers were. Married respondents of both sexes were also asked whether they could run the farm alone if something happened to their spouses. Women were asked which of a list of categories of farm tasks they did regularly, occasionally, or never (if the task was done on their farms), while married men were asked this for their wives. Further, women told the interviewers whether their names were on deeds or rental contracts for their land. We would expect independent farmers to be more involved in their farms and more optimistic about running the farms even without a spouse. To some extent, this set of variables tests the validity of our categories of farmers.

Class and Farm Characteristics

Following Mooney (1983), we consider class relations as defined by whether there is control over one's own labor, control over the labor of others, and ownership of and control over the means of production.[5] Mooney uses measures of land tenancy, indebtedness, contract production, off-farm employment, and hired labor as indicators of class relations. The women's data give information on all these conditions except contract production. Men were asked only about debt and their own off-farm employment. Additional farm characteristics included are size, indicated by number of acres, and commodity type, indicated roughly by region of the U.S. and percent of total sales from crops.

Family Characteristics and Labor Structure

In addition to operator status, we include variables that encompass other dimensions of household labor and the family life-cycle. For both sexes we know respondent's age. From women, we also have information on the number of children younger than six, the number of children age six to seventeen (and whether they regularly did farm work), the presence of a son eighteen or older who helped on the farm, and the presence of any other people who regularly helped with farm work and decisions. From these data, we will be able to see whether independent farmers really "go it alone," or whether other people at least partially substitute for a spouse in working the farm. None of the information on family composition and labor structure is available for the men.

FINDINGS

Relationship to the Farm

Not surprisingly, independent farm women are more involved in farming than are other farm women. Although they do not differ from other women in the proportion of their lives they have lived on farms (Table 10.2, part A), independent farm women do a wider range of farm tasks regularly or at least occasionally, are more involved in farm decision making, are more likely to be named on land deeds or rental contracts, and – if married – are more certain they could run the operation alone (Table 10.2, part B).[6] Even though unmarried women do not have a husband with whom to make decisions, many have someone else who is consulted – on average they make less than 40 percent of various types of farm decisions by themselves, and for about 40 percent there is another regular decision maker. Independent women have higher levels of farm involvement than other farm women, but even nonindependent women have relatively high levels of participation on their farms.[7] Independent men make a greater proportion of types of decisions alone than other farm men, although about 30 percent of men without wives have someone else who helps make decisions. Men whose wives do farm tasks are more likely to share decision making with them (Table 10.3, part B). (See also Rosenfeld 1985, chap. 4.)

Farm Economic Outcomes

Independent operations of women have significantly lower average net farm income than do other operations, including those of independent male farmers (see Tables 10.2 and 10.3, part C). The average net farm income for independent female operators is about $8,000, compared with $13,000 for other women's farm operations and $14,000 for operations of independent men (averaging together the figures for independent farmers by marital status in the tables). In part, this reflects the smaller size of independent farm women's operations – just over 300 acres on average, compared with 900 acres for other women's farms (Table 10.2, part E), a finding similar to Kalbacher's (1985). (See Tigges and Rosenfeld 1987 for an analysis of the effects of size and other variables on economic outcomes.)

Although the differences in farm income are consistent with Coughenour and Swanson's (1983) general conclusion that men's labor is more important to farm productivity than women's, one can ask whether differences in farm income reflect the presence of a spouse per se rather than a spouse's labor. Average net farm income for unmarried women is $8,822, not significantly different from the average net farm income for married independent women of $7,707. The size of unmarried women's farms is about the same as for independent married women farmers. Thus, for women, the economic effect of being an independent operator does not seem to be an effect of marital status. For unmarried men, average net farm income is $9,053, very similar to that for unmarried women and considerably below that for married men (independent or not). Their farms are also smaller than those of other men. Marital status is part of the story for independent men, perhaps because, as we suggest above, married men whose wives are not doing farm work are those who can afford this or who can invest a wife's off-farm income in the farm. Our data are consistent with Reimer's (1986) argument that conventional measures underestimate women's economic contributions to family labor farms. Women might contribute to farm profitability even if they do not directly contribute labor. Such a possibility cannot be discovered in studies examining farm couples only.

Independent male operators are in the best position of all groups in terms of relative debt, with an average debts-to-assets ratio of .16 (averaging together the figures for independent men in Table 10.3, part C). This is considerably lower than that reported by nonindependent men (.27) and women (.25) and somewhat below that for independent women (.20). While unmarried and married independent women operators have similar average debts- to-assets ratios, married independent male farmers have an exceptionally low average ratio of .13. (See Tables 10.2 and 10.3, part C.) Again, marital status differentiates among independent male farmers, but not among independent female farmers.

Family Income

Family income is lower for independent women operators ($19,724 with a standard error of $1,470) than for other operators (Tables 10.2 and 10.3, part C). Three times as many independent women operators as other women are sixty-five or older (Table 10.2, part A), and 43 percent of independent women operators lack a spouse. Thus, many do not have the opportunity to acquire off-farm income from their own or a husband's employment. However, older independent women may have additional income from transfer payments, such as Social Security, that are not included in our measures of family income. As a group, married independent women farmers are less likely than other women to have off-farm employment, but the unmarried women are more likely (part D), despite the large proportion of retirement age women in this group.

Many married independent female farmers, then, work only on the farm, while their husbands have off-farm jobs. Husbands' earnings, on average, are twice those of employed farm women (Table 10.2, part C). Perhaps half of the unmarried women, however, are farming on a "part-time" basis, with an off-farm job in addition to that of running the farm. These women earn somewhat more than other women (see Table 10.2, part C), perhaps because they are working more hours or weeks during the year (something about which we do not know) or because their somewhat higher education (Table 10.2, part A) gives them access to better jobs.

As was expected, despite this labor market activity on the part of unmarried women farmers, family income is higher for married women, independent or not. Among married women, family income does not differ by independent status. Here we are in agreement with other researchers' (such as Coughenour and Swanson's 1983) conclusions that farm households seek to maximize family income rather farm income and that this is accomplished by the most beneficial allocation of on- and off-farm labor activities of the couple. Overall, independent farm women receive lower economic returns from their farms, but the family incomes of those who are married are about the same as other married women's.[8]

Satisfaction with Farming

Independent operators do not differ from others in their enjoyment of farming as a way of life: around 90 percent of people in all categories are satisfied on this dimension. Given the economics of farming, it is not surprising that a smaller proportion are satisfied with farming as a way to earn a living. The pattern of responses to this question does not follow exactly actual farm earnings. Among male operators, unmarried men have the lowest farm income, and they are the least satisfied with this aspect of farming of all groups of operators. Men, despite having a love for farming per se, may judge their success and self-worth in economic terms. In contrast, unmarried women farmers are the most satisfied, despite their low farm (and family) income. They may gain satisfaction from doing this atypical job alone: being in farming may represent a stronger choice for them because it is unusual for a woman. In addition, because unmarried farm women are older and have fewer children in their households, their family economic needs may not be as great as other women's. For this group, farm income represents on average 58 percent of their estimated total family income. In comparison, only a third of married independent farm women's family income, on average, comes from the farm operation; the proportion satisfied with farming as a way to earn a living is lowest among this category of farm women. Nonindependent farm women are closer to the unmarried independent women in satisfaction and proportion of family income from the farm. Proportion of family income that comes from the farm thus may also affect satisfaction with farming as a way to earn a living, with those who have to depend to a larger extent on other income sources less satisfied.

Class, Farm, and Family Characteristics

In terms of their class position, independent farm women tend to have less involvement in capitalist social relations than other farm women (Table 10.2, part D): they are somewhat less likely to have hired labor, more likely to own all their land (as Kalbacher [1985] also found), and less likely to sell their labor power to others. On the other hand, the unmarried women, as mentioned above, are more likely to have off-farm jobs, and the husbands of the married independent women farmers are more likely than other husbands to be employed.

Independent women farmers rely on off-farm employment (by husbands when present) to supplement their lower farm income. Despite somewhat lower debts-to-assets ratios, independent women farmers are not less likely to be debt-free. This is in contrast with male independent farmers (Table 10.3, part D), who not only have lower debts-to-assets ratios than other men, but are also less likely to have any debt (nearly half are debt-free).

Independent male farmers are also less likely to be employed, whatever their marital status, than are operators with a wife involved in farm work (Table 10.3, part D). To some extent this may reflect a wife's earnings from off-farm jobs being contributed to the farm, allowing the husband to entirely devote his time to farm duties. Lodwick and Fassinger's (1979) category "peripheral helper" farm women includes many with off-farm jobs. Unmarried men are least likely to have off-farm jobs, but when employed, they earn more than married men. Thus, to some extent, independent farmers of either sex are somewhat less "proletarianized," which can mean fewer resources for expansion, but also less susceptibility to economic cycles.

Among independent farmers, women differ from men in the character of their product (Tables 10.2 and 10.3, part E). Compared with other men's operations, those of men farming independently have a relatively larger proportion of sales from crops and are more likely to be entirely devoted to crop production. Similar to Kalbacher (1985), we find independent women less involved in crop production. It is possible that women are somewhat more likely to engage in intensive rather than extensive farm activities (livestock in general requiring year-round care, many crops requiring large equipment). Unlike Kalbacher, we do not find an overrepresentation of independent women farmers in the South, but like her, we do find an underrepresentation in the Northcentral area. The discrepancy in regional distributions between Kalbacher and us could be because of the differences in our measures of operators and the nature of production across regions. It is possible that in the South widows are able to continue to control production, such as through controlling a tobacco allotment, because of the relatively small scale and intensive nature of such products. These women would be likely to show up as "operators" in the Census of Agriculture. We have a broader definition of operator (independent farmer) which picks up women running operations under other circumstances elsewhere. Such regional differences are probably also reflected in the average acreage by type of farm operator.

Our categories of women farmers differ in their life-cycle stages, and this is apparent in the nature of the family and family labor structure. Independent women farmers are less likely to have very young children in the home (Table 10.2, part A). Conversely, they are more likely to have an adult son regularly helping with the farm (Table 10.2, part F). In providing farm labor, children are somewhat more important for the married independent women farmers, whereas other household members are more important for the unmarried. For unmarried women, people other than household members, aside from hired labor, are also more likely to be helping with the farm labor (Table 10.2, part F). Thus, while independent farm women do not have the regular farm labor of a husband, they do have, on average, about three other people (including hired hands) who regularly do the farm work with them. Who these people are (household members, children) depends on marital status. On average, nonindependent women are on farms with about four other people doing farm labor: a husband, more hired hands, children, and people other than household members.

CONCLUSIONS

In general, women who operate farms largely on their own get lower economic returns from them than do other farm operators. This is true regardless of marital status. However, married independent farm women often have husbands employed off the farm, so that their average family income is about the same as that of farm women who are not independent farmers. Unmarried farm women, despite their somewhat higher levels of off-farm employment, have lower measured family income than do other groups. Married independent farm men have higher farm earnings than other farmers, while the unmarried men have lower farm earnings, nearly as low as those of independent women farmers. This finding suggests an explanation other than the technological one offered by Coughenour and Swanson (1983) is needed. The unmeasured contribution of a wife's labor, whether in the home or in outside employment, appears to make a significant difference in the economic outcomes of independent farming by men. A wife's labor may not be in farm tasks, but the farm benefits from her presence. As a farm woman in Fink's (1986) Iowa study stated, "A man really *needs* a wife on the farm" (p.207, emphasis in original). In comparison, the economic value of a husband comes in self- employment on the farm or in paid off-farm employment. His presence is important to family income, but only his farm labor appears to contribute to farm income. Coughenour and Swanson's (1983) argument about the importance of men's productivity on the farm for farm earnings makes sense when operations of farm couples are compared, but when unmarried men are also studied, farm productivity varies among men by marital status. Women's contributions to farm productivity do indeed appear to be underestimated in conventional measures, as Reimer (1986) and others have argued.

Married men whose wives are not doing daily farm work seem to have not only profitable but also viable farms. Their wives may have contributed farm labor earlier in the marriage, as well as off-farm income in 1980. Some women prefer not to do farm work unless they need to and are glad to get out of it when the farm makes a profit (Kohl 1976). On the other hand, Elbert (1982) argues that this choice may be the husband's: when the farm is prosperous enough, he chooses to organize farm labor so that he can have more control over production, even hiring outside labor to exclude the wife.

Whatever the reason for the wife's absence from farm work, married independent farm men are one of the groups most satisfied with farming as a way to make a living. They may now be reaping the benefits of past involvement in credit and labor markets. The other group most satisfied is unmarried independent women farmers. Their high level of satisfaction despite their low economic returns may be a result of the contribution of the farm operation to family income and possibly of their strong commitment to farming. They may have faced more problems in continuing farming than have men. Their relatively low average debts-to-assets ratio could be the result of not being able to get credit. Many of them need to work off the farm to supplement their farm income or even to keep the farm going. Yet they continue farming. For them, the satisfaction in farming may come from meeting the challenge of being a "woman farmer." While some married women independent farmers also make the choice to farm alone (with the husband uninvolved in the enterprise), it seems more likely that they are playing a part in a family (or husband's) decision about how to allocate family labor.

Although we defined women farming without a husband's labor as "independent," we found that they often are not alone. They use household and family labor in running the farm. They are more likely than other women to have an adult son in the household helping on the farm. People from outside the household who regularly do work and help with decisions also are important, especially for the unmarried women. These helpers could include adult children and other relatives outside the household. These data and the data on independent male farmers show the importance of family or friends' labor flexibility in the farm labor structure. At the same time, independent women farmers have fewer helpers (hired or otherwise) than do farm operations of other women. Their lower farm income may reflect this fact.

The number of farms has declined over this century and dependence of farm families on outside income increased. Women are contributing to the preservation of the family farm in their roles as farm helpers and income earners, but also as farm operators. In some cases, the woman takes over much of the farm management and labor while her husband goes into off-farm labor markets, but in other cases, a woman committed to farming continues the farm even without a spouse. Such women's farms are relatively small and contribute only a small proportion of farm output. However, they may be helping keep the land in farming for future generations (Fink 1986; Russell et al. 1985). It seems often that when a certain kind of work pays off (economically), men do it; when it does not, women do it. If family farms survive, we may continue to see increases in the proportion of farms run by women. If the family farm disappears (which Friedland [1987] believes is likely), women may lose their positions as operators and any influence in family or community life that accompanied such positions (Fink 1986; Salamon and Keim 1979). What happens to independent women farmers may be an indicator of what happens to family farming.

TABLES

Table 10.1 *Comparison of Definitions and Data on Farmers*

Source and Data	*Category and Definition*
Decennial Population Censuses	"Farmers and Farm Managers":
1950 2.7% female	Persons principally employed in
1960 4.7% female	these occupations, regardless of
1970 5.0% female	operator status.
1980 9.9% female	
Census of Agriculture	"Farm Operator":
1978 5.2% female	Person with primary responsibility
1982 5.4% female	for running the farm (sex of
	operator not asked until 1978; only
	one operator per farm).
Lodwidk and Fassinger (1979)	"Independent Producer":
N=66	Major laborer and manager.
Independent 2% of women	"Agricultural Partner":
Partner 15% of women	Coexecutor of labor and
	management.
1980 National Farm Women Survey	"Independent Operator":
16.4% of men	*Male.* Does not have a wife *or* has
9.2% of women	a wife who never does farm tasks,
	except errands and gardening.

Source: Adapted from Tigges and Rosenfeld (1987)

Table 10.2 *Description of Farm Women by Whether They Are Independent Operators:[a] Means (s. e.)[b]*

	Married Independent Operator (N=125)	Unmarried Independent Operator (N=95)	Not Independent Operator (N=2277)
A. Demographic/Family Characteristics			
Age	48.94	55.50	46.89
	(1.14)	(1.46)	(.26)
Over 65 (1=yes, 0=no)	.13	.24	.06
	(.03)	(.05)	(.005)

Table 10.2 *(continued)*

	Married Independent Operator (N=125)	Unmarried Independent Operator (N=95)	Not Independent Operator (N=2277)
Education (1=1-8th grade; 8=Ph.D, M.D. or other professional degree)	3.64 (.16)	3.86 (.19)	3.54 (.03)
Race (1=white, 0=non-white)	.95 (.02)	.97 (.02)	.98 (.003)
% of life lived/worked on farm	58.10 (3.16)	63.44 (2.98)	62.90 (.63)
Total children ever had (ever-married women only – includes step-children, adopted children)	3.99 (.24)	3.04 (.24)	3.32 (.04)
Any children < 6 years (1=yes, 0=no)	.08 (.03)	.05 (.02)	.17 (.008)
# children currently < 6 years	.13 (.04)	.08 (.04)	.24 (.01)
Any children 6-17 years (1=yes, 0=no)	.53 (.05)	.25 (.05)	.45 (.01)
# children 6-17 years not regularly doing farm work	.41 (.07)	.21 (.06)	.40 (.02)
B Relationship to Farm			
% farm tasks does regularly	45.24 (2.39)	47.49 (3.01)	27.66 (.43)
% farm tasks does at least occasionally	65.39 (2.34)	65.45 (3.10)	51.38 (.53)
% farm decisions makes alone	11.23 (2.19)	37.29 (4.26)	.95 (.15)
% farm decisions makes alone or jointly	66.69 (3.19)	75.68 (3.79)	45.28 (.77)
Other nonspouse decision makers (1=yes, 0=no)	.19 (.04)	.41 (.05)	.26 (.009)
Own name on land deed or rental contract (1=yes, 0=no)	.90 (.03)	.87 (.04)	.79 (.009)
Could run operation without husband (only currently married) (1=yes, 0=no)	.83 (.03)	- -	.58 (.01)
Is one of main operators (1=yes, 0=no)	1.00 (.00)	.80 (.04)	.52 (.01)
C. Economic Outcomes And Satisfaction			
1979 net farm income (negative values coded 0) (000's)	7.707 (1.48)	8.822 (1.88)	13.286 (.70)
Farm debts-to-assets ratio	.21 (.03)	.19 (.03)	.25 (.01)
Total farm value (000's)	231.717 (41.67)	251.945 (31.03)	315.712 (13.19)
Total farm debt (000's)	45.89 (15.94)	35.158 (7.85)	52.640 (3.11)

Table 10.2 *(continued)*

	Married Independent Operator (N=125)	Unmarried Independent Operator (N=95)	Not Independent Operator (N=2277)
Own 1979 off-fram income (000's)	7.006	10.878	8.110
(those with nonzero response)	(.74)	(1.65)	(.29)
Husband's 1979 off-farm income			
(000's) (husband reported with	18.661	-	16.714
nonzero income)	(1.37)	-	(.55)
Family income (net farm income			
plus own income plus husband's	23.179	15.074	25.124
income) (000's)	(1.96)	(2.08)	(.81)
Satisfaction with farming as a way			
of life (1=very of somewhat	.94	.94	.92
satisfied, 0=other)	(.02)	(.02)	(.006)
Satisfaction with farming as a way			
to make living (1=very or	.47	.72	.64
somewhat satisfied, 0=other)	(.05)	(.05)	(.01)

D. Class Characteristics
Labor:

No hired hands (1=yes, 0=no)	.62	.58	.55
	(.04)	(.05)	(.01)
# hired hands (including 0)	1.43	1.57	1.95
	(.49)	(.40)	(.11)
No debt (1=yes, 0=no)	.35	.39	.37
	(.05)	(.06)	(.01)

Tenancy:

Own all land (1=yes, 0=no)	.65	.73	.55
	(.04)	(.05)	(.01)
Rent all land (1=yess, 0=no)	.03	.07	.08
	(.02)	(.03)	(.006)
Neither own nor rent	.02	.46	.38
(1=yes, 0=no)	(.01)	(.009)	(.004)

Off-farm work:

Had off-farm job 1979-80	.24	.46	.38
(1=yes, 0=no)	(.04)	(.05)	(.01)
Has husband with off-job (only	.57	-	.37
currently married) (1=yes, 0=no)	(.05)	-	(.01)

E. Other Farm Characteristics

Total acres	364.06	316.50	901.76
	(88.26)	(86.28)	(87.24)
Percent of sales from crops	50.62	48.37	54.22
	(5.08)	(4.80)	(.99)
All sales from crops (1=yes, 0=no)	.37	.28	.34
	(.06)	(.05)	(.01)

Table 10.2 *(continued)*

	Married Independent Operator (N=125)	Unmarried Independent Operator (N=95)	Not Independent Operator (N=2277)
Region:			
Northeast	.31	.32	.25
	(.04)	(.05)	(.009)
Northcentral	.20	.19	.28
	(.04)	(.04)	(.009)
South	.22	.21	.22
	(.04)	(.04)	(.009)
West	.27	.28	.25
	(.04)	(.05)	(.009)
F. Farm Labor Structure (other than hired hands)			
# children 6-17 who help	.58	.25	.49
	(.09)	(.06)	(.02)
Son ≥ 18 who helps (1=yes, 0=no)	.21	.16	.13
	(.04)	(.04)	(.007)
# other household members who	.07	.24	.08
regularly do farm work	(.03)	(.05)	(.007)
Other, nonhousehold regular workers	.21	.38	.28
(1=yes, 0=no)	(.04)	(.05)	(.009)
# other, nonhousehold regular	.36	.72	.56
workers (including 0)	(.08)	(.12)	(.03)
Total (including husband)	1.24	1.37	2.22
	(.14)	(.13)	(.04)

a An independent woman operator either (1) has no husband present, or (2) has a husband not regularly involved in day-to-day farm work, and the woman considers herself one of the main farm operators.
b Based on weighted data.

Table 10.3 *Description of Farm Men by Whether They Are Independent Operators:[a] Means (s. e.)[b]*

	Married Independent Operator (N=125)	Unmarried Independent Operator (N=95)	Not Independent Operator (N=2277)
A. Demographic/Family Characteristics			
Age	54.18	49.75	48.94
	(1.54)	(2.19)	(.58)
Over 65 (1=yes, 0=no)	.14	.18	.11
	(.04)	(.06)	(.01)
Education (1=1-8th grade; 8=Ph.D,	3.19	3.26	3.48
M.D. or other professional degree)	(.21)	(.24)	(.08)

Table 10.3 *(continued)*

	Married Independent Operator (N=125)	Unmarried Independent Operator (N=95)	Not Independent Operator (N=2277)
Race (1=white, 0=non-white)	.93	.98	.96
	(.03)	(.02)	(.009)
% of life lived/worked on farm	73.79	73.85	70.87
	(3.39)	(4.13)	(1.37)
B Relationship to Farm			
% farm decisions makes alone	75.21	76.21	50.37
	(4.50)	(5.91)	(1.78)
% farm decisions makes alone	94.67	97.04	96.84
or jointly	(2.43)	(2.10)	(.56)
Other nonspouse decision	.28	.31	.21
makers (1=yes, 0=no)	(.06)	(.07)	(.02)
Could run operation without wife	.95	-	(.92)
(only currently married)	(.03)	-	(.01)
(1=yes, 0=no)			
Wife's % of farm tasks done at	10.83	-	54.53
least occasionally (only	(.90)	-	(1.13)
those with wife present)			
C. Economic Outcomes And Satisfaction			
1979 net farm income (negative	17.140	9.053	12.016
values coded 0) (000's)	(2.95)	(1.63)	(1.12)
Farm debts-to-assets ratio	.13	.22	.27
	(.03)	(.04)	(.02)
Total farm value (000's)	364.237	205.272	365.658
	(60.55)	(24.66)	(28.99)
Total farm debt (000's)	56.092	36.789	77.018
	(23.76)	(11.62)	(7.83)
Own 1979 off-fram income (000's)	14.360	40.954	20.176
(those with nonzero response)	(1.61)	(29.27)	(1.17)
Satisfaction with farming as a way			
of life (1=very of somewhat	.93	.92	.89
satisfied, 0=other)	(.03)	(.04)	(.01)
Satisfaction with farming as a way			
to make living (1=very or	.70	.49	.58
somewhat satisfied, 0=other)	(.06)	(.07)	(.02)
D. Class Characteristics			
No debt (1=yes, 0=no)	.58	.34	.30
	(.07)	(.07)	(.02)
Off-farm work:			
Had off-farm job 1979-80	.43	.23	.50
(1=yes, 0=no)	(.06)	(.06)	(.02)

Table 10.3 *(continued)*

	Married Independent Operator (N=125)	Unmarried Independent Operator (N=95)	Not Independent Operator (N=2277)
E. Other Farm Characteristics			
Total acres	883.81	605.73	1427.55
	(215.93)	(443.78)	(338.74)
Percent of sales from crops	68.31	60.35	52.95
	(5.62)	(6.49)	(2.08)
All sales from crops (1=yes, 0=no)	.51	.43	.32
	(.07)	(.08)	(.02)
Region:			
Northeast	.22	.31	.28
	(.05)	(.07)	(.02)
Northcentral	.21	.36	.29
	(.05)	(.07)	(.02)
South	.40	.17	.19
	(.06)	(.06)	(.02)
West	.17	.17	.25
	(.05)	(.06)	(.02)

a   An independent woman operator is one who (1) has no wife, or (2) has a wife who never does listed farm tasks (except errands and gardening).
b   Based on weighted data.

NOTES

[1]Authorship is alphabetical. The authors are grateful for the support of the Carolina Population Center and the helpful comments of Gary Green. This research was supported in part by NICHD, National Research Service Award 5 T32 HD07168 from the Center for Population Research.

[2]Coughenour and Swanson do not actually measure "performance" in standard economic ways. That is, they do not consider outcomes relative to inputs. Instead, they have an input (acreage) and an outcome (farm sales) as dependent variables and consider both as indicators of performance. True performance would be sales per acre.

[3]This question had been included to identify independent women farmers, with the expectation that at most around 10 percent would say they were main operators, but 55 percent of the NORC women replied "yes." (See Rosenfeld 1985, chap. 7.)

[4]Although 155 women and forty-one men indicated that their operations had net losses in 1979, only twenty-nine women and eleven men were able or willing to specify how great these losses were. To minimize missing data, we coded all

negative farm incomes as 0. In the analysis, we also excluded a few outliers on this and the other variables.

[5]We recognize that not all will agree with Mooney's definition of a simple commodity producer as one who retains surplus value within the household (pays no rent or interest and has no contract production or off- farm work), controls investment and the means of production, and has no control over the labor power of others. Friedmann (1981), for example, argues that the major defining characteristic of simple commodity production is the combination of ownership and labor in enterprises subject to the law of value. Simple commodity production has no class relations within the enterprise, according to Friedmann, and it almost invariably involves family rather than individual labor. The participation of family members in off- farm work to expand production, or the hiring of seasonal help on the farm, does not seem to disqualify an operation from simple commodity production in Friedmann's theory.

[6]To test whether differences between groups are more than just random sampling fluctuations, one can use a t statistic:

$$t = (mean_1 - mean_2)/ \text{ square root } (s.e.1^2 + s.e.2^2).$$

With large samples, a t value of about 1.96 or more indicates that the difference in means is (statistically) significantly different from 0 in either direction (Hays 1981). A value of 1.65 indicates a statistically significant difference in a given direction. We used t-tests (results not shown) to guide our discussion of group differences.

[7]Note that the measure of involvement in farm tasks and decisions gauges the types of activities in which a woman takes part, not how many or for how many hours. Some women with relatively low levels of involvement by our measures may spend large amounts of time on specialized tasks or decisions. (See Rosenfeld 1985, chaps. 3 and 4.)

[8]One problem with the comparisons for women is that a large amount of data is missing on net farm income, assets, and debts. Thirty-three percent of the women did not give net farm income; 38 percent, total farm value; and 23 percent, total farm debt. The women who provided this information are different from other women. For example, they are more involved in their operations' tasks and decision making. To see whether this selection influenced our results, we followed a procedure developed by Ray, Berk, and Bielby (1981), using logistic regression to predict the presence of data on net farm income or on assets and debts, then using the coefficients from the logits to calculate predicted probabilities of having these data. We included this predicted probability in regression equations for women's net farm income, debts-to-assets ratio, and family income (Tigges and Rosenfeld 1987). Even with this control for selectivity, the farms of independent women operators differ significantly from those of other women in terms of their net farm income, debts-to-assets ratio, and family income. (Not only did fewer men have data missing on these variables, but also it was not possible with their data to develop a logit equation with any predictive power for the presence of these data.)

BIBLIOGRAPHY

Buttel, Frederick H., and Gilbert W. Gillespie, Jr. 1984. "The Sexual Division of Farm Household Labor: An Exploratory Study of the Structure of On-Farm and Off-Farm Labor Allocation among Farm Men and Women." *Rural Sociology* 49 (2): 183-209.

Coughenour, C. Milton, and Louis Swanson. 1983. "Work Statuses and Occupations of Men and Women in Farm Families and the Structure of Farms." *Rural Sociology* 48 (1): 23-43.

Deseran, Forrest A., William W. Falk, and Pamela Jenkins. 1984. "Determinants of Earnings of Farm Families in the U.S." *Rural Sociology* 49 (2): 210-29.

Elbert, Sarah. 1982. "'The Farmer Takes a Wife, the Wife Takes a Child': Women in American Farm Families." Cornell University, Ithaca, N.Y. Photocopy.

Fink, Deborah. 1986. *Open Country, Iowa: Rural Women, Tradition, and Change.* Albany: State University of New York Press.

Flora, Cornelia B. 1981. "Farm Women, Farming Systems, and Agricultural Structure: Suggestions for Scholarship." *The Rural Sociologist* 1 (Nov.): 383-87.

Friedland, William H. 1987. "Women and Agriculture: A State of the Art Assesment." Paper presented at the annual meeting of the American Sociological Association, 17-21 Aug., Chicago, Ill.

Friedmann, Harriet. 1981 "The Family Farm in Advanced Capitalism: Outline of a Theory of Simple Commodity Production in Agriculture." Paper presented at the annual meeting of the American Sociological Association, 24-28 Aug., Toronto, Canada.

Geisler, Charles C., William F. Waters, and Katrina L. Eadie. 1985. "The Changing Structure of Female Agricultural Land Ownership, 1946 and 1978." *Rural Sociology* 50 (1): 74-87.

Gladwin, Christina. 1985. "The Increase in Women's Farming: A Response to Structural Change." Gainesville, Fl.: Department of Food and Resource Economics, University of Florida, Bulletin 66.

Haney, Wava G. 1983. "Farm Family and the Role of Women." In *Technology and Social Change in Rural Areas*, ed. Gene Summers, 179-193. Boulder, Colo.: Westview Press.

Hays, William L. 1981. *Statistics.* 3d ed. New York: Holt, Rinehart, & Winston.

Jones, Calvin, and Rachel A. Rosenfeld. 1981. "American Farm Women: Findings from a National Survey." Chicago: National Opinion Research Center, Report 130.

Kalbacher, Judith Z. 1985. "A Profile of Female Farmers in America." RDRR-45. Washington, D.C.: United States Department of Agriculture, Economic Research Service.

Kohl, Seena B. 1976. *Working Together: Women and Family in Southwestern Saskatchewan.* Toronto: Holt, Rinehart, & Winston of Canada.

Lodwick, Dora, and Polly Fassinger. 1979. "Variations in Agricultural Production Activities of Women on Family Farms." Paper presented at the annual meeting of the Rural Sociological Society, 24-26 Aug., Burlington, Vt.

Mann, Susan A., and James M. Dickinson. 1978. "Obstacles to the Development of a Capitalist Agriculture." *Journal of Peasant Studies* 5: 466-81.

Maret, Elizabeth, and James H. Copp. 1982. "Some Recent Findings on the Economic Contributions of Farm Women." *The Rural Sociologist* 2 (2): 112-15.

Mooney, Patrick H. 1983. "Toward a Class Analysis of Midwestern Agriculture." *Rural Sociology* 48 (4): 563-84.

_____. 1986. "The Political Economy of Credit in American Agriculture." *Rural Sociology* 51 (4): 449-70.

Moore, Keith M., and Eugene A. Wilkening. 1982. "The Allocation of Family Labor On and Off the Farm: Its Conditions and Consequences." Paper presented at the annual meeting of the Rural Sociological Society, Aug., San Francisco, Calif.

Pearson, Jessica. 1979. "Note on Female Farmers." *Rural Sociology* 44 (1): 189-200.

Ray, Subhash, Richard Berk, and William Bielby. 1981. "Correcting Sample Selection Bias for Bivariate Logistic Distribution of Disturbances." University of California, Santa Barbara. Photocopy. (Revision of a paper presented at the annual meeting of the American Statistical Association, 1980.)

Reimer, Bill. 1986. "Women as Farm Labor." *Rural Sociology* 51 (2): 143-55.

Rosenfeld, Rachel A. 1985. *Farm Women: Work, Farm, and Family in the United States.* Chapel Hill, N.C.: University of North Carolina Press.

Russell, Candyce S., Charles L. Griffin, Catherine Scott Flinchbaugh, Michael J. Martin, and Raymond B. Atilano. 1985. "Coping Strategies Associated with Intergenerational Transfer of the Family Farm." *Rural Sociology* 50 (3): 361-76.

Sachs, Carolyn E. 1983. *The Invisible Farmers: Women in Agricultural Production.* Totowa, N.J.: Rowman & Allanheld.

Salamon, Sonya, and Ann Mackey Keim. 1979. "Land Ownership and Women's Power in a Midwestern Farming Community." *Journal of Marriage and the Family* 41 (Feb.): 109-19.

Scholl, Kathleen. 1983. "Classification of Women as Farmers: Economic Implications." *Family Economics Review* 4 (Oct.): 8-17.

Tigges, Leann M., and Rachel A. Rosenfeld. 1987. "Independent Farming: Correlates and Consequences for Women and Men." *Rural Sociology* 52 (3): 345-64.

FARM WOMEN
AND RESOURCE CONTROL

11

FARM CONTINUITY
AND FEMALE LAND INHERITANCE:
A FAMILY DILEMMA

Sonya Salamon
Karen Davis-Brown[1]

Farm families planning intergenerational farm transfers confront a dilemma: how to treat all members equitably without destroying the farm in the process. Since female heirs typically do not farm, the dilemma focuses on how to respect the rights of daughters while maintaining enterprise continuity. Historically, some ethnic groups resolved the problem by giving land only to sons and giving daughters cash or other resources. Today, most farm families share the American value for treating all children alike. This essay examines solutions to this dilemma drawing upon field data from two Illinois groups that share similar soils, German backgrounds, and farming commitment, but hold differing religious ideologies for governing the family. Both groups, Mennonites and Apostolic Christians, are committed to an agrarian way of life and equal treatment of heirs, yet they diverge in their beliefs about female family status and control of female inherited land. Because they share many important characteristics yet differ in their treatment of women and land ownership patterns, these small ethnoreligious agrarian groups provide insights into how the choices of female heirs influence family-farm viability.

REVIEW OF THE LITERATURE

Female heirs present a particular problem for family-farm continuity. A son is a potential farmer, but a daughter may either marry a farmer or marry a non-farmer and leave agriculture. Either way, any land she inherits could be lost to the natal family before the next intergenerational transfer (Keim 1976; Salamon and Keim 1979). Among many American farm families, continuity has become secondary to the goal of equality in intergenerational transfers of farm resources (Salamon, Gengenbacher, and Penas 1986). According to Fink (1986), this reflects a general shift of commitment from the extended farm family to the nuclear family that occurred after World War II; individual desires came to be emphasized over family priorities. The shift reflects the emergent societal ideal for providing each child with equal resources and an equal opportunity in the world (Farber 1973) and an emergent child-rearing philosophy minimizing differences arising from age, sex, or education (Rosenfield 1979). The changing customs resulted in farm daughters inheriting equally with sons.

Despite equal inheritance values and the enhancement of women's right to hold property, the amount of farmland controlled by women in the nation has not increased substantially. As an illustration, only 17 percent of Illinois farmland is owned by women (Geisler, Waters, and Eadie 1985). No explanation for this seemingly illogical state of affairs has been posited. Inheritance may not be the key, but what women do with inherited land, or their discretionary freedom, might account for the continued dominance by male owners. For example, an early Wisconsin study documented a process whereby owner-operatorship moved out of families as intergenerational transfers were influenced by cumulative "natural" circumstances such as timing of retirement and children leaving the farm. The consequences of equal inheritance by both the farming son and the nonfarm siblings were generally negative for the heir to the family occupation (Salter 1943). Thus, the socialization of women, as a variation on a Salter natural circumstance, may shape a woman's commitment toward herself versus the family – as symbolized by the farm.

Household studies err in tending to assume a consensus model; the household is viewed as unanimously sharing collective goals which are pursued by all for a common good (Yanagisako 1984). Cross-family patterns emerge from male and female negotiations, necessitated by the fact that these classes of individuals possess personal goals and imperatives that challenge those of the kin group (Laslett 1984; Yanagisako 1984). By combining kinship and work relationships, farm families highlight the interplay between the goals an individual member holds and those the family has for enterprise functioning (Bennett 1982). How the outcome among these sets of goals is determined derives from the family cultural context – occupation, ethnicity, and religion; resultant patterns, such as those relating to inheritance and land tenure, are products of interchanges between the collective and its individual members (Laslett 1984).

Farm family goals, management strategies, and family organization are correlated with ethnic descent among midwestern farmers (Salamon 1985a, 1985b). Yeoman goals, often held by groups of German origin, define agricultural success as intergenerational continuity of the family farm and use risk-aversive financial practices. Yeomen possess a strong commitment to farming as a way of life; this agrarian ethic sometimes also serves as the means to an end such as preserving religious or ethnic identity (cf. Maurer 1925) or rural values (Davis-Brown, Salamon, and Surra 1987). Women, whose feminine socialization often symbolizes religious or ethnic ideals (Michaelson and Goldschmidt 1971), can by their decisions about inherited land help or hinder the realization of yeoman goals. Thus, farm households can be viewed as a "knot of individual interests" (Laslett 1984), daughters' interests potentially conflicting with family-continuity interests when the household decides what to do with inherited farm resources. The daughters' land is likely to pass out of the natal family. How the daughters are socialized is therefore a critical variable in the continued viability of the parental farm.

In this study we first describe the religious ideologies and yeoman agricultural goals of two Anabaptist sects. Next we delineate variations in the position of women in the family and on the farm in relation to how religious beliefs affect daughters' handling of the parental farm resources they inherit. Finally, we discuss the social and economic implications for each solution.

METHODOLOGY AND SAMPLE

Davis-Brown lived in a north central Illinois agricultural county carrying out the study from January to October 1985, examining the impact of family factors on the local land market. A promise of anonymity to our informants requires the disguising of the county and the communities. Former owners of land transferred in three distinct areas of the county (eleven of twenty-nine townships), conducted between 1979 and 1984, as reflected in the Illinois Department of Revenue Real Estate Transfer Tax Record, constituted the sample interviewed. Davis-Brown also conducted semi-structured interviews with local clergy, business people, lawyers, realtors, farmers, and other informants.

We compare two of the three areas. Constituting seven townships, the two areas were selected because they enabled us to hold soils constant (the soils are the most productive in the county, but not in the state) and because they were dominated by different Protestant sects of Germanic origin – Apostolic Christians and Mennonites – that embrace a common yeoman ideology but differ in their treatment of women. Both groups are comprised of several churches or conferences, spanning a socially liberal to conservative continuum; our involvement was with the larger, more liberal subgroups.

Because the original research design focused on land transfers, we did not survey the many communities constituting each area, and thus we failed to obtain desirable group-level statistical data. This problem is compounded by census data aggregated at the township level that tends to mask the internal variations we are seeking. Thus, we could not determine what proportion of the survey area's population each religion represented. However, the areas we term Apostolic Christian and Mennonite did show up as predominantly German in the population census – 58 and 64 percent, respectively (U.S. Bureau of the Census 1980). We obtained familial demographic data from church clergy regarding the characteristics of congregations, family size, and the proportion of families in farming. We used county histories, local newspapers, and religious documents shared by families and others to provide a historical context for our qualitative findings. Plat maps were examined to trace differences in religious-ethnic ownership trends over the past ninety years. Genealogical sources (principally Smith 1956) were used to establish plat-map surname ethnicity.

Most of our data on women derives from local informants and from qualitative interviews and participant observation with four families – two in the Apostolic Christian area and two in the Mennonite area. Each family was extended by two or three generations. The four families each represent twenty to forty contact hours, spaced over four to seven visits. The operations of this sample ranged from 440 to 700 acres – in the middle range of Illinois farms, but slightly larger than the county average of 342 acres (Salamon and Davis-Brown 1986). The Mennonite operations clustered at the smaller end, and the Apostolic Christian, toward the larger. The operations were of the part owner category;

most rental land was obtained from relatives. Davis-Brown participated in every-day family activities and attended church regularly with families, gaining in-sights into the relationship between agricultural values, religious beliefs, and the socialization of women.

RELIGIOUS BELIEFS AND LAND TENURE

Mennonites and Apostolic Christians are similar but unrelated Anabaptist sects that emerged in seventeenth-century Germany and nineteenth-century Switzerland, respectively. Their practice of baptizing adult believers conscious of their choice (rather than infants as advocated by the established churches) and their refusal to participate in government or the military led to persecution and subsequent immigration to the United States. Exclusive groups seeking to sepa-rate themselves from the sinful world, they chose farming as an occupation that enabled them to maintain isolation and therefore a simple lifestyle, antimaterial-istic values, and a cohesive group identity.

Historic commonalities of these theologically conservative groups, based on religious writings are: (1) a strong division of labor according to gender in church and household, with men as the sole occupants of leadership positions; (2) proscriptions against extensive socializing or marriage with nonmembers; (3) elected, sometimes unpaid, ministers and elders with little or no formal training; and (4) formal, group discipline of errant members, and the tendency to split churches rather than accept internal differences when faced with divisive issues (Kauffman and Harder 1975; Klopfenstein 1984).

Churches and sects can be positioned on a continuum according to the rela-tive acceptance (church) or rejection (sect) of the dominant social environment and culture (Johnson 1972). Both Apostolic Christians and Mennonites have historically been sectarian. Nonetheless, in their struggles to strike a balance be-tween belief and survival in twentieth- century American society, Mennonites have been more open to dominant cultural influences, so that they are currently similar to mainstream Protestant churches in their religious behaviors and everyday lives. Meanwhile, Apostolic Christians have succeeded in retaining a closed society where church doctrine limits and channels behavior, thereby maintaining group distinctness. Over the century since settlement in Illinois, re-stricted consumption, the equation of work and Christian virtue, and a commit-ment to mutual assistance have produced prosperity for both Mennonites and Apostolic Christians (Weber 1958: 155-83).

Apostolic Christians, Religion, and Farming
Although Apostolic Christians were artisans in Switzerland (Ruegger 1949), they became farmers after migration to the United States. Early in the 1860s, the group established a church in rural central Illinois. According to a church elder, farming is a means to an end: "A way of life that's helped us to preserve our be-liefs. It's conducive to our values. . . . I'm not saying you have to farm to be saved. We have plenty of members who don't farm. . . . Farming has helped preserve our way of life." He estimated that their church was once almost all farmers, but out of the two hundred households it still holds, about one hundred

households farm. In the half of the congregation that farms, seventy- five are under fifty years of age, indicating that young people are still entering farming.

The church retains a patriarchal structure, segregating women and men and with male leaders elected by the congregation. Women teach only lower-level Sunday school classes. Daily family life is also structured according to religious ideals. Homes reflect the sect's life of self-denial; most families reject television, radios, smoking, drinking, or card playing. Head coverings are worn by women at all times as the symbol of their submission to their husbands, in accordance with church teachings (Apostolic Christians of America n.d.), pants are seldom worn.

Apostolic Christian families perceive their agrarian way of life as a means of maintaining religious ideals. A middle-aged farmer recalled rejecting the overtures of a coal company that wanted to mine his farmland: "We just told them we feel we're taking care of that land for our families; for those generations who farmed it before we did. . . . to be good for the next generation." Apostolic Christian parents are committed to successful agricultural succession, with some fathers even establishing small businesses or taking off-farm jobs so that their sons can take over the farm at a relatively young age. Stated an Apostolic Christian in his mid-forties: "My brothers and I, we started this business mainly so our boys could start farming. Why should the son . . . work off the farm, when the father can just as well?" Education was not encouraged by previous generations, and it is still considered useful only for obtaining practical skills such as those appropriate to successful farming. Involvement of children in the family farm is a conscious strategy to help preserve a closed, church-focused community.

Mennonites, Religion, and Farming

In the 1840s, Illinois Mennonite settlements were founded by descendants of eighteenth-century Pennsylvania immigrants from Germany and the Low Countries (Smith 1983). Like the Apostolic Christians, Mennonites view their rural life as furthering religious values, but they are more accepting of fundamental changes occurring in society. According to a minister, "Mennonites have traditionally been a rural people, and they've held values that are easier to maintain in a rural setting. Now that we're becoming . . . less rural we just have to turn our faces to the cities. . . . We can't change it; we just have to look forward." A Mennonite pastor commented on the changes in his congregation:

> Ten or fifteen years ago, I could've said 97 % [were farmers], but now it's only about 25 %. About 60 % of the congregation used to farm, and now they rent their land out and live in town. Only about ten or twelve families farm actively, and many of them are in their fifties. There's only about three [families farming] that are under fifty. I'd say that's pretty true for the other Mennonite churches in this area; for the area as a whole.

According to our survey of local Mennonite ministers, his estimate was accurate: the mean congregation size for the five area churches was seventy-four households with just 38 percent of these farm households; the mean age of farm household heads was fifty-six years, three years older than nonfarmers.

Mennonites espouse a linkage between religious values and agriculture similar to that of Apostolic Christians but focus on a more universal form of stewardship. Observed a Mennonite farmer:

> I don't think it's farming itself [that the church is concerned with preserving] as much as the values that go with farming, the church, the family, and personal relationships. . . . My land is how I make my living, but it's also a national resource. Ultimately it belongs to God, it's just been loaned to me. . . . It's more important how it's being taken care of than who owns it.

Mennonites extend such religious values to cooperative business relationships. One philosophical Mennonite farmer explained, "Mennonites don't have enough of what I call the 'killer instinct,' the competitiveness that the Apostolic Christians do."

Mennonite churches have become more professionalized; they have recently moved to employing full-time ministers formally trained at the national level rather than local elders from among their own ranks (Smith 1983). Local congregations reflect the national democratization of the Mennonite church. Mennonite women play a more active church role than is permitted Apostolic Christian women, serving as committee heads and Sunday school teachers, though in rural areas they are generally not yet accepted as deacons, elders, or pastors. A young Mennonite farmwife expressed satisfaction with this situation: "I don't know why I think that, but I think there's an order in the home and in the church and men should be the leaders." The contrast with the Apostolic Christian situation is that women do have more autonomy and the possibility of being chosen for leadership, so that a structure exists in the Mennonite church that permits women to question and act to affect the church and family.

Land Tenure

Both Mennonites and Apostolic Christians espouse the yeoman goal of agricultural continuity. According to an area banker, "neither of them let any land get away." However, when we examine land transfers and land tenure, critical differences emerge between the areas dominated by the two sects, with implications for continued family-farm viability.

Table 11.1 delineates gradual changes in ethnoreligious land ownership by comparing plat map listings for the areas identified with the Apostolic Christians and Mennonites, respectively. Tract-size figures are conservative because we considered all tracts owned by the same person, if in the same section, a single tract.

The proportion of German owners increased and tract size decreased in both areas over the period from 1893 to 1984, though the change was slightly steeper for the Mennonites. The tendency toward tract fragmentation in association with increased numbers of owners is characteristic of other Illinois yeoman-Germanic groups (Salamon 1985b). Note that land controlled by Germans in the Mennonite area remained almost static over the better part of a century while that in the Apostolic Christian area showed a substantial increase, almost doubling between 1893 and 1949. Though Mennonites arrived in the county twenty years earlier, Apostolic Christians were more aggressive land buyers over the long-term. This contrast has continued into the present. Distinctive management styles are apparent to the religious group members, and to local agricultural professionals. Apostolic Christians are considered "very successful" farmers, typified as astute and "aggressive businessmen." In contrast Mennonites are uniformly called conservative and reputed to be sparing, even stingy, spenders.

Land markets in both areas are said to be tight, as evidenced by the small amount of any added German-owned acres between 1949 and 1984 (Table 11.1). An inability to expand between 1950 and 1984, due to equally persistent yeoman neighbors, led Apostolic Christians to move according to a Mennonite farmer into less competitive, non-German, areas of the county. To test the accuracy of this folk observation on Apostolic Christian expansion, we examined plat maps for twelve sections in two non-German-dominated townships close to both Apostolic Christian and Mennonite areas for changes in ethnic ownership between 1969 and 1984. Non-German ownership remained approximately stable in the area, but German owners more than doubled from nine (1969) to twenty (1984). German controlled land in the area also doubled, at the expense of Yankee (largely English-ethnic) owners, from 13 percent to 26 percent. Of the new German owners, five had recognizable Apostolic Christian surnames; none were Mennonite.

Transfer Tax records between 1979 and 1984, which better document recent expansion, show thirty-three total land transfers in the townships where German invasion occurred. Germans (n = 10) sold a total of 770 acres in contrast to the 2,570 sold by non-Germans (n = 25). Germans (n = 15) bought a total of 1549 acres compared with the 1791 bought by the more numerous non-Germans (n = 19). Proportionately Germans bought more land than they sold. Of the fifteen German buyers, the majority (n = 9) had identifiable Apostolic Christian names. Thus, the folk observation was supported by documented expansion of Apostolic Christians into previously unentered territory.

Over the years, both groups have provided for both farm viability and their daughters' futures. Religious beliefs, carried out by socializing group members to give priority to the interests of the family or those of the individual, cast light upon the land tenure contrasts delineated above.

RELIGION AND SOCIALIZATION OF WOMEN

Apostolic Christians, Religion, and Women

Apostolic Christian family organization reflects that of the church – it is patriarchal and gender-segregated. Women are considered to be under the authority and protection of men, for both guidance and security. For example, one Apostolic Christian farmer whose father died young perceived his duty as that of caring for his widowed mother and unmarried sisters, as well as for his own

TABLE 11.1 *Ethnoreligious Land Tenure Patterns from the Plat Map Record**

	1893	1949	1984	% Change
A. Apostolic Christian Area				
Total owners**	107	122	150	+40
German owners	29	53	83	+35
Average German tract (acres)	141	141	95	-33
% German-controlled area	24	44	47	+96
land (ca. 17,000 total acres)				
Total German acres	4,100	7,492	7,961	+94
B. Mennonite Area				
Total owners**	132	154	196	+48
German owners	75	94	125	+66
Average German tract (acres)	134	105	82	-39
% German-controlled area	58	57	59	+2
land (ca. 17,000 total acres)				
Total German acres	10,042	9,860	10,220	+2

*   Analysis based on a randomly selected sample of twenty-seven sections for each area, representing twenty-five percent of the community area used in the transfer transaction survey. Tract size should not be confused with farm size, which may include many tracts, both owned and rented.

**   Yankees are the other predominate ethnic group, typically being the majority of owners on the early maps and declining to as low as one-third by 1984 in the Apostolic Christian area. Some Irish and a few Scandinavian owners are also represented in both areas.

family: "That left me with a lot of responsibility. . . . I worried if something would happen to me." Only his oldest son, having "grown to manhood," has eased the burden; women could not shoulder the weight.

Church endogamy is required, and extensive visiting among various congregations facilitates marriage links. At marriage, young women tend to enter a patrilocal extended family some distance from their natal home. While extended families are not coresident, father and son usually farm together, so that extensive household cooperation is expected of wives and mothers. Being an in-marrying bride in a patriarchal family reinforces a woman's subordinate position (Michaelson and Goldschmidt 1971).

Because the church values large families, "women watch the calender, but they don't use birth control," explained an Apostolic Christian farmer. According to a church elder, three-quarters of the two hundred households have more than three children. A married woman's mission in the Apostolic Christian church and family is to produce children; pregnancy is a welcome and publicly celebrated event. "What's marriage without children?" exclaimed a mother of a large family.

The mean number of children born to women between the ages of fifteen and forty-four was a larger 2.1 in the Apostolic Christian townships compared with 1.9 in the Mennonite area (U.S. Bureau of the Census 1980). Even local Catholics note Apostolic Christians' fertility. Commented a priest: "They don't try to convert other people. . . . I think their goal is to hold their own. . . . Their church is growing slowly, just because they have large families and most of the children join the church."

Apostolic Christian women are regarded principally as "homemakers" and are not regularly involved in field work; a large family precludes their availability for farm work (Salamon 1982). One Apostolic Christian husband expressed a typically protective view toward women when commenting about his wife, "I don't like a woman . . . doing heavy, dirty work." However, women are involved in the farm operation by coordinating far-flung male family members via phone or CB radio, and by doing the farm operation bookkeeping.

Women's social participation outside the home is circumscribed, consisting of work, church, and child-oriented activities. A local non-Apostolic Christian woman who held home parties to sell domestic items reflected on the outsider view of Apostolic Christian women's economic dependence on their husbands: "Someone will say, 'She couldn't come, her husband wouldn't let her.'. . . Another will come, but her husband only gave her $5."

Many more women than men join the church prior to marriage and thus effectively rule out non-church members as potential mates. Explained an elder, "There's no marriage with nonmembers because of our belief about an unequal yoke. [This refers to a quote by St. Paul that Christians should not be joined by marriage or other partnerships with non-Christians.] If a member decides to marry someone outside the faith, they would leave the church." As a result, there are numerous unmarried women in Apostolic Christian congregations. For example, in the church previously cited, an elder estimated that 20 percent of women in the congregation are unmarried. Family farms have benefited from the celibate women in every generation who contribute household labor and salaries to the family enterprise while living under the control of father or brother.

Mennonites, Religion, and Women

Many Mennonites oppose women with young children working outside the home: "That's not good for a family," said one farmer. However, women's assistance in the fields during busy seasons is accepted as normal, and some women choose heavy involvement. "A lot of women get out in the field and work right alongside their husbands, especially when they don't have any children – even older couples," commented a farmer. We encountered a number of cottage industries that allow women to contribute financially without leaving home. Women reported husbands' willing assistance with household tasks, including baby-sitting and cooking. Such aid exemplifies Mennonite acceptance of gender-role exchanges.

Both men and women receive education in Mennonite families; education is valued as a worthy investment of enterprise profits. A local banker reflected that because the Apostolic Christians have only recently sought higher education for children, that group, "didn't have their own schools. Mennonites, on the other

hand have always encouraged education, and each conference has its own college
. . . and they send their children to these schools." Many Mennonite couples
reported meeting their mates at college, and not feeling constrained by a belief in
religious endogamy.

WOMEN AND LAND

Apostolic Christian Inheritance

Inheritance in Apostolic Christian farm families has twin goals: maintaining economic security and the continuity of a religious way of life. Family
teachings socialize children to hold group welfare and land ownership as high
priorities. Explained a middle-aged farmwife with a large family: "We've tried to
teach our children that we're a family, and that means things aren't always fair.
Sometimes one gets more than the other, then another time the other gets more.
They need to work together for the whole group." Men bear heavy responsibilities to assure security for women; but as nonfarmers with patrilocal residence,
women seem to make the most sacrifices for group welfare priorities. For married women, social and economic security is derived from husbands. For unmarried women, brothers are the males who manage their land and protect them from
the world.

In the past, when an Apostolic Christian husband died first, land was placed
in a life estate for the surviving widow, and eventually transferred in equal undivided shares to children. Siblings were free to determine equity among themselves, but it was assumed that sisters would either rent or sell out to brothers.
Though this custom was followed, large families has made inevitable some
division of land. This transfer pattern has continued to be the norm. An example
is seen in a middle-aged Apostolic Christian farmer who despite his intention to
incorporate the farm "To be fair to the girls," assumes his sons will farm the
land: "Then they can work out with their brothers whether they'll rent to them or
whether the boys will buy their sisters out." Thus, control does not actually re-
side in females even when they inherit land. However the question of ownership
is resolved, fairness is mitigated by a priority for the land to remain undivided
and with the patrilineal line; a woman's husband seldom farms the land she inherits. By not retaining personal control of inherited land, Apostolic Christian
women give up options for self-support and an economic lever for influencing
household politics (Salamon and Keim 1979).

Mennonite Inheritance

Mennonite families are highly committed to fairness among children; they
define fairness as exactly equal treatment. A generation ago, land was passed undivided down to children regardless of gender. Reflected a middle-aged farmer,
"My parents said 'You'll have to figure out what to do with it; work it out
among yourselves'. . . . They did it a good way for them, but it's not the best
way for us." Now fair treatment is equated with individual choice and heirs are
assumed to have complete use or sale autonomy over the land they inherit. An
active farmer explained that division of inherited land is a manifestation of this
priority: "Then if one decides to sell, the others don't have to." This also means

that, unlike Apostolic Christians, when a Mennonite woman inherits land she and her husband, rather than her brother or father, typically farm it.

Mennonites recognize that the land division that occurs with intergenerational transfers, while fair, causes a land fragmentation detrimental to farm efficiency and thus survival. Said a farmer, "Most try to farm the little bit of land they can obtain from family and others, but most just can't manage on such a small amount. A lot do sell out [to siblings]; so only a few in each family can farm." Those heirs not selling out to farming siblings could account for the static situation apparent for the Mennonite area (Table 11.1). More fragmentation can be expected during the next intergenerational transfer from the rising number of German owners prior to 1984, and lack of evidence of expansion into other areas. In the Apostolic Christian area, fewer owners and a more gradual land fragmentation indicate more land turnover within families, suggesting that in this area heirs sell to natal family members.

Mennonites seem acutely concerned with fairness in domains other than land inheritance, so that constant monitoring occurs between farming and nonfarming siblings. When one retired farmer provides labor for his son's operation, he gives the cash equivalent of his labor to the other children "so there won't be any resentment; so everything will be fair." The recipient of a grandmother's largess in the form of gifts for her children told the older woman: "I don't want any trouble because you gave something to our kids and didn't to some others." In some families, the fairness concern prevents current farmers from finding out what parents intend to do with the farm. Talk about the eventual land transfer is avoided so that parents will not think that children are greedy or question parental estate plans.

Socialization related to religious values creates differing priorities for each religious group, despite their shared basic yeoman goals. This is seen particularly in women's discretionary control over inherited land. Mennonites socialize individualistic values in women both in the church and at home, whereas Apostolic Christians train women to be submissive to the interests of farming and male family members. We now turn to the question of how women's discretionary control over land is related to the Apostolic Christian expansionist tendencies on the one hand and the Mennonite static or dwindling land control, on the other.

Women and Land Tenure

Different inheritance customs potentially influence land ownership patterns. Land inherited by Apostolic Christian women remains under the control of the natal family (that is, it is rented or sold to brothers), whereas equally divided Mennonite estates result in women controlling land. We expected the 1979-1984 Transfer Tax records to show greater female ownership in the Mennonite area as a consequence of these distinctive traditions. We did find fewer Apostolic Christian women owners 27 percent of total area owners (n = 41) compared with 34 percent Mennonite (n = 67) – but the difference was not significant. More Mennonite-area tracts were jointly owned (n = 7) compared with Apostolic Christian-area tracts (n = 3), suggesting joint purchases among the more egalitarian Mennonite couples. A partial explanation for the greater than expected

Apostolic Christian-area female owners is perhaps the existence of more women whose land is rented rather than bought by farmer brothers.

As noted previously, celibate Apostolic Christian women help families achieve farming goals by providing natal relatives with land and capital. According to an Apostolic Christian realtor, "a lot of women who own land around here are old maids. . . . They worked all their lives, and they didn't have anything to do with their money. . . . Land was the only investment they believed in. Then they'd rent it to their brothers." A farmer said, "There's one family, there was a couple of boys and about five sisters that never married. They [the men] all work together, buy land together, and their sisters worked too." Unmarried sisters financially help brothers buy land, as well as independently purchasing land for brothers to farm. Although women own the land, control is ceded to the male head of the extended family (Salamon and Keim 1979). In one case, several unmarried sisters were involved in a series of land purchases, trades, and sales that enabled their brothers to consolidate family holdings. One sister interviewed knew little about the land involved – for example, the quality of the soil – and even less about farming, but her earnings provided the capital to undertake family enterprise expansion.

Mennonite women landowners, however, do not give up management prerogatives. An elderly widow whose grandson farms her land is clearly involved in management decisions despite her advanced age. Reported the grandson, "I explain everything I do on her land and how I do it. She understands and asks questions; she has a lot of input especially about government programs. . . . She wants to know what is going on. . . . She doesn't miss much."

Apostolic Christians take an instrumental attitude toward land. It is a means to earn a living and to provide family security; ownership of a particular piece of land is not regarded as sacred. They readily buy, sell, and trade family acreage. A young farmer commented on whether land once purchased was kept in family hands: "Acres do, but not specific tracts. People buy and sell and trade so much, trying to get land closer to home." Married Apostolic Christian women are similarly pragmatic when they sell inherited land to brothers to generate capital for their husband's operation. Mennonites, however, are more deeply attached to particular pieces of land. "Mennonites hang on to land until the last dog dies. They don't sell unless they have to, and then it's to someone in the family," said a local agricultural lender. Neither Mennonite women nor men tend to sell inherited land, even when estate divisions result in very small tracts. As a result, "Most people rent a lot more than they own. They rent from family – aunts, grandmothers, parents," commented a young Mennonite farmer. Women thus contribute to the development of different land tenure patterns for each religious group.

Table 11.2 compares women's position in the Apostolic Christian and Mennonite family and church, and summarizes how these contrasts link with land tenure.

The sheltered way of life that submits women to men's authority and encourages large families to fulfill religious ideals demands that Apostolic Christian males assure family economic security by expanding farm operations to maintain viability. An outsider saw Apostolic Christians as forced to be

TABLE 11.2 *Women's Position According to Ethnoreligious Membership*

	Apostolic Christians	Mennonites
Church teachings	submission to males	equality
Position in church	segregated and subordinate	integrated, some leadership roles
Family hierarchy	patriarchal	egalitarian
Inheritance	joint tenancy	individual shares
Discretionary control over inheritance	limited	complete
Land inherited	bought by or rented to natal family	used by marital family
Family size	large	controlled
Involvement in farm	minimal	by choice
Employment after birth of first child	none	some self-employment

competitive because of their commitment to large families: "I think they . . . have pressure to get more land because they have bigger families and they want their kids to stay on the farm." Mennonites advocate family cooperation but also value individual autonomy and equality between the sexes. Thus, female Mennonite farm family members are not as pressured as their Apostolic Christian counterparts to place natal farm continuity above personal or marital family rights and desires. Both groups keep land in the family, but how families make use of this capital differs. Apostolic Christians who farm are provided with a predictable amount of land and often additional capital from unmarried sisters. This has provided the basis for continued expansion in contrast to the continually divided land base that the Mennonites face.

DISCUSSION

Yeoman farming goals are demonstrable for both the Apostolic Christians and the Mennonites, both of whom view farming as a way of life permitting the realization of religious and family ideals. Nonetheless, greater expansion, slightly less fragmentation, and, by implication, more viable farms occur among Apostolic Christians. A major contrast between the groups is how women are treated, as a consequence of religious attitudes regarding equality between the sexes and the primacy of individual or group welfare. The religious values affecting the socialization of women have led to differing solutions for the dilemma of farm viability versus equal treatment of children. Consistent with religious tenets, Apostolic Christians resolve the dilemma in favor of the family farm; among Mennonites, individual women's rights are favored.

Apostolic Christians, in their submission of women to men and of individuals to the welfare of the family group, resemble a family model more typical of past generations. Yet their economic practices firmly integrate Apostolic Christians in the market, making them resemble individualistic entrepreneurs as they meet yeoman goals. The Mennonite emphasis on equal treatment of the sexes integrates them more firmly into the wider society that favors a family model placing individual welfare and the nuclear family above that of a group or extended family. Mennonite yeoman farming choices, particularly in regard to the equal division, lack of consolidation, and sale of family land, threaten farm viability in spite of the sect's agrarian ideology.

As long as males are perceived as occupational heirs to the family farm enterprise, equal treatment of men and women in intergenerational land transfers will demonstrate that what is good for women as a class of individuals in the family is not necessarily the best policy for insuring farm continuity. More than Mennonites, Apostolic Christians achieve the yeoman goals of retaining an agrarian way of life and of maintaining the farm operation through the intergenerational transfer process. Apostolic Christians are also considered more successful farmers in the judgement of local informants and their expansion into non-Apostolic Christian areas indicates an ability to remain competitive through accumulating more land. Apostolic Christian women have less autonomy than their Mennonite counterparts, but the closed society in which Apostolic Christians function rewards female submission of discretionary land control to male kin with social and financial security. Mennonite women possess more autonomy and control over whether to sell and who farms their land than do Apostolic Christian women. Due largely to this, Mennonite farms are smaller. Aging church congregations with diminishing numbers of farmers suggest that the priority for individual choice has resulted in entire families moving out of agriculture and educated young Mennonites choosing other occupations.

This examination of religious ideology and farm family practices demonstrates that individualism and equality, when taken to their logical conclusion in the family context, can endanger the achievement of yeoman agricultural goals. Apostolic Christian women have sacrificed their autonomy to assure security and family farm continuity. Mennonites have begun to realize what Apostolic Christians have always practiced: "Being fair is not always being equal, and equal is not always the best way to go" (as expressed by a Mennonite farmer). To give equal shares of land to the farming son and his nonfarming siblings, expecting the farmer to buy equipment and maintain continuity is now regarded as unfair and defeating of yeoman continuity goals. Threats to Mennonite agricultural continuity are rooted in women heirs socialized to place individual interests before those of the natal farm; with many of them marrying nonfarmers, the potential for family land being sold is greater. These two religious groups reflect the dilemma facing families in agriculture – individual versus enterprise welfare.

The negative effects of each resolution, whether in land tenure or personal autonomy, are sobering in their social and economic costs to women family members.

NOTE

[1]This study was carried out with the support of U.S. Department of Agriculture Cooperative Agreement No. 58-3195-4-00236 and the Research Board of the University of Illinois. Edward V. Carroll assisted with the tax records and Katy Heyman with coding. The authors express their gratitude to Wava Haney for comments on an earlier version of the paper, and to Cornelia B. Flora for the original impetus for the chapter – an examination of farm welfare versus the individual rights of farm women. Calvin L. Beale suggested looking at the effect of declined fertility on farm continuity and provided the unpublished U.S. Census materials. A special thanks is owed to Frederick C. Fliegel who gave the manuscript his typically detailed and scathingly critical reading shortly before he died. We are indebted to him.

BIBLIOGRAPHY

Apostolic Christians of America. n.d. *Statement of Faith.* Eureka, Ill.: Apostolic Christian Publication.

Bennett, John W. 1982. *Of Time and the Enterprise.* Minneapolis: University of Minnesota Press.

Davis-Brown, Karen, Sonya Salamon, and Catherine A. Surra. 1987. "Economic and Social Factors in Mate Selection: An ethnographic Analysis of an Agricultural Community." *Journal of Marriage and the Family* 49(1): 31-55.

Farber, Bernard. 1973. *Family and Kinship in Modern Society.* Glenview, Ill.: Scott Foresman.

Fink, Deborah. 1986. *Open Country, Iowa: Rural Women, Tradition and Change.* Buffalo, N. Y.: SUNY Press.

Geisler, Charles C., William F. Waters, and Katrina L. Eadie. 1985. "The Changing Structure of Female Agricultural Land Ownership, 1946-1978." *Rural Sociology* 50 (1): 74-87.

Johnson, Benton. 1972. "On Church and Sect." In *Religion's Influence in Contemporary Society,* ed. Joseph Faulkner, 217-32. Columbus, Ohio: Charles E. Merrill.

Kauffman, J. Howard and Leland Harder. 1975. *Anabaptists Four Centuries Later: A Profile of Five Mennonite and Brethren in Christ Denominations.* Scottdale,Pa.: Herald Press.

Keim, Ann Mackey. 1976. *The Farm Woman: Lifelong Involvement with the Family Farm.* Master's thesis. University of Illinois, Urbana.

Klopfenstein, Perry A. 1984. *Marching to Zion: A History of the Apostolic Christian Church in America, 1847-1982.* Fort Scott, Kansas.: Apostolic Christian Church of America.

Laslett, Peter. 1984. "The Family as a Knot of Individual Interests." In *Households: Comparative and Historical Studies of the Domestic Group*. ed. Robert Mc. Netting and Eric J. Arnould, 353-79. Berkeley: University of California Press.

Maurer, Henrich H. 1925. "Studies in the Sociology of Religion. II. Religion and American Sectionalism. The Pennsylvania German." *American Journal of Sociology* 30 (4): 408-38.

Michaelson, Evalyn Jacobson and Walter Goldschmidt. 1971. "Female Roles and Male Dominance among Peasants." *Southwestern Journal of Anthropology* 27 (4): 330-52.

Rosenfeld, Jeffrey P. 1979. *The Legacy of Aging*. Norwood, N.J.: Ablex.

Ruegger, Herman. 1949. *Apostolic Christian Church History*. Vol. 1: *Old World*. Chicago: Apostolic Christian Publishing Co.

Salamon, Sonya. 1982. "Sibling Solidarity as an Operating Strategy in Illinois Agriculture." *Rural Sociology* 47 (2): 349-68.

_____. 1985a. "An Anthropological View of Land Transfers." In *Transfer of Land Rights: Proceedings of a Workshop on the Transfer of Rural Lands*, ed. D. David Moyer and Gene Wunderlich, 123-44. Washington, D.C.: U.S. Department of Agriculture, Economic Research Service.

_____. 1985b. "Ethnic Communities and the Structure of Agriculture." *Rural Sociology* 50 (3): 323-40.

_____. 1986. "Ethnic Determinants of Farm Community Character." In *Farm Work and Fieldwork: American Agriculture in Anthropological Perspective*, ed. Michael Chibnik, 167-88. Ithaca, N.Y.: Cornell University Press.

Salamon, Sonya and Karen Davis-Brown. 1986. "Middle-Range Farmers Persisting Through the Agricultural Crisis." *Rural Sociology* 51 (4): 503-12.

Salamon, Sonya, Kathleen M. Gengenbacher, and Dwight J. Penas. 1986. "Family Factors Affecting the Intergenerational Succession to Farming." *Human Organization* 45 (1): 24-33.

Salamon, Sonya and Ann M. Keim. 1979. "Land Ownership and Women's Power in a Midwestern Farming Community." *Journal of Marriage and the Family* 41 (1):109-19.

Salter, Leonard A. 1943. *Land Tenure in Process*. Agricultural Experiment Station Research Bulletin 146. Madison, Wi.: University of Wisconsin.

Smith, Elsdon Coles. 1956. *The Dictionary of American Family Names*. New York, N.Y.: Harper & Brothers.

Smith, Willard H. 1983. *Mennonites in Illinois*. Scottdale, Pa.: Herald Press.

U.S. Bureau of the Census. 1980. Census of the Population: Unpublished Tabulations on Ancestry.

Weber, Max. 1958. *The Protestant Ethic and the Spirit of Capitalism*. New York, N.Y.: Charles Scribner's Sons.

Yanagisako, Sylvia Junko. 1984. "Explicating Residence: A Cultural Analysis of Changing Households among Japanese-Americans." In *Households: Comparative and Historical Studies of the Domestic Group*, ed. Robert Mc. Netting and Eric J. Arnould, 330-52. Berkeley: University of California Press.

12

AGRICULTURAL MECHANIZATION AND AMERICAN FARM WOMEN'S ECONOMIC ROLES

Lorraine Garkovich
Janet Bokemeier

INTRODUCTION

Assessments of agricultural technological change have been numerous (Summers 1983; Havens 1986), most focusing on the industrialization of production with its acompanying rationalization of labor and the effects of these changes on the structure and organization of the agricultural enterprise and the agricultural economy. In general, technological innovations are viewed as an aspect of agricultural modernization that facilitates the incorporation of agriculture into industrial capitalism.

A growing scholarship on the effects of agricultural modernization on women's economic roles in Asia, Africa, and Latin America concludes that technology, in association with the emergence of industrial capitalism, marginalizes women's role in the household economy. Women, it is argued, lose access to productive land; they do not receive information on or access to new technologies; their opportunities to accumulate and invest capital are diminished; and development efforts are focused on commercial, not subsistence, commodities. Contemporaneous with those events is the breakdown of a preindustrial agrarian family structure – a family structure based on autonomous spheres of work and capital accumulation for men and women. Within many developing societies, ownership of land once was of "minimal importance" for land was communally held, and the tribe or extended family granted rights to utilize the land. Wealth was based not on ownership of land but on access to it and on the opportunity to retain the economic resources generated by the land (Dauber and Cain 1981).

Research on agricultural technological change and its effects on American farm women is less common and often reflects the interpretation of studies conducted in developing nations. To a great extent, this approach presumes that the effects of technological innovations, cash cropping, and export agriculture are universal. Yet this perspective may underestimate the influence of sociocultural forces and patterns of historical development on the unfolding of agricultural modernization. For example, in the United States, with the exception of a few experimental communities, land always has been privatized rather than held communally. As a result, women have always had limited access to land, and usufruct rights, typical in African societies, have not been an accepted legal concept. Moreover, women's opportunities to accumulate wealth have been circumscribed by inheritance practices and limited economic opportunities. Finally, technological innovations have been readily adopted in America, even during the period when susbsistence production dominated the agricultural system.

This chapter examines the relationship between agricultural technological change and American women's economic roles on independent family-owned farms. Our purpose is twofold: (1) to present a conceptual framework within which to analyze the family farm household; and (2) to use this framework to interpret the effects of modernization, specifically agricultural mechanization, on the farm household and farm women's economic roles.

A CONCEPTUAL FRAMEWORK OF THE AGRIFAMILY HOUSEHOLD

A traditional view of the farm enterprise is offered by Bennett and Kohl (1982, 129 passim). The "agrifamily unit" they describe is composed of a "nuclear family household" managed by the wife and an "agricultural enterprise" managed by the husband; "[a]ny contribution that women might make to [agricultural] production is viewed as an informal, personal service." In other words, the household is seen as distinct from the enterprise although these two entities usually coexist spatially.

Matthaei (1982) broadens this description to encompass the following points. Women's primary "work" is reproducing the farm labor force, but it also includes agricultural activities that generate cash income and agricultural products for home consumption and market sale. Despite this, according to Matthaei, women's work has not been defined historically as contributing to capital accumulation for the expansion of the farm enterprise. Thus, the traditional view of the farm enterprise defines farm women as adjuncts or "helpmates" to the men's domain – commercial agricultural production. Further, the work of farm women is defined, either implicitly or explicitly, as subsidiary and subordinate to the work of their husbands. Agricultural technology, the mechanism by which the enterprise increases the efficiency of its production and captures a larger share of profits, represents the man's sphere of influence in the farm enterprise.

As an alternative to the traditional framework one can view the farm family and the farm enterprise as interdependent social subsystems linked through the agrifamily household. From this perspective, the agrifamily household is a social institution situated within a particular historical, social, and cultural milieu and composed of a complex network of interpenetrating and mutually dependent roles. As an institution, the agrifamily household is an adaptive system "centering on special contexts of life with their own objectives and rules." The household functions according to a "texture of maps, rules, or diagrams for the performance of certain acts when certain conditions are present" (Bennett 1976, 260, 262). As an adaptive system, the agrifamily household adjusts its functioning and sometimes its structure to changes in the larger sociocultural milieu.

Within the agrifamily household, members negotiate role behaviors that satisfy their role obligations to both the family and the agricultural enterprise.

Both the role performances and the household goals are grounded in the particular sociocultural milieu of the time. This establishes parameters on socially approved behaviors as well as socially approved ends. The nature of these culturally based expectations will change to reflect social, economic, political, and legal transformations in society. In effect, both role expectations and dominant social goals are guidelines for behavior that reflect cultural mores, values, and attitudes and change in response to structural conditions. Figure 12.1 presents a schematic view of this framework.

A variety of factors influence the structure and functioning of the farm enterprise subsystem. Factors internal to the enterprise, such as size, type of commodity, type of labor input, technological level, and farming goals, affect both the expectations and the latitude given to the enterprise role performances of family members. For example, the size of the enterprise and the types of commodities produced determine the timing and sequencing of the labor demands on family members. Who contributes how much of their labor to what particular farm tasks is a function of (1) type of labor input (hired, family, technological) the enterprise utilizes, (2) competing role expectations held by the farm family, and (3) factors external to the enterprise such as economic conditions or dominant social trends. Illustrative of this latter point is the research on the sexual division of farm tasks which suggests that dominant cultural assumptions about appropriate sex role behavior influence how farm tasks are allocated among husbands, wives, and children (Bokemeier and Garkovich 1987; Fassinger and Schwarzweller 1984; Ross 1985).

Farming goals are the operational manifestations of the farm family's ideology, and they influence, in turn, the role expectations and performances of family members by determining the ultimate ends toward which the farm enterprise is operated. To illustrate, consider Salamon's (1985, 326) distinction between farm families oriented toward reproducing a "viable farm and at least one farmer in each generation" and farm families oriented toward optimizing "short-run financial returns," even when this may risk the intergenerational transmission of the enterprise. It may be assumed that the expectations for family members' participation in the enterprise will differ in these two types of families due to their different goals.

The structure and functioning of the farm family subsystem reflect the individual and joint influences of a host of factors including the following: personal variables (age, education, residential background, role concept, etc.); life cycle variables (marital status, number and age of children, etc.); social class variables (family income, tenure status, etc.); ethnic or racial heritage; family power structure (decision making, authority, etc.); and farm family ideology. Different configurations of these factors will produce different types of farm family and farm enterprise subsystems, and, hence, agrifamily households. Two examples will illustrate this point.

Research on ethnic variations in Illinois farm families (Rogers and Salamon 1983; Salamon 1980, 1984, 1985) demonstrates that there are ethnically based cultural differences in farm family goals, definitions of the sexual division of labor, attitudes toward land, and inheritance patterns that produce different styles of enterprise operation. German farm families with a "yeoman" farming ideology

oriented toward the intergenerational transmission of the land generally develop a
farm organization that is smaller than average and diversified (mix of livestock
and cash grains). In contrast, the "entrepreneurial" farming ideology of "Yankee"
farmers (descendants of early British Isles settlers who migrated from the East to
the Midwest), emphasizes farming as a business and generally produces "larger
than average operations" based on "monoculture cash grains" (Salamon 1985,
326).

The research on family power suggests that different arrangements of family
power – egalitarian, male-dominated, or female-dominated – yield different types
of decision-making styles (Ross 1985). Studies on farm family decision making
demonstrate that the relative influence of husbands and wives depends on the type
of decision to be made (e.g., production vs. investment vs. household)
(Wilkening 1958; Wilkening and Bharadwaj 1967). Hence, farm families negotiate their individual and joint actions under varying conditions (power arrangements, farming ideologies, and definitions of sex roles) that produce different
farm family structures and modes of functioning.

We have, then, an "agrifamily" household that engages in both production
(the agricultural enterprise) and reproduction (the family enterprise). Within this
household, members negotiate role performances that satisfy their role obligations to both the family and the agricultural enterprise as defined by household
goals. These role performances reflect the expectations of other household members as structured by the demands of the enterprise and the family. Furthermore,
the sociocultural milieu within which the agrifamily household operates establishes parameters on the development and enactment of individual role performances and influences the definition of household goals.

The sociocultural milieu constitutes the sum of cultural, political, economic, and social conditions that define the emergent structure and functioning
of the agrifamily household. To some degree the nature of the sociocultural milieu reflects the constraints of the environmental system. The environmental or
biophysical system is composed of the types, quantity, and quality of resources
available to the sociocultural system for transformation into socially desired
goods and services. The interaction of the environment, the sociocultural milieu,
and the agrifamily household is illustrated by Pfeffer (1983) in his analysis of
three agrifamily systems in America.

Three distinct agrifamily systems – corporate farming in California, sharecropping in the South, and family farming on the Great Plains – emerged initially "under conditions of concentrated ownership of land" (Pfeffer 1983, 540).
But the natural conditions of crop production set special demands on the allocation of labor, and the possible ways of dealing with the need for labor varied
with the social context within which the farm operated. The predominance of
family farming on the Great Plains reflected the absence of wage agricultural laborers in this region. Agricultural wages did not compete with urban industrial
wages (Danhoff 1966), and those who did migrate to the Great Plains came to
settle their own lands, not work for someone else. "Bonanza farms," large-scale
specialized farms that emerged during the early settlement years on the Great
Plains, failed due to the high cost of environmental risks (droughts, insects,
floods) (Pfeffer 1983). The family farm avoided the labor management problems

of corporate systems by relying on family labor that could be quickly allocated in light of new contingencies. Moreover, family farms could diversify their operations to take advantage of changing markets and thus, better utilize family labor inputs. Hence, Pfeffer's (1983, 560) conclusion that "specific social circumstances lead to the development of distinct systems of social production" illustrates the interactive effect of environmental and sociocultural conditions on the agrifamily household.

This framework is only one of many that can be utilized to interpret farm women's economic roles. It emphasizes the active participation of agrifamily household members in the construction of social actions designed to achieve household goals. Stressing negotiation of role performances and goals among household members, the model does not necessarily assume satisfaction with outcomes, for in the negotiation over goals and household strategies, individuals bargain and make trade-offs.

Given this view of the agrifamily household, it will be argued that agricultural modernization represents a change in the technological level of the farm enterprise with consequences for the agrifamily household and its members. The key to understanding this process is provided by the model. The changes in the technological level (e.g., tractors, mechanical harvesters, improved seed varieties, electricity, automated milking parlors, irrigation systems, wells) of the farm enterprise may lead to substantial or relatively insignificant changes in the farming practices of the enterprise. The effects of these changes on the farm family and the household will vary with the sociocultural context within which the household functions. While the introduction of a particular technological innovation may "marginalize women by reducing . . . women's control over productive technology" (Haney 1983, 180) in one sociocultural setting or in one type of agrifamily system, it may not necessarily produce the same outcome in another place and time. Hence, to understand the consequences of agricultural modernization on the economic roles of American farm women requires a consideration of the specific innovations and the sociocultural context at the time of their introduction. The next section will describe farm women's roles prior to agricultural mechanization on the Great Plains.

FARM WOMEN'S ECONOMIC ROLES

To understand the effects of agricultural mechanization on farm women's economic roles it is necessary to establish the nature of the agrifamily household prior to mechanization and the incorporation of agriculture into industrial capitalism. This discussion will focus only on farmer-owner agrifamily households, since a consideration of the wide range of agrifamily household types is beyond the scope of this chapter. The numerous accounts of family farm life on which this chapter draws represent the lives of predominantly white middle-class women, who with their families settled the Great Plains and established independent family-owned farms. The commonalities in their accounts suggest these women reflect the reality of everyday life for women of similar ethnic and class status in this region.

Throughout most of American history, women's economic roles within the farm household have encompassed three types of activities: (1) production for household consumption, (2) production for commodity sales and/or exchange, and (3) other activities designed for generation of economic resources for the farm household. The tasks involved in each of these aspects of farm women's economic roles are detailed below.

First, women performed production activities for household consumption. These activities included working a large kitchen garden, raising poultry for meat and eggs, caring for dairy animals, producing homespun cloth for articles of clothing, repairing and fashioning of cloths for household use, rendering animal fats for soaps, and producing specialized items for home use (such as baskets or quilts) (Fink 1986; Jensen 1981).

Second, women produced goods for commercial sales. Women often used surpluses from goods produced for household consumption to produce goods they could either sell to local store owners directly for cash or trade to them for in-kind purchases. The primary commodities in this market production were eggs and dairy products, but women also transformed other products of their household labor, such as baked goods, clothing, or crafts, into exchange commodities.

Women also performed field labor to produce the farm goods sold to commercial markets. As one Kansas farm woman commented: "It was wheat, corn, cattle, dairying, hogs, poultry. How much hard work that meant for the women folks only those who have tried it can understand" (Stratton, 1981, 60). This labor occurred not only in periods of peak labor demand; in particular circumstances, women assumed primary responsibility for field production.[2]

Women's participation in commodity production enhanced the economic viability of the farm household in several ways. The sale and/or trade of surplus commodities women produced in conjunction with their household activities meant that expenditures for commercially produced household items were avoided and a cash flow vital to the agricultural enterprise's and the household's financial survival (Jeffrey 1979). Moreover, women's participation in fieldwork reduced the need for hired labor, enabling enterprises to expand without labor constraints (Jeffrey 1979; Stratton 1981).

Finally, women engaged in a host of other activities designed to generate economic resources for the farm household. Some farm women sought wage labor off the farm (Lerner 1979). Sometimes this involved wage employment for other farm operators, and other times women worked in nearby towns. Farm women also performed paid "homework" or "piecework" in their homes (e.g., sewing, laundering, or taking in boarders), for these activities "fit" into their other economic and family responsibilities. It is important to remember, however, that these two types of income-generating work – wage work for an employer and paid homework – differ greatly in the degree to which the employee is able to exercise control over the work product, the pace of work, and the wage received.

These historical notes suggest that in the premodern American agrifamily household, women engaged in a variety of economically productive activities. Yet it is clear that the bundle of activities that comprised farm women's economic roles at that time cannot easily be separated into those focused on her family and those focused on the enterprise. Rather, her economic activities linked the farm enterprise and the family within a larger social system – the agrifamily household. Two examples will illustrate the interpenetration of these spheres.

Hired labor worked for cash wages, for room and board only, or for some combination of these prior to the mid-1900s. (While not as common today, this still does occur.) Farm women's food production and preparation activities fed their families, but also helped pay the cost of hired labor. Furthermore, Fink's (1986a) study of Iowa farm women indicates that as part of the noncash wages of hired labor many women also made and repaired work clothes.

In those regions where additional labor was hired during harvest times women spent between between ten and fifteen hours a day cooking the meals for harvest crews as part of their noncash wages (Armitage 1986; Fink 1986a). One study of Whitman County, Washington, reports that including food preparation in the calculation of women's contributions to the farm enterprise increased women's labor time to thirty-eight hours rather than the ten hours normally credited to them in most farm and housework time studies (Armitage 1986). These examples illustrate that many aspects of women's labor for the enterprise were intricately tied to their labor for the family.

The particular mix of economic activities in which women were engaged in this premodern era depends on the specific nature of the agrifamily household. Women on the Great Plains performed a wide variety of econmic activities for the independent family farm. Their work was not marginal to the economic survival of the agrifamily household; rather it contributed substantively to the economic stability and viability of the household.

THE SOCIOCULTURAL CONTEXT OF AGRICULTURAL MODERNIZATION

In order to understand how agricultural modernization affected the historical economic roles of American farm women, we need to consider not only the specific technological innovations that have altered the nature of the farm operation but also the broader sociocultural milieu within which these innovations have been developed and utilized. Hence, it is important to begin by considering the sociocultural context of agricultural modernization.

The "cult of domesticity" has been identified as the dominant cultural interpretation of women's roles in mid-nineteenth century society (Jeffrey 1979; Reiner 1985). Jeffrey's (1979) study of frontier women in the trans-Mississippi West from 1840 to 1880 demonstrates that "the early years of settlement, in fact, would test many facets of the cultural framework which women had brought west with them. The test suggests how firmly women clung to the framework and the meaning which it could provide for their lives even on the frontier. . . . The domestic ideal was a goal toward which women could direct their efforts."

While women did participate in numerous ways in the heavy fieldwork essential to the establishment of an ongoing agricultural enterprise on the plains, their involvement reflected a reluctant adaptation to the environmental and economic conditions of the early years of settlement. Women and men expanded the concept of "domesticity" to include these less appropriate role behaviors in the definition of household labor so as not to risk the women's "femininity." In most cases, women and men defined women as "helpers" and so the fieldwork was not their primary responsibility. When women did assume primary responsibility for particular enterprise activities, such as raising poultry, the activity was redefined from farm work to household work (Fink 1986a).

Thus, during the years of settlement, the cult of domesticity, reinforced through religious pronouncements, educational texts, and the popular media provided a set of behavioral norms that defined the ideal role of women within the context of the household rather than the context of the field (Reiner 1985). However, dominant cultural assumptions that identified "male" and "female" spheres of work and daily activities as well as clearly differentiated between appropriate male and female role performances were flexible enough to expand the boundaries of women's household activities to include fieldwork when conditions warranted.

This cultural definition of sex roles was deeply embedded in American society. Carr and Walsh (1979), in a study of seventeenth-century Maryland, illustrate the early roots of the cult of domesticity. They state: "Most immigrant women expected, or at least hoped, to avoid heavy fieldwork , which English women – at least those above the cottager's status – did not do. . . . The wife in a household too poor to afford bound labor . . . might well tend tobacco when she could. Eventually, the profits of her labor might enable the family to buy a servant, making greater profits possible" (Carr and Walsh 1979, 29, 41). Women worked in the fields in periods of labor shortage, but once economic security was established bound labor replaced the farm owner's wife in the fields, enabling the wife to return to her own sphere. Thus, the American cultural expectations that women's role behaviors would center on the family and/or household maintenance were derived from the English roots of many early immigrants.

These comments also point to a second aspect of the sociocultural context that must be noted – the influence of dominant social values related to economic growth, progress, individual success and achievement, and material comfort on both personal and family goal orientations. Most Americans, including farm families, have desired to improve their economic position to achieve what has come to be defined as the "middle-class" standard of living. The pursuit of this status has influenced the "cultural definitions of basic material needs" (Hoskins 1985, 131) and attitudes toward harsh, uncertain, and difficult working conditions. Moreover, awareness of the amenities of an urban industrial lifestyle was made universal through newspapers and other periodicals, and later, through Sears and Montgomery Ward catalogues, the expansion of specialized retail stores, and still later, through the electronic media.

Hoskins's study of the Oklahoma farming frontier from 1890 to 1907 illustrates the impact of "new definitions for 'necessary' goods" on the "number and variety of status-objects" that would satisfy the family. Hoskins identifies the types of possessions those settling the Oklahoma Territory in the late 1880s and early 1890s brought with them and comments that the "articles that bounced across the plains to Oklahoma in heavy farm wagons reflect the growing national propensity to invest in more efficient devices and partially processed goods in order to save labor in the home as well as in farming and business. . . . Home production of rural domestic needs had largely died out by the time Oklahoma was settled. The availability of manufactured goods had caused an economic and cultural adjustment prior to emigration to Oklahoma" (Hoskins 1985, 123-124). One farm woman commented on these changing aspirations in this way in 1919: "I mean to put in a vegetable garden this year, but we shop in town every week now. Imagine! Well, you can't grow corn flakes, can you? and Hatty [her daughter] has decided she must have corn flakes, as the town girls do" (McNall and McNall 1983, 107).

The importance of the mass media in establishing the criterion of a "minimally acceptable standard of living" cannot be overestimated. Rural electrification in the 1930s and 1940s introduced farm families, through radio and television, to the opportunities and luxuries of the urban world. Dorner (1983, 79) comments: "Farm children were no longer isolated from urban society. Rural electrification gave near-universal access to radio and later television. . . . Young men and women on the farm would not stay home if it meant falling behind in income and sacrificing the amenities urban life seemed to offer. If a farmer did not mechanize and expand, he fell behind in income and his children left the farm for city jobs."

The importance of land ownership within this value system must also be noted. The private ownership of land and the intergenerational transfer of the family land have been important social and individual goals among many segments of the agricultural community (Elbert 1981; Rogers and Salamon 1983) and the society at large. While the specific cultural meaning of land – as a home and hearth, or economic enterprise, or economic investment – may vary, ownership of land has figured prominently in our national ethos. Land ownership has been seen as a basis of wealth and individual control over one's fate, and, in the context of a Jeffersonian agrarianism, as the basis for the democratic system of government.

The third aspect of the sociocultural milieu that must be considered is the transformation of the national economy. Industrialization, the shift from an extractive to a manufacturing economy, and later from a manufacturing to a service economy, and the integration of local economies into regional, national, and eventually international markets profoundly altered the economic environment within which the agrifamily household functioned. The preindustrial agricultural enterprise, functioning as a relatively self-sustaining subsistence unit integrated into local markets through barter rather than cash, did exist in some areas of the nation prior to the Civil War (Henderson 1981). However, the plantation agriculture of the early South was clearly oriented toward cash – production and trade on an international market (Carr and Walsh 1979; Jensen 1981). And in later years, the value of national farm "exports rose from $12.2 million in 1860 to $305 million in 1897" (McNall and McNall 1983, 25). Moreover, as urbanization proceeded, commercial markets for grain and livestock expanded, driving up the demand for agricultural products. Thus, the farm economy was increasingly tied to the national and international economies during the late 1800s, establishing constraints on and providing incentives to expansion.

Several other important changes are associated with the urban industrialization of society. The price of land and equipment during the nineteenth century influenced the nature of economic development. Railroads aggressively advertised "land in the West selling for between $2.50 and $6.00 an acre" (McNall and McNall 1983, 10). Hicks, Mowry, and Burke (1965, 169) "estimated that the average northern farmer of the pre-1900 period had to invest about $785 in machinery" in order to operate a farm and this, with the cost of land, led Shannon (1945, 185) to estimate that in 1880 the outstanding mortgage on the average owner-operated farm was $1,224.

Farmers during this era (1860 to 1910) also faced an unfavorable credit market. Interest rates of 36 to 50 percent were not uncommon for farmers, and the interest was usually taken out of the principal before the money was lent because farmers were considered poor risks (McNall and McNall 1983, 23-25). Moreover, local banks often could not provide sufficient capital for all the farmers in an area so "eastern dollars" became a major source of Midwestern farm credit.

Furthermore, although domestic urban and international markets expanded during the nineteenth century, it is also important to recognize that the proportion of total per capita income spent on food declined "from about one third in 1870 to one fifth by 1890" (McNall and McNall 1983, 26). Indeed, by the early 1900s, the farm economy was staggering from a seemingly endless series of depressions. Farm prices were declining steadily but operating costs were rising. Foreclosures were becoming more commonplace, as was tenancy.

Finally, the focus on modernization within the farm enterprise has led many to overlook the modernization of the household that also occurred beginning in the late 1800s and continuing into the 1950s. As already noted, rural electrification brought the radio and later the television to isolated rural communities. As simple an innovation as the piping of water to the house profoundly altered the work demands on farm women. Rural telephone systems and rural free delivery as well as the emergence of speciality stores in a proliferating number of trade centers all contributed to the absorption of the agrifamily household into a mass consumer society.

Hence, the socioeconomic context within which the agrifamily household functioned was changing. While farmers participated to varying degrees in a cash economy prior to the mid-nineteenth century, industrialization and urbanization from that time onward deepened the integration of the agrifamily household into a national economy. The availability of cash, access to credit, and access to markets increasingly set parameters on the opportunities of the agrifamily household to establish, maintain, and, when desired, effect the intergenerational transfer of the farm enterprise. While many other aspects of the sociocultural milieu are important (e.g., rates and composition of immigrant streams or the abolition of slavery), the three factors discussed here – the cult of domesticity, dominant social values, and the nature of industrialization – provide a basis for interpreting the consequences of agricultural modernization for farm women's economic roles.

MECHANIZATION AND FARM WOMEN'S ECONOMIC ROLES

Although agricultural modernization includes both changes in the technology of production (e.g., chemicals, mechanization, biogenetics, farm implements) and the application of scientific knowledge to the operation of the enterprise (e.g., crop rotation, soil conservation, selective breeding), the change in the technological level of the enterprise of concern here is mechanization, specifically the introduction of the tractor.

Prior to the twentieth century, changes in the technological level of farming had typically been through improvements in implements. For example, the moldboard plow and barbed wire made the agricultural development of the Great Plains possible (Webb 1931). However, the most significant and far-reaching change in the technological level of farming in the early twentieth century has been the introduction of the tractor. The tractor, introduced during the 1920s, increased production by reducing both the time and the labor requirements of fieldwork. The tractor enabled farm families to expand the size of their field operations significantly and increase productivity, but not without some increases in costs (Dorner 1983). Williams (1985, 145) notes: "Farmers who mechanized seldom used their horsedrawn equipment with their new power source. Mechanized farms had high capital requirements." In other words, mechanization entailed not only the purchase of a power-driven tractor, but also the acquisition of the field production equipment that could be used with the tractor.

Why did farms mechanize? Williams (1985) analyzes the "Great Debate" over the relative economic advantages of horses and tractors in field production that continued into the early 1950s. From the 1920s onward, he notes, farmers were given examples of "successful mechanical farmers" who operated large farms and realized real improvement in profits due to economies of scale permitted by mechanization. However, the relationship between the size of the enterprise and the ability of the farmer to mechanize was often ignored. In other words, were larger farmers able to pay the costs of mechanization and so reap the higher profits due to economies of scale? Or, did mechanization enable small- or middle-sized farmers to earn profits that allowed them to expand their operations? Williams suggests that given the capital requirements of mechanization, the former is more likely.

Williams also argues that there were overriding noneconomic reasons for the adoption of tractors, such as reducing the harshness of farm labor and acquiring the status of a progressive farmer. Williams further suggests that while the economic advantage of tractors over horses for fieldwork remained a point of debate during these decades, the advantages of tractors *vis-à-vis* the achievement of other highly valued ends were clear.

Given the constriction in the agricultural market, mechanization, for those who could afford it, provided a competitive edge in the marketplace. Yet, the key phrase here is "for those who could afford it." The acquisition and use of modern technologies demanded a greater cash flow or more access to credit than were required for farming in earlier times. This meant that the agrifamily household had to develop strategies for increasing cash resources. Such strategies included expanding production, improving marketing, and securing off-farm sources of income. The particular strategy or mix of strategies selected by household members reflected the structural constraints of the enterprise, the imperatives of the family, and the intersection of individual, family, and community role expectations.

Consider the choice of off-farm employment. Historically, off-farm employment was a conscious strategy for adapting to both the chronic need for cash in a market economy and the chronic shortage of cash on the frontier. But the decision as to who will work off the farm reflects the influence of individual and social expectations regarding role performances and the structural constraints of the household as much as it does the availability of off-farm employment opportunities. At the time farmers' need for cash was increasing, electrification and the piping of water to the farm household were reducing somewhat the amount of time required for household tasks, freeing women to engage in alternative household activities, to become more involved in farm work, or to seek off-farm employment (Fink 1986a; Meiners and Olson 1986). By reducing the physical rigors of farm work, mechanization made possible a more fluid sexual division of labor both on and off the farm.

The economies of scale – afforded by mechanizing fieldwork – enabled farm households to increase their family incomes and improved their opportunities to acquire the culturally defined necessities of life. An associated consequence was the opportunity to establish an enterprise large enough and prosperous enough to attract at least one of the children to farming. In other words, mechanization provided a means of offering children a competitive alternative to leaving the farm for employment in the cities. The importance of this goal for many farm women is seen in their participation in the acquisition of new technologies. Jensen (1981, 108) notes: "By 1910, women on the plains of Montana were using butter money to buy windmills necessary for the survival of farms in the waterless land." Fink (1986a) documents the monetary contributions of Iowa farm women to the improvement of their enterprises, while Colman and Elbert (1984) comment that farm women define their economic activities as contributing to the intergenerational transmission of the farm.

Mechanization also transformed agricultural labor, changing it from "stoop work" to "mechanical work" just as it transformed industrial labor in the factories of the cities. It is not by chance that the concept of "factories in the field" appeared around this time. In effect, the acquisition of power-driven field equipment signaled the presence of a "modern" farmer and enhanced the social status of the operator. But the social significance of mechanization went beyond this. Macheski (1986) suggests that the ideals of middle-class domesticity dictated that wives should not have to perform heavy fieldwork. Mechanization reduced the demand for women's participation in the harshest and dirtiest aspects of farm production and meant that if they did do farm work, it would not have the stigma of stoop labor. Hence, mechanization symbolized the agrifamily household's movement toward a desired middle-class standard of living.

The importance of this association between mechanization and middle-class status was not overlooked by farm equipment manufacturers who directed advertising toward farm wives. Armitage (1986, 43) calls attention to a Caterpillar tractor pamphlet from the early 1930s that carried the slogan: "At last we wives can have vacations." Inside, the pamphlet were testimonials by women in the Palouse region of Washington State about the positive changes brought by tractors, including "fewer hired hands to cook for, fewer and less constant chores for both husband and wife, less worry about small children being injured by large farm animals, more surplus farm income to spend on home furnishings, and more time for family activities, and vacations."

Finally, even as mechanization reduced women's stoop labor participation in the fields, as it did that of all family members, it opened up a variety of new farm tasks to women. Although the physical labor requirements of most farm tasks did decline, the number of activities required to maintain and operate the farm increased. Mechanization generated new farm tasks, such as the maintenance of farm machinery, the acquisition of the technical information necessary to use modern agricultural technology, improved record keeping, and consumption tasks (the day-to-day "gofer" activities necessary to keep the industrial farm operating). Farm women's labor contributions to the enterprise increasingly involved all but the first of these (Bokemeier and Garkovich 1987; Fassinger and Schwarzweller 1984). Hence, the bundle of activities that constituted women's role performance in the farm enterprise shifted with mechanization, mirroring, to some degree, the changes in the nature of work occurring in the urban industrial marketplace.

SUMMARY AND CONCLUSIONS

American farm women have engaged in a wide variety of activities in the performance of their economic roles for the farm enterprise. The economic viability of the agrifamily household has depended on all of the work activities of farm women, not just their participation in fieldwork. The type of household analysis proposed here broadens the interpretation of the process by which household members develop the content of their economic role performances. The framework emphasizes that the interdependence of the economic roles of household members as they negotiate a set of work roles maximizes the economic resources available to the agrifamily household. As Jeffrey (1979, 61) suggests: "As their economic enterprises, their letters, and their journals indicate, women were both practically and emotionally involved in economic matters as they sought to improve the family economic status."

Selection of the particular activities that compose the economic role performances has been shaped, in part, by the forces of technological change that altered the structural context of the farm operation as well as the nature of family life. Increasing dependence on the market economy altered the rules for economic survival. The urban industrial society offered job opportunities and fostered a consumer economy. The adoption of labor-saving technologies enabled family members to negotiate and redefine their role performances in order to take advantage of these new opportunities. Sociocultural values and goals provided the context within which household members devised role performances. Opportunities presented by social and technological changes interacted with individual values to produce a desire to participate in the advantages of the larger society. This could only be accomplished by increasing the household's cash flow and entailed increasing productivity, expanding the operation, securing off-farm sources of income, or some combination of these. Farm women, according to Armitage (1986), welcomed new farm technologies for they broadened the role choices available to household members.

Did these changes in the economic activities performed by women necessarily reduce the value of women's contributions to the enterprise or the household? Although traditional activities such as producing goods for home consumption or exchange in the marketplace diminished in importance, these were replaced by new activities that also contributed to the economic success of the household. The tendency to define some of these activities (e.g., bookkeeping, information gathering, gofering) as of less value may reflect an inappropriate dichotomy in the context of the farm household between the "use" and "exchange" value of labor. In the agrifamily household, the distinction between production (enterprise) and reproduction (family) activities is blurred and as a result, women's work that in another context may not contribute "value" to the products of an enterprise becomes significant.

The framework presented here represents only one of many approaches to the interpretation of the changing American farm family. It is not our intention to suggest that this perspective applies to all farm families at every historical stage in the development of the American agricultural system. However, it does fit a household process that both farm women and men have suggested in their own writings and words.

Finally, this review of the changing economic roles of farm women following the introduction of the tractor raises an alternative research question to that traditionally posed. Typically, the question asked is: "Why has technology reduced women's involvement in the farm enterprise?" This assumes that women once participated actively in all phases of the farm operation and that mechanization disenfranchised women from a sphere of work that they had once defined as their own. This review of women on family farms on the Great Plains suggests that both women and men have defined women's participation in fieldwork as "helping," and that the cult of domesticity could and did expand the definition of women's sphere of work to encompass certain kinds of farm work when economic and other conditions demanded this adaptation. Hence, perhaps the more appropriate research question to be answered is: "What can explain the persistence of inequality in men's and women's spheres of work on the farm given the tremendous changes in the technology of farm work and the changes in the sociocultural milieu (e.g., women's participation in the wage labor force, development of feminist ideologies)?" It is the persistence of separate spheres more than the change in the activities associated with men's and women's sphere of work that should be the focus of future research.

Figure 12.1 *A conceptual framework of the agrifamily household*

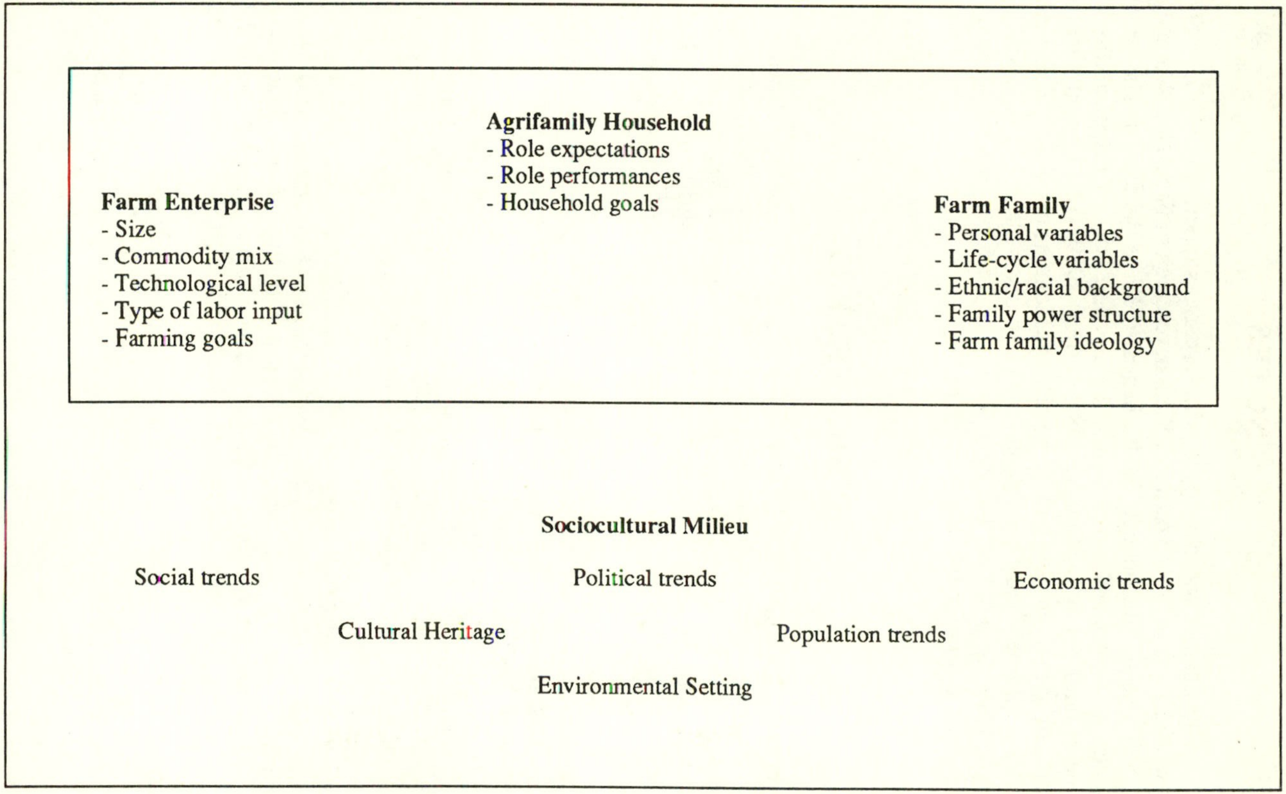

Agrifamily Household
- Role expectations
- Role performances
- Household goals

Farm Family
- Personal variables
- Life-cycle variables
- Ethnic/racial background
- Family power structure
- Farm family ideology

Farm Enterprise
- Size
- Commodity mix
- Technological level
- Type of labor input
- Farming goals

Sociocultural Milieu

Cultural Heritage

Political trends

Population trends

Economic trends

Environmental Setting

Social trends

NOTES

[1]This chapter was developed with research support from the University of Kentucky Agricultural Experiment Station, research projects Nos. 829 and 840.

[2]It was not uncommon for husbands to leave the farmsteads for several months or longer and wives would then assume primary responsibility for the general farm operation (Jensen 1981; Jeffrey 1979). In Mormon Utah, wives were left to maintain the farm or ranch for as long as two years while their husbands performed church missionary work in other places. In other cases, men would leave to work off the farm for wages, to hunt, to participate in cattle drives, or to serve in the state legislature.

BIBLIOGRAPHY

Armitage, Susan. 1986. "Farm Women and Technological Change." In *Plainswoman: An Anthology*. Grand Forks, N. Dak.: Plainswoman.

Bennett, John W. 1976. *The Ecological Transition*. New York: Pergamon Press.

Bennett, John W., and Seena B. Kohl. 1982. "The Agrifamily System." In *Of Time and the Enterprise: North American Family Farm Management in a Context of Resource Marginality*, John W. Bennett (ed.), pp. 128-47. Minneapolis: University of Minnesota Press.

Bokemeier, Janet, and Lorraine Garkovich. 1987. "Assessing the Influence of Farm Women's Self-Identity on Task Allocation and Decision Making." *Rural Sociology*, 52(2): 13-37.

Carr, Lois Green, and Lorena S. Walsh. 1979. "The Planter's Wife: The Experience of White Women in Seventeenth Century Maryland." In *A Heritage of Her Own: Toward a New Social History of American Women*, Nancy F. Cott and Elizabeth H. Pleck (eds.), pp. 25-57. New York: Simon and Schuster.

Colman, G. and Sarah Elbert. 1984. "Farming Families: The Farm Needs Everyone." *Research in Rural Sociology and Development*, 1:61-78.

Danhoff, Clarence H. 1966. "Economic Validity of the Safety – Valve Doctrine." In *Readings in United States Economic and Business History*, Ross M. Robertson and James L. Pate (ed.), pp. 185-94. Boston: Houghton Mifflin Company.

Dauber, Roslyn, and Melinda L. Cain (eds.). 1981. *Women and Technological Change in Developing Countries*. Boulder, Colo.: Westview Press.

Dorner, Peter. 1983. "Technology and U.S. Agriculture." In *Technology and Social Change in Rural Areas*, Gene F. Summers (ed.), pp. 73-86. Boulder, Colo.: Westview Press.

Elbert, Sarah. 1981. "The Challenge of Research on Farm Women." *The Rural Sociologist*, 1(6):387-90.

Fassinger, Polly A., and Harry K. Schwarzweller. 1984. "The Work of Farm

Women: A Midwestern Study." *Research in Rural Sociology and Development*, 1:23-40.

Fink, Deborah. 1986. *Open Country Iowa: Rural Women, Tradition and Change*. Albany: State University of New York Press.

Haney, Wava. 1983. "Farm Family and the Role of Women." In *Technology and Social Change in Rural Areas*, Gene F. Summers (ed.), pp. 179-96. Boulder, Colo.: Westview Press.

Havens, A. Eugene (ed.) 1986. *Studies in the Transformation of US Agriculture*. Boulder, Colo.: Westview Press.

Henderson, Hazel. 1981. "Foreword: Seeing Our Global Economy Whole." In *Women and Technological Change in Developing Countries*, Roslyn Dauber and Melinda L. Cain (eds.), pp. xvii – xxii. Boulder, Colo.: Westview Press.

Hicks, John D., George E. Mowry, and Robert E. Burke. 1965. *The American Nation*. 4th ed. Boston: Houghton Mifflin.

Hoskins, Deborah J. 1985. "Brought, Bought, and Borrowed: Material Culture on the Oklahoma Farming Frontier, 1889 – 1907." In *At Home on the Range: Essays on the History of Western Social and Domestic Life*, John R. Wunder (ed.), pp. 121-36. Westport, Conn.: Greenwood Press.

Jeffrey, Julie Roy. 1979. *Frontier Women: The Trans-Mississipppi West, 1840-1880*. New York: Hill & Wang.

Jensen, Joan M. 1981. *With These Hands: Women Working on the Land*. Old Westbury, N.Y.: The Feminist Press.

Lerner, Gerda. 1979. "The Lady and the Mill Girl." In *A Heritage of Her Own: Toward a New Social History of American Women*, Nancy F. Cott and Elizabeth H. Pleck (eds.), pp. 182-96. New York: Simon and Schuster.

Macheski, Ginger. 1986. "Technology and the Changing Role of Women in the Farm Labor Force." Paper presented at the Second National Conference on American Farm Women in Historical Perspective, 16-18 October, University of Wisconsin-Madison, Madison, Wis.

Matthaei, Julie A. 1982. *An Economic History of Women in America: Women's Work, the Sexual Division of Labor, and the Development of Capitalism*. New York: Schocken Books.

McNall, Scott, and Ann McNall. 1983. *Plains Families*. New York: St. Martin's Press.

Meiners, Jane, and Geraldine Olson. 1986. "Household Work Demands and Farm Women: A Fifty Year Perspective." Paper presented at the Second National Conference on American Farm Women in Historical Perspective, 16-18 October, University of Wisconsin-Madison, Madison Wis.

Pfeffer, Max J. 1983. "Social Origins of Three Systems of Farm Production in the United States." *Rural Sociology*, 48(4):540-62.

Reiner, Jacqueline S. 1985. "Concepts of Domesticity on the Southern Plains Agricultural Frontier, 1870-1920." In *At Home on the Range: Essays on the History of Western Social and Domestic Life*, John R. Wunder (ed.), pp. 39-56. Westport, Conn: Greenwood Press.

Rogers, Susan C., and Sonya Salamon. 1983. "Inheritance and Social

Organization Among Family Farmers." *American Ethnologist*, 10(3):529-50.

Ross, Peggy. 1985. "A Commentary on Research on American Farm Women." *Agriculture and Human Values*, 2(1):19-30.

Salamon, Sonya. 1980. "Ethnic Differences in Farm Family Land Transfers." *Rural Sociology*, 45(2):290-308.

_____. 1984. "Ethnic Origin as Explanation for Local Land Ownership Patterns." *Research in Rural Sociology and Development*, 1:161-86.

_____. 1985. "Ethnic Communities and the Structure of Agriculture." *Rural Sociology*, 50(2):323-40.

Shannon, Fred A. 1945. *The Farmer's Last Frontier: Agriculture 1860-1897*. New York: Farrar & Rinehart.

Stratton, Joanna L. 1981. *Pioneer Women: Voices from the Kansas Frontier*. New York: Touchstone Books.

Summers, Gene F. (ed.). 1983. *Technology and Social Change in Rural Areas*. Boulder, Colo.: Westview Press.

Webb, Walter Prescott. 1931. *The Great Plains*. New York: Grossett & Dunlap.

Wilkening, Eugene A. 1958. "Joint Decision-Making in Farm Families as a Function of Status and Role." *American Sociological Review*, 23(2):187-92.

Wilkening, Eugene A., and Lakshmi Bharadwaj. 1967. "Dimensions of Aspirations, Work Roles and Decision-Making of Farm Husbands and Wives in Wisconsin." *Journal of Marriage and the Family*, 29(5):703-11.

Williams, Robert C. 1985. "Farm Technology and 'The Great Debate': The Rhetoric of Horse Lovers and Tractor Boosters, 1900-1945." In *At Home on the Range: Essays on Western Social and Domestic Life*, John R. Wunder (ed.), pp. 137-56. Westport, Conn.: Greenwood Press.

13

THE IMPACT OF CHANGING TECHNOLOGIES ON THE ROLES OF FARM AND RANCH WIVES IN SOUTHEASTERN OHIO

Virginia S. Fink[1]

INTRODUCTION

Today's family farm is a unique place, where two work areas, farm and home, intersect. The work of a farm and ranch wife is less fragmented than that of other wives. The urban or nonfarm rural wife, working from nine to five, comes home to additional domestic work and family responsibilities. The farm or ranch wife does not leave the farm to do much of her work. While she may go to work, she also works in several areas on site; she performs many commercial and domestic tasks simultaneously, often integrating housework, care and socialization of the children, and feeding the hogs or milking the cattle into the same hours. Her work in some aspects, is not fragmented into public and private, as is most industrial workers, but is more like the home based production of the past. Interestingly, this *home* based aspect of her work is similar not only to work roles in the past but also to those predicted for men and women in the future. Based on existing trends, it seems that work may in the future commonly be performed in the home, using the current technology of the telephone and computer in new ways (Robertson 1982, 83).

The farm and ranch wife's role has incorporated considerable technological changes in the past fifty years. Electricity, telephones, trucks and automobiles, supermarkets, the computer and the microwave have altered the standard matrix of tasks once performed by women in this role. Over the years, since World War II, farm labor has become increasingly mechanized, while the total number of people and animals working on farms has greatly decreased.

The process of change – from the older family-based farm roles to contemporary agribusiness – and the impact of this change on farm women's roles are both underdocumented. At the beginning of this century, there were many gender specific tasks on farms (Voegler 1981; Shover 1976). Women worked in the home, milked the cows and cared for the chickens and separate areas of the farm, and men worked in the barn and fields. Data obtained in recent studies such as that by Fassinger and Schwarzweller (1984) have confirmed that there continue to be strong gender specific patterns on farms, with household tasks more sex segregated than farm tasks.

This study focuses on the period from World War I to the present, a time of radical change within the agricultural production system (Shover 1976; Vogeler 1981; Summers 1983). Rural sociology has begun to look more closely at the role of the farm and ranch wife (Kohl 1977; Sachs 1983; Fassinger and Schwartzweller 1984). Researchers are beginning to question the assumption common in older studies of farms that the farmwife's role is a marginal one (Boulding 1980; Wilkening 1981; Bokemier, Sachs and Keith 1983; Sachs 1983).

My study is exploratory, looking at perceived role changes over time in a small county in southeastern Ohio. The results are not intended to be used to generalize to larger segments of the population but to illuminate areas for further indepth studies. I began by wanting to know how the farm and ranch wife's role has changed over time, with the increasing mechanization and rationality in farming. Have the number of tasks performed by farm women actually increased rather than decreased? Or have the changes been more in the type than in the number of tasks performed? And what did the women themselves perceive as the important technological changes? My concern was to look at the farm and ranch wive's role from the point of view of the women themselves, to discover how women who had participated in the change process described it.

THEORY

Both manual labor and women's work tends to be invisible in our society. The work of farm and ranch wives is thus doubly invisible. Marcia Millman and Rosabeth Kanter (1975) and Gerda Lerner (1986) contend that sociologists and historians alike have overlooked the many contributions of women. As a result much contemporary theory about stratification, communities, family roles and farm systems may well be incorrect because it is based on an incomplete knowledge base.

The current farm and ranch wives's role set is influenced both by the older patriarchal agrarian role set and by the new technologies and methods of production in the agricultural system. The patriarchal set of rules limits the range of ways in which the new technology can be incorporated into gender segregated roles. The pervasive rules organize thought patterns of possible new behaviors to technological innovation. Although this chapter focuses on how major technological changes have shaped the wives' roles on farms, this changing technology has of course affected men's farm roles as well as women's. The role of farm and ranch wife is considered foremost a role within the family, yet it is also an economic role in the agricultural sector. To understand the full scope of farmwives' role changes one must look at the technological changes in agricultural production, processing and distribution, as well as in domestic tasks. Education, specifically in newer farm technology and accounting, has become more critical for family farms. At the same time, one must examine the societal change in attitudes toward women and their appropriate positions in society that has accompanied the change in women's material conditions (Reskin 1986).

Marketing and promotional activities done by farmers seem to be gendered at least in the women I interviewed and especially in the new agribusiness controlled agriculture. Women, although they generally are thought of as more educated and independent, seem now to be excluded from the marketing transactions. Where once they had marketed their products, currently this type of business activity is labeled by the younger women as men's work.

METHOD

This study uses the interpretive method, stressing a form of ethnomethodology, to examine the ways in which farm and ranch wives construct their reality. The emphasis is on the words and methods they use to order and make sense of their social life and work. The focus is on the verbal methods used by farm and ranch women to construct everyday meaning. This type of theory has also been labeled interpretive sociology by Lengermann and Wallace (1985), who identify Peter Berger (1967) as the most significant current proponent. Traditionally this type of sociological inquiry originated with the sociologist Max Weber. I selected this approach because of its potential to highlight discrepancies between the current sociological model of the farmwife role and the older biased descriptions, often by male investigators, which were subsequently used to develop theory.

This analysis is based on taped, standardized interviews conducted with nineteen farm and ranch wives during the summer of 1985 in a rural county in southeastern Ohio. I asked questions about the following: type and size of farm; major changes in commodities produced; types and amounts of equipment used; date of acquisition of new major technology such as electricity, tractors, and household electrical and mechanical aids; involvement in overall farm activities for subsistence and market; types of housekeeping activities; childcare and off- and on-farm nonfarm work; involvement in farming marketplace activities; and community involvement. In addition, I asked the interviewees which of the changes that had taken place since they began farming they considered most important (Fink 1985). The interviews offer insight into the farm and ranch wives, construction of reality and the social structure within which they work. During the analysis of my interviews, I became aware of several words and phases used recurrently by the middle aged and younger farm and ranch wives to describe their roles. Their notions of who was a "real" farmwife and their evaluation of their own work roles in terms of being "on call" or "filling in in a pinch" reflect attitudes and construction of reality and shed light on the farmwife's invisibility as discussed by Boulding (1980), Haney (1982), and Sachs (1983).

SAMPLE

My primary criterion for interviews was that the women be farm or ranch wives or widows who had farmed during their active years. I obtained names of women for my interviews first from the county extension agent and the director of the local Agricultural Soil Conservation Service office. A few additional names were obtained by the snowball process, using names cited by the women I initially interviewed.

The women I interviewed lived throughout the county and represented a range of different commodity groups, including a grain operation, cow and calves, sheep, hogs, and dairy. I obtained a balanced sample with respect to age, farm size and type. The older women were actually giving an oral history of their farm experience (Henige 1982). Time and life have edited some of their information, but it does have value, since I focused on the perceptions of the individual. Thirteen of the nineteen husbands in the total sample had worked or were working off-farm – four in the older group, six in the middle group, and three in the younger group. These men had worked in a variety of jobs: as coal miners, painters, mechanics, school bus drivers, county road maintenance workers, truck drivers, plant supervisors, and extension agents. The women said their husbands had found jobs that were available and compatible with farming schedules.

Older Group
The six women in the older group had started on farms with mixed commodities, including small dairy herds, chickens, hogs, and sheep; small fields of wheat, oats and corn; and large vegetable and fruit crops. These women had started to farm with their husbands near the beginning of World War I. They ranged in age from seventy-two to eighty-four. Their farms ranged from 80 acres to 470 acres; the average farm size for the older women was 155 acres. All were born on farms. They all had children, with the range being from one to six children. The educational level for the older women varied from eighth grade to one year of college. Two had worked off-farm, one had an on-farm business that was not farm related.

The older group saw the introduction of electricity as the technological change that had the most profound effect on their role as farm wives. Introduced in the 1940s, electricity radically and progressively altered the types of tasks done and the amounts of time expended by women on farms. Before that several larger farms had electricity, using "Delco" battery systems to power lights and water pumps. Before this time much of the "work" was done by human labor and simple machines such as hand-operated cream separators, wood cooking stoves, churns and wash-boards and later wringer washing machines using gas motors.

Electricity was added to all aspects of the house and barn. It was used to pump water, to heat and light the home and the barns, to refrigerate, and separate milk and cream, grind animal feed, sharpen grinders, freeze produce, ventilate the barn, and power saws and drills. It replaced human labor and allowed for new forms of storage, marketing and distribution of grain, produce, meat, and milk based on refrigeration.

In the home, electricity powered the vacuum cleaner, stove, washing machine, lights, clothes dryer, iron, water heater, and indoor fan. It replaced men's and women's physical labor and altered the natural rhythms of the days and the seasons. New approaches emerged for cleaning house and processing and preparing food. Although there is currently a debate about whether household chores actually decreased or increased, it is generally agreed that these mechanical changes were "labor saving" and that women had more free time. The newer work patterns are based on increasing consumption of fossil fuels (Cowan 1983, Strasser 1982).

This free time was purchased. In order to use electricity or gas and oil regularly, a farm family needed a steady source of cash income. This income was acquired with more cash crops or by off-farm employment. Off-farm employment for women in the older group began in the 1930s with two women who took jobs as teachers. Husbands' off-farm employment also began during this period. Many of the women found themselves with increasing responsibility for farm chores previously done by their husbands, such as milking, mending fences and feeding the stock. Along with these added responsibilities was the need to continue cooking large meals to feed their family and the hired farm workers.

Besides changing the type and nature of the tasks performed, electricity often enabled these farm men and women to labor longer each day. Whether in the newly lighted barn milking or incubating chickens, or in the newly lighted home sewing or canning produce.

The other technological change which is considered paramount by women in the older group was the tractor, which seems to have come relatively late to this area. Although the tractor and the fields are typically considered a man's area, the majority of the older women I interviewed had worked with horses and operated tractors to perform farm field jobs, "helping" or "filling in" when needed.

Middle Group

The eight women in the middle-aged group ranged from forty-nine to sixty-seven years old and had from two to eight children. All but one of the women had been born on a farm. Their educational attainment ranged from eighth grade education to a registered nurse's diploma. These women began their farms just before and after World War II. They described starting out with mixed commodity farms and gradually eliminating "her" chickens, "his" hogs or the dairy cattle. The farms in this group are now one- or two-commodity farms. They were working on-farm, off-farm and doing nonfarm work on their farm site.

Two changes occurred together, during this time near the war, which altered the gendered division of labor. The local commercialization of farmmade food products like butter, cheese, and eggs occurred as these women began to farm; these had traditionally generated cash income for farm wives. The older women said they had used this income for children's school needs and household supplies. The middle group women said this income seemed to contribute so little to the overall farm operation that they soon stopped producing these products as there was no profit in them. Women in the middle group also described obtaining automatic washers, clothes dryers, indoor toilets. Often they spoke of giving up their chickens or turkeys to help with his beef or his hogs since these had gradually become the profitable commodity. The introduction of labor saving appliances and the commercialization of their traditional products freed them up to help with other farm chores. They continued to care for children, clean house, cook meals, and can or freeze meat, fruits and vegetables.

Radio and television advertising became popular at this time and allowed the mass merchandising of "name brands" for such items as bread, ketchup and pickles. Ability to purchase "store bought" products was often a sign of prosperity and a status symbol and, as more basic consumer products were commercially produced, the need for a reliable cash supply also increased.

Farm equipment – hay balers and larger and more powerful tractors – was added. Women in the middle group were currently working on-farm in nonfarm jobs – one as a cosmetic salesperson and the other as a caterer – to help with the debt from equipment purchases. Two women were now working off-farm, one as a salesclerk and the other as a nursing supervisor. One was working full-time on-farm as the bookkeeper and clerk for the grain operation. There was only one couple in this group where both worked off-farm, and it was a smaller truck farm.

There were two other unique characteristics of this group. All the women in this group said proudly that they were the farm's "gofer," the person who went to town for farm parts and supplies and took food and supplies to the fields when they were needed. This was also the only age group in which some women I telephoned did not want to be interviewed as farm wives. These women were performing the role as I defined it, helping on-farm like the other women I interviewed and also working at another job; however they stressed that they did not think of themselves as "just farm wives," it was important for them to be known by their nonfarm jobs.

Younger Group

The five women in the younger group all began to farm after 1967 on farms producing one or two commodities. The largest farm seemed to have incorporated most of the modern farm machinery currently available. The women ranged in age from twenty-seven to thirty-eight. The farms varied in size from eighty to fifteen hundred acres. All but one of the women had been born on a farm. All had two children. The women were working both on- and off-farm, and on-farm in nonfarm related work. Most had worked off-farm until their children were born, and several planned to go back to work off-farm when their children were in school. Two of the women worked off-farm full time, one as a pharmacy clerk, the other as a bookkeeper – and one worked off-farm part-time as a crop insurance adjustor. Three of the younger women had high school educations, and two had college degrees, one in teaching and the other in agriculture.

Increased capital is essential to remain in farming, and many U.S. farm families have become evermore dependent on nonfarm sources of income. Off-farm income is used to pay electric bills and purchase farm inputs such as fertilizers, pesticides and insecticides and appliances such as air conditioners, automatic dishwashers, microwave ovens, blenders, freezers for vegetables, fruits and meat in the home and barn cleaners, fans and conveyor belts in the barns. Off-farm employment was wide spread among farm families by the late 1950s.

The trend toward off-farm employment was present in the younger group. In two of these couples both partners worked in nonfarm jobs and these were smaller farms. All of the younger women described the jobs of bookkeeper and "gofer" as a major part of their contribution to the farm. Older subsistence type farm practices have almost disappeared. Only one of the younger women kept a cow for family use, and no one raised chickens. All the women continued to can and freeze large amounts of fruits and vegetables. Some continued to sew for themselves and their children.

The younger women did not talk with the same familiarity as the older and middle-aged women about marketing the commodities they helped to produce. The younger women said that while they accompanied their husbands to the markets, often groomed the cattle or hogs for showing, knew the approximate price they would receive, and usually recorded the sale when they came home, they did not participate in the actual transaction, as that was "men's work." Two of these women regularly participated in supermarket and fair promotion activities for marketing their products, which required travel throughout the state and into neighboring states; however, they did not participate directly in the buying and selling of the beef or hogs. The higher level of education needed to farm was what these women saw as the important change in agriculture.

DISCUSSION

All women in the older group had at one time performed separate, gender-based, tasks that generated income. They had produced, processed, and distributed cream, butter, and cheese, vegetables, or eggs and chickens; they described personally marketing these products in nearby towns.

For middle group women the marketing role set changed. Early on they had marketed their eggs or chickens and then stopped because "their husbands didn't like chickens." The men, it seemed felt the women's time and materials would generate more profit if she helped with his beef or hogs or if they expanded the dairy cattle. Male-sphere tasks which produced income – such as the raising of beef cattle – seemed to increase in importance and these women spoke of spending more time "helping" in this area as they grew older.

One woman in the middle group was currently catering using some farm products, in some ways she retained the marketing function of the older women. She was politically active in the county government and in state wide farming activities. Another middle group woman locally marketed vegetable produce, but middle aged and younger women on cow-calf, hog and sheep farms all said marketing was their husbands' area.

Women in the middle group who had started to farm between 1949 and 1960 were currently working in the widest range of roles as homemakers and mothers, volunteers in the community, and employees on-farm, off-farm and on-farm in nonfarm jobs. This was due to the dynamics in agriculture at large and in this county and to their stage in the family life cycle. Their children were more independent than the younger womens' and they described their work on- and off-farm as necessary for the health of their farm operation. Although a few kept some chickens and cattle for their family, none were marketing the products that the older women had marketed, such as butter or eggs.

The incorporation of electricity and mechanical aids in the home and farm, the commercialization of bread, canned and frozen fruits and vegetables, and butter and eggs, generally smaller families and fewer live-in hired farm hands – all these – decreased the total time and energy needed to produce, preserve, and prepare food. Yet these developments seemed to "free" these women for more work in the *male sphere* of the barn and fields, the demands of which had increased as the need for cash grew. Here the women described themselves as "helpers," available "on call" to "fill in" when needed. When this "filling in" "in a pinch" was explored it turned out to often involve seasonal field and barn labor on a regular basis. It was often in addition to the "gofer" job which tied them to the seasons and the farm. All middle group and younger women were also performing the bookkeeping for their farms and caring for the sick or the very young animals.

The role sets, while still divided by gender, have changed and fit into a wider matrix of agricultural production. The current agriculture system is based on a centralized commercial production system. Older women spoke of local markets and local processing of their produce. Now, the grain grown or the hogs raised in Ohio may be shipped many miles before being processed or consumed. This switch to a world wide distribution of food, enabled by transportation innovations, began gradually, but has recently accelerated bringing many changes in its wake (Danhoff 1969).

With these changes came a shift in attitudes toward work roles. Attitudes changed as some tasks became more important to the farm's survival in a strong market economy. Some tasks disappeared; others changed radically. Many tasks in the traditional male role set gained in importance and required increasing investments of time – for example, bookkeeping, field chores, and the care and marketing of cattle, sheep and pigs. These changes have brought a gradual change in attitudes toward traditional feminine roles; they are devalued. To understand current attitudes, it is necessary to look first at the feminist concept of patriarchy.

The feminist concept of patriarchy can help explain how technological innovation will be implemented. It describes the deep rules that are followed when roles change. Patriarchal cultural ideals dictate that men's work is more important, men should direct or tell women what to do, and men should not do women's work (Sachs 1983). While these rules are often considered "natural" and "right," it is important to understand what this changing "natural division of labor" looks and sounds like to the women who experience it. This social fact of patriarchy can affect attitudes toward changing tasks and subsequent role evaluation due to changing technology within the system. Patriarchal rules act as a method to order daily reality.

For example, middle and younger women often stated that there were other women in the county who would be better examples of a farmwife because they were doing *more* or different kinds of chores on their farm. Some women in each age group were referred to as "real." These were women who continued to can or freeze large quantities of meat, or women who cared daily for many animals and worked regularly in the fields. The criteria the women themselves used are interesting to note. Other women who were doing traditionally *male chores* or older types of female chores were labeled as *"real farm wives."*

The women's downplaying of their own substantial contributions could be viewed as a polite humbleness or as a sign of a confusion about the purpose of my research, or alternately and more importantly, it could indicate a system of jointly held meaning. A role blurring is created as the tasks have changed from the traditional gender divisions to newer but also gender-based divisions. Due to patriarchy, value is given to male tasks, they seem like work. The traditional popular accepted definitions of the farmwife role may be far removed from the current roles performed by women. Some of the actual tasks which remain have changed so radically in scope, such as the gofer, that it may be difficult for modern women to identify with the traditional title. The actual time women spend in accounting, a less wifely task, may be many hours more than twenty years ago.

The preoccupation with what was considered "real" was evident in many ways. Mrs. B. an eighty-two year old, vivacious woman, related a revealing incident. Years ago, in the 1950s, the B's were discussing their plans for retirement and moving into town. Mrs. B. had a large flock of chickens and had marketed eggs and dressed chickens for many years, while her husband had raised beef cattle and worked off-farm. "Things had gotten too much for him she explained, now that his health was bad. Now, he would have time to do all the things he had wanted to do like fishing and reading." She said to him that she had not decided just what she would do when she retired; maybe she would continue to keep a few chickens. He then said that she didn't need to think about retirement as she had never really worked. At first she laughed and thought he was joking; later she came to understand that he had meant what he said. Since she had not worked at the same jobs he had in the barns and fields, from his point of view she had not *worked*.

When Mrs. B. came to this realization about twenty years ago it was a painful time in her life. She had thought that this would be a time when they would grow closer to each other, but it was not, once she understood that her husband did not value her work. He had taken for granted the meals she cooked, the clean house and the income from the chickens and boarders. On their five acres at the edge of town, which they retired to, she had about four hundred chickens per year for sixteen years and several regular boarders for twenty years.

Not all men would be so blind to their wives' contributions and many women are not so articulate as this woman, but several older women said they missed the independence of having their "own thing," such as butter or eggs. The incident related by Mrs. B. illustrates how the invisibility of women's work, and with time farm and ranch wives' work has become even less distinct. In addition to the domestic chores, women absorb the slack or fill in where needed, staggering their other farm and home chores to allow for planting and harvesting needs.

Most people behave and speak in ways that reflect their understanding of the social world. They construct a meaning based often on unstated rules, then behave accordingly.

The meanings are learned through a circular process between the individual and collective life, wherein meanings or beliefs are made visible through words, actions and products. These externalized ideas then become a part of the social world of others, where they are internalized (Lengermann and Wallace 1985, 13). In this paper, the use of new technology and the words used to describe roles become incorporated in a farm and ranch wife's system of reality ordering. This is reflected in the choice of words they use to describe their roles.

Complex technological factors influence the changing reality of the role of the farm and ranch wife, and there are mechanisms in our society which stabilize and limit the change. Changes in social arrangements, such as the division of labor, lag behind changes in technology. This process is labeled a feedback process in systems theory. The existing feedback mechanisms from the existing structure determine the direction the system will take (Summers 1983, 2). Patriarchal rules act as a powerful feedback mechanism, defining which tasks are "women's work" and which are "men's work." These rules also say that men's work is the most important or instrumental, that men have the right to direct women's work, that women are therefore "helpers" and not partners with an equal voice in decisions. Many of our current divisions of labor are based on a patriarchal paradigm that acts as a pervasive feedback mechanism limiting how the roles will change or how technology will be implemented.

When I specifically asked the older women if they had worked in the fields during their marriage, they usually responded, "He didn't *make* me do the field work; I liked to do it." I had not asked if they liked it or if they had been made to do it. The middle-aged and younger women did not respond in this manner. Some aspects of the patriarchal ordering have decreased. The middle and younger women referred to themselves usually as helpers and only one called herself a partner. They said that they worked in the fields more than their mothers had because they "must" for the farm to survive.

If these women were helpers in most of the male farm chores, they were the main source of labor for the domestic chores, which the men did not help with in any group. I asked if they were helped by their husbands in household chores; one older woman answered with a laugh and said, "No! His father would have kicked him out of the kitchen." The kitchen and home were and continue to be "women's work."

Marketing now seems to have become strictly "men's work." Is this because it involves unstated rules not known to women or is it because it is an adversarial situation involving large sums of money? Are women biologically unable to compete in the market place? Is this just an instance of male prerogative and a marking by exclusion of women? A gendering of work to keep the power balance. Why as local markets closed were women excluded? How are young boy farmers taught the rules of the market place and young girl farmwives excluded and taught to be generalized helpers.

CONCLUSIONS

The intertwining of *varied tasks* of production, processing, and distribution of food with homemaking and childcare makes assessment of the full range of farm women's tasks and change for this role difficult. Two other factors also contribute to the invisibility and confusion about this role. First, unlike nurses, secretaries or teachers, the farm and ranch wife performs much of her work *out of the view* of most of the general public. Very few adults in the current generation were raised on farms, so they have little participating knowledge of either farm life or the specific work of farm and ranch wives. To them the production of food is a mystery. Or it is strictly a mechanical process. Secondly, women's participation in field work may be downplayed to maintain status in the local community. Men have higher status if they keep their women out of agriculture (Sachs 1983.) Inasmuch as a woman's status is linked to that of her husband it is not difficult to understand why a farm woman would tend to *downplay her contribution* saying she did it "just in a pinch."

As male tasks increased in a market economy and women's decreased, women's work was devalued even more than the traditional patriarchal notion of it as less important; women were incorporated in more subservient "helper roles." Even though the helper is vital to the operation and often has a commitment and overall knowledge of the operation, since the role was performed by a woman, the helper was not "in control" or the prime decision maker; this was the male job. Even as more men work off farm and women pick up the slack, absorbing the new tasks and using the new technology, they don't usually become the boss.

The above factors act as intervening variables that affect the total range of behaviors for the farm and ranch wife role. Technology is an independent variable that has not been incorporated into this role in isolation. Before the new technology, farm labor was divided by sex. How technological innovation has and is incorporated is greatly influenced by extraneous larger agricultural economic factors and patriarchal filters. Add to the above a general societal devaluation of most manual labor and the under-evaluation of women's domestic roles, and a model for the current invisibility of the role emerges.

The invisibility of this role seemed to extend to wide segments of the local population, both male and female, if the reactions of many local "in town" people – often the community leaders – are accurate indicators. Many of the people living and working in the county seat were not aware of the range of work these women continue to perform or of the role that farming had in the past or present economy of this county.

The statements by the women I interviewed, their perceptions of what is considered "real work" and how they are "absorbing the slack" are important to consider for subsequent research about this role. Important questions would be:

1. Was this a unique sample, particular to this economically depressed, hilly area, or are these patterns found across regions of the United States and in developing countries?

2. What else intervenes to suppress and distort the status of this female role?

3. Do present sociological survey instruments used to understand this role tap the role confusion and the newer "absorptive qualities" of this role?

4. It would also be important to trace the history of recent innovations for the farm family such as artificial insemination or genetic manipulation and their connection to patriarchy and gendered farm roles.

5. Are farmwives participating in market activities? If so, how, and how are the rules for this area gender-linked?

Looking closely at the *common words* and themes that reoccur in a limited set of interviews is not a highly quantitative scientific measure, and a more sophisticated index of patriarchal attitudes in farming and homemaking can be developed. Yet words and conceptual patterns are part of the method that these women use daily to make their world a coherent whole as they work and interact within their family and within the larger agricultural production system. The linkages for women into a farming system which requires increased education and knowledge of market structures and their apparent exclusion from the market transactions are areas that need to be explored. As farming is integrated into the business of agribusiness – often a male dominated field – will women be more invisible and less equal or will new gendered, but equal, partnership roles emerge?

NOTE

[1] I thank Girard Krebs, Robert Sheak, Murray Milner, Wava Haney, James Hunter and Lori Kent for their valuable comments.

BIBLIOGRAPHY

Bernard, Russell H. and Pertti Pelto. 1972. *Technology and Social Change*. New York: Macmillian.

Berardi, Gigi M. and Charles C. Geisler. 1984. *The Social Consequences and Challenges of New Agricultural Technologies*. Boulder, Colo.: Westview Press. 9-23.

Boulding, Elise. 1977. *Women in the Twentieth Century World*. New York: Sage Press.

_____. 1980 "The Labor of Farm Women in the U.S.: A Knowledge Gap." *Sociology of Work and Occupations*. 7:3. 261-290.

Bokemeier, Janet L., Carolyn Sachs, and Verna Keith. 1983. "Labor Force Participation of Metropolitan, Nonmetropolitan and Farm Women: A Comparative Study." *Rural Sociology* 48:4.

Cowan, Ruth Schwartz. 1983. *More Work for Mother*. New York: Basic Books

Danhoff, Clarence H. 1969. *Agriculture in the Northern United States*. Cambridge, Mass.: Harvard University Press.

Dillman, Don and Daryl Hobbs ed.. 1982. *Rural Sociology in the U.S.: Issues for the 1980's*. Boulder, Colo.: Westview Press. 124-135.

Fassinger, Polly and Harry Schwarzweller. 1984. "The Work of Farm Women: A Midwestern Study" in *Research in Rural Sociology and Development*. Harry Schwarzweller ed.. Greenwich, Conn.: JAI Press.

Fink, Virginia S.. 1985. "Impact of Technology and Patriarchy on the Roles of Farm/Ranch Wives in a Southeastern Ohio County." Master's Thesis, Ohio University, Athens, Ohio.

Hacker, Sally. 1977. "Technological Change and Women's Role in Agribusiness." *Human Services in the Rural Environment*. Spring/Summer.

Haney, Wava. 1982. "Women" in *Rural Sociology in the U.S.: Issues for the 1980's*. ed. Don Dillman and Daryl Hobbs. Boulder, Colo.: Westview Press. 124-135.

Kohl, Seena.. 1987. "Women's Participation in the North American Farm." *Women's Studies International Quarterly.* 1:47-54.

Lengermann, Patricia Madoo and Ruth A. Wallace. 1985. *Gender in America: Social Change and Social Control.* Englewood Cliffs, N.J.: Prentice-Hall. 38-50.

Lerner, Gerda. 1986. *The Creation of Patriarchy.* New York: Oxford University Press.

Millman, Marcia and Rosabeth Moss Kanter. 1975. *Another Voice: Feminist Perspectives on Social Life and Social Sciences.* Garden City, N.Y.: Anchor Press.

Robertson, James. 1982. "The Future of Work: Some Thoughts About The Roles of Men and Women in the Transition to the She Future." in *Women in Futures Research* ed. Margrit Eichler and Hilda Scott. Oxford: Pergamon Press. 81-83.

Ross, Peggy Johnston. 1985. "A Commentary on Research on Agricultural Farmwomen." *Agriculture and Human Values.* 11:1, 19-28

Sachs, Carolyn. 1983. *The Invisible Farmers: Women in Agricultural Production.* Totowa, N.J.: Rowman & Allanheld.

_____. 1985 "Women's Work and Food." Paper presented at the Rural Sociological Society Meeting, August 21-24. Virginia Polytechnic Institute and State University. Blacksburg, Va.

Schlebecker, John T. 1975. *Whereby We Thrive: A History of American Farming 1607-1972.* Ames, Iowa: Iowa State University Press.

Shover, John L. 1976. *First Majority – Last Minority: The Transforming of Life in America.* Dekalb,: Northern Illinois University Press. 144-172.

Strasser, Susan. 1983. *Never Done: A History of American Housework.* New York: Pantheon Books.

Summers, Gene F.. ed. 1983. *Technology and Social Change in Rural Areas.* Boulder, Colo.: Westview Press. 2-9.

Vogeler, Ingolf. 1981. *The Myth of the Family Farm: Agribusiness Dominance of U.S. Agriculture.* Boulder, Colo.: Westview Press. 204,287-291.

Wallace, Ruth, and Allison Wolf. 1980. *Contemporary Sociological Theory.* Englewood Cliffs, N.J.: Prentice Hall.

Wilkening, Eugene A. "Farm Families and Family Farming." in R.T. Coward and W.N. Smith eds. *The Family in Rural Society.* Boulder, Colo.: Westview Press. 27-37.

FARM WOMEN IN COMPARATIVE AND HISTORICAL PERSPECTIVE

14

WOMEN AND FARMING: CHANGING STRUCTURES, CHANGING ROLES

Sarah Elbert[1]

Less than one hundred years ago, rural America *was* America. Today, although 900 million acres are still classified as farmland in this country, an expert observer speaks for many people when she claims that "recent years have favored an evolution away from farming as a 'way of life' to farming as a 'business venture'" (Scheuring 1983). In the contemporary model of Social Darwinism, natural history seemingly selects that species of farmer most competitively adapted to survive in it.

Farming families used to be recognized as active shapers of American history, not passive victims of unnatural selection. They fed an expanding nation, and their produce dominated the U.S. export trade throughout the nineteenth century (and still amounts to some $33 billion [20 percent of all U.S. exports]). Farming families commanded respect from historians and politicians alike, because a nation of immigrants was certain that family ownership and operation of commercial farms was the basis of American republicanism, guaranteeing national self-sufficiency and a sense of voluntary community. The term "family" or "household," of course, glossed over the question of precisely which family members owned the land and received payment for major cash crops. Still, despite Euro-American patriarchy, women, in a diversified agricultural society, produced and reproduced. They and their work were visible if not equally rewarded. Euro-Americans' passion for individualism was equated with universal progress. Sweeping away native Americans' traditional agricultural practice of collective kinship with their natural environment was an ominous foreshadowing of modern alienation – a society in which boneless, skinless chicken appears to be grown in plastic wrap. There was still hope despite the patriarchal pattern of land holding; individualism and community could not become totally divorced so long as fathers husbanded their land, and water, and stock, and seed to pass it on to their sons. And farmers needed farmwives for all of this. Farming and the farm way of life were synonymous.

The rise of farming as solely a "business venture" in the twentieth century, has resulted in a decline in the number of farm families in numbers while the total number of acres tilled in the United States remains stable. An abundance of food in markets and cupboards hides the farm crisis from an urbanized nation. From 1960 to 1970 alone, the farm population diminished from 15.6 million to

8 million. Four hundred thousand people left farming in 1985 (U.S. Census). For census purposes the definition of a family farm is relatively simple: a family-managed farm that uses less than 1.5 (hu)man years of hired labor per year is a family-operated farm business (family farm). Family farmers are an endangered species.

FARMERS AND CONSUMERS: COMMON GROUND

Farmers and consumers are finding themselves in a common, though not clearly visible, vise. Parents find food additives responsible for Johnny's hyperactivity and Mary's continually running nose. The tobacco industry is subsidized while the Surgeon General declares smoking hazardous to your health. The American Heart Association urges a cholesterol watch, and millions of Americans are spending nearly one-third of their food dollars at fast-food restaurants consuming salt, sugar, fat, and refined flour – the very things the National Health Institute warns us against. Artificial fertilizers disrupt the trace mineral balance of the soil which reduces the nutrient value in crops eaten by animals and people. Finishing our hamburger beef on grain gives us a side of beef with 30 percent fat and 50 percent lean. We can then pay again and go to an exercise club to take off the storage-type fats we consume. Or we drink skim milk and long for television-advertised pizza and pastries made with the dairy surpluses of butter and cheese. These 'improvements' in agriculture do not result in long-term benefits to farmers, and they certainly do not benefit consumers even though grocery bills stay low in comparison with other industrial populations (Fox 1986).

Researchers enter the contested terrain on one side or the other; while Ann Foley Scheuring sees agri-industry as a species naturally evolved from farm families, Ingold Vogeler bitterly denounces the process as a rapacious social-historical plot. Vogeler denies that the farming family is still an entrepreneurial unit in the traditional sense and argues that farm families are merely occupying an "ecological niche." In other words they have been allowed to produce (through hard family labor and enormous indebtedness) the petty commodities deemed unprofitable for larger corporate investments (Vogeler 1981).

Whether one sees the declining numbers of family farms as an inexorable stage in a natural evolutionary struggle or in terms of the uneven development of modern industrialism, there is certainly a historical trend evident, both in the recurring farm crises and in public policies toward agriculture, from World War I to the present. With additional help from current surveys and business reports, there is now some consensus on *which* family farms stand in most immediate danger of going out of business and *why*.

Farm women's participation in agricultural production, as well as their responsibilities for households and their off-farm work, is being newly recognized in the context of the farm crisis. The strategic choices being made by farming families occur within a context of gender hierarchy, and, in the most threatened farm households, the struggle for survival may well require an understanding of American agricultural history in both its public and private spheres. Let us examine the "public" history of the recent farm crisis first. Then we can uncover the "private" side, what Carolyn Sachs identifies as women's "invisible" contribution to farm production and women's equally "invisible" contribution to reproducing the agricultural labor force (Sachs 1983).

Only a small share of the consumers' expenditures for food or clothing goes back to the farm – 13 percent in 1982, and that share is decreasing. Consolidation in the food industry reduces competition and leads consumers to pay an estimated extra $18 billion a year. Nine percent of the consumer's checkout slip goes for food and beverage packaging – $34 billion a year. Three to four cents on every dollar goes to pay for advertising – $7 to 9 billion a year. We pay taxes for price supports, subsidies, storage of surplus produce. Production goes up and up; costly inputs accelerate, and real farm income decreases.

Net farm incomes decline over the long haul as farms become larger, more specialized, and more dependent on fossil fuels and new agri-industry technology. Farms have to enlarge to produce more to cover the cost of increased inputs necessary to produce more. And so the vicious cycle continues. American middle-sized farms – the most productive, efficient units in the world – must adopt industrial practices to survive, and, with cruel irony, agri-industry is killing agriculture.

The farm crisis is popularly viewed as 'merely' a leverage crisis for some 580,000 family farms earning between $40,000 and $200,000 annually from farm produce sales. These are the medium size farms that account for 38.5 percent of the value of all U.S. agricultural output. Those farms producing below $40,000 in sales stay in business largely because of their off-farm earnings, and a good proportion of these are women's earnings. The 112,000 largest farms have a cost structure that virtually guarantees their high profitability, at least in the short term (*Farm Journal* 1985, Salant 1983).

The U.S. Department of Agriculture notes that the value of American farm land fell 12 percent in 1984, the largest one-year decline since the Depression (*Farm Journal* 1985). But land values have been dropping since 1981, and this adds to the financial squeeze on middle-level farmers because much of the money they borrow to operate is backed by their land. The lower the value of the land, the more precarious their financial position and the less they can borrow. In other words, they have less leverage. Farmers who sell land may well need to rent it back to keep up production, and others who need to expand acreage under production by renting land are in trouble because more farm operators have to rent land rather than buy it in a crisis. Younger farmers are especially hard hit because income flow from farming usually will not cover the principal and interest payments during the early years of a farm loan and beginning farmers must also support themselves and bear the cost of starting a family from low farm earnings. They are in competition not only with older farmers, who have higher equity in land, equipment, and stock, but also with non-farming investors who, because of their high income tax liabilities, want to invest in farmland for income tax advantages. Experts' advice, rising land prices, rising commodity prices, and liberalized credit all encouraged farmers to risk debt in the 1970s. But by the 1980s, the rising price of oil and gasoline helped raise farm production costs, high interest rates and falling asset values collided, and the exploding rise of the dollar hurt exports of agricultural products.

THE STRUCTURAL TRANSFORMATION
OF AMERICAN AGRICULTURE

All of this is evidence of a rapid decline from what is called the golden age of American farming from 1900 to 1920. Agricultural research by state and private agencies introduced fertilizers, labor-saving machinery, hybrid seeds, disease and pest control, and artificial insemination during this period, but, as Mann and Dickinson (1980) and others have documented, the golden age is more than a little tarnished when one looks at the concentration and centralization of firms supplying farm inputs already well under way. Farm machinery manufacturing firms declined in number from 1,943 to 910 in the 1880s alone. And the reduction of risks and uncertainties in producing some commodities led to greater penetration of those enterprises by agribusiness. As Jane Knowles powerfully describes the "golden age of farming," women's work, as reported in United States Department of Agriculture surveys and in a dramatic survey by *Good Housekeeping* in 1909, was almost totally lacking in labor-saving machinery. Farm women lacked access to telephone service and basic sanitation, and they desperately sought the opportunity to earn or to control cash incomes to help meet family needs. Their plight was as much social as it was private household grief, and ultimately they looked to home economics and the Cooperative Extension Service for solutions to their problems (Knowles 1987).

William D. Heffernan (1984) describes the transformation of poultry production as one illustration of the concentration of ownership and control of a food production system by agribusiness firms. Diversified family farms commonly kept a flock of chickens, and women's control of their "egg money" was proverbial (Jensen 1981). Hatcheries and feed stores were common in farming communities, providing off-farm jobs for men and women. There were many competing firms that would purchase broilers and/or eggs. Poultry flocks produced year-round, start-up time was short, and the weekly income was a welcome addition to farm families largely dependent upon seasonal enterprises.

In the past twenty-five years, over 95 percent of the commercially produced broilers and eggs have become part of an integrated production, processing, and distribution system. The farmer, called a "grower," signs a contract with the integrating firm that supplies chicks and feed, deducting their cost from the guaranteed price paid to the grower. Broiler firms market under their own brands in supermarkets, and some of them market into fast-food outlets and take-out centers as well (Heffernan 1984). By 1981 there were only 137 such firms in America, and by 1985 each of four firms had 15 to 18 percent of the market. Heffernan describes an international industry in which even these giants are losing to the multinational conglomerates that dominate milling and grain trade. Two of the four leading integrated firms are already subsidiaries of conglomerates.

These giants are not interested in limited-resource farmers. They want growers who can supply one family member full-time to poultry production, and growers must supply poultry buildings equipped with feeding systems, ventilation, and watering systems that meet the firm's specifications. To provide full-time work for an adult family member, growers usually need two or three equipped buildings at a total cost of over a quarter of a million dollars. Growers borrow for construction, mortgage land, and must pay off their loans over twenty to thirty years while contract agreements, including price, are based on each batch of chickens. In other words, the farmer-growers must renegotiate their incomes about five times a year. Growers keep producing in order to pay off their buildings, and then they often go out of business rather than face the costs and the loans necessary to modernize or replace buildings and equipment. While they are in business, one or both of the adult family members has an off-farm job to subsidize farming as a "way of life."

Fertilizers are supplied to farmers by one of the "largest and most concentrated capitalist industries" (Perelman 1977). Two giant companies producing hybrid seeds control 50 percent of the market for seed grains, and while production has dramatically increased, the quality of produce has declined. The protein content of corn, oats, and wheat grown from hybrid seeds has declined over the past fifty years (Mann and Dickinson 1980).

We could go on, thinking about Sand Livestock Corporation in Columbus, Nebraska, which wants to build a "hog hotel" that will produce nine thousand hogs annually in closed, dark, crowded conditions. Hotel-housed sows feed their litters while confined in narrow crates, lying on concrete floors with no bedding. Small piglets will get their tails chopped off to avoid cannibalism from their stressful housing conditions. Odor problems will devalue land values around the "hotel," and maybe three or four local, displaced farmers will be employed to oversee the mechanized care and feeding of nine thousand hogs. Of course, 110,000 bushels of corn will be needed to feed the hogs. It will be grown on contract – making farmers subcontractors of the hotel corporation. Farm women who have demanded and taken courses in swine raising as a positive (and humane) means of keeping the family farm will be out of business. In addition, there is the danger of epidemic diseases from such intensive, confined, industrial farming, the manure-disposal problems, and the likelihood of poor-quality, even dangerous, pork produced by feeding hogs water and feed from recycled manure slurry (Fox 1986).

The most serious consequence of the structural transformation in American agriculture from the point of view of surviving farm families, however, has been the recurring cycle of agricultural overproduction as farmers attempt to compensate for their inability to control costs and markets. Farm families went into debt to increase production for wartime demands between 1917 and 1919. When prices declined over 40 percent after the war, bankruptcy and foreclosures on farms preceded the national Depression. Agricultural surpluses continued to pile up as farmers struggled to stay in business. Finally, the New Deal inaugurated the Agricultural Adjustment Acts in 1933 and 1938, hoping to curtail production by using public monies to make payments to farmers who participated in acreage allotments and marketing quotas. Parity payments were authorized to farmers to make up the difference between the prevailing low market prices and the "target" or support price that might give farmers the same purchasing power they had prior to World War I. The Commodity Credit Corporation was set up to buy, handle, store, and sell surpluses. Farmers received nonrecourse loans for their surpluses. The system has endured with some modification to the present time. If the market price does not go up, farmers can take the government support price. If the market rises, farmers can sell the commodities themselves and pay off the loan.

The problem is that government price supports are distributed in proportion to the share of total production each farmer controls. The largest farms get the most government payments; those farms in the less than $40,000 sales category get virtually no support. Overproduction has not been curtailed because middle and large farmers intensify production with fertilizers and no-till corn practices combined with herbicides, and, of course, they often cease crop-rotation conservation practices in order to maximize cash crops. They also divert their least productive land to meet acreage allotments and land retirement programs. The result is a leverage crisis, great price fluctuations, and unstable, declining farm incomes.

Nevertheless, the most important question is not why so many farmers must leave the land, despite their years of hard work and their sincere acceptance of "scientific" advice about the best farming and business practices. Frederick Buttel asked the most cogent question in 1982: "why the family labor [farm] can be so persistent in an advanced capitalism dominated by large-scale corporate production?" (quoted in Sachs 1983). The answer lies in the continuing struggle of farming families to integrate farm and family roles in the face of proliferating wisdom that insists family labor is an anachronism and modern farm women's work is reproductive rather than productive.

WOMEN'S ROLE ON FAMILY FARMS

In the early decades of this century, everyone in farming families played a crucial role as a producer and citizen. Indeed, the balanced spheres of farm and home seemed to provide a model means toward the enormous task of reorienting American culture to modernize it. Farm women and children in the first half of the century were important producers. Although New York State rural school leaflets for use in 1909 publicized white-uniformed male technicians making cheese at the New York State College of Agriculture, the leaflets also acknowledged that of the 115 million pounds of butter produced annually in the state, nearly two-thirds was made on farms. Although cheese was now made in factories, farm-home-produced commercial butter was still the particular work of women and girls (Cornell Rural School Leaflets 1909). The early leaflets and the Reading Courses for the Farm Home evidence considerable conflict between promoting more efficient means of household production for market and promoting a balanced separation between the spheres of home and work.

Rural school and home economic extension workers proselytized modern scientific farming and homemaking while reminding their clients that the participation of women and children in production was a last historical remnant of primitive cultures. There was a significant struggle going on between rural women who eagerly, sometimes desperately, sought advice in order to maximize their productive roles and experts who, while sympathetic, nevertheless believed in the inexorable progress of civilization through a functional gender separation of spheres. The family in which men played productive roles and women played newly elevated reproductive roles in rural life was promoted as the path to abundance and social harmony. A wealth of historical evidence documents that struggle between 1900 and the present, including rural school leaflets, home economics extension bulletins, and correspondence between educators and political leaders, and experts and producers. A rich and often contradictory prescriptive literature on home production for children as a learn-by-doing process teaches young people the craft of scientific milk testing, hygienic butter and bread making, cultivation of yeasts, poultry raising, and sheep shearing. The lessons are sometimes gender-segregated: both bread- and butter-making contests, for instance, are for girls alone. Sometimes, however the curricula are integrated, as in nature-study projects or home and school gardens. This literature is accompanied by students' and teachers' reports on their projects. Children and teachers report back to the experts, and adult student groups or clubs also follow study guides and report back. Even more importantly, many readers in each category ask for specific advice and freely describe their own situations. Rural women in particular pleaded for research publications and advice on the means to productive autonomy within the farming enterprise. Whether married, widowed, or single, many of these women wanted the integration of rural life and work, and they said so – demanding, pleading, cajoling experts for the means to such integration. Agricultural colleges and universities were going in another direction – reinforcing, perhaps even leading the way toward, industrial agriculture, which they argued would produce an abundance for market sufficient to make women's productive skills and their desire for autonomy superfluous. A "modern" industrial model of agricultural production would necessitate expert homemakers. Women's roles were to be transformed, specialized for reproduction in an educated blend of nature and culture. This chapter only begins to outline a small part of the struggle over shaping the relationship between home economics and rural work. *It was a struggle* – rural women and children did not really ever part, I argue, with their productive skills and their desire for integration of home and work. *Only a continued role in production could insure equality*; if they could not remain producers, they were doomed to dependency, and they knew it. Home economics potentially offered an opportunity for vocational training, development of markets, and even expert help in building cooperative enterprises and genuine farming partnerships between men and women. Such a potential democracy was never realized; separate spheres were not equal and they masked the integration of production and reproduction that actually made family farms efficient and rewarding to farming men, women, and children.

Instead, agri-industry and a newly vigorous gender separation of farming spheres had their roots in a muscular campaign called "The Country Life Movement" in the early twentieth century. By 1911, reformers, including President Theodore Roosevelt, were fearful of the degradation of the Anglo-Saxon race by the vast immigrant population, including Southern and Eastern Europeans, Asians, and Latin peoples – the "huddled masses" whose hands ran the machines of progress. Many leaders of agricultural progress joined in the Country Life Movement, hoping to enhance and preserve the character and habits of "Jeffersonian," native-born farm families (Bailey 1911). Liberty Hyde Bailey,

Director of the New York State College of Agriculture at Cornell, wrote a small history of the movement, detailing its analysis of the contemporary American condition and its goals for the future.

He accepted the new urban hegemony and stated matter-of-factly, "We shall never again be a rural people." And he was precise about the kind of agriculture suitable to a modern America: "The real problem before the American people is how to make the country population most effective, not how to increase this population; the increase will be governed by the operation of economic law" (Bailey 1911). Rural life proponents and their allies, the euthenics advocates, assumed the inevitability of a time

> when there are no new lands, and when we shall have taken away all the first flush of the earth's bounty; then the future farmers of America must truly be a superior race; the character of the farm man, therefore, becomes of supreme importance, and all of the institutions of society must lend themselves to this personal problem. . . . It is perfectly apparent that the fundamental need is to place effectively educated men and women in the open country. All else depends on this (Bailey 1911).

Agriculture was concerned not only with the production of materials but also with the making of homes on the land where production took place. Family farms must not yield to corporate, distanced ownership. The reason, as Bailey honestly put it, lay deep in the faith of American reformers that the "virgin land" had made their country's fate different from that of older civilizations, past and present. He said:

> Civilization oscillates between two poles. At the one extreme is the so-called laboring class, and at the other are the syndicated and corporate and monopolized interests. Both these elements or phases tend to go to extremes. Many efforts are being made to weld them into some sort of share-earning or commonness of interest but without very great results. Between these two poles is the great agricultural class, which is the natural balance force or the middle-wheel of society. These people are steady, conservative, abiding by the law, and are to a greater extent than we recognize a controlling element in our social structure (Bailey 1911, Bowers 1971, Ellsworth 1960).

There is nothing new, of course, about American reformers being right for the wrong reasons. Fearful of "race suicide" and "mongrelization," many Progressives saw American farm families as a conservative bulwark against the tide of vigorous, diverse, ethnic and racial immigrants. Reformers argued that the farm home should be as modern and comfortable as the city or suburban home to refresh educated farmers and rear the future farmers of America. Such a campaign might have freed farming women from household drudgery and contributed to full gender equality in production and ownership. But the "controlling element," or racial bias, inherent in the movement also had unhappy prescriptions for American farm women of several races and ethnic heritages.

Liberty Hyde Bailey stressed that "farming is a co-partnership between a man and a woman." What did he mean by the word "partnership" in the "golden age of agriculture"? Bailey sent a letter to five thousand New York State farmwives whose husbands were already enrolled in a Cornell Extension program designed to educate farmers in scientific farming methods. He invited their wives to take a reading course through the "university extension of agriculture." He called it a "partnership" course because he made two assumptions: (1) that "we never think of an unmarried farmer" and (2) that "of a hundred widows with a family of children and a farm, we are sure a larger percentage will make a success in the single-handed struggle than would the same number of widowers in the same condition" (Bailey 1911). The reading course for farmwives was widely advertised in the *Ladies Home Journal*, *The Rural New Yorker*, and the *Delineator* from 1921 to 1926. It was a phenomenal success, ultimately servicing between fifty and seventy thousand readers.

Martha Van Rensselaer, supervisor of the course, was Cornell professor of home economics between 1900 and 1920. The course is of some interest to us for several reasons: it is representative of the home economics movement; it is part of the Progressive dream of cultural uplift and assimilation; and it reveals, in letters from the women who took the course, what some women hoped their role in modern American agriculture might be. These women were not likely candidates for women's colleges' liberal arts programs. Women's colleges avoided courses in domestic science or home economics as unlikely to "furnish a serious or profound course of training for really intelligent women" (Newcomer 1959). For rural wives, mothers, and daughters, who could not afford to attend private women's colleges, extension courses such as the Cornell Reading Course were a blessing. The pamphlets were free to New York State residents, and the women who took them wanted both culture and vocational training.

Home economics education entered colleges in the 1870s after the Morrill Land Grant. Ever since Catharine Beecher published *A Treatise on Domestic Economy* in 1841, many advocates of education for women had promoted professionalization of women's roles as wives and mothers. Teaching was a natural extension of woman's sphere, and professionalization of homemaking would ensure that women's traditional crafts such as nursing, sewing, and cooking might offer cash in a wage-labor force.

By the 1880s, domestic science was a mainstay of public schools, private schools, and settlement house courses. It Americanized, promoted a single middle-class standard for home life, and institutionalized the notion of woman's proper, indeed her professional, place in household economics. Less obviously, it also extended women's sphere to include problems of sanitation, nutrition, child care, schooling, and farm-home industries. Land grant colleges in the West enthusiastically took up domestic economy and domestic science. Along with eastern institutions, they emphasized scientific principles and research. By 1899, eastern and western proponents of home economics met at the first Lake Placid, New York, conference. For ten years they met annually, and by 1908 they cre-

ated the American Home Economics Association. Anxious to establish themselves and their students as professionals in the new American "culture of
professionalism" (Bledstein 1976), they distinguished between home economics,
at the college level, domestic science in the high schools, and introductory programs in domestic economy in the elementary schools.

Interestingly enough, Ellen Richards, the first president of the American
Home Economics Association (1908) and instructor of sanitary chemistry at the
Massachusetts Institute for Technology, linked rural women and immigrant
women together as a targeted clientele in need of the science of "euthenics, an
essential preliminary to the study of the better race, a study to which Mr. Francis
Galton has given the name Eugenics" (Richards 1908). The obstacle to scientific
improvement of home life, she said, "seemed to be in the woman herself"
(Richards 1908). It was necessary for housewives to understand the home as a
place for the nurturance of children and "for those personal qualities of self sacrifice for others for the gaining of strength to meet the world" (Richards 1908) and
to understand economics as the science of efficient time and energy use as well as
the management of family income. The social work and public education directed
at assimilating and homogenizing diverse immigrant groups between the end of
the nineteenth century and the First World War are well known. The effort of the
same Progressive movement to enlist farm women as students in agricultural,
evening, and vacational schools, extension programs, and farmers' institutes is
less well known. The standard upheld to both immigrant women and farm
women was a new pseudoprofession, unpaid and unlicensed – housewifery. This
new, scientifically trained profession was only available to one sex. Women
were born home economists and yet not provided by birth alone with the skills
necessary to their "natural" professional roles. Education and technology could
streamline their daily chores and provide the tools necessary to train them for
their "expressive" roles, thereby uplifting not only individual families but the
entire society.

THE CORNELL HOME ECONOMICS PROGRAM

Cornell curiously procrastinated in developing its Reading Courses for
Farmers Wives into a Home Economics Department. Nearly all the land grant
colleges had departments by 1900 (Bevier and Usher 1912). Director Bailey,
Flora Rose, the home economics students and the farmers, wives have all left
their records of what women wanted and what they got. The first students in
home economics at Cornell contributed a handwritten "History of Home
Economics at Cornell," as an introduction to their class scrapbook (1911, 1912,
1913). Dedicated to Liberty Hyde Bailey, the account bears his inscription on the
first page with his own rationale for home economics: "The department of Home
Economics was organized to train a woman in efficiency and to develop her outlook to life. Such a department is a necessity as a means of developing societies.
It stands for the evolution of woman's work and place."

Bailey's inscription is followed by an expression of appreciation to Martha
Van Rensselaer and Flora Rose, co-directors of the Home Economics

Department. Under their photographs is the students' version of the history. They wrote that in 1900 Liberty Hyde Bailey recommended a series of pamphlets be sent to farmers' wives, comparable to the reading course for farmers. Martha Van Rensselaer was asked to organize the women's course, and two thousand women enrolled. "It soon appeared, however, that these farm women who were taking this course wanted to talk with their neighbors on the subjects represented in the reading course lessons. As a result Cornell study clubs were organized and suggestive programs for their use were prepared by Miss V.R." So successful were these reading courses and clubs that, as the students put it, "It seemed desirable to develop further the work that the college could do for the women of the state." They then offered a winter course in home economics in 1906. The next paragraph is ingenuous and intriguing:

> The interest shown in home economics by women *outside* the college led to the belief that the college girl might also be interested in the subject. During the year 1906 a general course in home economics with three hours credit was given by Miss Van Rensselaer. The course was attended by about fifteen *men and women* from the College of Arts and Sciences and the College of Agriculture. Instruction was planned which would give students a practical knowledge of home-making and would prepare the way for more permanent teaching.

More permanent teaching resulted when permission was given for a Home Economics Department within the College of Agriculture in 1907. Clearly rural women wanted home economics training – they wanted information on home production and marketing, food preparation, sanitation, child care, and vocational training to earn additional income.

Martha Van Rensselaer became interested in rural women when she was a rural school commissioner between 1894 and 1900. She knew of the farmers' course, and she was certainly involved with Anna Comstock, and John Spencer's famous nature study programs. These programs for rural schools and youth clubs deserve greater study because they evidence a magnificent attempt to integrate agriculture, nature, and rural community life. Van Rensselaer had organizational skills and she was familiar with rural politics, but she did not have a college degree. Bailey appointed Van Rensselaer and Flora Rose, who did have a master's degree in science, as co-directors of the program.

The letter sent by Liberty Hyde Bailey and John Spencer announcing the reading course for women mentioned that the first topic was "Saving Steps." It was clearly the home economics version of the now infamous Taylorism, or scientific management, movement. The industrialization of farming had its start in reading courses for farmwives! Two thousand women replied that they wanted the first bulletin, "Saving Steps," and they were encouraged to send in comments that would be published annonymously in subsequent bulletins. Martha Van Rensselaer was a bit broader in discussing her goals. She thought that home economists might

assist women living on farms in solving their many household problems . . . relieve the monotony which in some isolated parts of the
state affects the attitude and health of its women . . . [and create] better sanitary conditions and more healthful living. Besides the farm
acts as a stimulus to high living as well as to approved methods of
housekeeping.

Education and Information for Farm Women

The idea that farm life was a stimulus to higher living came partly from the
rural school leaflets, which unashamedly recognized close ties with nature as a
great moral and aesthetic farm asset (one that modern women in agriculture also
value). The bulletins published by the Cornell Department of Home Economics,
were published irregularly at first and then by 1912 came out monthly. In addition to encouraging appreciation for the rural environment, the study course bulletins covered history, child care, rural schools, self-education, physical exercises, gardening, food preparation, laundry, interior decorating, and women's
civic responsibilities, as well as canning, baking, and preparing poultry for market. From 1901 to 1922, the enrollment grew, and the title changed from
"Cornell Reading Course for Farmers' Wives" to the "Cornell Reading Course
for the Farm Home," signaling a more distinct separation of male production
and female home-making in the minds of experts. To emphasize this, the
farmwives' progressive reading course included a pamphlet entitled "The Life of
Primitive Women." It made clear that women's labor in fields and in home production was an important but unenviable early stage of human evolution. Higher
civilizations were marked by gender specialization and separate spheres; women's
highest role was – professional homemaking. The farm partners proposed division of labor marked a higher evolutionary stage than native Americans, immigrants, or farm women had previously known.

Martha Van Rensselaer quotes Dean Bailey's address to the Girl's Club of
the College of Agriculture:

The farm and the home are the two underlying factors in the country-
life development. As the strength of a chain is determined by its
weakest link, so will the development of rural civilization be determined by the weakness of the farm as an economic unit or by the
weakness of the home as a social unit. It follows, therefore, that the
woman has equal and coordinate part with the man in the redirection
of rural society. Not only will she be able to create a sentiment for
better farming itself, but it is to be expected that her best contribution will be to create a quickened sentiment in respect to the homemaking and householding end of country life, I do not mean to restrict woman's activities, but we must recognize the law of nature
that certain activities are primary and others are secondary. . . .

> Whatever a woman may gain, she must never lose her domesticity. Her effectiveness as a social agent depends directly on her retaining the natural womanly qualities (Van Rennsselaer 1913).

By 1920, sixty-five thousand readers had been enrolled, and women who took the course often mailed their answers to discussion questions to Martha Van Rensselaer. Study clubs met twice a month to discuss the bulletins and enjoy refreshments and their own musical or recitation entertainments. Van Renssalaer encouraged a personal identification with the courses and with Cornell, and her students responded with news of their own personal lives and with thoughts about the subjects raised in bulletins and study groups. Indeed, some of the postal exchanges went on over a period of several years. Approximately one hundred letters survive in a file labeled "Reading Course: Letters from Readers" in the Cornell Archives Collection of Home Economics. The archives are unusually rich in detailed correspondence with ordinary rural women because the Cornell Reading Program distributed questionnaire forms for "discussion papers" which invited readers to answer by relating readings to their own experiences. The blank spaces provided for answers were not only filled in by readers, their handwritten replies often overflowed the allotted spaces, circling round the paper and filling the available margins. Not only did they explain the integrated circumstances of their lives and work, they often apologetically related that precisely these circumstances prevented their following the progressive practices encouraged in the reading courses.

Single women, married women, and widows asked for vocational guidance. They wanted to use home economics to earn money on the farm or nearby. Van Rensselaer excerpted some of the letters in her *Delineator* columns. Asking for more bulletins, one woman wrote: "I am very ambitious and wish to learn all I can about the *house and farm*" (Miss E. Brunjes to Cornell Reading Course, 11 April 1917). A twice-widowed woman wrote asking how she might run her farm to generate an income and produce her own sustenance (Mrs. Jem Robertson Richardson Clevenger to Cornell Reading Course, 12 January 1914). Cornell bulletins did indeed suggest ways for women to earn money by selling produce from fruit orchards or poultry flocks or goods canned at home. Such advice may well have aided farmwives to supplement family income, but the letter writers were not all in the same economic circumstances. City women unable to earn their livelihood or to continue stressful work wrote to Cornell, having read of the bulletins in women's magazines. An urban widow with only a few hundred dollars wrote asking Van Rensselaer if she might be able to settle in the country with her daughter and support herself there.

Another woman wrote asking about vocational training in agriculture because she was too ill to work in domestic service and she thought she might raise chickens somewhere in the country to support herself. A woman named Mary Ryan who had a husband and three children longed to take "a complete graduate course in the school of home economics at Chicago." She wrote often, and perhaps her most heartbreaking letter admitted that while she needed to earn a living for her family, she wanted so much to make something worth while out of my life. Is there any way on earth that Cornell can help me? Either fitting me for a teacher of home economics while I remain at home and perform my many labors of love, or fitting me in some way to earn a few dollars each week at home toward the future education of our girls.

Again she wrote

My dear Miss Van Rensselaer isn't there *some* kind of work for me which I can do at home. I find so much time while doing my house-work to just think, think, think. I try to keep my thoughts pleasant and useful but there are times when – well, I just get painfully downcast, discouraged and lonely (Mary Ryan to Martha Van Rensselaer, 14 September 1917).

Rural women included mill girls, too. From Manchester, New Hampshire, a former Cornell student wrote to Van Rensselaer that she had started a study club. All the town's domestic science teachers and many nurses attended, and there were so many interested women that they were short of bulletins. She added that the audience was "mostly young married women who worked in the mills and they are the ones that are so eager for it." She went on, "After the meeting I found one frail looking young married woman who works in the mills here, in tears. She said 'this is the first chance I ever had to learn anything like this and the bulletins were all gone before I could get one.' Needless to say I gave her my own copy." Yantis reported also that at least fifty other "young working women who keep homes and most of them babies, came up and took my hand and said it was the first chance they ever had of this kind and asked me to thank you for the bulletins." Effie Yantis was stirred to go on with the extension education: "I came home feeling I must weep or pray but decided to get out all my old notes which I took during that year's work with you, and all the old bulletins and go to work instead getting ready for the next lesson" (Effie Yantis to Flora Rose, 12 November 1915). Small towns and cities evidently still had some space for gardens and domestic animals. One reader wrote: "You see it is just people like us, the working class that need those lectures, and we make good use of them too, we have two acres of ground and will appreciate reading about inside and out of house" (Mrs. Joseph Dennler to Martha Van Rensselaer, 16 May 1917).

Some of the letters complain bitterly of farm life and women's lot. One writer insisted that all "the men want is pork, pie, and doughnuts." Another reiterated: "Men, men, mud, mud and my cellar. I wonder we are alive. Poor me. I know if everything had been kept properly my children would all be alive and well" (Discussion Papers returned to Martha Van Rensselaer, March 1905). At least one woman reported illiteracy in her community and suggested courses in reading, writing, and mathematics. She was seconded by a woman who said, "Please tell us how to begin and then give us all the aid you can. As you would do for the very young, some do not know how to read yet nor to write – only their names. Hardly legible at that" (Discussion Papers returned to Martha Van Rensselaer, April 1912).

Self-improvement, sociability, vocational training, housekeeping advice, child care methods, and earning money on the farm and in the village were all motivations for women's home study. Only one woman correspondence student was an independent farmer, and she and two sisters had inherited shares of the family farm and managed to buy out their siblings. There were, of course, widows who inherited their farms and a few women who were clearly farm partners with their husbands. But most respondents had, at best, an indirect claim on the land. All of the suggestions offered by Cornell for earning a living in agriculture depended upon access to land. None of the home production projects could hope to accumulate enough capital to purchase a working farm. The women who wrote nevertheless clearly expressed their vision of self-sufficiency and a hope for the development of local and regional markets for their products.

One of the most visionary writers, Mrs. Allen, wrote from California in 1913. Her committee of the California State Federation of Women's Clubs suggested that farmers and their wives and children might develop a mail order fruit and vegetable business. Dealing directly with their customers would guarantee a lower price for consumers and more profit for farmers. She hoped that Cornell might research the design and manufacture of containers for such a business. She was quite precise and emphatic, underlining her request:

> What *we need and need at once*, while the people at large are interested in this new line of transportation, is a regulation size crate that with its contents will not weigh over the 11 pounds, made suitable both for dry vegetables and also for those like peaches and plums which are apt to leak more or less juice. We also need either glass or heavy cardboard (waxed) for butter, lard, cheese, etc. etc. also cardboard (waxed) or some other suitable material for fruit and particularly berries. . . . Miss Rose will remember that our California cherries and currants and blackberries are much more solid and capable of being shipped greater distances than the Eastern fruit.

Mrs. Allen had an even broader vision; identifying herself with older women in need of employment, she wrote that such direct shipping of food might be an

> opportunity given to us with a small piece of land either in city or country of being able to specialize in any one of the many branches and will open possibilities to women of forty years or over of having a home and congenial work after she is too old for office, school and many other lines of city work" (Mrs. Clark Allen to Cornell Reading Course, 21 February 1913).

Another woman wrote,

> We have reached the point where no woman dares say that her education is finished. I also realize the necessity of constant polishing to

keep abreast of the times, to keep up with the children, to preserve a
joyous spirit and to expand our sympathies, and I heartily endorse the
desirability of basing the occupations of the Farmers' Wives on scientific principles, as well as to relieve them with a thought of poetry,
history or fiction and to pursue such a course has never been within
my reach before. So can you imagine the grip with which I grasp this
opportunity? Why it comes as an oasis to the traveler of the desert
(Nellie H. Mahanto, Cornell Reading Course, no date).

Surely the writers hoped for far more than Cornell's home study courses or home
economics, itself a young field, could offer them. In retrospect, their requests
seem far more visionary than anything proposed by educators and reformers.
Rural women rarely validated separate farm and home spheres in their descriptions of daily life. One more letter sent to Cornell makes this point vividly.

I weigh 120 pounds. I milk seven or eight cows night and morning;
run a separator; get breakfast, dinner, and supper; do most of the
cooking for five people; do all of the washing and cleaning; do most
of the garden work and rake some in haying. I feel very good most of
the time, only when I get too tired I have a headache and pain in back
of neck. I mend, read, and such but I don't have time to rest as we
have a 200 acre farm (quoted in Rose, Stocks, and Whittier 1969).

Martha Van Rensselaer, herself a rural woman, was both a teacher and a
student. She finally had to get a college degree herself in order to teach in a university department of home economics. She received a Cornell A.B. in 1909, and
the Cornell faculty records for October 1911 state that the university faculty,
"while not favoring in general the appointment of women to professorships, in-
terpose no objection to their appointment in the department of home economics
in the College of Agriculture" (Cornell Archives, Faculty Minutes, October
1911).

The separate course that evolved in the Agricultural College for women as
home economics grew into a separate college eventually. As long as the department still allowed non-home economics majors to take its nutrition courses,
men attended them in impressive numbers. But when a shortage of funds limited
student enrollment to majors, the men dropped out, for none of them were planning to be housewives, and the remaining fields open to qualified home economics majors were female-identified careers in dietetics, teaching, and the like.
It is not sufficient to attribute the current separation of responsibilities and skills
in farm families to the prescriptive campaigns of the short-lived Country Life
Movement or to the efforts of the more successful and often liberal home economics movement. Nor will it suffice to explain farming's gender hierarchy
purely in terms of a Progressive ideology that hoped to fashion a "steady, conservative, law-abiding" class of farm families as the balance wheel of society –
even if we admit that women were supposed to guarantee the conservative nature
of those families. Our understanding of the present status of farmwives and farm
families can be enhanced, however, by considering what Liberty Hyde Bailey

called the "solution to the farm-labor problem" – a capital-intensive system of agriculture. Scientific education in agriculture and home economics consciously if unwittingly promoted vertical integration of agri-industry.

CONCLUSIONS

Rural analysts generally acknowledge that farm households are now as fully mechanized and modernized as urban households of comparable income. Yet there is a catch-22 in this triumph of euthenics. The mechanization of agriculture that might have freed women's labor for other pursuits due to its superior efficiency has instead displaced both men and women farmers from their contemporary farms.

In 1967, Cornell College of Agriculture researchers returned to local farms in order to learn from farm families (Colman and Elbert 1984). Over a fifteen-year period, we found that the complexity of modern farm technology eliminated many traditional tasks of the farmwife, such as feeding the old-time harvest crew. But the farm chores had changed for male farmers as well. A great variety of modern farm tasks now took place in the home-farm office, and farm women were utilizing computers, directing or coordinating farm tasks on CB radios, and taking phone calls from sons and daughters away at college learning agricultural engineering, farm management, herd management, pomology, and horticulture, among other things.

The social science literature has insisted that farm work and household work are totally separate, and indeed, that the greater the separation of spheres, the more modern, efficient, and hence successful agri-industry would be. The reality is better presented by the women we interviewed. When asked whether washing the family clothes represented "farm work" or "housework," one woman threw up the lid of her washing machine in disgust, pointed out the "dark" wash mixture of barn suits, children's jeans, and furniture slipcovers tumbling about in the soapy water, and invited me to help myself to sorting farm wash from home wash. It took several years of lengthy visits to confirm that farm woman's view of her own integration of tasks, information, and roles. And, as Morrison and Wilkening (1963) sensibly noted, husbands and wives often report differently on their respective roles in farm labor and decision making. A husband may see his wife's contributions as limited to the family and the housework while she assumes that what she does is farm work.

Male farmers, we discovered, still depend upon a family labor force. The nature of their coordination and control of labor power depends upon the stage of the family cycle and the stage of farm development. Small to middle-sized dairy farms and grain farms, as well as stock-raising ranches, utilize a simple mode of labor control. The farmer or "boss" exercises power personally, sets the pace himself, hires and fires and uses "incentives and sanctions in an idiosyncratic and unsystematic mix" (Edwards 1979). Depending upon the form of land and enterprise ownership, the level of a woman's education, and her ability and willingness to combine household management, child care, and farming, this simple control can develop into a genuine partnership between husband and wife. Indeed, in times of crisis, the farming family's willingness to shift gender roles, to split time between on- and off-farm work, and to share child care often saves the family farm.

When the farm moves to a larger scale of operation and a corporate control model, the farmer may use impersonal language to assert that "the farm" does not "require" the services (and, incidentally, the challenging authority and expertise) of a farmwife and/or grown children. Family members have usually been crucial to that farm's operation in earlier stages. Nevertheless, they acceeded to the farmer's control of their labor not only because of the traditional pattern of male dominance within the family, but also because women share with men the goal of effecting an intergenerational transfer of a going farm enterprise. To many farm women, the phrase "he's the boss" is of secondary importance to the recognition that farm women play an important role in "doing it" (farming) and "passing it on." Ellen Richards counseled self-sacrifice to farm women. But modern farm families are often characterized by mutual sacrifice. When they lose the sense of personal responsibility for land and the larger natural environment traditionally associated with the farming way of life, they also lose their willingness to sacrifice their health, leisure, and imagination to produce our nation's food. Women in agriculture have not been self-sacrificing so much as they have been self-actualizing through the sense of "us" and "ours" that characterizes family farms. Herd health, flocks that are well fed and comfortably bedded, land that remains arable because it is naturally fertilized and allowed to rest and rejuvenate, have all been part of a system of agriculture that has rested upon a sacred "way of life."

In examining women's role in the shifting structure of American agriculture, we may be able to return *home* economics to its rightful place within economics – thus awakening that "dismal science" from its long hibernation. Economics must be prodded awake because women in agriculture demand an agenda that includes both progressive public policy to save our land and our way of life and private domestic reform because natural resources include people – our population of men and women. Michael W. Fox has called the industrialization of American agriculture "agricide" (Fox 1986). The farm crisis is not only the agony of American farm men and women; it presents a major threat to America's security. *Agriculture* is regenerative; agri-industry is exploitative. It destroys land, water, air, animals, and people. And agri-industry is, indeed, killing agriculture.

Family life and family farming are integrated, and women's productive and reproductive work cannot be neatly separated without losing the holistic reality of farm families, family farms, and their location in a world system. "Way of life" is not a sentimental term. The tendency of researchers and policy makers to analyze the impact of work on the family obscures the family itself as a changing structure that shapes and constrains production. The personal ties linking owner-operators to family workers on family farms have often enhanced production because "way of life" and "passing it on" remain primary goals of farm families. More specifically, passing on both their skills, values, and the farm itself remains a primary goal of *women* in farm families. Farm ownership, to be sure, remains a largely male terrain and women still have to contest access. But farm women are already on the site, and they are contesting and cooperating at the same time. They want individual recognition and smoother integration. For over one hundred years, they have demonstrated a form of feminism that reaches beyond any simple definition of autonomy or individualism – farming women have claimed the right to integrate work and family life with an enduring respect for the earth which is, after all, one sphere.

NOTE

[1]The author gratefully acknowledges the help of archival staff, fellow scholars and editors who include: Archivist Kathleen Jacklin and Peggy Pack of the Cornell University Archives; Gould Colman, Cornell University Archivist and initiator-guiding light of the Farm Family Documentation Project; Wava Haney, Jane Knowles, and Cathy Loeb of the University of Wisconsin who provided precise and imaginative editing; and Jean Morton and Cindy Curtiss of Cal Poly, San Luis Obispo, who tirelessly processed, revised, and re-processed this study.

BIBLIOGRAPHY

Bailey, Liberty Hyde. 1911. *The Country Life Movement*. New York: Macmillan.

Bevier, Isabel, and Susannah Usher. 1912. *The Home Economics Movement*. Boston: Whitcomb & Barrows.

Bledstein, Burton. 1976. *The Culture of Professionalism: The Middle Class and the Development of Higher Education in America*. New York: Norton.

Bowers, William L. 1971. "Country-Life Reform, 1900-1920: A Neglected Aspect of Progressive History." In *Agricultural History*, 14, No. 3, 211-221.

Colman, Gould, and Sarah Elbert. 1984. "Farming Families: 'The Farm Needs Everyone.'" In *Research in Rural Sociology and Development*, ed. Harry K. Scharztweller, vol. 1, 61-78. Greenwich, Conn.: JAI Press.

Edwards, Richard C. 1979. *Contested Terrain: The Transformation of the Workplace in the Twentieth Century*. New York: Basic Books.

Ellsworth, Clayton. 1960. "Theodore Roosevelt's Country Life Commission." In *Agricultural History*, 34, No. 2, 155-72.

Farm Journal (Eastern Ed.) 109 (Mar. 1985), 13-17.

Fox, Michael W. 1986. *Agricide: The Hidden Crisis That Affects Us All*. New York: Schocken Books.

Heffernan, William D. 1984. "Constraints in the U.S. Poultry Industry." In *Research in Rural Sociology and Development*, Vol. 1, 237-60.

Jensen, Joan M. 1981. *With These Hands: Women Working On the Land*. Old Westbury, N.Y.: Feminist Press; New York: McGraw-Hill.

_____ 1983. "New Mexico Farm Women, 1900-1940." In *Labor in New*

Mexico, ed. Robert Kern, 61-81. Albuquerque: University of New Mexico Press.

Jones, Calvin, and Rachel A. Rosenfeld. 1981. *American Farm Women: Findings from a National Survey.* NORC Report No. 130. Chicago: National Opinion Research Center.

Knowles, Jane B. 1987. "It's Our Turn Now: Rural American Women Speak Out, 1900-1920." Chapter in *Women and Farming, Changing Structures, Changing Roles*

———— 1984. "The United States Cooperative Extension Service: The Origin of the Gender Gap." Paper presented at the Conference on American Farm Women in Historical Perspective, New Mexico State University, Las Cruces, N. Mex.

Mann, Susan, and James Dickinson. 1980. "State and Agriculture, in Two Eras of American Capitalism." In *The Rural Sociology of Advanced Societies*, eds. Frederick Buttel and Howard Newby, 283-325. Totowa, N.J.: Allanheld, Osmun & Co.

Morrison, Denton, and Eugene A. Wilkening. 1963. "A Comparison of Husband's and Wive's Responses with Respect to Who Makes Farm and Home Decisions." In *Marriage and Family Living*, vol. 3, 349-51.

Newcomer, Mabel. 1959. *A Century of Higher Education for American Women.* New York: Harper & Bros.

"Cornell Reading Course for Farmers' Wives," New York State College of Home Economics Collection, 1900-1922, Cornell University Archives, Ithaca, N.Y.

Richards, Ellen. 1908. "Ten Years of the Lake Placid Conference on Home Economics: Its History and Aims." *Proceedings of the Tenth Annual Conference* (Lake Placid, New York).

Rose, Flora, Esther H. Stocks, and Michael W. Whittier. 1969. *A Growing College: Home Economics at Cornell University.* Ithaca, N.Y.: Cornell University Press.

Sachs, Carolyn E. 1983. *Invisible Farmers: Women in Agricultural Production.* Totowa, N.J.: Allanheld, Osmun & Co.

Salant, Priscilla. 1983. "Farm Women: Contribution to Farm and Family," Agricultural Economics Research Report No. 140, Economic Research Service, United States Department of Agriculture and Mississippi State University.

Scheuring, Ann Foley. 1983. *A Guidebook to California Agriculture.* Berkeley, Calif.: University of California Press.

———— 1983. *Tillers: An Oral History of Family Farms in California.* New York: Praeger.

Taylor, Marcia Z. 1985. Lecture given at Farm Crisis Conference, Washington State University, Pullman, Wa.

Van Rensselaer, Martha. 1913. "Home Economics at the New York State College of Agriculture," *The Cornell Reading Courses*, vol. II, No. 37, Rural Life Series No. 3.

Vogeler, Ingolf. 1981. *The Myth of the Family Farm: Agri-Business Dominance of U.S. Agriculture.* Boulder, Colo.: Westview Press.

15

PUBLIC POLICY AND WOMEN IN AGRICULTURAL PRODUCTION: A COMPARATIVE AND HISTORICAL ANALYSIS

Cornelia Butler Flora[1]

INTRODUCTION

Women's roles in agricultural production show enormous variation across time and space. This paper attempts to describe that variation and analyze it in terms of differences in the structure of agriculture and the policies that affect those differences. It is the hypothesis of this paper that policy generally affects women in agricultural production indirectly through its impact on the structure of agriculture. It is also hypothesized that major macroeconomic policies, rather than agricultural policies per se, have the largest impact on women and agricultural production.

I first delineate the nature of agricultural production and the ways public policy influence it. I then explain the unique role of the household in some types of agricultural production, discussing the interaction of internal household dynamics with changing structures of agricultural production.

Next, I present contrasting agricultural production systems, the policies that influence them, and women's response to those policy-generated shifts. The objective of the paper is to develop a model that links macroeconomic policy actions with those events that affect the role of women.

THE NATURE OF AGRICULTURAL PRODUCTION

Scholars have recently identified a number of characteristics that distinguish agricultural production from industrial production. Agricultural production must be done sequentially (Brewster 1950; Pfeffer 1983). The degree to which the rule of sequentiality holds varies by animal, crop, climate, and agricultural organization. In general, however, it is necessary to plow before one can plant and plant before one can harvest. In contrast, in industry production can take place simultaneously. The engine can be assembled at the same time the hubcaps are being attached at a different place in the same factory.

Sequentiality in agriculture is related to the time it takes for biological processes to occur. While one can plant immediately after plowing (if the moisture conditions are favorable), one cannot harvest immediately after planting. The seed must germinate, the seedling must develop, the plant must flower, and the fruit or grain must set and mature. As a result, there is a disjuncture between labor time and production time (Mann and Dickinson 1978). That disjuncture implies that labor must be mobilized at key periods in the agricultural cycle – and supported or dispersed at other periods.

Those characteristics have important implications for the gender of agricultural labor. In certain agricultural situations, women are a major reserve labor force. In other situations, migrant males perform the seasonal labor.

Sequentiality and seasonally lumpy labor requirements, caused by the biological base of agricultural production, have implications for land and capital as well. Women's multiple use of small plots and other income-generating activities serve to subsidize basic crop production and provide capital for the periods between planting and harvesting, making possible land-extensive production enterprises. Women are absorbers of risk and providers of capital in a variety of agricultural systems, from traditional peasant economies to highly mechanized commercial enterprises.

Public policies related to access to land influence women's productive roles in agriculture. When women have no clear title or right to land use, their options as producers are severely limited. Even more important are policies affecting the third factor of production, capital. Whereas policies influencing land and labor may be written to affect women's access to and control over land, labor (including their own), and the conditions under which they work, policies influencing capital seem on the face of it gender-neutral. Yet the indirect impacts of policies related to capital may be greater than the direct impacts of labor or land policies that specifically mention women. Policies related to capital may be more insidious in limiting women's options in agricultural production.

GENDER ANALYSIS

Gender is a more useful category of analysis than *women* for approaching women's role in agriculture and agricultural development because gender is a relational term (Carloni, 1987, Feldstein and Poats, 1985). Gender relationships can best be illustrated by first considering a stylized version of peasant agriculture. There is no one culture that this stylized description fits perfectly, yet the general characteristics fit traditional agricultural production systems in Asia, Africa, and Latin America. We will then look at changes from peasant farming systems to more capitalist forms of agricultural production. Those changes come about as a peasant farming system is increasingly linked into a world system of exchange. Although increases in these linkages generally result from the policies of both center and periphery nations, the relation of policies of trade, tariffs, foreign relations, exchange rates, and the like to the gender division of labor in agriculture and the options available to women in agricultural production is seldom considered. Changes in national and international linkages transform gender relationships because of the way the increasing international dependence affects control of land, labor, and capital.

This paper hypothesizes the following relationships between public policies and women's participation in agricultural production:

1. Policies affecting land.
    a. Policies that privatize land, particularly liberal reforms related to the alienation of land, decrease women's options in agricultural production.
    b. When land reform and titling takes place, unless women are specifically included, and official policy requires their systematic inclusion, their options in agricultural production decline.
    c. Policies, including tax policies, that encourage the separation of land ownership from land management (as in corporation farming) decrease women's options in agricultural production.
2. Policies affecting labor.
    a. Policies that lower the cost of labor increase women's participation in agricultural production, both as paid and unpaid workers.
3. Policies affecting capital.
    a. Policies that decrease the factor costs of capital decrease the options of women in agricultural production.
    b. Policies that encourage capital-intensive agricultural development, particularly agricultural specialization, decrease women's options in agricultural production.

PEASANT AGRICULTURE

Custom, rather than policy, determined the relations of production, including the gender relations of production, in early forms of agricultural production.

In peasant agricultural systems in the developing world, and in frontier agriculture in the United States, custom and necessity determined agriculture to be a family affair. Family labor is uniquely flexible in maximizing diversified survival strategies and minimizing risk. Labor can be mobilized when it is needed and sustained when it is not. But the family is not a "collectivity of reciprocal interests, a pooling of efforts in the benefit of all members" (Stolcke 1984, 265). Some members' interests may be in conflict with others. Benefits for some family members may be costly for others. Custom, including the obligation to participate in agricultural production and the right of access to the fruits of participation, often protects the less powerful members of the family unit. When custom is replaced by law, implying the imposition of public policy, a disruption of the gender balances derived over generations generally occurs. It is only recently that policy has begun to explicitly address women's rights and obligations in agricultural production, through such mechanisms as laws affecting labor, land ownership, and capital availability. However, many of the policies that have served to disrupt women's productive activities in agriculture have no direct remedial policy options.

The social division of labor (Durkheim [1893] 1964) in most peasant societies has two major dimensions: age and sex. What men do in some societies, women may do in another. Except for a few tasks, men's and women's work varies from one society to another. Although everyone does not do the same thing in traditional farming systems, everyone is productive. In certain Native American groups, when individuals felt that they could no longer work, they would walk out onto the prairie and patiently wait to die. Universal participation as a productive member of society is absolutely vital to the survival of the social unit in circumstances of high risk and little surplus production.

Gender- and age-based tasks interdigitate and are complementary in peasant agriculture. Generally men are in charge of such tasks as clearing fields and killing lions, while women manage work like seed selection and planting. Everybody harvests. Women often do the postharvest processing of food. Older women and older men do the lighter tasks. Wild as well as domesticated plants and animals are all part of the system. Knowledge of where to find wild plants and animals (which in some cultures include worms and bugs, key sources of protein and oil during the hungry season) is passed on from father to son and mother to daughter.

Because the risk is very high, traditional farming systems develop strategies aimed at the minimization of risk, including constant modification of the *multiple enterprises within the farming system* (Johda and Mascarenhas 1984). These modifications generally require little capital input and a flexible labor source – and are often controlled by women.

In peasant farming systems, land generally has use value. Men and women have equal access to the land they need. There are "his" crops, "her" crops, and "their" crops. Some of "their" crops might be sown on collectively held land. Capital inputs are generally low. These are labor-intensive systems, and the inputs are generated through the labor of the family.

COLONIAL AGRICULTURE

Policies that link traditional farming systems to the world system drastically change gender relationships and gender relations to land, labor, and capital.

Disequilibrium is introduced in traditional peasant farming systems by the accumulation of surplus outside the production unit by indigenous empires and by colonialism. Colonialism and neocolonialism have introduced disruptions in traditional farming systems through policies that have favored monoculture exports.

In most of the developing world, colonization was not an overt policy of the imperialist countries, particularly Spain and France. Only in rare cases, as in North America, were colonizers sent to the newly "discovered" continents to build a new country. Instead, administrators were generally sent on finite assignments to protect the imperial nation's policy interests, which included maintaining the flow of capital back to that country both through taxes and the extraction of raw materials. Later, policy also attempted to secure colonial nations as markets for the industrial goods produced in the imperial countries.

POLICY AND THE CONTROL OF LABOR: IMPLICATIONS FOR GENDER ROLES

Early colonial policy was oriented less to control over land than to control over commodities, particularly minerals and agricultural products. The limiting factor in controlling commodities was usually labor. The land needed for mining was generally not good agricultural land. However, the mines did require labor, as did plantations growing crops such as sugar, bananas, and cotton. These crops tended to be grown in lowland malarial zones, where most Indians had difficulty surviving. Labor, the male peasant agriculturalists or slaves from Africa, had to be brought to those areas. (Africans were genetically able to resist malaria due to the presence of a recessive sickle-cell gene.) In neither case was the labor provided willingly. The labor needed to work the mine, harvest the bananas, and cut the sugar cane was already well integrated into traditional peasant production systems. Men had specific productive roles in carrying out various agricultural, hunting, and gathering tasks that maintained the local social groups. There was no felt need for the wages paid by the mines and plantations.

The colonial powers initially used two major policy tools to insure the needed labor: taxes and enforced labor laws. For example, the Hut Tax in Africa provided a major new need for capital that forced African males to work in the mines to generate cash to pay the tax.

The imperial powers imposed taxes in many parts of Latin America with the same goal. To earn cash to pay taxes, one had to work in the Crown's mines, the Crown's plantations, or in the case of Central America, the plantations of the British or the North Americans. When the tax alone did not work, further negative sanctions were used, such as vagrancy laws. In Guatemala, the vagrancy laws defined any male Indian in the countryside not harvesting bananas as vagrant, subjecting him to arrest. Once imprisoned, gangs of prisoners were sent to work in the mines and plantations. The labor mobilized by tax and vagrancy policies for the plantations and mines was male labor.

Direct coercive policies were applied primarily to men. The representatives of the colonial powers had a very distinct norms about proper male and female roles. The Spanish, who conquered Latin America soon after driving the Moors, with their Islamic notions of women, from the Iberian penisula, felt women were to be in the house (*casa*) and men in the street (*calle*). Women were to be protected, as they were the carriers of the family honor. If they were exposed to men, they became the source of family shame (Youssef, 1974). Therefore, it was inconceivable that women should be exposed to the outside through productive work. It should be noted that these constraints were only possible for upper-class women, and the reality that women worked in agriculture and trade made no normative difference. That the policies requiring male labor for export agriculture actually increased women's productive work in many agricultural areas was ignored.

Similar norms were brought to Africa by the Victorian-Age British. Their view of the world was that of the upper-class Victorian family. It dictated that a woman should be at home, with her water colors and her tatting, playing sonatas on the pianoforte; taken care of by a man out doing battle in the rapacious world, the woman should prepare an environment to sooth his weary brow after he conquered the world. This notion of female "leisure" was brought to Africa by the imperialists. The taxation system, aimed at males, reflected the ideology that men take care of women and if they don't, they should. By making the men pay taxes, the imperial powers "helped" those men become "responsible."

Labor demands for most export crops is seasonal. Periodic male out-migration in Africa and Latin America was disruptive of the complementary farming system. The men often were not on the farm at key times in the agricultural cycle when their labor was needed.

In plantation societies, the fact that the men were often absent made it extraordinarily difficult for nonplantation agriculture to continue at all. For example, in the Caribbean, where export agriculture required a great deal of land as well as labor, subsistence production was reduced to small gardens (Chaney 1983). Women tended to become household heads and carry on various small-scale enterprises in addition to farming. In other places, such as Africa and Central America, the women were left to produce as best they could. Men tried to come home when it was time to clear the fields and harvest the crops. The complementary gender-role system began to break down, but in a highly differential pattern, depending on the degree of colonial penetration. While economic penetration was a private-sector phenomenon, it was facilitated at both origin and destination by public policy decisions.

Pfeffer (1983) shows how in the United States, where commercial agriculture has dominated, different policies in combination with different ecological circumstances and cropping systems led to different uses of labor. By extension, we can see implications for labor by gender.

Early plantation agriculture in the New World depended on slave labor, requiring public policy that sanctioned ownership of human beings and permitted slave trade. Such a labor force has built-in diseconomies pointed out by Weber (1978). The slave owner must provide for maintenance of the population when agricultural activity is not taking place and for the reproduction of the labor force, particularly the support of young children and the elderly, when they are not capable of peak physical production. In situations of slavery, or its functional equivalent in such institutions as the *huasepunguero* system in Latin America, both male and female labor were used in production. In field work, there was little division of labor by sex, although males predominated. In the production of horticultural crops and animals, differential and complementary male and female production patterns emerged. As slavery gave way to free labor in areas of plantation production, often in response to specific public policy, temporary male migrants replaced slaves. The cost of reproduction and maintenance of the labor force thus fell on the family rather than the plantation owner, and new patterns of female agricultural production developed, including production for home use and marketing channels. The types of agricultural production done by women varied according to their access to land.

Commercial agriculture in the West of the United States, supported by a public capital investment to provide irrigation water, required seasonal labor to be profitable. Public policy facilitated the provision of that labor through control of immigration. The government opened the way for the immigration of the Chinese, then the Japanese, then Filipinos, through government-to-government agreements. Finally, particularly after the Depression, Mexican workers, through the *bracero* program jointly administered by the United States and Mexican governments, brought contract workers to the western United States until 1965 (Pfeffer 1983). Whereas during the Depression, both males and females of midwestern origin picked the agroindustrial crops in the West, the immigrant workers tended to be male. The fact that these workers left their families in their native countries assured that the costs of reproduction of the labor force would be borne elsewhere. Agricultural employers had only to pay slightly more than transportation and maintenance costs while the migrants were in the field. The 1987 policy fining employers who hire undocumented workers may lead to more women working in the "factories in the fields" in the Southwest of the United States.

In the labor-scarce Midwest, where land-intensive agriculture predominates, the family provides the majority of the seasonal labor demands, with the exception of male harvest crews. Even for those crews, women in the past were hired to do cooking and laundry (maintenance tasks). Females provided the necessary labor and subsistence production that allowed cash grain farming to prosper (Flora and Stitz 1988).

LAND USE AND GENDER ROLES

The second factor of production affecting the gender balance in agricultural production is land. In some countries, such as Costa Rica, Brazil and Colombia, the major export crops at the time of independence from Spain and Portugal were tree crops, such as coffee and cacao. There are few economies of scale in such production. A large coffee producer is no more efficient than a small coffee producer. In fact, small production units may be better than larger units in terms of mobilization of labor. The small production units utilized the labor of the entire family, with women "helping," and generated a family income although a percentage went to the landlord. Gradually, however, those family production systems were absorbed by elite-controlled land accumulation, facilitated by government policies encouraging credit which led to debt foreclosure and land loss. In Brazil, there is an attempt to return some coffee production to sharecropping to increase efficiency, as individual wages and total lack of access to land left women aware of the low return to their labor and their husbands' inability to provide for the family (Stolcke 1984). In these smallholder or tenant systems, subsistence crops were intercropped between coffee or cacao trees. Women were extremely active as agricultural producers, on both the export crops and their own agriculturally related enterprises. As in the frontier United States, policies that favored maximum access to land by medium and smallholders tended to maximize women's options in agricultural production.

Where land was owned and operated by large landowners, export crops competed for land with subsistence crops. Increase in export agriculture on *haciendas*, where peasants had traditionally exchanged labor for use rights to land, removed peasants from the land, forcing both men and women to become seasonal laborers. While women's labor as agricultural producers increased in such situations, their agricultural options declined (Leon and Deere 1986).

GENDER AND CAPITAL
IN THE TRANSFORMATION OF PEASANT AGRICULTURE

Political independence brought a desire for economic independence in both Africa and Latin America. Economic independence was interpreted as increasing industrialization, which required major capital investments. Policies aimed at industrialization put a new set of pressures on peasant agriculture during the 1950s and early 1960s. Previously the peasantry could be temporary wage laborers and then fall back on their peasant plots for subsistence production in times of economic hardship, whether their access to land was through ownership or use rights. However, because of the prevailing development model and the policies implemented to bring it about, that fallback position for the masses began to be eliminated in many countries during the 1960s.

Import substitution as a policy tried to confront the old imperialist notion that the role of developing countries was to provide raw materials to the "mother" country and serve as markets for that country's exports. The advantage of the major world powers in Europe, Japan, and North America seemed to be due to industrialization. Many newly independent governments, as well as governments experiencing a new sense of independence, implemented national policies designed to bring about industrialization, including policies establishing high tariff barriers to protect infant industry, instituting differential and preferential exchange rates to encourage exports, and promoting direct government investment in industry (or, in other cases, governmental loan guarantees). Import substitution policies were widely accepted by nationalists in many developing countries, as well as by those who supplied the capital to these countries. Industrialization is substitution of capital for labor. The needed capital had to be generated from internal savings, which were in local currency, or from external sources. External sources included both direct foreign investment and loans. Internal savings alone could not propel industrialization, as the industrial machinery (and often raw materials) had to be purchased, at least initially, from developed countries. That required foreign exchange.

The import substitution strategy in developing countries was built on export agriculture. The need for foreign exchange pushed economies and national governments into policies that largely favored export agriculture over subsistence food production.

Import substitution, with its pressure on agriculture to export, forced changes in land use patterns, and as an unforeseen result, changes in gender relations. Land that had been used extensively or for subsistence production now had to be coerced, through policy mechanisms, into higher productivity.

Land reform sounds like redistribution of the land to the people who cultivate it. However, such reform almost never gave women title to the land they farm (Deere 1987). The slogan for land reform in many countries was "land to the tiller." But the results were quite different.

Land reform as public policy was triggered, particularly in Latin America, by three main forces. First, peasants who had been maneuvered out of their land during the liberal reforms of the late nineteenth and early twentieth centuries when land was made alienable began to invade land and to make demands to gain land titles and control. Particularly in Latin America, the Cuban revolution of 1959 convinced some peasants that organizing and demanding land might yield positive results.

Second, international institutions interested in political stability attempted to sponsor land reform. The Kennedy administration, galvanized by the 1959 Cuban revolution, put forward a foreign assistance package to help finance land reform in order to deter future peasant revolutions. In some areas, the Catholic Church became involved in land reforms to prevent another Cuba in the hemisphere.

Urban elites were the third source of political pressure for land reform. They desperately needed foreign exchange. In country after country, land reform legislation was worded in terms of increasing production rather than equity. If land was being used up to its productive potential, it would not be expropriated. If, however, the land was not being fully utilized, the state would take it over. The most convincing argument to change land use was that expropriated land would be compensated based on the value the owner had declared on the tax roles, which everybody knew was far below its real value. Only in cases of continued inefficient land use would land be expropriated and divided among the local peasants. When it was divided, it was almost always titled to men (Deere 1986).

Instead of making land available to peasants, land reform legislation forced the *hacendados* to use their land much more intensively in export crops – another disruption of the complementary system of peasant production. Although when the land was extensively used, it was titled to the *hacendado*, the *hacendado* usually lived with his family in the city. The farm was run by a *majordomo*, or manager, and it depended on peasant labor. The peasants had use rights to the land. They were ceded a small parcel where they could grow subsistence crops. In exchange, they provided labor to the *hacienda* for whatever the *hacienda* needed. Both men's and women's labor was required. The resulting exchange relationship kept the complementary set of gender relations in place (Balarezo et al. 1984).

Land reform policies were really policies for more intensive land use, because export crops could generate the foreign exchange needed by the industrializing elites. With the new "reform," land was once again taken away from the peasant producers. They were displaced physically, because land where they once lived, land where they once sowed subsistence crops to sell in a local market, now went into export crops such as cotton, coffee, and sugar cane. While some of the export crops utilized women as wage labor, others did not.

AGRICULTURE AND WOMEN IN THE DEVELOPING WORLD

The history of agriculture in the developing world is one of entry and exit of different crops from different areas into world markets, from indigo to coffee to bananas to flowers. The different crop mixes at different historical periods have greatly influenced the roles women have played in agricultural production. Public policy has shaped these cropping mixes, the labor relations under which they were produced, and the technology used, including packaging and transportation, which in turn have influenced the type of articulation with the world market as well as the form of women's participation in the production process.

Semiproletarianization of the peasantry has increased. Peasants are rapidly becoming part-time wage workers. The combination of small peasant plots and part-time work, which often requires long migration periods, allows food to be produced for the nation, export crops to be grown to generate foreign exchange, and relatively low wages to prevail, facilitating capital accumulation (de Janvry 1981). Semiproletarianization tends to put an especially heavy burden on rural women. Never a policy goal, this burden often results from policies aimed at increasing export agriculture.

Agro-industries that require the most highly developed technology and transportation systems are those producing fruits, vegetables, and flowers. These export enterprises, generally owned by multinational firms, often use strict division of labor by sex – and the differential wage scale that accompanies it – to their advantage. In the new international division of labor, many nations (but not all) have introduced policies that that stress exports and comparative advantages. Often that comparative advantage, even in agricultural production, lies in the low cost of labor, often provided by rural women. Studies of these enterprises, which increase women's wage labor in agricultural production but lower their overall options as agricultural producers, show such employment gives little advantage to women, as they are unprotected by unions and are doubly burdened by the double day of labor market participation and full responsibility for domestic chores (Roldan 1982; Cuales 1982).

Women's roles in rural-based agro-industries are more in the area of food processing (packing and handling) than production (Arizpe and Aranda 1977; Medrano 1982; Lago and Olavaria 1982). Except for flower producers, food processing industries are highly seasonal, and women move in and out of agricultural production with hardship, but without protest. Often cited as examples of successful development of nontraditional exports, these industries enjoy substantial goverment support through subsidized inputs, preferential exchange rates, subsidized credit, and policies discouraging labor organization.

Livestock production for export is growing in much of the developing world, including Africa and Latin America, as part of the drive for foreign exchange. Beef export has been a policy objective of both national governments and international lenders. These enterprises tend to be land extensive and labor displacing, proving particularly disadvantageous for women (Hecht 1985).

Changing policies in developed countries in mid-twentieth century also disadvantaged women. The 1950s and 1960s marked the replacement of women's crops and animals – their on-farm risk reduction activity – by industrial-type production and market dependence (Fink 1986). Government policies, particularly related to sanitation and marketing, were partially responsible for that shift. As a result of the demise of women's crops in developed countries, a differentiation of farm women occurred – between the minority, who in the 1950s and 1960s became de facto partners in their husbands' monocultural enterprises, and the majority, who, deprived of their on-farm production role, began to engage in either on-farm consumption reduction or off-farm employment to provide capital for the expanding – and capital-intensive – enterprise. These women were marginalized from the farm operation at the same time their work load increased.

An increased need for capital further disrupted the gender balance in both developed and developing country agriculture beginning in 1973. The effective action of OPEC (The Organization of The Petroleum Exporting Countries) and the multi-national oil conglomerates to restrain production and increase oil prices changed the world terms of trade and triggered an unprecedented period of worldwide inflation. All commodity prices increased. For the period between 1973 and 1980, the terms of trade favored commodity producers. High prices for commodities and increased availability of capital stimulated international lending, especially to developing countries with relatively high levels of mineral or agricultural wealth. They also encouraged heavy borrowing by farmers in developed countries, a trend that favored male-controlled, capital-intensive enterprises. These loans, in turn, stimulated export production to facilitate repayment. In the early 1970s, President Nixon unpegged the U.S. dollar, allowing the dollar to drop against foreign currency and giving an advantage to U.S. exports and those of nations whose currency is pegged to the dollar. At the same time, a shift in the terms of trade and increased commodity prices meant a shift in location of purchasing power to commodity producers, particularly developing countries. More dollars were being circulated internationally, feeding worldwide inflation. High rates of inflation led to low real interest rates. As a result, many developing countries shifted from a development strategy seeking external investment to one of international borrowing. Policies basing development on indebtedness encouraged capital-intensive development both nationally and internationally. The ready availability of capital spawned large development projects, which tended to ignore women's production activities, and investment in machinery, which tended to be operated by males.

Although it was felt that relatively high commodity prices served as loan collateral, inflation itself guaranteed loan servicing. Developing countries could simply roll over their loans, borrowing a little extra to pay the up-front fees and interest, planning to repay with dollars worth less each time. The 1970s produced an increasing indebtedness on the part of some (but not all) developing countries. Appreciating assets in the form of high-priced commodities presumably insured repayment. Further, the type of development favored by cheap capital – the choice of capital over labor, with capital investment a male monopoly – disadvantaged women in agricultural production.

Developing country exports of luxury crops (part of the "comparative advantage" strategy of the 1970s which replaced import substitution as a development strategy) led to increasing reliance on imported grains from developed countries. To provide for these new markets, the United States in the mid-1970s implemented a series of policies that led to an increased marginalization of women in U.S. agriculture, particularly in grain-based farming systems.

Grain monoculture was directly encouraged by policy in the United States. Farming corporations were formed both to facilitate capital flow and reduce the costs of intergenerational property transfer caused by the high inflation of the value of farm assets. Tax policies rewarded capital investment, as all interest payments were deductible. The corporations formed in response to the shifting role of capital tended to leave women out. Women's activities became less production and management oriented.

Increasing indebtedness, shifting terms of trade, relatively cheap U.S. exports, including food (which made U.S. agriculture even more dependent on the world economy), helped by over-valued local currencies and the high prices of commodities, encouraged more land to be put into export commodity production. Women's crops were displaced, and women's simple commodity production was replaced by women's wage labor, often of a seasonal nature.

During the 1970s, the high prices of all commodities brought marginal producers into the marketplace, often through an overreliance on capital. Such capital-intensive production systems tended to be male-dominated. Even on U.S. farms, women were marginalized in the production process, except in animal production. While women participated in many phases of agricultural production, their participation in the United States was often in "helper" roles (Rosenfeld 1985). Costs of production were high, and prices fluctuated more and more widely.

Increasing supply eventually saturated the demand. By 1981, the house of cards created by inflation and high commodity prices was ready to tumble. The debt crisis hit most of the developing world and agricultural producers in the developed world. The high degree of specialization of agricultural production, where little produced was consumed locally, had definite implications for women. Under austerity measures imposed as government policy, often at the urging of local or international lenders in response to the highly leveraged positions of both countries and agricultural enterprises, women more than men bear the burden of investment cutbacks.

The worldwide recession of the 1980s retarded the development of demand. Most agricultural products have a relatively inelastic demand. Policies in many developed nations have responded to low commodity prices by making up the difference between the world price and the costs of production. Such policies have further aggravated the surplus and have made women's position as agricultural producers even more marginal. In many agricultural production units in both the developed and the developing world, women's major contribution to agriculture is through off-farm work to generate capital, not through direct agricultural production.

While the traditional subordination of women kept them out of key agricultural production roles in systems of subsistence production as well as in the latifundio-minifundio production systems of the colonial and postindependence period, increasing integration of agricultural economies into the world economic system has further subordinated women (Ward 1984). Research such as that of Rubbo (1975) on the incursion of sugar cane for industrial production on cacao smallholders in Colombia suggests that the result of this integration into the world economic system has made women more dependent on men, reduced women's flexibility, and diminished their control over their own lives. The patriarchal forms of traditional societies have been absorbed and utilized by contemporary societies in such a way as to intensify women's oppression. Women's dependence and subordination in agricultural production are not new, but have taken new and harsher forms. Division of labor by gender in agriculture is profitable for the owners of the means of production. Thus, women's increasing wage-labor employment in agricultural production is accompanied by a decline in their agricultural options (Roldan 1982; Spindel 1982).

POLICY RESPONSES TO WOMEN'S DISADVANTAGE

As capital penetrated rural areas, the breakdown of the traditional farming unit in developing countries left women in charge of subsistence agriculture, which provided basic foods for the family and local markets. But policies were not implemented to provide women with access to either capital or land. Rather, development programs to reduce the food deficit were oriented to men. Programs designed to increase productivity and maintain income in developing countries have been de facto male oriented. Likewise, emphasis on bushel subsidies through deficiency payments rather than payments to maintain farm income, U.S. farm policy has been made capital intensive, and as such, has disadvantaged women by reducing production options.

The crisis in agriculture in many developing countries is a problem of food production and requires dramatic policy change. To be effective, those policies must recognize women's role in agriculture and their need for separate income streams and separate access to resources. The crisis in agricultural production has resulted from draconian shifts in the terms of trade worldwide. Economic policies that made sense during the 1970s encouraged high indebtedness in both the public and private spheres, an indebtedness spurred not only by low real interest rates, but also by tax policies that rewarded a highly leveraged position. Policies that encouraged substitution of capital for labor, combined with a "comparative advantage" strategy, allowed developing countries to export high-priced commodities and import U.S. grain. In the 1970s, the reduced options for women in agricultural production were not of concern because the world economy was expanding. Farmers in both developing and developed nations seemed to be doing well. In the 1980s, those same policies have brought increasing disarticulation of farming interests worldwide. Further, the detrimental impact of those policies on women in agricultural production now stands out in bold relief.

Concern with debt seems gender-neutral. Yet policies in both the United States and the developing countries tend to remove women from direct access to productive resources. The resulting agricultural structures may demand increased female labor, but without concomitant mechanisms to insure women's access to and control over the profits from their own labor. Gender analysis of the current situation demonstrates the negative impact on both individual welfare and sectoral production that has resulted from male-biased policies.

CONCLUSIONS

Women in both developing and developed countries have seen a growing limitation of their agricultural roles as their countries and the products they produce become integrated into the world economic system. Women's traditional farm labor has been that which is most regular and repetitive, such as poultry production. That labor, unlike male labor with field crops and large animals, lends itself to industrialized production forms. The crops that generated women's separate income streams in both developed and developing countries have become commodified and are now purchased from the market (Fink 1986). Policies that have favored corporate ownership, bulk marketing, high sanitation standards, and tax write-offs for borrowing for inputs have removed women from production arenas where their comparative advantage was low input costs and regular labor inputs.

In developed countries, women still provide a reserve army of labor for peak labor periods when policy shifts limit male migrant workers. In developing countries, where land reconcentration is occurring in response to policies favoring export agriculture, women provide seasonal labor for planting, harvesting, and packing. Women are valued for their nimble fingers and their low wages. For family farms all over the world, women's off-farm labor increasingly serves to provide the capital necessary to maintain the enterprise.

Women's work in agriculture has changed in response to macro government policies. But more important than the things women do are the labor relations under which they do them. These relations have changed even more radically. Women are now less likely to determine their own working conditions or control the fruits of their labor as the result of policies that have contributed to the increasing separation of capital, land, labor, and management in both developed and developing countries.

NOTES

[1]Contribution No. 88-14-B, Kansas Agricultural Experiment Station

BIBLIOGRAPHY

Arizpe, Lourdes, and Josefina Aranda. 1977. "The 'Comparative Advantages' of Women's Disadvantages: Women Workers in the Strawberry Export Agribusiness in Mexico." *Signs: Journal of Women in Culture and Society* 7: 453-73.

Balarezo, S., Osvaldo Barsky, Lucia Carrion, R. Rosero, and Lucia Salamea. 1984. *Mujer y Transformaciones Agrarias.* Quito: Centro de Planificacion y Estudios Sociales.

Brewster, John M. 1950 "The Machine Process in Agriculture and Industry." *Journal of Farm Economics.* 32: 69-81.

Carloni, Alice Stewart. 1987. *Women in Development: A.I.D.'s Experience, 1973-1985.* Vol. 1 *Synthesis Paper.* A.I.D. Program Evaluation. Report No. 18: Washington, D.C.: Agency for International Develpment.

Chaney, Elsa. 1983. "Scenarios of Hunger in the Caribbean: Migration, Decline of Small Holder Agriculture and the Feminization of Farming." Women in International Development Paper No. 18, East Lansing, Michigan State University.

Cuales, Sonia M. 1982. "Accumulation and Gender Relations in the Flower Industry in Colombia." *Research in Political Economy* 5: 109-37.

Deere, Carmen Diana. 1987. "The Latin American Agrarian Reform Experience." In *Rural Women and State Policy: Feminist Perspective on Latin American Agricultural Development*, ed. Carmen Diana Deere and Magdelena Leon, 164-90. Boulder, Colo: Westview Press.

de Janvry, Alain. 1981. *The Agrarian Question and Reformism in Latin America*. Baltimore: The John Hopkins University Press.

Durkheim, Emil. [1893] 1964. *The Division of Labor in Society*. Reprint. New York. The Free Press.

Feldstein, Hilary S. and Susan Poats. 1985. "Case Studies for FSR/E Training: Concepts and Format. Paper presented at Kansas State University Farming Systems Research and Extension Symposium. Oct. Manhattan, Kansas.

Fink, Deborah. 1986. *Open Country, Iowa: Rural Women, Tradition and Change*. Albany: State University of New York Press.

Flora, Cornelia Butler and John Stitz. Forthcoming, 1988. "Female Subsistence Production and Commercial Farm Survival among Settlement Kansas Wheat Farmers." *Human Organization* 47.

Hecht, Sussana. 1985. "Women and the Latin American Livestock Sector." In *Women as Food Producers in Developing Countries*, ed. Janie Mouson and Marion Kalb, 51-70. Los Angeles: UCLA African Studies Center.

Johda, N.S. and A.C. Mascarenhas. 1984. "Adjustment to Climatic Variability in Self Provisioning Societies: Some Evidence from India and Tanzania." *Family Systems Newsletter* No. 16, (January-March): 11-43.

Lago, M. Soledad and Carlota Olavaria. 1982. "La mujer campesina en la expansion fruticola chilena." In *Las trabajadores del agro*, ed. Magdalena Leon, 179-299. Bogota, Colombia: Asociacion Colombiana de Estudios de Poblacion.

Leon, Magdalena and Carmen Diana Deere. 1986. *La mujer y la political agraria en America Latina*. Bogota, Colombia: Siglo Veintiuno/Asociacion Colombiana de Estudios de Poblacion.

Mann, S.A. and J. M. Dickinson. 1978. "Obstacles to the Development of Capitalist Agriculture" *Journal of Peasant Studies* 5: 466-81.

Medrano, Diana. 1982. "Desarrollo y exploitacion de la mujer: Efectos de la proletarizacion feminina en la agroindustria de flores en la Sabana de Bogota." In *La realidad colombiana*, ed. Magdalena Leon, 43-55. Bogota, Colombia: Asociacion Colombiana de Estudios de Poblacion.

Pfeffer, Max J. 1983. "Social Origins of Three Systems of Farm Production in the United States." *Rural Sociology* 47: 540-62.

Roldan, Marta. 1982. "Subordinacion generica y proletarizacion rural: Un estudio de caso en el Noroeste Mexicano." In *Las trabajadoras del agro*, ed. Magdelena Leon, 75-102. Bogota, Colombia: Asociacion Colombiana de Estudios de Poblacion.

Rosenfeld, Rachel A. 1985. *Farm Women: Work, Farm and Family in the United States*. Chapel Hill: University of North Carolina Press.

Rubbo, Anna. 1975. "The Spread of Capitalism in Rural Colombia: Effects on Poor Women." In *Toward an Anthropology of Women*, ed. Rayna R. Reiter, 333-57. New York: Monthly Review Press.

Spindel, Cheywa R. 1982. "Capital, familia y mujer: La evolucion de la produccion rural de base familiar, un caso en Brasil." In *Las trabajadores del agro*, ed. Magdelena Leon, 227-46. Bogota, Colombia: Asociacion Colombiana de Estudios de Poblacion.

Stolcke, Verena. 1984. "The Exploitation of Family Morality: Labor Systems and Family Structure on Sao Paulo Coffee Plantation, 1850-1979." In *Kinship Ideology and Practice in Latin America*, ed. Raymond T. Smith, 264-46. Chapel Hill: University of North Carolina Press.

Ward, Kathryn. 1984. *Women in the World System: Impact on Fertility*. New York: Praeger.

Weber, Max. 1978. *Economy and Society*. 2 vols. Berkeley: University of California Press.

Youssef, Nadia H. 1974. *Women and Work in Developing Societies*. Populations Monograph Series No. 15. Berkeley, California, Institute of International Studies.

16

FARM WOMEN AND THE STRUCTURAL TRANSFORMATION OF AGRICULTURE: A CROSS-CULTURAL PERSPECTIVE

Kathleen Cloud

All over the world rural women play important roles in agricultural systems. Most are agricultural producers; they may be mothers, housekeepers, healers, wage laborers, market women, entrepreneurs, and community leaders as well. In some ways their roles and responsibilities are very much the same. In others, what women do and how they do it varies substantially.

Some of women's roles are biologically based: only women can bear children. In societies where bottle feeding is not practical, women must also nurse infants if they are to survive. Other differences between men's and women's roles are socially constructed: what is women's work in one community may be men's work in another. Women are the traditional farm managers in some systems; in others, women assume management roles when husbands and sons migrate to cities. In still other systems, women have little to do with field crops but may be very involved in poultry and dairy production, piggeries, or production of fruits and vegetables. In some systems, young girls do field work or herding while boys go to school; in others the opposite is true. Older women may be very powerful, supervising the work of others in the household, or very marginal, doing long hours of hard work to survive.

The causes and effects of such variations in gender roles have been the subject of intensive research and discussion over the past two decades, and a better understanding of factors influencing gender roles is gradually taking shape.

This paper addresses a number of these factors, noting the strengths and weaknesses of the available data and of current analysis. A discussion of the current state of international knowledge about the work of rural women is followed by a discussion of the factors influencing differences in gender roles and responsibilities at the household level. In the final section, the paper addresses the process of structural transformation of agriculture, and our current understanding of the ways in which that process interacts with gender roles and responsibilities.

THE WORK THAT FARM WOMEN DO

The past decade has seen an explosion of micro studies documenting the range and importance of women's agricultural activities (Cloud 1985). An in-

281

creasing number of surveys have also been done in the United States and Europe documenting women's agricultural roles (Cernea 1979; Croll 1981; Jones and Rosenfield 1981; Ministere du Travail 1974). Such small and mid- scale studies are complemented by Dixon's macroanalysis on three types of national census data to produce more reliable estimates of women's agricultural work in eighty-two developing countries (1982). For all the countries combined, the proportion of women in the agricultural labor force was 42 percent. For Sub-Saharan Africa the regional average was 46 percent, for North Africa and the Middle East, 31 percent and for Asia, 45 percent. There were important differences within regions, and, indeed, within countries.

The composite picture that emerges from these complementary types of data is not complete, but generalizations can be made with increasing confidence. Many adult women work in the paid agricultural labor force, twenty five million in India alone. Many others work as unpaid family labor. Of these, some contribute routinely to the production of the family food supply, others work only during the peak labor seasons. In addition, many girls between the ages of ten and fifteen do substantial amounts of agricultural labor, particularly in North Africa and the Middle East.

Women not only provide labor, they may manage cropping enterprises producing poultry, small ruminants, dairy products, vegetables and tree crops that provide them with separate income streams. Many also participate in managing the total farm operation. Others manage the total enterprise themselves, either because they are household heads or because of male out- migration.

Although there is evidence that many farm women earn money through off-farm employment and small enterprises, there is not yet a strong international base of data on women's off-farm work. We do know that in the industrialized world, educated farm women may generate a significant portion of the household cash income through work as teachers and nurses, or work in businesses and government agencies. Women with less education may work in local factories or service businesses (Huffman and Lange 1983, see also Sachs, this volume, McCarthy *et al.* this volume).

With the exception of women working in perishable export crops such as fruits, vegetables, flowers, and tea, women in the developing world generally have more limited access to rural labor markets, especially for steadier or more highly skilled work, and receive much lower salaries than men. In response to these sex-segregated labor markets, large numbers of women try to make money in the informal sector, selling products such as eggs, dairy products, cooked or processed food, home-brewed beer, and handicrafts. They also provide paid services such as sewing, laundry, hairdressing, cleaning, healing, home nursing, midwifery, and child care. Many of these informal sector activities are also undertaken by American farm women (see D. Fink, this volume), but given the large number of women who participate, there is still too little empirical data on the economic contribution to farm income from this sector.

Household production is a major activity of women all over the world. For agricultural households in much of the developing world such production may include not only food preparation, laundry and the care of the house, but also provision of fuel and water, the processing of crops for storage, health care, and midwifery.

Whatever the extent of farm women's work in agriculture and the generation of off-farm income, this work must be interwoven with household and child care obligations. Whatever else they are doing, women also have the major responsibility for child care, and for the nature, degree and timing of household investments in children. Several papers for this conference note the lower rates of off-farm employment of North American mothers with young children. Not only are women primarily responsible for the health and safety of children, but in large measure, they are also responsible for their education. In traditional societies most education takes place in the normal course of daily activities. In modernizing societies where increasing numbers of rural children attend school, it is still women who teach language, cognitive skills and social norms to their children through conversation and stories. Women's degree of skill in this role has profound effect on their children's school success and total life chances.

Although there are many similarities, women's roles and responsibilities also differ from system to system. Looking at these differences at the household level is one way of understanding the factors influencing the work that men and women do. The next section addresses gender roles from a household perspective, using the tools of economics to discuss the range and variation in farm women's roles across a variety of systems.

HOUSEHOLD LEVEL ANALYSIS

Few people live alone in rural societies. Agricultural production is basically a collective endeavor, with the agricultural household as the most common unit of production and consumption. It is within the household that decisions are made about what will be grown and how, who will work for wages, who will go to school. Because of this, economists and anthropologists use the household as a basic unit of analysis in the study of agricultural systems. Farm households can be defined as kinship-based groups engaged in both production and consumption with corporate ownership of some resources and a degree of joint decision making among members (Cloud and Overholt 1983).

Traditionally, anthropologists have been interested in the structure of household roles and responsibilities, the links between households, and how these are understood by the culture in which they exist. Economists have been interested in understanding and predicting the decisions households make in response to changing conditions, particularly changes in prices. As economists have come to realize that internal processes affect household decisions and anthropologists have realized that social arrangements have economic content, interdisciplinary cross-fertilization has occurred.

Both disciplines agree that farmers know what they are doing and that most manage their resources very well, given the constraints under which they operate. Farm households are seen as "efficient by necessity." Yet not all households share the same goals. Small farms may use a safety-first strategy that minimizes risk, while larger, more affluent farms may be able to take the risks that result in greater profits. Some households develop labor-absorbing production patterns which provide an on-farm role for all members. Others encourage some of their members to work off-farm.

Economists have developed and refined a series of increasingly sophisticated models to explain the rational basis underlying the decisions of agricultural households. Differences in household goals are accommodated by assuming that households are seeking to maximize not simply profit, but "utility" – a combination of economic factors and preferences. In order to make mathematical analysis possible, such models hold everything constant except prices.

> Farm households base their consumption and production decisions on farm input prices, cash and food crop output prices, the prices of consumer goods from the market, the opportunity cost of member's time either in outside labor markets or in farm production (including household work), and the demand for leisure. (Timmer, Falcon and Pearson 1983, 78)

The earliest models focused on the way the household allocated its resources to produce crops for market. Such models had serious limitations for understanding household behavior in the developing world, where much of the land and labor are devoted to subsistence production – to food, clothing, and equipment that are consumed without ever passing through the market. Gradually these early models have been expanded to include production for use as well as for sale, and some reflect both consumption and production behavior. As economists have become increasingly clear that the home and the fields compete for capital resources and family labor, they have expanded their definitions of the "products" of the farm enterprise to include increasing amounts of women's productive activities.

While such models do not explain everything about farm household behavior, they are very useful for illuminating certain aspects. In particular, recent models have made farm women's productive work more visible, both because women's labor time can be included as a rationally allocated resource and because enlarging the definitions of farm household production assigns economic value to the goods and services produced by women, even when these do not pass through the market.

Research is increasingly convergent in its definition of the output of the family farm firm. The following formulation of five categories of agricultural household production (Cloud and Overholt 1983) integrates recent work by Acharya and Bennett (1982), Binswanger et al. (1980), Evenson (1978), Folbre (1983), Da Vanzo and Lee (1978), Barnum and Squire (1979), Cain (1979), Cernea (1979), Huffman and Lange (1983), and Ahn, Singh and Squire (1981):

1. *Agricultural Production*: the farm firm's output of crops and livestock for home consumption or market sale (cereals, livestock, vegetables, tree crops, dairy crops and poultry)
2. *Wage Labor*: paid employment in agriculture or other sectors

3. *Self-Employment*: in the formal and informal market sectors including activities such as marketing and personal services
4. *Household Production*: goods and services produced within the household for household consumption (food processing and preparation, collection of household water and cooking fuels, laundry, cleaning health care and maintenance)
5. *Human Capital Production*: childbearing, child care, and the transmission of skills and knowledge

RESOURCE ALLOCATION WITHIN THE HOUSEHOLD

The uses of time

Economic models of the farm household assume that households move labor and resources among productive sectors to gain for themselves the maximum amount of welfare and satisfaction (utility). By the late 1970s, models utilizing Becker's (1965) theories of the value of time in household production were including women's household and child care work as products of the agricultural household. The more recent models (Barnum and Squire 1979; Ahn, Singh and Squire 1981; Huffman and Lange 1983) include household and human capital production as Z goods, and in somewhat different ways, each of the models permits analysis of the allocation of household capital resources and labor supply, reflects household consumption of leisure goods and services, and predicts outputs of both farm and household under differing conditions. Some also permit modeling of choices between different cropping patterns (Ahn, Singh and Squire 1981). Such models unify production and consumption decisions by making them simultaneous and thus interactive. Because the models focus on resource allocation during a single cropping season, they tend to eliminate fertility decisions, treating household composition as a given.

An important feature of these models is their emphasis on time as a productive resource which is rationally allocated within the household as well as on the farm and in the labor market. It is assumed that the value of time is determined by the price it brings on the market. In the developing world, where farms are small and tools are simple, the time of household members is often the major resource possessed by the poor. Time can be sold for wages or invested in squeezing greater production from household land. It can be used for work on other people's land, or in their households, in return for goods and services. In the slack seasons, handicrafts can be made. Foods can be processed and sold in the local markets. Family members may migrate to other areas to lighten the burden on family resources, and perhaps to send money back.

Through the year, time must also be invested in the ordinary tasks that keep the family alive and functioning. Grain must be ground into flour, meals cooked, laundry and cleaning done, the young and the sick cared for. Two reasons are commonly given for the fact that in rural societies these household and human capital tasks are overwhelmingly assigned to women. One is biologically based; it is argued that such tasks are compatible with women's role in pregnancy and nursing, while men have more of the upper body strength required for certain agricultural tasks such as land clearing and plowing with draft animals. There may be a biological reality underlying the division of labor in traditional systems characterized by high fertility, animal traction agriculture, and low levels of technology. But as technology changes and women live longer, have fewer children, and have more acceptable substitutes for breastfeeding, such biologically based reasons become less compelling, and societal choice plays a larger role.

The second reason given for women's responsibilities in household and human capital production is undoubtedly socially constructed, although it tends to be treated as if it proceeded inevitably from the biological. Women command lower wages in local labor markets. Therefore, it is presumed that there is a comparative economic advantage to the household in having women engage in essential but unpaid household and human capital production while men generate an income stream through field crop production or work off-farm (Evenson 1978, Becker 1965).

Rural institutions are often structured on the assumption that it is desirable to preserve this norm of gender linked comparative advantage. The procedures of these institutions discriminate against women, permitting them less access to land title or use, to credit, agricultural extension, and new technologies, as well as to an income stream from employment. Such arrangements retard women's increased productivity in agriculture and business and often reinforce gender patterns that have outlasted their usefulness.

Many households are headed by women, and many others need all the income they can generate. So in spite of the economists, most farm women add work in agriculture and the informal sector to their household production and child care, making due with the resources they can squeeze out, taking the best wage they can achieve, making each hour as productive as they can with the means at hand.

Yet time is not an unlimited resource; there are only twenty-four hours in a day. Time has an opportunity cost.

> The value of additional time spent in food preparation or tending the children must be balanced against the productivity of an additional hour weeding the rice, driving the ducks or tending the home garden. The opportunity to spend some of that time working for cash on a neighbor's farm, or in a rural wage-labor market places a lower bound on the value of household-farm time, and the value of leisure ultimately places a limit on the willingness to work, especially at low productivity tasks. But for households with inadequate land . . . and with limited outside employment opportunities . . . even tiny increments to output can be valuable. (Timmer, Falcon and Pearson 1983, 89)

As a result of time pressure, women make constant trade-offs in fulfilling their obligations to themselves, to kin and community (Nerlove 1974). One common response is to work long hours, longer than men in the same community (Szalsi 1975, Minge Klevana 1980). Another strategy is to do two or three things at once, particularly when there are children in the household.

All over the world the pattern of farm women's work differs from that of men. While men characteristically devote several hours to one task, women often engage in joint production, managing three or four shorter tasks simultaneously. After several hours hoeing maize, an African woman may be carrying her youngest child on her back, milking, keeping an eye on the cooking pot, and discussing with a neighbor whether she needs to take a sick child to the clinic. After a day spent teaching school, an American farm woman may be feeding her youngest child, supervising the older children in doing the chores, cooking supper, and discussing a farm management decision with her husband.

The flexibility of response demanded by farm women's roles has been noted in many of the papers in this volume. Farm women must shift attention frequently, accommodate unplanned interruptions, prioritize and reprioritize tasks, and maintain both intellectual and emotional balance while doing so. Mead Cain (1980) noted that for farm women in Bangladesh, this pattern of briefer, more diverse interrelated activities demands substantial management skill and judgement, yet this skill is undervalued by society. The same might be said of American farm women.

Decision making within the household

Most economic models of the farm household do not deal with how decisions are arrived at within the household. They assume that all resources of land, labor and capital are pooled and then allocated where they will be most useful to the household. This assumption is referred to as the household utility function.

But in fact, each household is a collection of individuals, and these individuals may be responsible for enterprises that compete for resources. From system to system, there are different patterns of participation and responsibility for women and men. In much of Africa, women have the obligation to grow the food the families eat; these crops may compete for land and labor with the cash crops of their husband, or his father. Men and women, the young and the old may have shared, separate and opposing interests within the household, and may wish to use the same resources in different ways. A woman may wish to use cash income for an improved stove, while her husband may wish to use the income for fertilizer.

This conflict of interest is addressed in many societies by arranging for individuals to manage small enterprises which generate personal income. Children may raise animals and sell them to pay school fees. Young adults may have their own cropping enterprises and save their income to establish their own households. Women may grow or process crops of their own and control the resulting proceeds; income from vegetables, dairying, eggs and poultry, street foods and home brewed beer is common. Profit may be reinvested in that enterprise or used for other things. Such money often goes to investments in human capital – to improving family nutrition or to payment of clinic and school fees. It may be invested in better technology for household production, for example, a washing machine, an improved stove or the kerosene to fuel it.

In some systems the amount of unpooled resources is small enough so that economists have been able to overlook its effects on household decision making. However, such resources are an important consideration in African systems.

There, economists have begun to work with agricultural production models that reflect the unpooled resources and competing interests within the household (Jones 1983). By contrast, economists working with Asian data have begun to analyze the links between income and the ways in which consumption goods are distributed within farm households – who gets enough to eat, and who goes without (Folbre 1983).

The notion of a household utility function not only ignores unpooled resources, it also obscures the fact that what is in the best interest of the household may not be in the best interest of particular members. This dilemma is well illustrated by the Salamon and Davis-Brown paper in this volume. The unpaid family labor of women or younger members may increase farm production or contribute to the purchase of additional land or livestock, but they may not receive an equal share of the benefits. Children who work on the farm instead of going on to school, the son who works alongside his father for years and then farms for a sibling corporation, the woman who marries the son, all may contribute a greater share to an agricultural household than they receive in return. Unfortunately, what works to the benefit of the family farm may not work to the benefit of all members of the farm family.

The way in which households actually allocate land, labor and capital between competing uses is certainly based on economic rationality. Most farm households are indeed "efficient by necessity"; they cannot afford to waste resources (Schultz 1964). But power also plays a role in the way resources are allocated and used, and many household level decisions benefit some at the expense of others. Household goals, and the ways in which they are implemented, are affected by the power relationships within the household, which tend to reflect those of the larger system within which the household exists.

EXTERNAL FACTORS INFLUENCING GENDER ROLES IN HOUSEHOLDS

Although models of agricultural households focus their attention on the way households respond to relative price changes, it is clear that many other factors influence households. Each household operates in a larger context affecting its decisions: the natural resource base may be good or poor; the climate reliable or capricious; the city nearby or far away; the country rich or poor; the government well managed or inefficient, committed to improving agriculture, or to exploiting it. Systems vary greatly in the equity of their relationships. In many traditional and governmental systems, resource allocation decisions are relatively equitable. In others, the strong exploit the weak for their own advantage.

Countries, in turn, may be situated so that they can profit from their place in the increasingly interdependent world economic system, or they may, because of their history, their natural resource base, or the world geopolitical situation, be at a serious disadvantage in providing a just economic environment.

Because these contextual circumstances influence the way in which households manage their resources, they undoubtedly affect both the content and the execution of gender roles and responsibilities. These interactions are not yet well understood, but as research accumulates, some patterns are emerging.

Cultural, political and ideological factors such as religion, social norms, and legal patterns of property and inheritance, have always been seen as important influences on gender roles. Indeed, until recently such factors were often treated as the only influence. Traditional norms are changing under the pressure of circumstance, but they are still very powerful in influencing who women marry and when, how many children they have and which ones go to school, whether family labor is paid or unpaid, whether couples live with their in-laws, and if so, which ones.

Both traditional practices and public institutions influence the pattern of control over resources. The hierarchial distribution of social power, income and productive resources by class has been extensively explored in the development literature. There is a second system of stratification present in many societies – that of patriarchal relations between the sexes. Mead Cain (1980) defines patriarchy as " a set of social relations with a material base which enables men to dominate women. . . . The material base of patriarchy is men's control of property, income, and women's labor. The structural elements of patriarchal control are interlocking and include elements of the kinship, political and religious systems (1979, 2).

As noted earlier, rural institutions are commonly structured to give males relatively greater access to productive resources such as land title, technology, capital, credit, education and information. To the extent that class or patriarchal stratification characterizes an agricultural system, women's access to productive resources, and thus, their roles, will be constrained by their household's class status, their gender, or both.

Over the past decade it has become increasingly clear that a number of material conditions also have consistent effects. Among these are cropping mix, the technological mode of production, farm size, the subsistence/cash crop mix. and the gender specific opportunity structure in the rest of the economy. Fertility patterns also affect gender roles in many ways.

These variables interact, and it is not always easy to separate their effects. The needed information base is still fragmentary; both the sources and the types of data vary, with some variables receiving more attention in one literature than in another. As both comparative and longitudinal data accumulate, greater clarity of analysis should become possible. In the meantime, some tentative comments can be made.

Insights into the relationships between gender roles and the cropping mix have come primarily from two sources: anthropology and farming systems research. Comparative statistical analysis of large numbers of traditional agricultural systems has been undertaken by anthropologists to understand which factors influenced gender patterns of responsibility in agricultural systems before these systems were heavily influenced by the world economy (Burton and White 1984). Other current anthropological work examines the interaction between gender roles and cropping mix in one area over time (Guyer 1984).

Farming systems research is done by interdisciplinary teams of agricultural and social scientists on experiment stations and farmers' fields in the developing world. Farming systems research looks at farmers' current problems in order to generate solutions to fit their circumstances. Because it is experimental research and the outcome measure is farmer adoption of recommended innovations, it provides considerable insight into the reasons households allocate their land, labor and capital as they do, and into the ways they are willing to change. Although the focus of research is at the micro level, the increasing body of knowledge generated across many systems permits some tentative generalizations (Feldstein 1987).

Climate has a major effect on the cropping mix, and the labor demands of the various crops have a major effect on gender roles. Burton and White (1984) found that in the rainey tropics where root crops are common and the labor demand is spread rather evenly across the year, women do much of the farming. In climates with a long dry period, cereal production is more common, and there is more dependence on domesticated animals for food and traction. In most cereal systems, men have primary responsibility for field crops. Women continue to do agricultural work, but the nature of the work changes. In addition to vegtable and fruit production much of their time is spent caring for animals and processing both cereal and animal products. Across systems women's average hours of agricultural labor per day stay constant at about 4.5 hours, but their household and human capital production time increases from 3 to 6 hours a day, while men's agricultural work increases from 5 to 7.5 hours a day (Burton and White 1984).

Intensive cultivation of cereal crops with animal traction and the plow demands substantial initial investment of labor in land preparation, removing roots, stumps and rocks, and possibly building terraces or irrigation channels. At the point where such investments are demanded, land tenure usually shifts from use rights to some form of longer-term control that encourages these investments. Land title generally goes to those who clear the land, that is, to men. Such a shift occurred in the United States with homesteading, and is now underway in many parts of Africa.

The labor demands of cereal crops vary, but all demand bursts of intensive work at certain points, in plowing, planting or harvesting. It is possible to hire help during these periods or to move every available household member into the fields. Systems differ in the gender-specific strategies they choose to address these labor bottlenecks: some hire extra men, some extra women; some draw upon the unpaid family labor of women and girls, others call home the members who have migrated to off-farm work.

Many traditional farm households also even out their labor flow and increase their total production by using a cropping mix that provides productive work for its members over a greater part of the year. Such systems may mix cereals, vegetables, tree crops, legumes, and animals. Systems that include animals tend to involve women in the more skilled operations, such as care of the young, or to assign certain animals entirely to women. Women's management of poultry, goats, and pigs is especially common. A number of papers in this volume note a negative correlation between women's involvement in on-farm animal production and off-farm employment. Both absorb labor, and in many systems, returns to women's labor may be greater in animal production than in low-wage off-farm labor markets.

The technology of production is related to crop mix, but the issues should not be confounded. Many of the crops traditionally cultivated by women with the hoe in Africa, such as millet, maize, beans, cassava, and yams, are mechanized crops using primarily male labor in other parts of the world. Currently, systems based on crops such as wheat, which are easily mechanized, utilize women's field labor much less than systems based on crops such as rice, which still demands a great deal of hand labor at several points in the production cycle. In Indonesia, as rice production is gradually being mechanized, paid male labor is replacing women who worked for a share of the crop. Yet in Japan, where the opportunity structure is different and there are well-paying jobs available to men off- farm, women's involvement in rice production has increased with mechanization (Kada n.d.).

Given the current data base, it is hard to predict accurately the degree to which mechanization will shift a crop or a task from female to male responsibility. Boserup's argument (1970) that women's agricultural production is primarily done with the hand and the hoe, does seem to be true up to a certain point. Very little animal traction is utilized by women. Yet women in many highly mechanized systems do use substantial amounts of sophisticated machinery, from milking parlors to cultivators. It may well be that there is a U shaped curve in with high involvement of women in low and high technology systems, and lower involvement of women in systems dependent on animal traction.

Two factors may influence this pattern. One is the relative attractiveness of off-farm work available to men and women. The other is the flow of the labor demand relative to its supply in the household. In systems where farmers have to get crops into the fields or out of them in a hurry and where there are not many adults in the household, women are more likely to end up in the milking parlor or on a rig.

With regard to farm size, the subsistence/cash crop mix, and the opportunity structure of the economy, one study stands out. In 1983, Dixon sought to illuminate the features in national production systems that influence women's participation in agricultural production. Using the adjusted female participation data established in her earlier study as the independent variable, she examined the relationship between the sex composition of each national agricultural labor force and three features of each rural economy: the distribution of land holdings by size, the market orientation of agricultural production, and the relative attractiveness of urban employment activities. She found women most involved in systems characterized by smallholder agriculture oriented toward subsistence production and sale to local markets. The pattern of landholding explained 44 percent of the total variation in sex composition of the agricultural labor force and 80 percent of the variation due to regional differences (Dixon 1983, 365) Two other factors acting both independently and in concert were low levels of urbanization and male-dominated out-migration.

By contrast, Dixon found lowest female participation where land distribution is highly skewed toward a few large farms, where agricultural production is export-oriented, and where out-migration, particularly of females, is high. The error of estimation is large, due to measurement error in both labor force data and the structural variables, and there are a significant number of countries that did not fit the patterns. Yet the robustness of the findings permit confidence that underlying regularities do exist.

Finally, patterns of fertility and life expectancy have a profound effect on gender roles. In systems where human labor is an important source of energy, having large numbers of children is important for survival. Women are valued for their fertility and strive to bear many children. As structural transformation unfolds, life expectancy increases dramatically, and a generation whose parents died in their forties may expect to live into their sixties. Their children also face a much higher chance of surviving.

In response, many farm households are shifting the way they allocate their child rearing resources: "Use of non-traditional inputs, increased reliance on markets, improved labor markets, and increased awareness of opportunities outside the agricultural sector lead many farm households to have fewer children, and to make greater human capital investments in the nutrition and education of each" (Nerlove 1979). Farm households are shifting their intergenerational strategies, preparing some children for participation in science-based agriculture, and others for other parts of the rural and urban economies. This demographic transition from resource- extensive investments in many children to resource-intensive investments in fewer children has occurred since the turn of the century in the United States and it is currently occurring in farm households in all areas of the world except Africa.

Such a change in child raising strategies has profound implications for gender roles because it demands that the mother focus much more time and attention on each child. Her skill in teaching, health care, sanitation, food preparation and preservation become as important as her fertility in producing the next generation. When there are young children in the house, it affects mother's time use substantially. Yet the proportion of a women's total life span devoted to the care of young children is much smaller, leaving time for other roles during other parts of her life cycle.

THE STRUCTURAL TRANSFORMATION OF AGRICULTURE

As the discussion of fertility demonstrates, the world changes, and gender roles change with it. The structural transformation of agriculture involves changes in technology, infrastructure, economic and social structures. Over the past two hundred years, a substantial body of knowledge has been built up that helps in understanding the systematic changes that occur in the economy and the society as agriculture becomes more productive (Johnston and Kilby 1976). This section discusses the changes briefly from the perspective of classical and neo-classical development economics, and then moves to a discussion of the current state of knowledge about the shifts in gender roles during the change process. Ways in which current thinking about gender roles during structural transformation may provide a framework for thinking about the history of American farm women will be suggested.

One of the most commonly used indicators in describing national economies is the percentage of the population engaged in agricultural production. This number often tells a great deal about the productivity of the farm sector and the extent of the non-farm economy. Countries range along a continuum from developing countries in Africa where 96 percent of the population is in agriculture, to highly industrialized countries such as the United States where 4 percent of the population produces the nation's food. Although a few oil-rich states are able to purchase their food abroad, for most countries, increasing the productivity of agriculture is a necessary part of national development. Businessmen, factory workers, university professors, bus drivers, and bureaucrats all need to eat. If a country wants the services they produce, then farmers must increase their productivity to feed them.

Increased agricultural productivity comes in part from changes in the technology of production. Although many governments now actively encourage farmers to adopt new technologies or improved versions of traditional ones, technological change has been occurring since long before there were governments to encourage it. Over time, food production techniques changed from hunting and gathering to slash-and-burn agriculture, and sedentary hoe cultures. In many places, the plow then replaced the hoe, and techniques of irrigation and drainage were developed to control the water supply. Many systems now use sophisticated machinery. Hoe, plow, and machine-powered systems all rely increasingly on the new "soft" technologies; higher yielding seed varieties, commercial fertilizers and pesticides are in use all over the world.

If farms are to produce more food than they consume, and provide the surplus to those who do not farm, then there must be infrastructure: roads to move products on; markets to sell them in; merchants, millers, butchers and dairies who will buy them, process them, and move them on the consumer. As cities become bigger, and demand for food greater, these systems become more complex, with wholesale as well as retail merchants, and regional and national markets as well as local market towns. Banks, coops and other credit institutions become more important. Merchants sell increasing amounts of consumer goods and production inputs to farmers who now have cash to buy, at least in the good years. Schools become increasingly important as farm families prepare some of their children for work in the towns and cities, and even more important as the pace of technological change quickens, and science based agriculture becomes common. Government agencies are increasingly present in rural areas, both to provide services such as extension and credit, and to extract surplus in the form of direct and indirect taxes.

As the farming sector becomes more commercialized and complex, the rural social structure inevitably changes. At the very least, there are more layers, with tradespeople, wage earners and bankers, as well as farmers. In some circumstances the benefits and costs of change are distributed relatively equitably. In others, the rich get richer, the poor get poorer. The causes and effects of these different outcomes are now fairly well understood, and there is a substantial body of knowledge available on how to design and execute policies which promote growth with equity.

We are at a much earlier stage in our understanding of changing rural gender roles and relationships. Engels aside, it was as recently as 1970 that Ester Boserup, the Danish economist, made the first attempt at a comprehensive view of women's roles in agricultural development. She posited that population growth was the engine that drove agricultural intensification. People moved to hoe cultivation when population density made hunting and gathering inadequate, and to the plow when the hoe would no longer produce enough food. Using comparative data from Africa and Asia, she argued that women's status tends to get steadily worse as this progression unfolds. Although women continue to do important work in agricultural households, she noted that in the transition from the hoe to the plow, women lose independent access to land as it becomes increasingly scarce and valuable. She argued that the loss of control over the means of production reduced women to the role of (often unpaid) laborer.

Although Boserup went on to argue the economic efficiency of increasing women's productivity through improved access to education and employment, it was the paradigm of women as victims of development that provided the primary theoretical framework for the first decade of research on women in development. Much of the early work was done by anthropologists and sociologists who generated a great deal of data on gender roles in traditional societies. Both framework and data were useful in supporting equity arguments for attention to gender roles in developing economies.

But as feminist scholars entered into dialogue with the development establishment, with economists in particular, they found they had to reexamine their arguments. Although many in the development community ignored questions of gender entirely, a significant number had begun to address these issues using other analytic frameworks and tools (Binswanger et al 1980; Cain 1980; Cernea 1979; Evenson 1978; World Bank 1980). These and other scholars (Mellor 1966; Schultz 1964; Timmer, Falcon and Pearson 1983; Wharton 1968) drew upon a long analytic tradition within development economics that emphasizes the relationship between equity and efficiency.

Such analysis has been influential with donor agencies and national governments in promoting policies of growth with equity. The pressure on feminist scholars to think in terms of efficiency as well as equity, together with the sheer weight of the newer data, made more sophisticated analysis of gender roles imperative.

The accumulating data makes it clear that women's roles and power are very different in different farming systems, and that not all systems fall neatly along the continuum from low productivity/high status to high productivity/low status. Status itself has become an increasingly slippery concept, and many scholars now prefer to talk in terms of women's access to and control over concrete resources such as cash income, credit, education, land, improved technology, labor time, and leisure. Objective measures of life expectancy, fertility rates and school enrollment are also used. Such concepts are measurable and provide a more empirical data base for comparative studies.

Traditional agricultural systems present a more complex picture than Boserup predicated. Two decades of accumulated data make it clear that the amount of agricultural work women do is not directly related to their status. By 1974 anthropologists had concluded that where women do more than 70 percent of the subsistence production, their status is likely to be low (Sanday 1974). Some farm women produce subsistence crops primarily for family consumption, others produce and process crops that produce a substantial income stream. Some women trade while their husbands farm, in other systems, the reverse is true. Women's power in household decision making seems to be affected more by the income producing potention of their work that by its sheer quantity (Acharya and Bennet 1981; Huntington 1975). In Latin American where traditional systems have been impacted by modernization, the results for women are mixed, varying by location, class and ethnicity (Deere and Leon, 1987).

Systems practicing modern scientific agriculture also deviate from the early paradigm. Boserup had not included them explicitly in her analysis, but there was a tendency in the literature to assume that high technology agriculture, by definition, was not good for women. Yet there are several patterns of women's involvement in high technology agriculture that seem to serve both women and their country's economy reasonably well.

In the United States large family farms are a common unit of production. and though historically there has been plenty of land, women have never owned much of it. Their participation in unpaid agricultural work varies, but appears to be increasing. Yet by commonly used measures such as life expectancy or education, their status is reasonably high compared to farm men, and most express satisfaction with their roles, if not their legal relationship to the farm enterprise (Jones and Rosenfield 1981).

But the American pattern is not the only one possible in high-tech agriculture. Japan more closely approximates Boserup's pattern; population density is high, and family farms are small and highly mechanized. Here again, women do not hold title to much land. Nevertheless, they are the principal farm managers as well as the laborers. Measures of their education, access to technology and capital are reasonably high, (Kada, n.d.) while female infant mortality is lower than male, and women's life expectancy is greater (Population Reference Bureau, 1980). Much of Eastern Europe presents still another pattern. Here women do much of the farm labor on large mechanized state farms while their husbands work in factories. Although much of the management of these farms remains in male hands, women's rates of education are roughly equal to men's, their life expectancy relatively higher, and female infant mortality rates lower (Population Reference Bureau, 1980)

If Boserup's original paradigm was too simplistic, where does that leave us? I would suggest that we face two related tasks. The first is to gain a clearer understanding of the key variables influencing gender roles and relationships in agricultural systems. The second is very careful observation of what happens to gender relationships when one or more of these key variables shifts. Neither of these tasks is simple, and assimilating the data from them into manageable form presents formidable challenges. Nevertheless, work has begun in both areas.

A number of these variables have now been clearly identified. The productivity of agriculture, the types of available technology, crop varieties and the subsistence/cash crop mix, farm size, fertility patterns, the availability of education and the opportunity structure in the rest of economy, have been discussed in the international context. The importance of social and cultural norms has also been noted. All have changed radically in the United States over the past two hundred years; both infrastructure and social structure have changed with them. The importance of gender based patterns of access to and control over land and capitol have also been discussed. These appear to have remained somewhat more stable in the American contest.

An examination of the history of American farm women in terms of these variables could be very productive, both for American historians, and for development practitioners. The wealth of information in the studies for this volume provide a useful starting point.

BIBLIOGRAPHY

Acharya, Meena and Lynn Bennett. 1981. *Women and the Subsistence Sector, Economic Participation and Household Decision Making in Nepal.* Washington, D.C.: The World Bank.

Ahn, Choong Yong, Inderjit Singh and Lyn Squire. 1981. "A Model of the Agricultural Household in a Multi-Crop Economy: The Case of Korea." *The Review of Economics and Statistics* 63:4 520-25.

Barnum, H. and Lyn Squire. 1979. *A Model of an Agricultural Household: Theory and Evidence.* World Bank Occasional Paper No. 27. Baltimore: The World Bank

Becker, Gary. 1965. "A Theory of the Allocation of Time." In *The Economics of Women and Work*, ed. by Alice Amaders. New York: St. Martin's Press.

Beneria, Lourdes and Gita Sen. 1981. "Accumulation, Reproduction and Women's Role in Economic Development: Boserup Revisited." *Signs* 7:2. 279-98.

Binswanger, Hans, Robert Evenson, Consuelo Florencio and Benjamin White, eds. 1980. *Rural Households in Asia.* Singapore: Singapore University Press.

Binswanger, Hans and Mark Rosenzweig. 1981. *Contractual Arrangements, Employment and Wages in Rural Labor Markets: A Critical Review.* Series in Employment and Rural Develoment No. 67. Washington, D.C.: The World Bank.

Birdsall, Nancy and Susan Cochrane. 1983. "Education and Parental Decision Making: A Two-Generational Approach." in *Education and Development*, ed. by Lancelles Anderson and D.M. Windham. Lexington, Mass.: D.C. Heath.

Blades, Derek W. 1975. *Non-Monetary (Subsistence) Activities in the National Accounts of Developing Counries.* Paris, France: Organisation for Economic Co-operation and Development.

Blumberg, Rae Lesser. 1979. "A Paradigm for Predicting the Position of Women." In *Sex Roles and Social Policy.* ed. by Jean Lipman-Blumen and Jesse Bernard. London: Sage.

Boserup, Ester. 1970. *Women's Role in Economic Development.* New York: St. Matin's Press.

Burton, Michael, and Douglas White. 1984. "Sexual Division of Labor in Agriculture." *American Anthropologist* 86:3 568-83.

Cain, Mead. 1980. "The Economic Activities of Children in a Village in Bangladesh." in *Rural Households in Asia*, ed. by Binswanger, *et al.*

_____. 1979. *Class, Patriarchy and the Structure of Women's Work in Rural Bangladesh.* The Population Council Working Paper No.43. New York: The Population Council

Cernea, Michael. 1979. *Macrosocial Change, Feminization of Agriculture and Peasant Women's Threefold Economic Role.* Washington, D.C.: Agriculture and Rural Development Department. World Bank.

Cloud, Kathleen. 1985. "Women's Productivity in Agricultural Systems: Considerations for Project Design." In *Gender Issues in Development Projects: A Case Book.* ed. by Catherine Overholt, Mary Anderson, Kathleen Cloud, and James Austin. West Hartford: Kumarian Press.

Cloud, Kathleen and Catherine Overholt. 1983. "Women's Productivity in Agricultural Systems: An Overview." In *Rural Development, Growth Rural Development, Growth and Inequity.* ed. by B.L.Greenshields and M. A. Belamy. I.A.A.E. Occasional Paper No. 3. International Agricultural Economics Association: Aldershot, Hants, England

Committee on Status of Women in India. 1974. *Towards Equality: Report of the Committee on Status of Women in India.* New Delhi: Dept.of Social Welfare, Government of India.

Croll, Elisabeth. 1981. "Women in Rural Production and Reproduction in the Soviet Union, China, Cuba and Tanzania: Socialist Development Experiences." *Signs* 7:2 361-400.

Deacon, Ruth, and Wallace Huffman. 1986. *Human Resources Research, 1887-1987.* Ames, Iowa: College of Home Economics, Iowa State University.

DaVanzo, Julie and D.L.P. Lee. 1978. *Compatibility of Child Care with Labor Force Participation and Non-Market Activities: Preliminary Evidence from Malaysian Time Budget Data.* Rand Paper Series, 6126. Santa Monica: The Rand Corp.

Deere, Carmen Diane and Magdalena Leon. 1987. *Rural Women and State Policy: Feminist Perspectives on Latin American Agricultural Development.* Boulder,Colorado: Westview Press.

Dixon, Ruth B. 1982. "Women in Agriculture: Counting the Labor Force in Developing Countries." *Population and Development Review* 8:3.

_____. 1983. "Land, Labor, and the Sex Composition of the Agricultural Labor Force: an International Comparison." *Development and Change* 14 347-72.

Evenson, Robert. 1978. "Time Allocation in Rural Phillipine Households." *American Journal of Agricultural Economics* 60:2 322-30.

Dixon, Ruth B., Barry Popkin and Elizabeth Quizon. 1980. "Nutrition, Work & Demographic Behavior in Rural Phillipine Households." in *Rural Households in Asia.* ed. by Binswanger *et al.*

Feldstein, Hilary, ed. 1987. "Household Dynamics and Farming Systems: Case Studies in Agricultural Development." Ford Foundation, New York.

Folbre, Nancy 1983. *Household Production in the Phillipines: A Non-neoclassical Approach.* WID Working Paper No. 26. East Lansing: Michigan State University.

Guyer, Jane. 1984. Naturalism in Models of African Production. *Man* 19, 371-88

Heyzer, Noeleen. 1981. "Women and the Informal Sector: Toward a Framework of Analysis." *IDS Bulletin* 12:3. 3-8.

Huffman, Wallace, and Mark Lange. 1982. *Farm Household Production: Demand for Wives Labor, Capital Services and the Capital Labor Ratio.* Yale University Discussion Paper 408. New Haven: Economic Growth Center.

_____. 1983. "Off-Farm and Farm Work Decisions of Married Farm Males and Females." Ames, Iowa: Iowa State University, mimeo.

Huntington, Suellen. 1975. "Issues in Women's Role in Economic Development: Critique and Alternatives." *Journal of Marriage and the Family* 1001-12.

Hymer, Stephen and Stephen Resnick. 1969. "A Model of an Agrarian Economy with Non-agricultural Activities." *American Economic Review* 59:493-506.

International Service for National Agricultural Research. 1985. *The User's Perspective in International and National Agricultural Research.* A background document prepared for a CGIAR Inter-Center Seminar on Women and Agricultural Technology, Bellagio, Italy, March, 1985.

Jayme-Ho, Teresa. 1976. *Time Allocation, Home Production and Labor Force Participation of Married Women: An Exploratory Survey.* Institute of Economic Development and Research. Discussion paper No. 76-8. Los Banos: University of the Phillipines.

Johnson, Glenn. 1981. "Small Farms in a Changing World." Dept. of Agricultural Economics, Michigan State University, East Lansing. Mimeo.

Johnston, Bruce F. and Peter Kilby. 1976. *Agriculture and Structural Transformation.* New York: Oxford University Press.

Jones, Calvin and Rachael Rosenfield. 1981. *American Farm Women: Findings from a Survey.* Report No. 130. Chicago: National Opinion Research Center.

Jones, Christine. 1983. "The Mobilization of Women's Labor for Cash Crop Production; A Game Theoretic Approach." *American Journal of Agricultural Economics* 65:5. 1049-55.

Kada, Yukiko. n.d. *The Changing Role of the Extension Services in the Rural Development of Japan, Where Farming is Predominantly Conducted by Women on a Part Time Basis.* Master's Thesis. University of Wisconsin, Madison.

Krishna, Raj. 1968. "Models of the Family Farm." in *Subsistence Agriculture and Economic Development,* ed by Clifton Wharton, Jr. Chicago: Adelaine Publishing Co.

Levine, Robert A. 1984. *Maternal Behavior and Child Development in High-Fertility Populations.* Fertility Determinants Research Note No. 2. New York: The Population Council.

Lewis, W. Arthur. 1954. "Economic Development with Unlimited Supplies of Labor." *Manchester School* 22:2 139-191.

Mellor, John W. 1966. *The Economics of Agricultural Development.* Ithaca: Cornell University Press.

Minge-Klevana, Wanda. 1980. "Does labor time decrease with industrialisation? A survey of time allocation studies." *Current Anthropology.* 21:3 1-16.

Ministere du Travail, Comite du Travail Feminin. 1974. *La Formation du Femmmes en Milleau Rural*. Paris: Government of France.

Moock, Peter. 1976. "The Efficiency of Women as Farm Managers:Kenya." *American Journal of Agricultural Economics* : 831-835.

Nag, M., White, B., and Peet. 1980. "The Economic Value of Children in Java and Nepal." In *Rural Household Studies in Asia*, ed by Binswanger *et al.*

Nerlove, Marc. 1979. "The dynamics of supply: retrospect and prospect." *American Journal of Agricultural Economics* 874-87.

Nerlove, Sara B. 1974. "Women's Workload and Infant Feeding Practices." *Ethnology*. 13: 207-14.

Overholt, Catherine, Mary Anderson, Kathleen Cloud and James Austin. 1985. *Gender Roles in Development Projects*. East Hartford, Conn: Kumarian Press.

Population Reference Bureau. 1980. *World's Women Population Data Sheet*. Washington, D.C.

Rosenzweig, Mark. 1980. "Neoclassical Theory and the Optimizing Peasant: an Econometric Analysis of a Market Family Labor Supply in a Developing Country." *The Quarterly Journal of Economics* 31-55.

Rosenzweig, Mark, and Robert Evenson. 1977. *Fertility, Schooling, and the Economic Contribution of Children in Rural India: An Economic Analysis*. New Haven: Economic Growth Center, Yale University.

Sanday, Peggy. 1974. "Female Status in the Public Domain." in *Women, Culture and Society* ed. by Michelle Rosaldo and Louise Lamphere, Stanford: Stanford University Press.

Schultz, Theodore. 1964. *Transforming Traditional Agriculture*. New Haven: Yale University Press.

_____. 1982. *Investing in People: The Economics of Population Quality*. Berkley: University of California Press.

Strauss, John. 1984. *An Overview of Agricultural Household Models: Empirical Applications*. Economic Growth Center Working Paper No. 451. New Haven: Economic Growth Center, Yale University,

Szalsi, Alexander. 1975. *The Situation of Women in the Light of Contemporary Time-budget Research*. Report submitted to the World Conference of the International Women's Year, Mexico. New York: The United Nations.

Timmer, C. Peter, Walter Falcon and Scott Pearson. 1983. *Food Policy Analysis*. Baltimore: John Hopkins University Press for the World Bank.

Wharton, Clifton R. Jr. ed. 1968. *Subsistence Agriculture and Economic Development*. Chicago: Aldine Publishing Company.

White, Benjamin. 1975. "The Economic Importance of Children in a Javanese Village." in *Population and Social Organization*, ed. by Moni Nag. The Hague: Mouton.

World Bank. 1980. *World Development Report 1980*. New York: Oxford University Press.

FARM WOMEN'S COMMUNITY AND POLITICAL ROLES

17

'IT'S OUR TURN NOW':
RURAL AMERICAN WOMEN SPEAK OUT,
1900-1920

Jane B. Knowles

INTRODUCTION

The period 1900-1920 was one of unparalleled prosperity for American agriculture, especially that of the Middle West. It still stands as the basis for determining parity – the attempt to make prices charged for agricultural products bear an equitable relationship to the costs of their production.[1] Demand was up, fueled by the explosive growth of cities and by the requirements of World War I; at the same time, the number of farms grew very little after the effective close of the frontier around 1900, and the numbers of people actually resident on farms and hence available for agricultural work declined fairly sharply over the period. There were real fears, quite widely expressed, that American "agricultural production would be unable to keep pace with the growth of the nation." (Saloutos and Hicks 1951; Clutts 1961; Bowers 1974).

Despite these shifts in demand and supply, and the relative prosperity they produced, as the historians of agrarian discontent note, "During the late nineteenth century western agrarians had built up a philosophy of radicalism sufficient even to endure the acid test of good times" (Saloutos and Hicks 1951, 31). During this period of relative good times, however, the focus of rural protest began to shift from the need to increase agricultural production to a broader concern with the well-being of the whole farm enterprise, including prominently the farm family. To some extent the shift was one of degree rather than kind – no farm protest movement had ever completely ignored the well-being of farm families and some, like the Grange, had paid significant amounts of attention to the whole constellation of farm family issues. Nevertheless, after 1900 there was a new recognition of and response to the sorts of rural discontent that were producing a swell of rural-urban migration and evoking heretofore unheard expressions of dissatisfaction with the quality of American farm life. The net effect was the creation of a second stream of agricultural protest, complete with suggested solutions to what were seen to be the presenting problems. There were now two sets of actors:

303

1. Large prosperous farmers and their urban business supporters who viewed farming as a business enterprise and supported governmental aid to increase output, scientific farming practices, and organization for economic benefit

2. Other farmers and their urban supporters – many from the academic, church and social work communities – who saw farming as a way of life that transcended mere economics and advocated a broad-gauged approach to rural concerns

In 1919-1920 the dichotomy was crystallized with the formation of the Farm Bureau Federation, on the one hand, and the National Country Life Association, on the other (Clutts 1961, 14, 24-26; Bowers 1974, 20-23, 28-29).

Both the existing farm protest organizations and those formed in the decades 1900-1920 tended to focus on the economic issues – credit, marketing, freight rates, prices, and the like – though some (e.g., the Non-Partisan League) had a broader social and political program as well (Saloutos and Hicks 1951). It was agencies of government – especially the federal government – that provided the principal base of support and encouragement for those who were concerned with the overall quality of farm life. While it is too simplistic to think of these diverging streams of thought as representing "masculine" vs. "feminine" points of view, it is unmistakably the case that women's concerns about the quality of farm life only found significant expression in the second, newer sort of agricultural protest.

WOMEN'S VOICES

Individual

It was around the whole issue of the material conditions of farm life that women's voices began to be raised. Inevitably, these were largely individual expressions of discontent, since rural women were largely outside the complex web of women's organizations in which so many urban women were securely enmeshed.[2] Given their relative isolation, rural women had to await the creation and application of one of the most powerful tools of modern times – the survey.

It is in the work of the Country Life Commission (CLC) in 1908-1909 that we first see even a primitive application of survey methodology to the issue of the quality of rural life. Appointed by Theodore Roosevelt as one of the first national commissions (in what was to become a long and occasionally honorable line) set to investigate and report on some aspect of American life, the CLC was composed of seven men who had long been concerned with rural matters as farmers, educators, conservationists, and journalists. The commission represented both the best and the worst of what was later to be called Progressivism, and the impact of its *Report* on subsequent farm legislation and policy is the subject of dispute among historians (Clutts 1961, 62-66, 163; Bowers 1974 31-40, 128-34). Its significance for this discussion is (a) in its twofold solicitation of opinion about the status of American agriculture by means of a survey of more than 100,000 farm families and a series of thirty public hearings across the country, and (b) in its strong endorsement of the survey as a dependable means of securing information on rural conditions to serve as the basis for sound policy decisions (Clutts 1961, 86-87, 129, 163ff.; Bowers 1974, 86-88).

Although the CLC's survey instrument was not directed specifically to women, they seized on it – and on the public hearings – as a means of making their voices heard. The message they delivered to the commission was one of isolation, endless hard work, lack of any household help, poor health and sanitation, schools that did not provide a useful education for rural children, lack of women's organizations, and the declining significance of rural churches. The commission's response was to recommend a formal national survey of rural needs, a national agricultural extension system, and a campaign for rural progress including such amenities as improved roads, telephone service, and rural free delivery (Rasmussen 1975, 2: 1860-1906) – certainly a response sympathetic to women's concerns, but hardly a call to revolution.

In part, the response is symptomatic of the larger problems of the commission, briefly noted above, but in part it may have stemmed from the commission's make-up. That perpetual gadfly, Charlotte Perkins Gilman, demanded in the pages of the January 1909 *Good Housekeeping* (*GH*), "Why Are There No Women on the President's Commission?" Gilman noted that much of the commission's focus of inquiry was "distinctly the business of women" since it included "woman's long-defined province – the affairs of the home." She proposed that women choose a commission of their own – nine "distinguished authorities," "experts in domestic architecture and decoration, landscape gardening, household industries, sanitation, hygiene and physical culture, food preparation, aseptic cleaning, education and amusement." Given the lack of women's organizations in rural areas, she suggested public meetings in schools and churches to gather and tabulate information.[3]

GH went Gilman one better (taking a hint from the CLC) and organized its own survey of rural women – "a great National Inquiry," to be carried out by means of a questionnaire printed in *GH* itself and in three major farm publications. "This will be the first opportunity of the farm women of America to make their voices heard as a unit in a great cause – the best development of their home life and especially of their children." Subsequent to the survey, and using names suggested, *GH* would select a women's equivalent of the Country Life Commission (Gilman 1909).

GH was as good as its word. By April 1909 it could report receiving responses to its questionnaire. But the women did not speak "as a unit"; rather, there were letters of two types – those from prosperous farms whose womenfolk wanted or needed no investigation of their lot by anyone, and those from poorer units "in which the lot of womenfolk is a hard one." By June, the magazine had more than one thousand replies and letters, which it turned over to the General Federation of Women's Clubs to serve as the basis for a state-by-state inquiry into the condition of rural women. *GH's* editors considered such a survey to be of great potential significance since Congress had refused to provide funds for widespread distribution of the CLC's report.

The letters that *GH* chose to print do in fact give more sense of the unity of farm women than the magazine's editors acknowledged in April. Some women do speak of their contentment with rural life (often in terms of the relative freedom from social conventions like urban dress), but all want "betterment," and most see that in terms of more social life with other women which in turn will require labor-saving help and/or machinery ("New Era for Farm Wives" 1909):

> No woman can do the housework for a family of five, all sewing, spinning and knitting, take care of seventy-five hens, milk four to seven cows night and morning, make from fifty to eighty pounds of butter every week and help about other chores and still have time left for social life. (Vermont)

> Our wants are many and various. We want better roads; we want a parcels post; we want better schools. But what we need more than any of the above is *labor-saving machinery for the farm women.* (Iowa)

> I cannot be a social woman and tend to my household duties and a gang of hired men at the same time. California farmers as a rule do not know that they have a wife. A wife is merely a machine. (California)

> I do not have any time for social life; if there is one minute to sit down I must sew or mend. With twenty-five pounds of butter to make every other day, cows to milk, chickens and pigs to care for, besides my garden and various other little cares, and with two children, there is no time for pleasure-seeking. I have no drain, so have to carry all slop water away from the house to avoid disease, and there is a great deal of slop where milk is handled. . . . I have been to town three times in ten years . . . I am not slow in my duties, either, as I am small in build, weighing only ninety pounds . . . . (New York)

The historian William Bowers argues that urban women did take up the causes of their rural sisters, working for rural school improvement (including placing home economics in the curriculum), improved health and sanitation (including eradication of hookworm), and the provision of clean, comfortable "rest rooms" for rural women and children to use during their visits to towns.[4] However helpful the efforts of urban women, they did not make rural women less anxious to raise their voices the next time they were asked to do so.

In October of 1913 – the timing was dictated by the need to wait until after the pressure of harvest work – the United States Department of Agriculture (USDA), in deliberate preparation for the extension responsibilities it would have to assume when the Smith-Lever Bill passed Congress, wrote to "the housewives of 55,000 crop correspondents, asking them to suggest ways in which the Department could render more service to the farm women of the United States" (U.S. Department of Agriculture 1915a, 5). Crop correspondents were farmers to whom the department regularly turned for information on yields and costs; hence, they were probably at the middle level of all farmers in the country or above and did not equitably represent the wide range of economic conditions within U.S. agriculture. Just under 2500 replies were received by the end of 1913, but the number of individuals represented – both men and women replied – was greater than the response indicated since many women consulted others and wrote on behalf of several people. The department divided the replies into four large groups and used them as the basis for reports on the social and labor, domestic, educational, and economic needs of American farm women.[5]

The complaints are very much the same as those presented to the CLC and *GH*; expressions of satisfaction are found too in fairly substantial numbers. The USDA compiler noted (a comment reported by the *New York Times* ["Farm Women Find Life Hard" 1915]), that "the condition [being reported] is peculiar to individual farms rather than . . . to any general state of farming" (Report No. 103, p. 11), but that is not precisely accurate. There *are* very distinct common threads that run through many of these letters, across all regions of the country. The women's discontent focuses on three comparisons between the material conditions of their daily lives and those of others:

1. *Their mothers and grandmothers*: With the exception of the sewing machine, women's work in 1913 is little changed from that of previous generations, but there is now a shortage of household help for hire and a need to feed and care for field hands, neither an improvement

2. *Their husbands and sons*: Attention paid to farms by private industry and by government has focused exclusively on male tasks, making them both more productive and less labor-intensive

3.*Their urban counterparts*: Water, drains, and electricity are now an accepted part of urban women's homemaking, and their lives are demonstrably less burdensome as a result.[6]

Specific complaints included the following:

1. loneliness, monotony, and isolation

2. lack of household help and the extra burden of caring for farm laborers, often of undesirable character

3. lack of women's clubs to provide both an educational and a social function and the inability of farm women to organize these without government help

4. heavy work responsibilities in fields and home with no economic reward

5. lack of good, all-weather roads, of rural free delivery, and telephone service at reasonable cost

6. lack of labor-saving devices and any consideration of convenience in farm homes

7. lack of information on growing and marketing crops for which women were largely responsible, e.g., vegetables, fruit, poultry and eggs, butter and cheese

8. lack of information on and equipment to ensure basic sanitation in the home

9. lack of information on how the knowledge of domestic science might be used to ease work burdens and to make farm life more appealing to girls

10. lack of knowledge about good human (as opposed to animal) nutrition and proper medical and nursing care

11. poor schooling for the needs of rural children, including lack of instruction in domestic science for girls and agriculture for boys (and even an occasional hope that girls and boys could both study these subjects as they do academic ones)

12. lack of information on how to integrate the many aspects of their work life

13. lack of opportunities to earn – or, even more often, to control – cash incomes to help meet family needs.

USDA's leadership was clearly nonplussed by some of this outpouring because the department had for several years been attempting to provide at least some of the help these women sought. In each of the four volumes of the survey report, appendices prepared by USDA provided lists of appropriate Bulletins women could consult, and one (Report No. 103, Appendix A) included a very full discussion of the work already under way in Farmer's Institutes and other types of moveable schools and in agricultural clubs for children. The department's official report on the survey (Mitchell 1915) noted the women's unawareness of work already undertaken to help them, and the strength of their demand for government assistance in organizing themselves into clubs that could work for mutual betterment.

Both sides in this continuing dialogue – farm women on the one hand, and on the other those interested in their condition – increasingly looked to the long-anticipated Cooperative Extension Service (CES) to provide solutions to the women's problems. The Smith-Lever Bill, which created the CES, required it to diffuse "useful and practical information on subjects relating to [both] agriculture and home economics" by means of "instructions and practical demonstrations" and "publications" (Scott 1970, 46). The language about home economics was new to Smith-Lever; it was not present in either the Morrill (1862) or Hatch (1887) Acts which created the land grant university and the agricultural experiment station systems, respectively.

By 1914, when Smith-Lever finally passed, home economics or domestic science had attained the dual status of an appropriate field of study for women at both the secondary and collegiate levels and a respectable profession for women to pursue before or in lieu of marriage. The numbers of women it engaged had increased dramatically in previous decades, and they had organized themselves into a professional association in 1909, following a decade of the less formal Lake Placid meetings by leaders of the movement (Craig 1945; Croyle-Langhorne 1982; Hunt 1918; Ehrenreich and English 1979; Solomon 1985). The serial *Reports* of the United States Commissioner of Education document the growing numbers of women pursuing courses of study in domestic science in the land grant universities up to the time of Smith-Lever:[7]

Year	Number in Degree Programs
1906	833
1907	1030
1908	1319
1909	1443
1910	1617
1911	2258
1912	2506
1913	3074
1914	4018

The land grants had begun a biennial summer graduate program in agriculture in 1902; by 1912, home economics was one of the subjects offered (*Report of the Commissioner of Education for . . . 1912*, 1:215). And there were outreach efforts as well. The Farmer's Institutes, a semiformal educational program based on European models, were generally one- or two-day meetings held at a time and in a place convenient for farmers at which a few topics were covered in a series of short (often illustrated) lectures. The federal government supported and encouraged the institute movement. In the period of its greatest sophistication and effect (ca. 1900-1912), USDA's Office of Experiment Stations employed a Farmer's Institute specialist, who oversaw the preparation of lecture series and accompanying lantern slides. During roughly the same period, the land grant universities began to develop on-campus short courses for farmers, and before long the two activities overlapped (Scott 1970, 64-97, 154-57; U.S. Department of Agriculture, Office of Experiment Stations).

Over time, both the Farmer's Institutes and the short course programs attempted to deal with the concerns of the entire farm family. Initially, Farmer's Institute programs for women included some technical presentations on, for example, dairying, poultry, and beekeeping, along with domestic science-type programs on food preparation,sanitation, child care, and clothing construction, etc. In time, the emphasis came to be heavily on the domestic science side, with cooking schools a particularly popular offering, at least at the state level. In the federally created series of illustrated lectures, three of the fourteen – "Farm Architecture," "Farm Homes," and "Farm Home Grounds-Planting and Care" – were fully or partially addressed to women. The USDA paper that reviewed Institute programs for women cited their "need . . . for more definite instruction in domestic and sanitary science and household art than is given to mixed audiences of the Farmer's Institutes." In 1908, the year on which the document reported, twenty-one states had separate programs for women, and seven had female lecturers in their regular programs – all dealing with strictly domestic science programs. Short courses on land grant campuses followed much the same pattern.[8]

In the year 1909 alone, three states – Minnesota, Ohio, and Utah – mandated their public universities to establish outreach programs in domestic science that were accessible to all state residents, and Wisconsin organized a campus-based short course which attracted more than four hundred participants (*Report of the Commissioner of Education for . . . 1909*, 1:137-49). By 1911-1912, 491 men and 56 women associated with land grants were involved in extension work in some capacity; 43 institutions had directors of extension; and 220 moveable schools and 93 educational trains were in operation (*Report of the Commissioner of Education for . . . 1911*, 2:991-1046; *Report . . . for . . . 1912*, 1:264-80). In 1914, the U.S. Bureau of Education produced a special bulletin more than two hundred pages in length on "Education for the Home" by Benjamin Andrews (Assistant Professor of Household Economics, Teachers College, Columbia University) which reviewed all aspects of home economics education (U.S. Bureau of Education 1914). Clearly, the ground was prepared for the CES, and the service immediately recruited and put into the field female home-demonstration agents, who wasted little time in putting the by now well-recognized survey method to work again.

In 1919, home-demonstration agents working in thirty-three northern and western states undertook a widespread and quite scientific survey of the women in approximately 10,000 homes "to learn from the farm women themselves their real problems and how the extension service [could] aid in solving them" (Ward 1920, 1). This survey was different from previous ones both in its coverage – it was a deliberate attempt to cover *all* farm homes in the region served by the agents – and in the nature of the data it collected: there were no first-hand responses by farm women, but rather a careful tabulation of the answers to questions posed by the agents and interpretation of their meaning by the author, Florence Ward. The survey did show some slight improvements in women's conditions over time – there were more telephones and automobiles – but women still suffered under a burdensome work load (nearly twelve hours a day on the average) with no regular breaks, and exercised very little control over any income they earned from their labor. Few had even the basic convenience of running water, let alone power-driven home machinery (though in 42 percent of all the farms surveyed, and a far higher percentage in some regions, power was available for farm machinery). Household help was rarely available. Isolation was not significantly diminished. The survey identified the major problems of the women surveyed to be excessively long working days, heavy burdens of manual labor, lack of comfort in their homes, poor health of mothers and children, and lack of opportunities to earn income to use for home improvements (p. 16).

This survey's detached and scientific nature in comparison to earlier surveys does not disguise the fact that the overall condition of farm women during the most prosperous decades in the history of American agriculture had improved scarcely at all, despite the willingness of these women to address their problems whenever asked to do so.

Collective

Instances of collective action by rural women, even on their own behalf, are rare. Two such instances that will be discussed here are of particular interest in that each represents significant dissatisfaction with institutions to which farm women were regularly turning for help – the home economics movement within the land grant university community and the USDA.

Domestic science at a land grant university. In 1900, the University of Illinois recruited the chemist Isabel Bevier to revive its languishing domestic science program. Fresh from the Lake Placid conference of that year and quite solidly grounded in chemistry, Miss Bevier arrived to develop a program at Illinois that would emphasize basic science rather than a how-to approach to household studies. Her program was highly regarded by other land grant universities and the Carnegie Foundation, but her local base of support was less than solid. Before coming to Illinois, Miss Bevier was not acquainted with public universities and their outreach functions, and she found their politics somewhat difficult to master. In her early years at Illinois, she seems to have tried to work with those women in the local Farmer's Institutes who were conducting homemakers' programs. Nevertheless, Bevier's program incurred the organized wrath of the Household Science Department of the Illinois Farmer's Institute, which successfully demanded that the university close down her experimental house on the Champaign-Urbana campus and very nearly forced Bevier's resignation from the University. Bevier characterized the incident as part of "the age-old conflict between the cooking and sewing school adherents and those who believed in the scientific method of approach to the teaching of household science," and of course she was in one sense correct. But there were significant political overtones as well – for example, Bevier had refused to help seek a legislative appropriation the Farmer's Institute staff felt would have been forthcoming with her support. And it cannot be insignificant that many of her autobiographical statements about the incident, and about the Farmer's Institute women in general, reveal her contempt for the women and their program of work and her failure to comprehend their expectations of the university. The Farmer's Institute women, in turn, were clearly angry at the irrelevance of the fully electrified and equipped demonstration house (it drew eighty to one hundred sightseers a day) to the reality of their daily lives on farms (Bane 1955, 45-55, 86-87; Shapiro 1986, 181-85).

USDA. In 1915, one Representative Keating of Colorado introduced H.R. 21203 "[t]o provide for the establishment, operation and management of a bureau to be known as the Farm Women's Bureau in the Department of Agriculture."

The legislation was advocated by the U.S. branch of the International Congress of Farm Women (an organization that enjoyed the sponsorship of the International Congress of Dryland Farming), whose president was a resident of Keating's district. Under the legislation, which incidentally never reached the floor of the House, the bureau was to investigate the problems of farm women, serve as an advisory center for the land grant universities and the experiment stations, work with the Public Health Bureau on issues of health and sanitation, organize farm women into clubs, help to consolidate rural schools and to develop extension-administered programs of home study, work to solve the problems of domestic help, assist women to secure relevant agricultural publications, and construct and fully equip a model farm home. The bureau was to be headed by a woman with "at least 10 years' practical experience as a home-maker on the farm," with an initial annual budget of $200,000. Lettters of suport for the legislation, written by the president and vice-president of the sponsoring organization, made a number of challenging points: they argued that USDA should have been doing all this anyway but wasn't, and estimated that only $58,000 of the department's annual budget of $26 million was being spent on programs of direct relevance to women; they claimed that USDA and the colleges had paid too much attention to the business aspects of farm enterprises and not enough to the home; they argued that city women already had the help they needed while farm women's needs were unmet; they noted that women needed new economic opportunities to replace now lost home industries and that their legislation was favored by people "who realize the immense importance of the farm woman as an economic factor in the world's great work [of agriculture]" (Congress of the United States 1915).

THE GRANGE

Finally, there is the special case of the Grange, which admitted women as full members from the start, required their participation in all Grange activities, and provided them with a set of unusual opportunities (Buck 1913; Nordin 1974; Grosch 1876). It was in the activities of the Grange that rural women most closely approximated the urban club model of years of organized work with other women – on domestic issues, on more cultural or literary interests, and on such difficult political issues as women's suffrage. Participation in the Grange provided women with an opportunity to develop leadership skills, socialize with other women, participate in the ritual of the organization, and exert pressures for issues of particular concern to themselves (Blair 1980).

Individual women were actively involved in the Grange's organized support of improved rural education of all kinds, making public speeches and urging legislative action (Nordin 1974, 57-59). State Granges were active in promoting such women's issues as home economics instruction in schools and equal admission of women to land grant universities (Nordin 1974, 48-50, 76). Easing the work burdens and the isolation of farm women were high on Grange agendas from its earliest years, and there is anecdotal evidence that Grange members improved both the material conditions of their farms and their individual organizational skills (Grosch 1876; Buck 1913; Nordin 1974). The numbers of women (and men) involved were never very large, however, and even if one accepts the existence of a second surge of activity between 1880 and 1900, the Grange was not a strong force after that. Clearly, it did offer special opportunities to rural women for action on their own behalf – opportunities not easily found in other farm organizations that they eagerly took up.

CONCLUSIONS

This very brief overview presents three different means used by farm women during the period 1900-1920 to articulate their concerns with the material conditions of their lives:

1. individual women seizing a range of opportunities offered to state their views
2. ad hoc groups formed to deal with a special issue
3. groups with a broader and longer set of purposes, at least one of which fairly closely approximated the women's clubs available in urban areas.

The women's effort was a valiant one, and it did not go unnoticed. The Country Life Commission heard women and tried to deal with their concerns in its *Report*. USDA heard women and tried to deal with their concerns in its educational programs – bulletins, Farmer's Institute lectures, and the Cooperative Extension Service. The press heard and reported on women's attitudes toward rural life, usually quite sympathetically.[9] Nevertheless, very little changed in the lives of rural women.

The early years of the twentieth century saw massive structural changes in the delivery of basic social services. Health care can serve as one example: the number of hospital beds doubled between 1900 and 1920 (it took until 1970 to accomplish the next doubling); such preventive services as prenatal care and immunization of children became widely (and cheaply) available in towns and cities. Yet in 1919 farm wives were an average of 5.5 miles from the nearest doctor, 12 from the nearest nurse, and 14 from the nearest hospital; as a result, they spent an average of more than thirty days a year providing nursing care to their families, and rural infant mortality remained high (Cowan 1983, 76-77; "Why Some Young Women Are Leaving Our Farms" 1920, 56; "Some Solid Reasons for a Strike of Farm Wives" 1919, 78).

In cities, the age of consumerism was well underway. Homes were electrified and enjoyed central heat. Women could choose among a plethora of competing brands of appliances – washing machines (for those who chose not to use the many new commercial laundries), irons, ranges, and vacuum cleaners. Large department stores flourished, providing clothing and household goods, and groceries sold products once produced by hand at home. Many middle-class women had sufficient free time to be very active in club work or to participate in elaborate cookery demonstrations. All of these changes received wide publicity in the popular press and were clearly reflected in the mail order catalogues entering farm homes. By contrast, in 1919, 96 percent of the farm families surveyed did their own laundry by hand (68 percent of them without running water), 92 percent did all family sewing, and 94 percent baked all their own bread. In only 14 percent of the homes was there a hired girl, yet women had significant field work responsibilities in 24 percent, helped with the livestock in 25 percent, with the milking in 36 percent, with the kitchen garden in 54 percent, and with the poultry in 81 percent.[10] Grange-member Mary Ann Mayo's concerns, dating from the 1880s, about how farm women's excessive work loads prevented them from pursuing any personal improvement or civic activities were still well-founded in 1920.

Were farm women's concerns unreasonable? Hardly. Rural women clearly were disadvantaged in the material conditions of their daily working lives vis-a-vis both rural men and urban women. Moreover, the women were not proposing any significant changes in their farm and/or home responsibilities, but only that these be carried out in reasonably convenient fashion. Nor were they arguing for any special consideration at the expense of other farm-firm activities. Rather, they were anticipating one of the modern streams of argument about economic development and making what were clearly "efficiency" arguments for even minimal investments in the domestic side of the farm enterprise: the knowledge and ability to provide more nutritious food will in turn produce a generation of healthier farm laborers; more efficient homemaking equipment will free women's time to help with other farm tasks or to engage in income-earning activities.

In fact, the women were confronting a set of circumstances over which they could exercise very little control. First, changes in the material conditions of farm lives were primarily dependent on thousands of individual decisions about the most appropriate use of farm income – decisions on which women could have little effect since they controlled virtually none of that income, frequently not even that generated by their own efforts. Women clearly understood the nature of the problem, and they actively sought more income-earning opportunities.[11] The conservatism of farmers was – and is – legendary, and there was no reason for women to be sanguine about the sympathy they could generate in men who tended to distrust even such potentially beneficial undertakings as Farmer's Institutes and mutual cooperation, and who may have been financially hard pressed as well.[12]

Second, there were structural impediments to the women achieving their goals, chiefly the unwillingness of federal or state governments to raise rural living to urban standards by, inter alia, investing in rural electrification, roads, schools, and hospitals. The first of these awaited the New Deal and the Rural Electrification Administration; the remainder were even longer in coming.

Finally, women were in many instances badly served by the very profession to which they turned for help – domestic science. Rural women's expectations of domestic science were rather limited and quite simple: they wanted advice on how to manage their complex burdens more efficiently and in such a way as to improve the quality of their own lives and those of their families. Some home economists were able to deliver those kinds of services – Nellie Kedzie Jones of Wisconsin, with her immensely practical and sensible advice columns to farm wives; Martha van Rensselaer of Cornell who first surveyed farm women about their needs and then tried to design programs to meet them; Florence Ward of the

CES who plainly understood the complex web of work responsibilities borne by the women she and her agents surveyed in 1919. Others were both unable and unwilling to do so – especially those who had secured hard-won training in the sciences and who were deliberately trying to raise both their own status as professionals and that of women's work in general by demonstrating its scientific significance – exemplified, perhaps unfairly, by Isabel Bevier of the University of Illinois, but much more certainly by her teacher, Ellen Richards of MIT. In the long run, the scientific approach was more promising as a means to improve women's overall status, but in the short run it was the practical approach to daily problems that rural women so eagerly sought.

Annette Baxter, arguing from an urban context, notes a "striking difference in women's and men's perception of social ills at the start of the twentieth century" (Blair 1980, Preface). The same was largely true of rural women and men, but in neither context did all women speak with the same voice. The problems were too individual. Nevertheless, there was a strong commonality in rural women's concerns in these two decades, and they were clearly mobilizing themselves to organized effort on behalf of their families' welfare, an effort that is central to the current protests by farm people against what they perceive to be the indifference of government and many of their fellow Americans.

NOTES

[1]Nevertheless, the economic status of all farmers was not promising during this period. In 1916, when the federal income tax first took effect, only 14,407 of approximately 6,000,000 farmers earned the $3,000 minimum net income that was the requirement for filing a return, and nearly half of those had earned less than $5,000 (Bowers 1974, 14).

[2]By the 1914 biennial convention of the General Federation of Women's Clubs, some 1.7 million club members were represented by the more than 1000 delegates who voted overwhelmingly in favor of women's suffrage (Blair 1980, 113-14). Of course, this statement about a lack of rural organizations for women does not pay adequate attention to the experience of female members of the Grange. See the discussion of the Grange in this chapter.

[3]I know of no other place where the CLC's work is characterized as a "rural home inquiry."

[4]Blair 1980, in her very thorough history of the women's club movement, does not describe these activities.

[5]Unfortunately, none of the original documents on which these reports are based has survived. Virginia Purdy (National Archives Staff Member), interview with the author, Spring 1985.

[6]On the general comparison see, for example, Strasser 1982 and Cowan 1983. On the issue of a comparison between equipment available to women and men, see U.S. Department of Agriculture 1915b, 22, 29. Running water was a particularly sore point of comparison for rural women. By 1900, it was to be

found in virtually every urban home. In 1911, by contrast, Liberty Hyde Bailey, a member of the Country Life Commission, estimated that *"in twenty years' time all farm homes of the first class would have running water"* (Bailey 1911, 88-89; emphasis added).

[7]*Reports of the Commissioner of Education for . . . 1906, 1907, 1908, 1909, 1910, 1911, 1912, 1913, 1914*, 2 vols. (Washington, D.C.: 1907, 1908, 1909, 1910, 1911, 1912, 1913, 1914, 1915), 1906: 1:566; 1907: 2:909-912; 1908: 2:737-770; 1909: 2:1012-15; 1910: 2:998; 1911: 2: 1022; 1912: 2:332; 1913: 2:174; 1914: 2:281.

[8]Scott 1970, 116-18. Other lecture topics included "Milk," "Potato Diseases," "Acid Soils," "Profitable Cattle Feeding," "Silage and Silo Construction in the South," "Essentials of Successful Farm Experimentation," "Roads and Road Building," "Tobacco Growing," "Production and Marketing of Eggs and Fowl" (specifically addressed to poultry*men*, though the author does acknowledge "the woman in search of a livelihood" who may have some interest [p. 31]), "Wheat Culture," and "The Peanut." U.S. Department of Agriculture, Office of Experiment Stations; Hamilton 1909, Introduction; Bay 1961, 7.

[9]See, for example, "Issuing Bulletins for Farmer's Wives" 1915 (noting especially the rural-urban disparity in medical services), "Farm Wives Tell of Further Needs" 1915 (commenting on lack of even basic household amenities and of women's clubs), and "Farm Women Find Life Hard" 1915 (citing heavy work burdens and lack of hired help.

The World's Work (whose editor was a CLC member) carried "A Strike of Farm Wives" 1913, approving of a short story about a strike by farm wives for "running water and other conveniences" (144). *The Literary Digest* ran two pieces -- "Some Solid Reasons for a Strike of Farm Wives" 1919 and "Why Some Young Women are Leaving Our Farms" 1920 -- the first citing a survey of 1400 farm wives in New York State conducted by Martha van Rensselaer of Cornell University, the second citing Ward 1920; both accurately and sympathetically described women's complaints.

[10]The results of subsamples from the New York State survey noted above are not significantly different though the numbers are much smaller. Ward 1920; "Some Solid Reasons . . ." 1919, 48.

[11]See U.S. Department of Agriculture 1915d, which is especially eloquent on men's decision-making power (8-14) and on women's inability to control their own incomes (11-20). The urgency of women's continuing search for income-earning opportunities is clear in Ward 1920, and, according to Sarah Elbert (this volume), in the responses to Martha van Rensselaer's New York State questionnaire. In 1909 Bryn Mawr College conducted a conference on "the opportunities open to women for earning a livelihood in general farming, truck gardens, stock raising, poultry raising, fruit-tree nurseries, hothouse floriculture, beekeeping and landscape gardening." *Report of the Commissioner of Education for . . . 1910.* 1:272.

[12]U. S. Department of Agriculture 1915d, esp. 8-17. "A Remarkable Study of a Rural Community" 1912, citing a study by G. P. Warber of the University of Minnesota of a rural community in southeastern Minnesota where only 14

percent of farmers attended Farmer's Institutes, "and a majority [were] prejudiced against scientific methods of farming" (264). On the point about cooperation see Saloutos and Hicks 1951, and Bowers 1974.

BIBLIOGRAPHY

Bailey, Liberty Hyde. 1911. *The Country Life Movement in the United States.* New York: Privately Published.

Bane, Lita. 1955. *The Story of Isabel Bevier.* Peoria, Ill.: Privately Published.

Bay, Edwin. 1961. *The History of the National Association of County Agricultural Agents, 1915-1960.* Springfield, Ill.: Frye Printing Co.

Blair, Karen J. 1980. *The Clubwoman as Feminist: True Womanhood Redefined, 1868-1914.* New York: Holmes & Meier.

Bowers, William L. 1974. *The Country Life Movement in America, 1900-1920.* Port Washington, N.Y.: National University Press of America.

Buck, Solon J. 1913. *The Granger Movement: A Study of Agricultural Organization and Its Political, Economic and Social Manifestations, 1870-1880.* Lincoln, Nebr.: University of Nebraska Press.

Clutts, Betty C. 1961. *Country Life Aspects of the Progressive Movement.* Ph.D. diss.: Ohio State University.

Congress of the United States. 1915. *Congressional Record, 63rd Cong., 2nd Sess.* Appendix, 904-905.

Cowan, Ruth S. 1983. *More Work for Mother: The Ironies of Household Technology from the Open Hearth to the Microwave.* New York: Basic Books.

Craig, Hazel. 1945. *The History of Home Economics.* New York.

Croyle-Langhorne, Deborah Ann. 1982. *Men Will Brand It an Experiment: A Study of Undergraduate Women at Michigan State College 1870-1940.* Ph.D. diss.: State University of New York-Binghamton.

Ehrenreich, Barbara and Deirdre English. 1979. *For Their Own Good: 150 Years of Expert Advice to Women.* New York: Anchor Books.

Elbert, Sarah. 1986. "Women and Farming: Changing Structures, Changing Roles."

"Farm Wives Tell of Further Needs." 1915. *New York Times,* 4 April. Section 4, p. 6.

"Farm Women Find Life Hard." 1915. *New York Times,* 30 May. Section 5, pp. 14-15.

Gilman, Charlotte Perkins. 1909. "That Rural Home Inquiry: Why Are There No Women on the President's Commission?" *Good Housekeeping* 48 (Jan.), pp. 120-22.

Grosch, Rev. A.B. 1876. *Mentor in the Granges and Homes of Patrons of Husbandry.* New York.

Hamilton, John. 1909. *Farmer's Institutes for Women.* U.S. Department of Agriculture, Office of Experiment Stations Circular 85. Washington.

Hunt, Caroline L. 1918. *The Life of Ellen H. Richards*. Boston.

"Issuing Bulletins for Farmer's Wives." 1915. New York Times, 28 March. Section 4, p. 5.

Mitchell, Edward B. 1915. "The American Woman as She Sees Herself." *USDA Yearbook 1914*. Washington. Pp. 311-18.

"New Era for Farm Women: Our Farm Home Inquiry Taken Up by the General Federation of Women's Clubs." 1909. *Good Housekeeping* 48 (July), pp. 39-43.

Nordin, Sven G. 1974. *Rich Harvest: A History of the Grange, 1867-1900*. Jackson, Miss.: University Press of Mississippi.

Rasmussen, Wayne, ed. 1975. *Agriculture in the United States: A Documentary History*. 4 vols. New York: Random House.

"Remarkable Study of a Rural Community, A." 1913. *The World's Work* 26 (July), pp. 263-64.

Reports of the Commissioner of Education for . . . 1906, 1907, 1908, 1909, 910, 1911, 1912, 1913, 1914. 2 vols. Washington.

Saloutos, Theodore and John D. Hicks. 1951. *Agricultural Discontent in the Middle West 1900-1939*. Madison, Wis.: University of Wisconsin Press.

Scott, Roy V. 1970. *The Reluctant Farmer: The Rise of Agricultural Extension to 1914*. Urbana, Ill.: University of Illinois Press.

Shapiro, Laura. 1986. *Perfection Salad: Women and Cooking at the Turn of the Century*. New York: Farrar, Strauss and Giroux.

Solomon, Barbara Miller. 1985. *In the Company of Educated Women*. New Haven, Conn.: Yale University Press.

"Some Solid Reasons for a Strike of Farm Wives." 1919. *The Literary Digest* 63 (20 Dec.), pp. 74, 78.

Strasser, Susan. 1982. *Never Done: A History of American Housework*. New York: Pantheon.

"Strike of Farm Wives, A." 1913. *The World's Work* (June), p. 144.

U. S. Bureau of Education. 1914. "Education and the Home." Bulletin No. 37. Washington.

U. S. Department of Agriculture. 1915a. *Social and Labor Needs of Farm Women*. Report No. 103. Washington.

_____. 1915b. *Domestic Needs of Farm Women*. Report No. 104. Washington.

_____. 1915c. *Educational Needs of Farm Women*. Report No. 105. Washington.

_____. 1915d. *Economic Needs of Farm Women*. Report No. 106. Washington.

U.S. Department of Agriculture, Office of Experiment Stations. Various Dates. *Farmer's Institute Lectures 1-14 (1904-1912)*. Washington.

Ward, Florence. 1920. *The Farm Women's Problems*. U. S. Department of Agricul ture Circular No. 148. Washington.

"Why Some Young Women Are Leaving Our Farms." 1920. *The Literary Digest* (2 Oct.), pp. 56, 58.

18

"HELPING PAPA AND MAMMA SING THE PEOPLE'S SONGS": CHILDREN IN THE POPULIST PARTY

MaryJo Wagner[1]

INTRODUCTION

Prior to the 1892 presidential election, a little girl from Mississippi wrote to the editor of the *National Economist*, the official newspaper of the Southern Farmers' Alliance, published in Washington, D.C. Ella Naylor wanted to know why her sister, uncles, and aunts who lived in the city were Democrats and her father, a farmer, was a Populist. The National Economist's answer was brief: "Freedom does not thrive in cities."[2] Ella, her father, and the *National Economist* all agreed that the Populist Party (or People's Party as many called it) would reform the economic system and thus free American farmers from foreclosed mortgages and bankruptcy. And they all campaigned for James Weaver and James Field, the Party's candidates for United States President and Vice-president.

Ella's letter was not an isolated incident. The *American Nonconformist*, a newspaper widely read by radical Populists and published in Indianapolis, printed several hundred such letters from children in the months prior to the 1892 presidential election. These letters and several other factors indicate the extent to which the National Farmers' Alliance and the Populist Party in the late 1880s and early 1890s encouraged the participation of women, children, and entire families in the political process. By focusing on the period immediately preceding and following the 1892 elections, one sees clearly the influence of women in the Populist Party and especially the interest which children took in the political process. The origins of the People's Party were rural and given the nature of family farming in which all members of a family worked at farming, it is not unusual that entire families would then enter into politics. As the Party became more determined to win on a national level and as a consequence willing to compromise with the Democratic Party, it, not surprisingly, began neglecting its commitment to agrarian reforms. Grass roots support became less significant, and women's participation dwindled as men perceived women's interests, if not their outspokeness, as threatening.

319

FAMILY POLITICS: THE RECRUITMENT OF CHILDREN

Although most recent historians of Populism have ignored women and children in their studies of the Alliance and People's Party, Populist novelists of the late nineteenth century did document family particpation. Both Hamlin Garland and Fannie McCormick described Alliance and Populist gatherings. Garland's romantic and optimistic novel *A Spoil of Office*, published in 1892, tells of young Bradley Talcott, his conversion to reform politics, his romance with an Alliance woman orator (who was modeled after Mary Elizabeth Lease, the best-known female Populist orator), and his political campaign. While teaching Talcott the elements of reform politics, one of the politicians explains to Garland's hero some of the ways in which women and children are involved in politics. "See that old woman in the sunbonnet carrying that banner! Now don't make no mistake; the old girl knows just what that means; that's *right*! They're all reading these days, even the babies."[3]

Unlike the novels of Hamlin Garland, Fannie McCormick's novel *A Kansas Farm*, also published in 1892, has long since been forgotten; however, when the book first appeared, it was widely advertised in the reform press. The plot of this didactic novel is simple and predictable. A hard-working Kansas family nearly loses its farm when an evil banker attempts to foreclose on the mortgage. The family is saved by joining other farmers in similar circumstances by forming a sub-alliance in their community. Realizing the need for political action, the Alliance women and men support the Populist Party. A victory of the Populist Party would assure farm prosperity. McCormick's fictional depiction of the Alliance and the People's Party stresses family participation. She states:

> Men, women, and children sprang to the work with a courage born of necessity and an invincible determination to win the day. . . . [F]armers held their meetings during the campaign. They erected platforms in the groves, and held frequent mass meetings. Children recited and sang the doctrines of the Alliance from these platforms. The farmers' wives, sisters, and daughters took hold of the Alliance work with all their might, and rallied to the support of the People's party with all the energy they could command. They sang Alliance songs, gave readings and recitations for the benefit of the cause, and many of our women talked on the platform eloquently and well.[4]

McCormick's detailed descriptions of Alliance parades and picnics also include children. During the picnics, "perhaps a rosy-cheeked school-girl would step forward and recite the Alliance 'Ninety and Nine,' or that beautiful poem, 'The Promised Land To-morrow.'" Long processions precede the picnics, children ride along, some taking part in "tableaux on wheels" or floats. In one parade, a "large header" is crowded with children and labeled "over-production."[5]

In yet another popular reform novel of the nineties, *Shylock's Daughter* by Margaret Holmes Bates, John Longwood, the hero and a Populist political candidate, listens at a Populist rally to thirteen-year-old Katy Lee read a poem about hunger and poverty. "The plain words came forth in sing-song procession . . . and yet, there were strong men with tears glistening on their cheeks." Even Republicans wrote about Populist children. William Allen White's unsympathetic short story about a failed Populist governor, "A Most Lamentable Comedy," includes an Alliance procession with one group of children singing from hayracks and another group of children dressed in red, white, and blue singing political verses to the tune of "Near the Cross."[6]

Hundreds of newspapers, and not a few minute books, and Alliance constitutions corroborate that Populist families were involved in more than just parades and picnics, which were already common pastimes for families of all political persuasions. Most Alliance functions were planned intentionally for families. Everyone could sing, and even very small children could recite short memorized verses or speeches. One young person wrote a letter to the editor stating: "We are all Populists. My father sings at People's Party meetings; he composes his own songs. My sister sings at the Alliance." Another young person bragged that even her brother and sister belonged to the Alliance. Children were sometimes named after Alliance and Populist politicians. Benjamin Otis owed his election to the U. S. House of Representatives to the Farmers' Alliance. When his wife Bina had a baby, the women's Alliance newspaper, the *Farmer's Wife*, wondered what the new baby's name would be. By the next issue of the paper the editor reported happily that the baby had been named "Bina Alliance Otis." The children themselves named their animals after their favorite reformers. So, for example, one boy called his dog "Vincent" after the editors of his favorite reform newspaper, the *Nonconformist*.

In addition to riding on floats in parades, frolicking at Alliance picnics, and giving recitations, children were educated in economic principles and actively recruited as reform workers. Because children constituted the next generation of voters and politicians, they needed to be trained and recruited at the earliest age. The Ohio Farmers' Alliance manual gave specific instructions regarding the participation of children: "The exercises consist of readings, recitations, essays, addresses and discussions. Children of members may take part. Where there are too many for all to take part in one night the Alliance may be divided into two or more classes; one class to perform one night and the other the next." The Farmers' Alliance adopted a minimum membership age of sixteen at its national convention in Ocala, Florida, in 1890, further encouraging young people to join. Sixteen-year-old sons were considered "operative farmers" for membership purposes.[7] Obviously, Populists did not conform to the prevailing Victorian ideal of innocent and protected childhood; rather, they believed that children could and should be taught the harsh realities of farming, economics, and politics. Teenagers were given adult responsibilities; younger children helped.

From as far away as Los Angeles (hardly a Populist stronghold), Matilda Berra wrote to the *Nonconformist* in Indianapolis expressing the Populist faith in children. While attending a parade, she was impressed with an "immense float literally packed with women and children." She believed that women and children have "faithfully attended, and worked very hard in the pure political schools of 'Nationalism, Farmers and citizens Alliances, and People's party clubs.'" She further argued that "young boys and girls in this movement understood the economic questions better than any a senator in the country. . . . Women and children have learned that corrupt and rotten politics engender unjust and oppressive laws and that from these two pointed sources flow all the ills and sufferings with which they are crushed down!" She went on to say that the hard work and inspiration of the women and children combined with the righteousness of the cause could not fail to bring about a victory. "The two old parties do not dream what a gigantic help the children are."[8]

The newspapers of the National Reform Press Association frequently included a "children's corner." Some newspapers printed puzzles, games, and moralistic stories for children; other newspapers extended their political perspective to young readers. *The Voice of True Reform*, the *Farmer's Wife*, and the *Nonconformist* focused their children's material specifically on teaching children reform principles. Some editors instructed parents and teachers; another editor wrote for the children themselves and published their letters.

THE ALLIANCE HOME KINDERGARTEN

In 1891 a Kansas woman, Emily E. Lathrop, with the assistance of her husband, James H. Lathrop, a liberal minister, wrote the "Alliance Home Kindergarten, a series of lessons for mothers and teachers." Emily Lathrop published two introductory essays and lessons in the *Voice of True Reform* and the *Farmer's Wife*. Subsequent lessons could be purchased for a penny. The author believed that "true and radical education of the child must begin with the mother, whose thought and life will shape her offspring" because "the final solution of the great social, commercial, political, physical and religious problems of the day is dependent upon this change in the education of the race." As she argued, "*home* is the nursery of the individual for social relations, [and such] instruction should be given as will embrace the economic relations of a complete society." The author hoped that the Alliance kindergarten would become an established branch of the National Women's Alliance. Lathrop believed that her kindergarten was indeed the "grand effort to school the children in the issues of the day" and that such education was important to the success of reform work. Lathrop claimed that through the Alliance one could learn of the "great natural truths of life." Who better to teach these truths than mothers, and what better age to begin learning than early childhood? A mother could teach reform politics to her children during playtime.[9]

The lessons preached traditional Protestant values, the benefits of hard work, and the importance of spiritual development. Lathrop emphasized the undesirability of the pursuit of wealth for its own sake, which would benefit only a few, and the importance of sufficient financial return for hard but rewarding work. Lathrop admonished teachers to instill in their pupils the philosophy that the "*sum of life* is not to *gather wealth* in great abundance, and become narrow and sordid therewith." The Lathrop home lessons were designed for mothers to use in weekly classes with their children. A series of short questions and answers, similar to a catechism, comprised the lessons. The first lesson on the

"Rights of All Life" began with questions about the creation of life and empha-sized that the "right" to the "fruits" of one's labor was God-given, even though many did not receive this "right."

> Q. Do [sic] everybody have good clothes and food and homes who la-bor, even, ever so hard?
> A. No, the most of mankind in all ages have toiled too much, and got so little, that suffering, starvation, homelessness, crime, and war, has [sic] been the lot of most of the people.
>
> Q. Why have the people who labor gone so much without their rights to life?
> A. Because some have always been trying to live without labor, by plunder of those who toiled too hard.[10]

Lathrop buttressed the arguments of the Alliance by insisting that its reform principles were those rights that God intended in the first place.

The second lesson embraced the "Rights of Home." Contending that nature does and should provide a home for all life including oysters, snails, and birds and that humankind also has the right to a home, she formulated the following series of questions and answers:

> Q. Are all poor people as unwise and unfaithful in this world of plenty?
> A. No. The masses of the people are poor and unsettled about home, because the "wicked rule" and tax the willing workers on their occu-pancy of earth and natural rights, to support themselves in splendor and idleness.[11]

In answer to the question of how "natural" rights can be restored, Lathrop offered the standard Alliance/Populist solutions such as government ownership of the railroads and "exchange with a money that will unite all families together into one national Co-operative Union." She argued that such economic princi-ples were easy for children to understand if they had a "calf to feed or a cake to make."[12]

Lathrop anticipated that Alliance mothers would subscribe to the Home Kindergarten so as to "study the means of making and preserving the Home and Nursery as the basis of good society and a just government." Appealing to Alliance women by reiterating the prevalent ideology of domesticity and the moral superiority of women, Lathrop combined a belief in traditional women's roles with the radical economic views of the Alliance and the even more radical idea of teaching these views to children. And, despite her emphasis on the importance of the mother's role, that it belonged "to the Mother and Home to build society," Lathrop insisted that "Man should be her aid, support, counsellor and guard. He cannot shirk his responsibility of the same without equal loss to the community. The attention of both should be given equally to the home and

natural culture of those human scions in the Kindergarten of Life." In Lathrop's
view, mothers and fathers shared equal responsibility for raising children.[13]

Two months after the Alliance Kindergarten lessons appeared in the
Farmer's Wife, Fanny Tentrill contributed her essay on "Home Education." She
agreed with Lathrop that the home constituted one of the "most powerful agencies" for bringing about reform through the training of children by mothers, and
she quoted Pestalozzi to that effect: "'The reformation of a nation begins in the
nursery.'" She also credited school teachers with furthering the cause of reform:
"This cry of reform which had its birth in the school room--thanks to teachers,
those earnest, hardworked, unappreciated servants of the public--has become the
pass-word of the Republic. . . . "[14] Together Lathrop and Tentrill provided both
a rationale for educating children in reform politics and some practical ways of
accomplishing the task.

AUNTY ROSE'S COLUMN

The most direct and persistent recruitment of children was that of the
Nonconformist's children's editor, Aunty Rose. In her column, "Our Little
Folks," Aunty Rose wrote editorials specifically for children, printed children's
letters to the editor, and commented on them from January 1892 until after the
November election. Although not the first editor to print children's letters,
Rose's efforts produced the largest number of letters. Rose carefully explained to
the children their responsibilities to the People's Party:

> We are *Nonconformist* boys and girls. People's Party children and
> like the rest of the people must be doing, doing something to help
> the cause. . . . You have done splendidly in the work, my dear ones. .
> . . but now that the campaign is coming on, when every inch of this
> sheet is needed to convert men voting wrong . . . I don't want to give
> you up and I trust you will put your little heads together and just not
> be given up. You know we have said before that we can't vote, but
> maybe we can make votes.[15]

She continued flattering children by characterizing them as people who are
shorter but who are also people who can "work faster, and before long we may
have set hundreds to thinking."[16]

Aunty Rose encouraged the children to write about local Alliance and
Populist Party activities, to solicit subscriptions for the *Nonconformist*, and to
campaign for Populist politicians. She instructed the children to remind their fathers to renew *Nonconformist* subscriptions, told about her attendance at
Populist conventions, solicited money for her charity Easter dinner, explained
reform for the young readers, and gave prizes for new subscriptions. One subscription entitled the worker to a Weaver/Field hatband. Rose's readers worked
diligently as directed. By September the children had produced sixty-one new
subscriptions to the *Nonconformist* and by November 17 the total had risen to
three hundred.

The column was maternal, terribly sentimental, self-righteous, condescending, and at times harsh and judgmental. Aunty Rose's praise for good letters and zealous political work was as effusive as her criticism was blunt. She described a model letter as one in which the children should "tell us your plans--your work and play." She wanted original ideas and modesty. Despite harsh criticism of their letters if too long, too immodest, or lacking in political commitment, the children responded enthusiastically, if for no other reason than the opportunity to have their letters printed and possibly win prizes through the mail. One of the children, hoping her letter would be printed, complained that she had written two letters to the *Progressive Farmer* (another widely-read Populist newspaper), and neither had been printed. The children wrote from as far away as Washington, Texas, and Florida; the largest number of letters came from Kansas. Children as young as three years old "wrote" with the help of an older sibling or parent, and teenagers sixteen and seventeen often wrote to ask if they were too old to be "nieces" or "nephews." Rose took them all into her "happy band." She commented frequently that she had far more letters than she could actually print, despite the dozen or more that appeared each week.[17]

Some parable-like editorials preached reform politics to young readers. In other editorials Rose defined words and concepts. "Traitors" were men "who promise to do things for the people's good and then sell the interest of the people for dollars and cents." "Traitor" was a "wicked, mean, and ugly" word. In response to a letter from a Michigan girl who described a Lansing Populist convention and commented on the evils of the capitalists, Rose stated:

> Right you are, Madge dear. But the people are tired of giving all their earnings into the hands of the monopolists and have "put their heads" together to see if something can't be done. Oh, how happy we will all be to have People's Party men in power. That will mean "good times" for the poor laborer and control of his own pocket-book.

She also asked the children to do some of the teaching. When Ida Cain wrote from New Mexico, Rose asked her to describe the mining industries in New Mexico. "'Tis the laboring people in whom we are interested in--the ones we want to help. You may be able to tell us many interesting facts."[18]

Most of Rose's responses to the children's letters praised the work they were doing and pleaded for more help. When a Kansas boy wrote suggesting they have a history class, Rose replied "that the history class would be interesting, but just now I think it better if each of us enter into the campaign work and do all that little hands can do." A nine-year-old wrote telling of his pets and his enjoyment of the children's letters. Rose answered: "What has Carl been doing since he last wrote to make some other one happier? Are you helping to make votes for Weaver and Field, Carl?" To a girl from Indiana she replied: "Write often, little one, and in the meantime show us what you can do toward spreading reform. You are too energetic not to do something." Other girls wrote who had been working for the Alliance; one of them had procured a subscription. Rose was pleased with her effort but wanted more subscriptions. To one of these girls she replied: "That's right, my Elsie, go to work right away, dearie, lest some one gets ahead of you." Even after the election defeat in November, Rose persistently reminded the girls and boys that they should begin campaigning for the 1896 election.[19]

The children's letters followed a predictable pattern. They wrote about school, the number of siblings in the family, and their pets. The spelling and grammar were usually satisfactory, suggesting most had attended school regularly. Most of their parents belonged to the Alliance and read the *Nonconformist*; some were officers of a sub-alliance. The children wrote about Alliance meetings and picnics. Rosa Corkdale reported that both her parents belonged to the Alliance in Valley Falls, Kansas, and that "our Alliance is progressing finely." She feared her family's subscription to the *Nonconformist* had nearly expired and promised to convince her father to renew it. As the election drew nearer the children's praise of Weaver and Field increased.[20]

One can conclude from some of the letter that busy farm parents had probably not read their children's letters. When her older sister married, Ida Martindale complained that she "was sorry for that for her husband is a Republican party man." Eleven-year-old Mollie Hancock wrote from Texas where the People's Party was "booming." James Weaver and Mary Elizabeth Lease had made a campaign stop and delivered some "fine speeches." Mollie continued: "The People's Party has papa's name on the ticket for justice of the peace. Papa is a farmer and does not want the office." A sixteen-year-old from Iowa wrote to Rose that his papa and grandfather read the *Nonconformist* but his uncle did not. He complained about living on a farm and told Rose that he would surely fall in love with her since she was obviously just like his mother. Rose urged him to get his uncle to reading "this dear old paper." Sophia Wright also wrote about her uncle. "My uncle, Charlie Sharpe, has been attending school at the Butler College. . . . I don't know whether he is a People's party man or not, but he must be, as Mamma says 'he was always a good, sensible boy.' When this comes out in the *Nonconformist* we will send this paper to him."[21]

The children knew that the Populist Party was new and sometimes talked of their relatives'conversion from the "old parties." "My grandpa has been a democrat till he is seventy-three years old. Now he goes for the *Nonconformist*," wrote a girl from Indiana. Another little girl wrote:

> My papa says that he had been born and raised a democrat; brought up in good faith believing there was no one right but his own party. But I am glad to inform you that he is now a People's Party man all over, takes three reform papers, and I think he would like to take more if he could find time to read them.

A precocious six-year-old from Texas even credited herself with her father's conversion to the Populist fold. "I love to sing 'Good-bye, Old Party, Good-bye,' and the 'People's Ticket,' for I think I turned my papa with those songs and my speeches."[22]

Others wasted no time telling Rose just what their parents thought about politics. Jessie Bender wrote from Kansas: "I will tell you what papa thinks: He says that [if] the Alliance don't get there this time that he won't vote again for any of the old party. He thinks Powderly [Terence Powderly, Grand Master of the Knights of Labor] ought to be elected president." The children had their own strong opinions about the Alliance, the *Nonconformist*, and the new party. Adults had included them in political talk, and the children had obviously been listening to conversations, and to speeches at Alliance meetings and Populist rallies, and reading reform newspapers and novels. Two girls reported they had enjoyed reading *Which Wins* and *Richard's Crown*, popular reform novels. An eleven-year-old girl claimed that her family subscribed to sixteen reform papers and that she read each and every one of them.[23]

Virgil Wait wrote twice with unbounded enthusiasm for the People's Party. "I believe that this party is the right one, and I believe that God is with us. I think that the People's Party is the grandest thing ever invented in the world. It is grander than the Masons." His concern was not limited to farmers but included factoryworkers as well. "If the third party does not get into power it will ruin the people. I tell you the laboring people have been run over so long that they will stand it not longer." As the election approached, he wrote a second time with faith in the potential of the Populist Party and a naive concern for what he supposed would be the best interests of the supply merchant in tenant farming states:

> I hope Weaver and Field will be elected. It will help the farmer, the day laborer, the merchant, mechanic and mason. When the farmer comes to town and gets a good price for his cotton he will feel like a man. He can get what he wants for his little wife and children. Don't you suppose the merchant would feel better when he is handed the dollar than if he had to put it on a little book and didn't know for certain whether he would get his money – for the man mite [sic] skip the country.[24]

Virgil's letter, as did most of the letters of the children, including those from the girls who supported woman suffrage, reflected stereotypical thinking about sex roles. No matter how much heavy field work a woman might be doing, she could still be called the "little wife."

Grace Pyles, proud of her father's work in starting a Populist club, described the activities in Westport, Missouri:

> A little over four months ago papa started out in the field to work for the new party and to get signers and now he has a club of sixty or more started in our little town of Westport. They are all of the best men of our town. The whole place in and around here is all stirred up. The people feel and know how they have been run over and wronged in so many ways, and now are ready and willing to do their part to

bring a reform which will not only benefit us now, but for years to come. They want justice and freedom and will have it.[25]

Emma McDonald promised Aunty Rose to "be your friend and worker forever." A Weaver and Field club had been organized in Emma's township, and she was proud of her father, "a full-blooded third party man." The symbolism attached to the names of the candidates was noticed by Sarah Dixon in Ohio. "The names are so suggestive. Weaver is one who weaves cloth and Field is where we plant potatoes and grow good things to eat, you know."[26]

An eleven-year-old wrote modestly: "I think we [children] can help a little in the work of reform." Another stated:

> I am just a little girl but I want to do and will do all I can to help my papa and other papas to vote right next election time. I know ever so many men, who are good people, but they do look like they need waking up and if you will trust a little twelve year old girl with some paper she will use them to tickle the noses of those good sleepy fellows.[27]

And help the children did in more ways than simply selling subscriptions for the *Nonconformist*. Some worked at home: one little girl read a reform paper out loud to her grandmother. Others took part in community activities. Several children wrote about singing People's Party songs and providing part of the entertainment at gatherings. Nona Wallace enjoyed going to a People's Party club in Joplin, Missouri, and helping "Papa and Mamma sing the People's songs." Edna Riedliger belonged to a girls' band led by a woman. The girls were all daughters of Knights of Labor parents, and their band played for meetings of the Knights and the Alliance.[28]

Several children wrote about speaking out at Alliance meetings and giving formal speeches. Children as young as four were making "Alliance speeches." Agnes Aston, six years old, sent Aunty Rose a copy of her speech. It is doubtful that a six-year-old composed the speech without considerable help from older siblings or parents; however, it is likely that she did indeed memorize and give the speech at a local Alliance meeting. The speech emphasized the importance of Populism to the welfare of children and argued that even a child could understand such concepts as "selling out" for gold rings and pretty dresses.[29]

Girls often mentioned the famous women they had heard or seen at meetings and picnics. Several girls had heard Mary Elizabeth Lease speak and were favorably impressed. According to Harrie Hatton, nearly half of the members of the Farmers' Alliance in Blue Rapids, Kansas, were women, and she, herself, at the age of sixteen, was elected secretary, which pleased her. "I am proud of my office, and I try to do my duty fully. I hope all the Alliances are as good as ours. I would then know we will 'get there' at the election."[30]

If the children had any regrets, it was that they were not allowed to vote; nevertheless, they felt as Homer Young did when he stated: "I am a Populist too, although only a boy thirteen years old." The girls, well aware that it was not merely youth that prevented them from voting, were staunch supporters of woman suffrage and believed that by the time they were old enough to vote, woman suffrage would be won. One little girl declared: "Oh, if women could only vote. When I get to be a woman I would like to put in about twenty or thirty votes for the People's party." When another little girl expressed the desire to vote, Rose optimistically assured her that by the time she was grown up, women would vote.[31]

Children were also present at national Populist conventions. Aunty Rose told her young readers that she hoped to see them at the conventions, demonstrating that children were welcome and accepted at such events. Upon her return, she expressed disappointment that none of her readers had been there although she had seen their mamas and papas. She did, however, meet a three-year-old and encouraged mothers reading her column to "take the little ones with you."

> Mrs. [Fanny] Vickery was accompanied by her little three-year-old daughter who showed a beautiful admiration for the People's party and Alliance men. Like mother like daughter. The little one is being guided by a mind that is instilling into the baby mind an unselfishness and love for others that is commendable.[32]

It is questionable that this three-year-old absorbed much about politics, and more probable that her mother had no one to stay with the child during her absence.

Older children, however, could participate more actively. Even Lease, one of the least domestic Populist women, boasted that she took her older children with her on speaking tours. Her daughter, Louise, spoke at the convention in Omaha. Marion Todd, also an active and well-known Populist lecturer, took her daughter with her to Omaha. The daughter was described as "a lovely young woman who is following in the mother's wake." At one convention, S. B. Irvin and his daughter were "conspicuous in the large delegation from old Kentucky." A picture of the Nebraska state convention of 1892 shows several children in attendance.[33]

The letters to the editor and the participation of children at conventions and in other activities indicate not merely tolerance by adults for the presence of children at political events but adult encouragement for children's actual participation in Alliance/Populist politics. Small children sang at Populist meetings; slightly older children sold newspaper subscriptions and gave recitations; teenagers held elected offices in local sub-alliances. The letters also attest to the children's own interest in politics and their understanding of political issues as these issues affected their families and farms. As Robert Coles has noted, children around the world are aware, in ways most scholars and researchers have underestimated, of the political environment in their country, have opinions about it, and see politics as affecting their life. Populist children of the 1880s and 1890s were no less concerned about politics than the children Coles interviewed in South Africa and Ireland in the 1970s and 1980s.[34]

FAMILY POLITICS: GENDER ROLES AND FARMING

Children's participation also was naturally affected by the activities and ideology of mothers. Few children, especially under the age of sixteen, attended a political convention unless their mothers, who were elected delegates, were also in attendance. Although Populist women did attend political conventions and believed it within women's sphere to do so, they remained firm to the conviction that it was also a mother's duty to care for her children. Child care obligations surely explain one of the reasons some women took children with them to Populist conventions, Alliance meetings, and even on campaign tours. By accepting and encouraging the involvement of women, the party assumed that children would also be present. Otherwise, who would stay with the children? Political activity for women did not mean a shirking of domestic responsibility, a diminishing belief in domestic ideology, or a lack of concern for respectability and propriety. And, indeed, Populists prided themselves on the respectability of their conventions. Sobriety was valued among convention delegates who assumed that Republican and Democratic conventions were comprised of drunken mobs. A father could take his wife and children to a sober Populist convention but hardly to a drunken Republican or Democratic convention. Certainly, several factors contributed to the presence of children in radical agrarian politics. These factors might vary from family to family, but all rural familes were affected by gender roles and the work patterns of farming.

Although it remained unusual for traditional nineteenth-century political parties to involve entire families in the political process to the extent that the Farmers' Alliance and Populist Party did, the practice was consistent with the way many families worked together at farming. The nature of family farming best explains the ease with which children and their mothers participated in the Farmers' Alliance and the Populist Party. The financial prosperity of the farm often depended on the work of all family members except for babies and very young children. Consequently, all family members were knowledgeable about farm work and finances. Children and women worked in the fields, especially on less prosperous farms that could not afford hired help, and women often kept the farms' account books, even on the most successful farms. The Alliance acknowledged the farm as a family unit. Texas Populist, Bettie Gay, writing for the *Agricultural Digest* in 1891, described the Alliance as an extension of the family. Women and children were as central to the Alliance as to the family. Women like Bettie Gay optimistically assumed not only that the Alliance and People's Party would rescue family and home from financial ruin, but also that the salvation of the family farm, not the single issue of free silver, constituted the primary Populist goal. Editorials in the *Farmer's Wife* and the women's columns in other papers reinforced these sentiments.[35]

The story of Luna Kellie, an active Nebraska Populist, and her farming family illustrates the ways in which farming was a family business in the 1880s and the ways in which farmers then turned in the 1890s to politics as a family activity.[36] In 1882, Luna Kellie, with her three-day-old infant wrapped in a quilt, helped her husband J.T. and their young son Willie cut the broom corn.

J.T. helped Luna plan and lay out the garden. She drove the wheat to the grain elevator while her husband and other men were building a new house. Usually J.T. drew the water for drinking and washing dishes; sometimes Luna drew the water, and other times the older children performed the task. During a blizzard, J.T. cooked the meals. Luna, toward the end of her second pregnancy, drove the second-hand Marsh harvester while two men rode along and bound the grain. Her teenage brother John helped Luna with the washing during one of her pregnancies. Luna kept the account books. She knew that in one year she had sold 344 pounds of dressed chicken at five and six cents per pound and had sold or used seventy-one chickens at about twenty-five cents per chicken. J.T. gave her two cows to pay for the chickens and eggs the family had consumed. One of Luna's friends, recognizing her expertise in poultry raising, asked for advice concerning incubators. Luna recommended an Excelsior incubator; her friend ordered a Reliable incubator instead, believing it to have a better warming element. After 250 chicks died by mid-April, she decided that Luna had been right after all.

Luna and J.T. were both aware of the necessity of mortgaging the farm for $800 at 10 percent. They calculated together that it was costing $5.00 an acre to raise wheat that was bringing in only $4.50 an acre. When they traded the homestead to Luna's father for his timber claim, the family worked together planting fruit trees and strawberries. J.T. trimmed the trees off at the top and set them in holes, Luna filled in the holes, and Willie watered the new trees. J.T. fertilized the strawberry plot; Luna planted the berries, and Jessie, a toddler, thought she was helping by pulling up the strawberries to protect them from a rainstorm.

To be sure, there were distinctions between Luna's and J.T.'s responsibilities, between women's work and men's work. Luna might "help" J.T. with the harvest; J.T. might "help" her with the vegetable garden; nevertheless, farming was a task at which the family worked together. So was politics. In the 1880s, after several years of hard work, failing crops, and falling prices, the Kellies were ready for the Farmers' Alliance.

After Luna gave a speech entitled, "Stand up for Nebraska," at the 1894 Nebraska Farmers' Alliance Convention, delegates nominated her for the position of state Alliance secretary. Both the Kellies, accompanied by several of their children, and Luna's father, J. M. Sanford, had attended the convention as delegates. Luna won the election. Once home on a farm outside Hartwell, the Kellies converted a bedroom into an office for the Alliance, thus saving the Alliance the cost of renting office space. The children doubled up in one bedroom. The Kellie boys rode into town on a fast pony once a day to pick up the Alliance mail. When the Nebraska Alliance Executive Committee voted to publish a newspaper, Kellie and her daughter Jessie, no longer a toddler, took on the responsibility of editing it, frequently staying up past midnight together to work on the paper. Other children when old enough to read helped with the proofreading. When Luna went to Minden once a month to print the paper, she took Helen, the new baby, with her. The baby played in a wastebasket and napped on a pile of newspapers. The trip to Minden soon became such a hardship that Luna and Jessie purchased an old Washington hand press and some used type in order to print the paper themselves. Luna's father, the manager of the Alliance Aid and Mutual

Insurance Company, purchased enough advertising in advance to enable his daughter and grand-daughter to buy the press and type. The printing press occupied the family dining room; the family now took its meals in the crowded kitchen. Politics became as much a family business as farming.

Many historians subscribe to the view that women's, men's, and children's roles were rigidly segregated in nineteenth-century America; yet, Luna Kellie and her children were far from unique in their interest and involvement in, and knowledge of the Kellie farm. Women's and children's farming work, often essential, provided a basis for their participation in the traditionally male world of politics. A sharp distinction between the domestic, private sphere and the public sphere existed more commonly in urban areas where many husbands, including those who were self-employed, left the house and family each day to go somewhere else to work; however, in 1890, 42.3 percent of the United States population still lived on farms. One can estimate, therefore, that nearly half of the women in America in 1890 lived on farms. A substantial number of these women and their daughters were performing some "male" tasks on family farms and working alongside husbands and sons in the business of farming as Sandra Myres, Carl Degler, and others have shown. In contrast, fewer urban wives performed as integral a role in their husbands' occupations, financial successes, or failures.[37]

Sandra Myres has recently argued, based on an analysis of pioneer diaries, that many women and girls in the West did work side by side with the men in the fields. One farm woman stated: "The thing you learn on a farm is that the cultivating of crops and the butchering is man's work, while everything, including cultivating the crops, is woman's work, except the butchering." When husbands were away from home or ill, women did all of the work. One woman remembered how difficult it was to do all the farming, housework, and child care with no one to help her. Ben Clover's wife did not accompany her Congressman husband to Washington; she stayed home in Kansas and attended to "all the business of the farm."[38] Another woman worried that she should be helping with the haying but was too ill, and the family could not afford hired help. The blurring of gender roles does seem to have been most prevalent during hard times. During more prosperous times, fewer women worked in the fields as the family could afford hired hands. This was true for the Kellies. Around 1890, for a short time, they had enough money to hire help during harvesting and planting. J.T. remarked to Luna that although he was glad they were not as poor as when they first started homesteading, he missed having her help him. Still other women, unmarried or widowed, took on homesteading alone or with other women, assisted by the Homestead and other land acts that provided single women an opportunity to procure land. Degler estimates that at the end of the nineteenth century in some counties in Wyoming and Colorado as much as 12 percent of the land claims were made by women and that 42.5 percent of the women were able to keep their land compared to 37 percent of the men. A contemporary observer believed that as much as one-third of the land in the Dakotas was owned by women although not necessarily settled permanently by them. White women generally claimed land under the Homestead Act in the western states to the exclusion of black women; however, the large number of black women performing farming tasks or farming alone in the South after slavery has also been documented. One black widow was "capable of taking on her hands 130 acres of land, and raising one hundred and seven bales of cotton by force which she could organize." Another southern black woman "rented, cultivated, and solely managed a farm of five acres for five years." Sometimes two widows would work together. Minnie Brown described the situation of a Mrs. Jane Brown and a Mrs. Halsey who formed a partnership, leased nine acres and a horse, and cultivated the land.[39]

One of Luna Kellie's neighbors declared herself head of the household, even though married. (Her husband had failed at a business dealing in the East.) She filed for a homestead claim under her name and used money she had earned as a state agent for a corset business to have the fields plowed. Her husband and boys worked the farm; she saw to all of the business transactions of the homestead. After the Civil War, Bettie Gay worked in the fields with her husband and sold farm products at market. In 1880 her husband died; the farm house and 1,776 acres were mortgaged and her one son was not yet old enough to help. Another Alliance woman praised her work:

> Then it was that her extraordinary qualities, her industry and her business ability, were tested to utmost. In addition to her farm work, she took in sewing. . . . She raised and started in the world six boys and three girls, none of them having any claim of relationship upon her. . . . As a result of her indomitable energy and her executive ability, she raised the mortgage from her home, paid other outstanding debts, and educated her son.[40]

Although Gay had argued in her essay in the *Agricultural Digest* that woman's position was as the "companion and helpmeet of man," she never remarried but ran the family farm while concurrently working for the Alliance, the People's Party, woman suffrage, and temperance. She was not always the "companion and helpmeet of man."[41]

The Alliance organizers and reform press were not unaware of the work of women and girls on farms. One set of instructions for organizing a sub-alliance acknowledged the inclusion of women members because "there is nothing in any of the laws of the Farmers' Alliance which will prevent anybody who is in any way engaged in farming operations from becoming a member, and therefore, the ladies of the farm are eligible to membership."[42] In 1890 the *Chicago Express* reported on women farming in Kansas. One fifteen-year-old girl was described as having driven a binder over 1,200 acres. Another girl tended to her father's grape patch and picked the fruit on 1,000 apple trees. Still another young woman herded the family's cattle and sheep each summer. A father gave his daughter a farm; she lived on it, "looking after eighty acres without help, and last year cleared $1,000, besides buying clothes, machinery, and stock. This year she has a girl friend for a companion and a hired man." The *Express* concluded:

There are hundreds of bright women and girls who have taken up
claims in the western part of the State and lived on them until they
got a deed for the land. There are hundreds of women in the State who
manage to keep men depending on them from going hungry; there are
hundreds of women who can do anything a man can do, or has ever
done.[43]

The *Farmer's Wife* included under "Items of Interest to the Farmer and
Housewife" such topics as the feeding of dairy cows, care of trees, building
straw-stack stables, and raising crops that bring a good return. The newspaper
assumed that farm women were as concerned with farming as farm men. The
column "The Ladies Corner," however, included only the traditional domestic
topics. The editor admonished: "Men are not expected to read this column."
Reform novelists also wrote of the work farm women did. McCormick claimed
in *A Kansas Farm* that "the farmers' wives are not merely 'helpmeets' in subdu-
ing the wilds of this Western country, but have done their full share of solid,
hard work as *equal partners*; and if there is a credit balance on either side it is in
favor of the women." John Longwood's mother, in *Shylock's Daughter*, who
possessed "much more than ordinary business ability," kept the farm accounts.[44]

Myres argues convincingly not only that many women performed farming
tasks, understood both the mechanics and economics of farming, and often kept
the accounts but also that neither they nor their husbands resented such activities. Luna Kellie's memoirs and the writings of other Populist women support
Myres' argument. Myres found many families similar to the Kellies in which
men helped with "churning, washing, cleaning, 'fetching and carrying,' and other
housework." She also found numerous families in which, again similar to the
Kellies, wives and husbands made joint decisions about the farm. "It is clear
from women's diaries that in many families women's work was respected; their
role in the family's fortunes, and therefore in the decision-making process, was
an important one."[45]

Annie Diggs, a national Populist figure, asserted that it was specifically
women's work on the farm and the knowledge women had of farm finances that
caused many women to join the Alliance. She also contended that women's mo-
tives for political participation were more sincere that those of men. "Politics for
the [male] farmer had been recreation, relaxation, or even exhilaration, according
to the varying degree of his interest, or of honor flatteringly bestowed . . . at a
caucus or convention." She argued that women were not involved in partisan
politics for relaxation or honor but rather for the economic salvation of their
homes. "Women spoke right out in meeting, demanding explanation for the non-
appearance of the home market for the farm products. . . . These women in the
Alliance, grown apt in keeping close accounts from long economy, cast eyes
over the long account of promises of officials managing public business." And
once a member of the Alliance, women gained some degree of political power.[46]

Michelle Rosaldo suggested some reasons for this public political power.
She argued that women have more power in the public sphere where the distance
between the private sphere and the public sphere is minimized: "Women's status

will be lowest in those societies where there is a firm differentiation between domestic and public spheres of activity and where women are isolated from one another and placed under a single man's authority in the home." Rosaldo further contended that "women gain power and a sense of value when they are able to transcend domestic limits, either by entering the men's world or by creating a society unto themselves."[47] This hypothesis suggests that an egalitarian society would be one in which women entered male-dominated activities and men entered the female world of the home. The Alliance and early Populist experience supports this argument. Women and children did share farming tasks with men; men did not leave home to work, and women and their children not only entered the political arena on both local and national levels but also achieved some measure of power and respect--at least for a brief time.

CONCLUSION

Despite the dedication of entire families to the Populist cause, family politics was a short-lived phenomenon, and the women's hopes that the Populist Party would support women's issues died. As early as 1894 Populist politics began to resemble more closely the traditional parties with politics defined as a man's business. As more Populists became less radical, more willing to compromise with the Democrats in hopes of winning the 1896 presidential election, less concerned with farm grievances, and more concerned with the single issue of free silver, family involvement dwindled. Women's and children's work on the farm certainly did not change; the change occurred in the ideology and agendas of the Populist Party. With the fusion of the Populist Party with the Democratic Party, fewer party leaders were farmers or even politicians with farmers' interests foremost. Although few stated such, it is clear that as the Party changed its focus, women and their issues were seen as a detriment to winning votes. With the exception of Colorado, women lost suffrage battles in the 1890s. Pragmatic politicians shied away from the question of temperance. Fewer newspapers carried women's columns. Children's letters did not appear in the papers; children were no longer welcome. The *Nonconformist* stopped reporting on families at conventions, and editors stopped printing "women's issues," such as suffrage, on the front pages. The remaining women's columns devoted themselves once again to fashions and cooking, rather than women's rights, economics, and the political education of children. Many women, however, who were no longer welcome in the world of traditional male politics, did not cease working in the public sphere. Some continued campaigning for women's suffrage and temperance. Other Populist women became socialists and supported Eugene Debs for President. Populist farm boys had become used to seeing women in the political arena, and some would no doubt eventually vote for women's suffrage; some Populist girls would become the next generation of suffrage workers. Women and their children had gained valuable experience in journalism, organizing, and public speaking which they continued utilizing in the public sphere.

NOTES

[1]This work was supported, in part, by awards from the Center for the Study of Women in Society, the Martin Schmitt Fund, and the Graduate School of the University of Oregon. Additional research was supported by a grant from the Center for Women's Studies, The Ohio State University. The article has benefited from the comments and criticism of Gail Malmgreen, Kathleen Laughlin, Daniel Pope, and Randall McGowen. Michelle Speights and Susan Farquhar provided much appreciated clerical assistance.

[2]*National Economist*, 15 Oct. 1892.

[3]Hamlin Garland, *A Spoil of Office* (Boston: Arena Publishing Co., 1892), 5.

[4]Fannie McCormick, *A Kansas Farm* (New York: J. B. Alden, 1892), 127.

[5]McCormick, *Kansas Farm*, 140.

[6]Margaret Holmes Bates, *Shylock's Daughter* (Chicago: Charles H. Kerr, 1894), 66; William Allen White, "A Most Lamentable Comedy," in Strategems and Spoils (New York: Charles Scribner's Sons, 1901), 207-08.

[7]*Instruction Book for the Use of the Ohio Farmers' Alliance* (Columbus: Hann & Adair, 1891), 15-16; *National Farmers' Alliance and Industrial Union Constitution* (Ocala, Fla.: 1890).

[8]Matilda Berra, "How a Woman Sees It," *American Nonconformist*, 4 Aug. 1892. (Referred to hereafter as Nonconformist.)

[9]Emily E. Lathrop, "The Alliance Children's Home Kindergarten," and "Kindergarten Thought for Youth," *The Voice of True Reform* 1 (Oct. 1891): 52-54; and "The Alliance," Farmer's Wife, Dec. 1891, Jan. 1892.

[10]*Farmer's Wife*, Dec. 1891.

[11]*Farmer's Wife*, Jan. 1892.

[12]*Farmer's Wife*, Dec. 1891.

[13]*Farmer's Wife*, Jan. 1892.

[14]Fanny Tentrill, "Home Education," *Farmer's Wife*, Mar. 1892.

[15]*Nonconformist*, 30 June 1892. Despite several queries, Rose refused to identify herself to her readers. They did learn, however, that she was an "Iowa girl and a former resident of Wayne County [Indiana], where her mother now lives." Iowa City *Advance* as quoted by the *Nonconformist*, 10 Mar. 1892.

[16]*Nonconformist*, 28 July 1892.

[17]*Nonconformist*, 17 Nov. 1892; 10 Mar. 1892.

[18]*Nonconformist*, 11 Aug. 1892; 14 July 1892; 4 Aug. 1892.

[19]*Nonconformist*, 21 July 1892; 4 Aug. 1892; 1 Sept. 1892.

[20]*Nonconformist*, 10 Mar. 1892.

[21]*Nonconformist*, 10 Mar. 1892; 29 Sept. 1892; 28 July 1892; 11 Aug. 1892.

[22]*Nonconformist*, 21 July 1892; 25 Aug. 1892; 17 Nov. 1892.

[23]*Nonconformist*, 16 June 1892; Mary H. Ford, *Which Wins? A Story of*

Social Conditions (Boston: Lee and Shepard, 1891); Anna D. Weaver, *Richard's Crown* (Chicago: B. S. Heath, 1882).

[24]*Nonconformist*, 28 July 1892; 13 Oct. 1892.

[25]*Nonconformist*, 1 Sept. 1892.

[26]*Nonconformist*, 17 Nov. 1892; 25 Aug. 1892.

[27]*Nonconformist*, 4 Aug. 1892.

[28]*Nonconformist*, 21 Jan. 1892; 1 Sept. 1892.

[29]*Nonconformist*, 17 Nov. 1892.

[30]*Nonconformist*, 1 Sept. 1892.

[31]*Nonconformist*, 17 Nov. 1892; 25 Aug. 1892.

[32]*Nonconformist*, 10 Mar. 1892.

[33]Elizabeth Barr, "The Populist Uprising," *Standard History of Kansas and the Kansans*, ed. William Connelley (Chicago: Lewis Publishing Co., 1918) 2:1164; *Nonconformist*, 14 July 1892; 3 Mar.1892.

[34]Robert Coles, *The Political Life of Children* (Boston: Atlantic Monthly Press, 1986), 3-19.

[35]Bettie Gay, "The Influence of Women in the Alliance," *The Farmers' Alliance History and Agricultural Digest*, ed. Nelson A. Dunning (Washington, D. C.: Alliance Publishing Co., 1891), 309.

[36]This sketch of the Kellie family farm is summarized from two manuscripts in the Nebraska State Historical Society, Lincoln: Luna Kellie, "The Farmer's Alliance in Nebraska" (1926) and Kellie, "Memoirs" (1918).

[37]*United States Bureau of the Census, Historical Statistics of the United States, Colonial Times to 1957: A Statistical Abstract Supplement* (New York: Basic Books, 1976), 457. Statistics for the number of family workers in comparison to the number of hired workers are unavailable until 1910.

[38]Sandra Myres, *Westering Women and the Frontier Experience* (Albuquerque: University of New Mexico Press, 1982), 162; Annie Diggs, "Women in the Alliance Movement," *Arena* 6 (July 1892): 177.

[39]Carl Degler, *At Odds: Women and the Family in America from the Revolution to the Present* (New York: Oxford University Press, 1980),409; Minnie Miller Brown, "Black Women in American Agriculture," *Agricultural History* 50 (January 1976): 206-08.

[40]Diggs, "Women in the Alliance," 171.

[41]Gay, "Influence of Women," 309.

[42]*Western Rural Rules of Order and Rallying Song Book* (Chicago: Western Rural, 1882), 16-17.

[43]*Chicago Express*, 29 Nov. 1890.

[44]*Farmer's Wife*, Apr. 1893; Nov. 1891; Bates, Shylock's Daughter, 22.

[45]Myres, *Westering Women*, 164-65.

[46]Diggs, "Women in the Alliance," 162-63.

[47]Michelle Rosaldo, "Woman, Culture, and Society," *Woman, Culture, and Society*, ed. Rosaldo and Louise Lamphere (Stanford, Calif.: Stanford University Press, 1974), 36, 41.

19

BUILDING THE BASE:
FARM WOMEN, THE RURAL COMMUNITY, AND
FARM ORGANIZATIONS IN THE MIDWEST,
1900-1940

Mary Neth

INTRODUCTION

Neighboring has long been the basis of farm communities. While historians and rural sociologists have usually focused on institutions as the social basis of community, it was informal social life that gave institutions in farm communities their meaning and created the fabric of daily living during the first half of this century. Social neighborhoods, patterns of interaction, and the unwritten customs that were their foundation developed the sense of dependability, stability, and security that were the basis of resource sharing and economic exchange. Women were the primary organizers of this social world.

By creating this social sense of community, women built the base that was the key to success for both local institutions and farm organizations throughout the nineteenth and twentieth centuries. While men dominated formal offices and leadership roles at all levels of these organizations, women connected the political programs and formal structures to community traditions giving the organizations their grass-roots base and a cultural and social meaning that intensified loyalty and group cohesiveness. Women's importance to this social base gave them the resources and skills to challenge the dominance of men and to influence the directions of the programs of these farm organizations.

This paper will analyze farm women's participation in farm organizations during the first half of the twentieth century by examining the life histories of two Midwestern farm leaders. Although these two women are unique because of their state leadership positions, the paths they took to achieve this prominence reveal how women participated in and built rural communities and how they used their skills to increase women's voice in male-dominated farm organizations. Similarities illuminate experiences common to many farm women. Farm women were crucial to building neighborhood unity. They were skilled organizers, educators, and fund raisers. These skills were vital for farm organizations, and these two women used these talents as a base for their state political activities.

A comparison of these two women also highlights significant differences in the ways women used their community building skills. The different strategies they adopted to work toward greater participation came not just from their distinct personal backgrounds, but also from the economic conditions and family structures that shaped their work on the farm and influenced their views of women's relationship to the farm business and to men. In addition, the structure and ideology of the farm organizations they joined defined the perimeters for women's activities and the barriers that needed to be challenged. Women were excluded from full participation in different ways and this shaped the strategies they developed to gain entry to political power. Nevertheless, the various tactics were still based on the skills farm women learned from building rural communities.

WOMEN AND THE INFORMAL FARM NEIGHBORHOOD

The informal exchanges and social interactions of rural neighbors were the heart of the farm community and the source of women's influence on community life. While neighboring might seem to lack the permanence of schools or churches, local custom did include standards of acceptable and expected behavior that had continuity over time and provided a moral center for community social and economic relations.[1] Farm neighboring integrated the work, trade, and social lives of farm people. Farm people exchanged work, traded produce, and gave favors and gifts to neighbors. These exchanges helped redistribute the resources within a farm community. Neighbors could share labor and equipment in very flexible ways depending on the needs, resources, and intimacy of the individuals involved. The underpinnings of this trade were the social ties of the community. Because neighbors visited and built emotional ties, trust and shared values could emerge from the consistent repetition of friendly interaction. Favors and exchange took place within this familiarity and were based on an attitude of giving and helpfulness, rather than a sense of direct obligation that balanced debts and credits in a mechanical way. Values of farm neighboring integrated the economic and social lives of farm people into expected patterns of reciprocal aid and exchange.[2]

Women played an important part in building these links between the local economy and farm social life. Although women worked in all parts of the farm operation, their primary work products were often those most frequently exchanged in local markets. Farm women often traded poultry, dairy and garden produce, helping to balance work and machinery exchanges and to cement friendships. This made their work central to building the consistent patterns of resource and labor sharing within rural neighborhoods. Women also organized the primary social events that created a sense of community. When threshing day arrived, women made the meals and produced the festive atmosphere that made the day one of neighborhood sharing and unity rather than merely one of work. Women organized the celebrations that marked special life events, such as birthdays or marriages, and that commemorated community pride, such as school picnics and church Christmas pageants. Women used their work and organizing skills to integrate the social and economic life of the community.[3]

Neighboring also integrated an individual into a series of interconnected relationships that expanded and contracted to meet personal and community needs and to give individuals a sense of place and security.[4] Most ties were based on kinship. The family was the basic economic and social unit of the farm neighborhood. An individual's place in the community was first assigned through kin relations. These basic kin ties could expand outward to form large networks between families. This expansion gave to an individual a sense of place in the community and provided the base for larger work and trade exchanges. The larger networks also contracted to form smaller networks that could be based on kin, sex, or age, or even the ties between two neighboring families. These networks fulfilled needs for intimacy and provided a basis of security for sharing resources during both good and bad times.

Women defined their place in the community through ties of gender, family, and friendship. Rather than being sharply defined by a separate sphere of gender, women's identity encompassed their roles as women, as family members, and as friends and neighbors in the rural community.[5] While women's work was sometimes gender-defined, it was not segregated from the work of the family or the community.[6] For example, when farm families butchered, the work separated along gender lines, with men killing the animal and women preserving and preparing the meat. But the work was often exchanged with close kin or neighbors, linking gender networks to family and neighborhood networks. While women shared the responsibilities of organizing social and community events and this common activity developed intimate ties among women, the events they organized were designed to connect kin and community, not just women. Even a ritual as female-centered as birthing was shared by the community. Women shared the preparations for birth, the birthing experience, the child care, and the work, but the birth itself was welcomed by kin and community with rounds of family visits that included women, men, and children.[7] While gender did shape the lives of women, it was only one of their points of reference. Women were also connected to the community as kin and neighbors, and they used their work and skill as organizers to build these interconnecting links.

WOMEN, RURAL INSTITUTIONS, AND FARM ORGANIZATIONS

As women built the economic and social base of informal community life, they also built the economic and social base for local rural institutions through their formal women's organizations. These groups' activities spoke both to the particular needs of women and to the more general needs of the rural neighborhood. The groups had four goals – to build social cohesion and unity, to raise money for neighborhood improvements, to educate the community and the groups' members, and to improve women's working conditions. Often these goals overlapped. Women's organizations raised money for schools and churches, and the fund-raising events, such as box socials or dances, were also social get-togethers that increased community solidarity. Women's clubs provided libraries, playground equipment, free health examinations for children, restrooms in town for farm women, and hot lunches and milk for school children. Clubs also encouraged self-education on issues such as state and local history or laws affecting women, and provided education for the community by organizing debates and talks. Club women improved their own work by studying gardening or poultry, purchasing canning equipment, or sharing work. Some clubs even operated cooperative laundries.[8] Thus, when women organized, their activities followed the same lines as those in the informal neighborhood. They shared work experiences within gender networks, contributed to the economic creation of community sharing, and were primarily responsible for the social rituals that united the neighborhood. Their activities linked them by gender, but also integrated them into the local community.

Women used these same skills in general farm organizations. Historians, who are beginning to uncover the activities of women both in farm organizations and in other political groups, have found that women were at the center of grass-roots activities – raising funds, organizing locals, creating social cohesion and group loyalty, and educating the family and neighborhood on important issues.[9] The lives of two Wisconsin farm women, one a leader in the Farm Bureau and the other a leader in the Farmers' Union, illustrate how farm women used their economic and social skills to influence and shape the growth of farm organizations. Both women worked to improve their lives as farm women, as members of farm families and as a part of the farm community. Their experiences as women show a basic commonality even as the emphasis and definitions they chose demonstrate the variety of ways farm women worked for equality.[10] Although the two women used similar skills to work for themselves and the farm community, their strategies, tactics and goals differed because of their personal backgrounds, their work on the farm, their experiences as family members, their economic conditions, and the different ideologies and structures of the farm organizations of which they were members.

ISABEL BAUMANN AND THE FARM BUREAU

Isabel Baumann was born in 1906 in south central Wisconsin.[11] Whereas her father's family was English, her mother's family and the community of Dunkirk, where they lived, were Norwegian. The family farm was a small, eighty-acre general farm, which included ten to seventeen acres of tobacco as a cash crop. In her early farm experience there was little sex segregation of labor. In fact, according to Baumann, her mother was the farmer, and her father preferred carpentry. Because she was the oldest of five children and because tobacco is a labor-intensive crop, Isabel worked in the fields from the age of eight or nine until she married at age twenty-one. She knew from an early age that women were primary contributors to the farm economy. Even as her work became more gender defined after her marriage, she continued to be knowledgeable about the work of the entire farm operation.

Baumann's youth was clearly rooted in a shared women's culture from which she gained her strength and ambition. Women's access to farming generally depended on marriage to a farmer, and, as the oldest daughter, Isabel had to support herself. While her mother loved farm work, she also believed in education and was determined that Isabel get a high school education, despite the economic sacrifices required to pay for board and tuition. At school, Baumann was influenced by a home economics teacher named Sarah Leslie, who introduced her to the ideas of professional homemaking, encouraged her to go to high school, and provided an example of neighborhood organizing with her adult education programs for local farm women. Showing strong gender identification, Baumann described these two women – her mother and Sarah Leslie – as the strongest influence on her early life. Her mother provided a strong model for women as farm partners; her teacher a model of educator and organizer of women's groups. Both women emphasized the importance of education, and Baumann ultimately chose to become a teacher and attended Stoughton High School's teacher-training program. In 1925, she moved to Sun Prairie to teach. Teaching not only enabled Baumann to earn a living, but also to stay in a rural community that was near enough to the home farm to maintain these close kin ties and assist her family with cash and labor.

When Baumann married, her new work routines followed more traditional gender definitions than in her girlhood; however, she continued to make important economic contributions to the farm. In 1928, she married Dan McCarthy, quit teaching, and became a "farmer's wife." Her new economic conditions were very different from those on her mother's farm. The McCarthy farm was a 160-acre dairy farm operated by Baumann's husband with his brother and father. The larger operation, the switch from tobacco to dairy farming, and the availability of male labor made Baumann's farm contributions closer to those traditionally seen as "women's work." She cooked for three men, kept a garden, and cared for the yard and house. But Baumann also expanded the poultry operation, using skills she had learned from her mother. She contracted to furnish eggs to a Madison hospital, providing 120 dozen per week. Baumann kept this income and used it to buy home goods. As household manager, she made the decisions about home production. As the farm continued to expand, adding eighty more acres, Baumann shared in the improvements. The McCarthys alternated purchases for farm and home, showing both the farm's prosperity and the relative equality of the marriage partnership. This equality was based on a work relationship that was sex segregated but entailed a sharing of resources and prosperity.

Baumann's involvement in organizations began after her marriage. The organizations, like the organization of the McCarthy farm's labor, were generally sex segregated, but their activities linked them to the rural community which integrated men and women. Baumann's husband had been a member of dairy and breeders' associations and the Farm Bureau before their marriage in 1928. But at that time, the Farm Bureau in Dane County, Wisconsin, had no comparable organizations for women and did not include women in its general meetings. Baumann's first activities were in the local Mother's Club. This organization raised money to buy equipment for the school, such as chairs, books, pictures, hot lunches, and wiring for lights. To do this they organized community events, such as box socials and dances, or made quilts and held raffles. The club also had card parties and other purely social events for members and their families. Baumann's activities included economic support for local institutions and education, organizing the neighborhood to support these institutions, and in this way creating social unity and sharing.

Women who were affiliated with the Farm Bureau organized as women and used this separate position to meet their own needs and to push for more representation in the general organizations. This tactic was in part a reaction to the ways in which women were restricted from full participation in the Farm Bureau. The Farm Bureau structure and ideology assumed a sexual division of labor on the farm, the separation of the male business from the female social world, and separate organizations for women and men. Men participated in the Farm Bureau, which taught new scientific advances in farming and promoted agriculture as a business. Women participated in auxiliary Homemakers' Clubs that focused on new methods of performing household tasks and community service. While the separation and devaluation of women's work on a farm might be mitigated by face-to-face relations that integrated women in personal ways, such as equal participation in farm decisions or neighborhood solidarity, the segregation of women in a formal organization made women's concerns structurally marginal and subordinate. Baumann described the Women's Farm Bureau Federation as helping women gain a position where they could "express themselves and do things on their own." To her, women were equal partners on the farm, and the women's organizations promoted their interests and increased their influence. Although Baumann described farm women as equal members in the Farm Bureau, other statements indicated that this was not always the case. At one point, she stated that women in the 1970s were no longer "lunch preparers" and that women had previously been auxilary to the male-dominated organization. Her own career is evidence both of how women were auxilliary to the organization and how they used separate women's groups to gain influence in the Farm Bureau.

In 1934, the Farm Bureau began to organize auxiliary groups for farm women in Dane County. Baumann attended the first meeting at the county office, was elected treasurer, and was "never out of it from then on." The Farm Bureau organized women separately from men and at the county rather than local level. In this way it capitalized on the already existing local clubs and the Dane County Rural Federation which had been organized in 1927. Women worked to connect the larger Farm Bureau structure to the local base of the farm neighborhood. The Dane County Women's Farm Bureau Federation and the Dane County Rural Federation helped local clubs give programs, organize discussions of issues, and write and stage plays. These affiliated local women's clubs served as an education and social base for the male-dominated Farm Bureau, and farm women used this local base to take a larger role in the general farm organization. Women prepared the kick-off breakfasts for Farm Bureau memberships drives and participated in the teams that traveled through a community encouraging neighbors to join.

Baumann used her skills as an educator and organizer to work for the Farm Bureau and to move from a local to a state-level position in the organization. The visibility she gained as a local and county leader enabled her to move into state-wide positions designed for women when they were finally created. She participated most frequently in discussion programs and plays. In 1937, the county agent invited her and five other farm women to begin a radio program, the "We Say What We Think Club." Although it provided recipes and practical work tips for farm women, the program's primary purpose was to discuss public and agricultural issues. In 1939, she won the state speaking contest, speaking on "The Farmer's Stake in World Peace." When the work women had been doing was finally acknowledged by the Farm Bureau, it was in an institutional way, assigning a specific office to a women's representative. As chair of the Wisconsin Farm Bureau Federation's Women's Committee, Baumann, in 1959, became the first woman to serve in a permanent seat on the state Farm Bureau Board of Directors.[12]

When Baumann reflected on her work, her evaluation of its significance reveals her firm sense of women's place in an integrated community and her knowledge that women's work was not always valued. Baumann believed that her work as educator and organizer and that the quality of community life were important. In reflecting on her goals and accomplishments, she took pride in seeing former students still in the community and leading satisfying lives. She was gratified that she had helped create an informed membership and active local organizations. She was glad that she had lived in a time "when people had to determine what was going to happen to themselves and their community." But because the organizations in which she participated segregated women, Baumann's views show a strong awareness of both her strength as a woman and the general societal devaluation of women's work, including women's contributions to community building. At the end of her interview, Baumann wondered whether women ever really appreciated their own contributions to the community. Women have "done it without people realizing they've been doing it; been going along and just doing it."

Baumann evaluated the strengths of the Farm Bureau in women-centered ways as well. She did not discuss the Farm Bureau's economic or political policies in much detail but focused on how farm women found a more public voice. The Farm Bureau trained men and women (her emphasis) as leaders and spokespeople for agriculture. The women's clubs gave women a chance to grow and get "outside of the home" and do "something creative and worthwhile." When asked why this change had occurred, Baumann gave the credit to women. Women wanted to be more vocal, and "women changed it." She described the Farm Bureau as "willing" to put women on committees, but it is clear that women had to demand representation. The structure of the Farm Bureau required that women organize separately, and farm women, creators of a vibrant women's culture, developed these separate organizations and used them to influence the male-dominated structure. Baumann emphasized her identity as a woman, but she also drew her strength from her awareness of women's integral importance to the farm and the rural community. She used this strength to organize women for the betterment of themselves, their community and of farm people in general.

JEAN STILLMAN LONG AND THE FARMERS' UNION

Jean Stillman Long was born in 1891 in rural New York, but she was not a farm girl.[13] Her father was an engineer and inventor who worked in a series of jobs, cooper and lumber mills, a hat factory, and a paper-coating company. At the age of ten, Long moved with her family to Milwaukee, where she graduated from high school in 1909. Unlike Baumann, Long did not identify with a separate women's culture, except to rebel against its restrictions. Long recalled that she was an independent and rebellious girl. The sources of this rebellion she traced to her family heritage and her parents' indulgence. Her grandfather had been sold "into bondage" as a cabin boy, became a fervent abolitionist as an adult, and always spoke out for individual rights. Although her father was a more "conservative" Republican, he thought his daughter's independence was humorous. Her mother was busy cooking for the workers at the mills and gave her daughter a great deal of freedom, both because she was so busy and because she felt her daughter "could do no wrong."

Like Baumann, Long chose the teaching profession, but rather than using it to maintain gender and family ties, she used it to rebel against gender restrictions. After attending normal schools in Milwaukee and Genessee, New York, Long went to rural New York to teach. She found the community too restrictive. She could be criticized for riding a horse astride, going to a dance or having a date during the week, or for showing her ankles. In 1912, Long decided to go to Montana to teach and homestead. There she was "free to climb a mountain," while in New York, "they would help you climb over a fence." Besides giving her independence, Long's stay in Montana revived her radical political tradition. Cayuse Prairie, near Kalispell, Montana, was active socialist and Non-Partisan League (NPL) country. When Long went with a school board member to hear socialist leader Eugene Debs, she found that he "didn't say anything I didn't already believe in." She joined the NPL but eventually quit because the dues were too expensive and she disliked the Montana promoters. Long's political conscience and belief in freedom were based in part on a rejection of the restrictions placed on women and in part on a family political tradition. Her life in Montana fused these two elements.

Long's economic condition and ties to agriculture were, like Baumann's, determined by her marriage, but the results were quite different. In 1918, Jean Stillman married Clifford ("Cy") Long, the brother of her school board's treasurer, and moved to his farm near Downsville, Wisconsin. Long described her marriage not as an equal partnership based on mutually accepted gender work roles, but as a series of restrictions on her freedom, based on sexual inequality and her lack of knowledge about farming. First, she had four children in the first four years and ten days of her marriage. Second, the farm home was operated by Cy's mother, "Mrs. Long," who managed and allocated work in the household and set family standards. Third, the family's general attitude was that women should stay on the farm to work, rather than spending time socializing or joining community groups. Long recalled that it was five years before she visited a neighbor. Finally, the money that she had earned independently by teaching and selling her homestead went for the purchase of a herd of purebred Holsteins, and she was "not permitted to buy one thing for the house." The freedom that she had found on the frontier did not exist within her new marriage.

But this tale of restrictions was balanced by a tale of growing understanding of farm life and Long's discovery of ways to assert herself within the family. Part of her growing independence was due to changes in the family cycle. As her children grew older, they took less of her time and also assumed part of the farm work. Her three daughters and her son learned all the work of the farm and home and performed regular chores with very few gender distinctions, reflecting both Long's attitudes and her mother-in-law's example. Work on the Long farm was less sex segregated than on Baumann's, and despite continued conflicts with her mother-in-law, Long began to appreciate Mrs. Long's work skills, strength, and contribution to the farm's survival. While Long complained of her mother-in-law's opposition to the purchase of a washing machine, Long also recognized that Mrs. Long "washed better by hand than any machine" and "worked like a man," milking the cows twice a day and working in the barnyard. Long admired her mother-in-law's ability to raise things in the garden that the extension agent said were impossible to grow in that climate. Long was also glad that her mother-in-law taught the Long children how to identify and gather wild foods, such as spring greens.

This respect for her mother-in-law grew stronger as Long found her own place in the work of the farm. As an "educated fool," she had had to learn farming from scratch. But with the increasing use of machines, which everyone had to learn how to use, Long could gain entry to work at an equal level. While she never milked a cow by hand, she did tend the milking machine, because the hired man did not know how to operate it and her mother-in-law preferred milking by hand. Long also began to get some independent income from the sale of eggs. This gave her control of one farm operation as well as some cash to spend on household items. This work gave Long some autonomy, even though her mother-in-law still controlled much of the household work.

Long was never able to put household improvements on an equal footing with farm improvements as was done on the McCarthy farm. But the work structure and economic conditions on the two farms were quite different. The Long farm was less than half the size of the McCarthy farm. This made cash income more difficult to acquire and investments in the cash producing part of the farm a top priority. Long understood these priorities, saying "the cows were our living; the family wasn't." Moreover, because work was less sex segregated on the Long farm, women's labor, as well as men's, was lightened by farm investments. Rather than a partnership of two separated but equal parts, the Long farm was a single unit. The emphasis was on farm survival, and all were to contribute in any way possible to that goal.

Although work roles were flexible and women made equal contributions, this did not mean that the family structure was not patriarchal. Men made the decisions for the unit, and Jean, as a "greenhorn," rarely participated. It is unclear from the interview whether Mrs. Long influenced any decisions other than those pertaining to the household, but Jean generally described decision making as her husband's responsibility. Although she shared the values that put success of the family operation above the needs of individual family members, she also clearly resented her exclusion from farm choices. Because women performed more varied tasks on small farms, their labor was even more crucial to farm survival; yet, this did not necessarily lead to greater equality or more power within the family.[14]

Further freedom from the restrictions of Long's early married life came with her involvement in the Farmers' Union. Cy Long had been active in Equity and had helped organize local tobacco and creamery cooperatives even before his marriage. When a Farmers' Union organizer visited, he readily joined. Jean did not approve at first because she felt he was in too many groups and she still recalled her dislike of the Montana NPL organizers. Yet eventually she, too, became a supporter. Her direct involvement began when a Farmer's Union leader, who had heard that Long had directed home talent plays in Montana, asked her to direct a pageant. This activity was acceptable to her husband, and Long had an opportunity to be active again in the community. The Farmers' Union charged twenty-five to fifty cents admission to the plays and raised money for organization expenses. The play toured the region and state in about 1931 or 1932, and Long served as the play and the project's director. Like Baumann and other farm women, Long used her skills as an educator and organizer to create events to raise money for a local institution.

The structure of the Farmers' Union, unlike that of the Farm Bureau, integrated women and men into one local organization. Any farm family member over the age of sixteen could vote at the local, and all were encouraged to be knowledgeable and speak out on important issues. The Farmers' Union, like the Long farm, recognized the farm as a family unit whose functioning depended on the contributions of all its members. The Farmers' Union recognized women's importance to the farm and the community by incorporating them on an equal basis in its local organizations and by recognizing their education and social activites as fundamental to the group's survival. Long's activities as educator and organizer were integrated with the Union's political and economic ventures rather than segregated into a separate women's organization. Utilizing the skills gained at the local level and the access to the organization inherent in the Farmers' Union structure, Long expanded her work from the local to the regional and state levels of the group. While her husband worked to organize economic cooperatives in Dunn County, Long served as the county education leader, creating the social spaces to unite local neighborhoods, introducing Farmers' Union ideas to farm people, and raising money to support the organization. Long cooperated with the University of Wisconsin Agricultural Extension to set up workshops teaching skills in public speaking, running meetings, and discussing public issues. She organized youth groups in Dunn County that not only educated farm youths on the programs of the Farmers' Union, but also educated the larger community through youth speeches to area churches on such issues as peace and the prevention of war. For five years, Long worked as State Recreation Director for the rural segment of the Works Progress Administration (WPA) Workers' Education Program. This program provided speakers, discussion classes, and recreation for rural areas. Its folk dancers of various ethnic traditions toured Wisconsin, appearing at picnics or in town or church halls. Whenever Long organized an appearance, the local community had to form an organization to promote recreation, education, and discussion of public issues. Long also prepared radio programs on rural issues. After the WPA program ended, Long continued pursuing these kinds of activities, first as organizer for Central Cooperatives Wholesale and then, from 1949 to 1961, as Farmers' Union state education and youth camp director.

Although women were included in the Farmer's Union organization, the group's recognition of women did not lessen male control of its formal political offices, much as the importance of Long's farm work did not increase her influence on farm decision making. Except in the field of education, most state offices were held by men. Nevertheless, because women were accepted as equals in the local organizations and theoretically could be elected to office, there was no move to create a separate "woman's office" in the formal structure of the Farmers' Union. Long, however, used her official position as education director and her informal position as "farm leader's wife" to stretch her own influence and preserve the programs that gave women a base of influence in the organization locals. Although her husband Cy did not hold state offices, his local leadership and personal contacts often involved him in important leadership meetings. His insistence that she, as his wife, attend those meetings – even when women's presence was unusual – gave her access to the decision-making process. But, it was Long's skill that gained her acceptance and made her voice an important one. As she told the interviewer, "as long as I was there, as you know, I talk." She described her role as the person who could break a stalemate, get a laugh, encourage discussion, and iron out conflicts. Despite the respect she gained, Long constantly had to defend the importance of funding her education programs against those who thought economic cooperative matters, such as advertising, were more important. She was usually successful. Long increased the presence of women in the Farmers' Union by protecting the education and community programs that were women's strength at the local level, by actively holding state office, and by using her informal paths of influence to express her own ideas.

Long's evaluation of her work, like Baumann's, included a belief in the importance of education, organizing, and community strength, and illustrates that farm women viewed themselves as integral to an integrated community. Long felt personal satisfaction when former students or contacts recognized her work and acknowledged that the ideas she taught affected their lives. But her greatest satisfaction came from increasing large group participation and getting people to take an active part in their community and the Farmers' Union. Like Baumann, Long believed that people should shape their own communities, and building this involvement was her primary goal.

However, Long did not see her success in terms of what it did for women, but rather in terms of what it did for the Farmers' Union and the ideal of the "cooperative commonwealth." Despite the exclusion of women from most leadership positions, women were accepted in the Farmers' Union locals, and these locals were vital to the Union's bottom-up organization. Its structure rested on a firm social base that integrated women and men. Women built this social base and educated the family and community to accept and believe the ideals at the foundation of the organization's political and economic ventures. The organization assumed the importance of this base, and Long did not have to fight for this recognition. She believed that her activities in the WPA workers program saved the Farmers' Union. The membership had been falling in the mid-1930s, there was dissension in the state leadership, and there were few organizers in the field at the time. The education people, she believed, did more than the organizers. They made personal calls, got people to talk out their problems and grievances, and created the social occasions for people to meet, discuss issues, and unite. Long's role was not auxiliary; it was primary. Her success was promoting the cooperative ideal. This gave people "personal dignity" and a "sense of belonging," and these to Long, were at the heart of the Farmers' Union's significance.

Although Long clearly saw the restrictions that women faced, she did not believe in women's auxiliaries or separate women's clubs to address these problems. Long connected the restrictions she felt early in her marriage to those faced by women who organized separately. She connected the two by using similar phrases to describe each. As a woman, she had been "expected to stay within four walls." As members of auxiliaries, women could only do "petty little things within four walls." While Baumann found strength in segregated women's work on the farm and used this to build a separate base to influence the Farm Bureau, Long saw this sex segregation as the cause of restrictions for women and demanded that women work directly with men within the organization, just as they shared a common endeavor on the farm. Baumann and Long believed that women were and should be equal, but they chose different means to accomplish that end.

CONCLUSION

Personal, social, economic, and political differences are at the root of the two women's divergent attitudes. Baumann's experiences on the farm, the example of her mother, and the general equality and sharing of her marriage supported her personal recognition of the worth of women to the farm. The farm's prosperity led to a gender segregation of work, but also allowed a sharing of prosperity in both cash and home production. Sex segregation was also evident in the organization of the Farm Bureau, and, in this case, it led to a marginalization of women's work and concerns. Whereas the individual farm and local community could recognize the importance of women's contribution to the whole and reward it, the larger organization focused on the commercial and business side of farming and separated the farm as "business" from its family and community base. Women had to organize separately to have their work acknowledged as an integral part of the farm operation. They had less access to power within the organization, but they had a strong base from which to challenge the formal structure that excluded them as women.

Long's farming experiences had both confirmed the importance of women's labor and shown the limits of shared work as a basis for equality. Because the Long farm was less prosperous, women's labor was clearly necessary for the survival of the farm unit, and it was demanded in all parts of the farm operation. But because of the need to increase the farm's cash income, the value of women's contribution was clearly not equally rewarded through the purchase of home improvements or even with increased influence in decision making. The problem was not making women's work equal to men's but rewarding the farm unit enough to assure survival. Once survival was assured women then would benefit from the new prosperity as family members, as part of the farm family unit. The Farmer's Union recognized the family farm unit as its basis of membership and gave equality to all its adult members. Thus, Long had access to the organization and worked through it. While women were not equal in positions of leadership, the organization did recognize their work and the importance of a community and family base, which women generally organized. On the one hand, sexual integration made it easier for women to influence the direction of the organization; on the other hand, because women were not organized as women, they found it difficult to challenge directly the structures that kept them out of official power.

Despite their differences, both Baumann and Long worked to build a base for their farm organizations. Their demands for equality as women were based on their economic contributions to the family farm, their strong ties to the local neighborhoods, and their skills as educators and organizers. Women built farm neighborhoods economically and socially. They created trade and visiting patterns that developed habits of mutuality and strategies for economic survival. They raised money to support local institutions and organized the rituals and events that supported feelings of community sharing and unity. Farm organizations needed this economic and social base to assure broad-based support and loyalty – the keys to a successful organization. While men dominated the public and political arenas, the institutions they led were built largely on the structures women created.

NOTES

[1]Local customs and expectations of neighboring were flexible but fairly well defined. A good description of these standards of the "country code" can be found in Nellie Kedzie Jones, "The New Home and the Old Farm," an unpublished manuscript collecting articles published in *The Country Gentleman* between 1912 and 1916 in Nellie Kedzie Jones Papers, 1881-1950, Wis Mss RT, pp.66-68, State Historical Society of Wisconsin. The persistence of neighboring values in the present has been discussed by rural sociologists and anthropologists. See, for example, Seena B. Kohl, "The Making of a Community: The Role of Women in an Agricultural Setting," in *Kin and Communities: Families in America* ed. Allen J. Lichtman and Joan R. Challinor (Washington, D.C.: Smithsonian Institution Press, 1979) and Mary Ann Gardner, "Plain Country People: A Study of Values in a Kentucky Hill-Farming Community" (Ph.D diss., University of Texas, Austin, 1982). See also Nancy Grey Osterud, "Strategies of Mutuality: Relations Among Women and Men in an Agricultural Community" (Ph.D diss, Brown University, 1984). The discussion in this chapter is primarily based on my own research and is presented

in my dissertation "Preserving the Family Farm: Farm Families and Communities in the Midwest, 1900-1940" (Ph.D diss, University of Wisconsin, 1987).

[2]Steven Hahn describes these patterns of sharing in late nineteenth-century Georgia as "habits of mutuality" that enabled the local culture to resist the increasing changes in market relations until the failure of the Populist movement. See Hahn, *The Roots of Southern Populism: Yeoman Farmers and the Transformation of the Georgia Upcountry, 1850-1890* (New York: Oxford University Press, 1983), 50-85. Thomas Bender summarizes the growing literature on working-class and black community structures and social networks, which shows similar responses to lack of resourses or access to power. See Bender, *Community and Social Change in America* (New Brunswick, NJ: Rutgers University Press, 1978), 127-49. Both of these discussions emphasize these strategies as economic responses, but do not discuss their importance as social values or heritage. In "Making of a Community" Seena Kohl describes the sharing strategies of Saskatchewan, tracing their development to the settlement period when resources and labor were scarce and following their persistence into the 1970s. Reciprocity and mutual aid were preserved through generations not just because they were an economic necessity but also because they were shared goals and values.

[3]A good example of how women's trade helped build economic and social ties and how women organized social events is the diary of Anna Pratt Erickson, a Wisconsin farm woman who recorded daily entries from 1898 to 1959. Anna Pratt Erickson Diaries, 1898-1959, Microfilm 738, State Historical Society of Wisconsin. Women's work was not just tied to local markets, but larger commercial ones as well. One example is butter making; see Joan Jensen, *Loosening the Bonds: Mid-Atlantic Farm Women, 1750-1850* (New Haven, Conn.: Yale University Press, 1986), 79-91. The rich lore on women and threshing is best found in oral history collections. The following are good examples: Ethel Fosberg, North Dakota Oral History Project, TR8-0977 A & B; Jake and Clara Jacobs, North Dakota Oral History Project MN12-0657 A, B, North Dakota State Historical Society; and Walter and Emma Henderson, Iowa Century Farms Oral History Project, OH4-82, Iowa State Historical Society. Examples of women building social ties through gift exchange can be found recorded in most holiday entries in the Erickson diaries. Osterud in "Strategies of Mutuality" argues that women used their ties of kin and community to build the support networks necessary to compensate for the discrimination they encountered in the economic and legal structures of both agriculture and the family. For a theoretical discussion of the need to define the building of kin ties as women's "work" and to move beyond the artificial dichotomy of emotional versus economic purposes of kin or neighborhood networks, see Micaela di Leonardo, "The Female World of Cards and Holidays: Women, Families, and the Work of Kinship," *Signs* 12 (Spring 1987): 440-53.

[4]Similar types of networks existed in rural New York in the nineteenth century. See Osterud, "Strategies of Mutuality," pp. 14-16, 23, 183-210, 455-56,

490-513. While this paper emphasizes the integrative aspects of community building, this does not mean that rural neighborhoods were homogeneous or conflict free, or that all people were included in a neighborhood on an equal basis. Rural communities could be divided by such things as ethnicity, length of residence, race, economic status, or religion.

[5]Carroll Smith-Rosenberg argued the importance of gender networks and the development of a separate women's culture for middle-class women between the 1760s and 1880s in "The Female World of Love and Ritual: Relations Between Women in Nineteenth Century America," *Signs* 1 (1975): 1-30. Studies of rural women have modified and expanded her findings to examine other places and times and working-class women. Jane Pederson studied visiting patterns in rural Wisconsin. Her findings that women primarily visited women confirmed that the "homosocial" world described by Rosenberg still existed between 1890 and 1900 and had changed only slightly between 1900 and 1925. See Pederson, "The Country Visitor: Patterns of Hospitality in Rural Wisconsin, 1880-1925," *Agricultural History* (July 1984): 347-64. My own interpretation based on my research on twentieth-century midwestern farm women, more closely parallels the arguments made by Nancy Grey Osterud, describing nintheenth-century New York farm women. By examining not only how women relate to women, but how women relate to families, kin, and community, Osterud achieves a more complex view of women's networks. Although gender networks were important for emotional and financial support, and rural women shared certain work rituals and viewpoints based on gender experiences, Osterud finds their contact with men was not so foreign as Rosenberg describes, rather, the contact occurred in informal settings that integrated a neighborhood in spite of gender or age differences. Osterud goes on to argue that women used their social ogranizing skills to include men and build bridges of mutuality and shared experiences. See Osterud, "Strategies of Mutuality," pp. 5, 18-23, 183-210, 361-94, and 490-513. One reason that the "homosocial" relations Rosenberg described were acceptable even into the twentieth century was that they were closely integrated with ties to family, kin, and neighborhood, and were thus not a challenge to heterosocial roles and gender definitions. See also Kohl, "Making of A Community," pp. 183-5.

[6]Although work was generally assigned by gender, the performance of tasks was somewhat flexible. Women performed all sorts of work on the farm whenever the needs of the farming operation demanded it. Although women frequently did "men's work," men assisted with women's tasks much less frequently. See Osterud, "Strategies of Mutuality," 361-438; Delores Janiewski, *Sisterhood Denied: Race, Gender and Class in a New South Community* (Philadelphia: Temple University Press, 1985), 27-54; and Joan Jensen, *With These Hands: Women Working on the Land* (Old Westbury, NY: The Feminist Press, 1981) and *Loosening the Bonds*, 36-56.

[7]See, for example, Erickson, Diaries, March 7-24, 1903; June-September 1905; May-August 1908; March-May 1911; July-August 1912; November-December 1913; January-March 1917. Life experiences that were less gender

defined than birthing show even greater links between family and gender networks. See Erickson, Diaries, December 1917-March 1918. Osterud found similar trends; "Strategies of Mutuality," 18-19, 490-525.

[8]Examples of midwestern women's club activities can be found in Homemakers Club Histories Project, North Dakota Institute for Regional Studies, North Dakota State University; and in Anne M. Evans, "Memo and Report of Western Trip, Including Illinois, Kansas, and Iowa, June 10-30, 1916," "Significant Examples of Women's Rural Organizations," and "State Reports to the Farm Women's National Conference, October 23, 1917," Record Group 83, Field Reports, Box 4, National Archives, United States Department of Agriculture, Bureau of Agricultural Economics, Division of Farm Population and Rural Life. On cooperative laundries, see C.J. Galpin and D.W. Sawtelle, "Rural Clubs in Wisconsin," *University of Wisconsin Agricultural Experiment Station Bulletin* 271 (August 1916): 36-41

[9]Some of the new literature on women in farm organizations includes Osterud, "Strategies of Mutuality," 529-36; Karen Starr, "Fighting for a Future: Farm Women of the Non-Partisan League," *Minnesota History* 48 (Summer 1983): 116-37; Julie Roy Jeffrey, "Women in the Southern Farmers' Alliance: A Reconsideration of the Role and Status of Women in the late Nineteenth Century South," *Feminist Studies* 2 (Fall 1975): 72-91; Donald Marti, "Women's Work in the Grange: Mary Ann Mayo of Michigan, 1882-1903," *Agricultural History* 56 (April 1982): 439-52; Jensen, *Hands*, 142-54; and Mari Jo Buhle, *Women and American Socialism, 1870-1920* (Urbana: University of Illinois Press, 1983), 82-94. Women have played similar roles in other organizations. See Buhle, *Women and American Socialism*, and Sara Evans, *Personal Politics: The Roots of Women's Liberation in the Civil Rights Movement and the New Left* (New York: Vintage Books, 1979).

[10]Differences in the way women organize and promote social change, and evaluate their roles in social organizations, have begun to be explored by women's historians. Mari Jo Buhle located two traditions in organizations for socialist women. The native tradition drew from a separate women's culture and maintained a separate position from the male-mainstream socialist movement. The immigrant tradition worked closely with the movement, organizing women in auxiliaries which created family and community cohesion for the organization. Buhle locates women in the Farmers' Alliance and Populist Party as members of the first tradition, but this analysis is based on women leaders rather than grass roots activists and does not examine the later organizations such as the cooperative movement, the Non-Partisan League, and the Farmers' Union. In states such as North Dakota and Wisconsin, immigrants were an important part of rural organizations. Sometimes farm women formed separate auxiliaries, but in some groups women were members of the general organization as well. Buhle's conclusions need to be reexamined with more studies of farm women in the more radical farm organizations. Where Buhle focused on radical women and ethnic differences, other historians have found similar differences in women's organizations and self-evaluation based on class and race. The questions of how sex discrimination connects with race and class and how women define their

problems in relation to race, class, or sex are discussed in such works as Alice Kessler-Harris, "Where Are the Organized Women Workers?" *Feminist Studies* (1975): 92-110; Nancy Schrom Dye, "Creating a Feminist Alliance: Sisterhood and Class Conflict in the New York Women's Trade Union League, 1903-1914," *Feminist Studies* (1975); Gerda Lerner, *The Majority Finds Its Past* (New York: Oxford University Press, 1979), 83-111; Lerner, *Black Women in White America: A Documentary History* (New York: Vintage Books, 1973), 561-614; and Janiewski, *Sisterhood*. Many women primarily defined themselves by the economic, racial, or ethnic character of their families and communities rather than by their status as women within the family structure. This was probably not an either/or definition, but more a matter of defining priorities and emphasizing one or the other in different contexts.

[11]Isabel Baumann, interviewed by Dale Trelevan, April and May 1980, Wisconsin Agriculturalists Oral History Project, Tape 809A, State Historical Society of Wisconsin. As leaders in state farm organizations, Baumann and Long are obviously not typical farm women. However, their work on family farms and their roles in local community institutions and networks are representative of the activities of many Midwestern farm women in this time period. Studying thier move from "common" work roles to active political leadership is one way of analyzing the gender-defined structures of farm organizations and the processes women used to gain power in political groups that traditionally excluded them.

[12]The first woman to serve on the Wisconsin Farm Bureau Board of Directors was Mabel Douglas of Green County, who served in the 1930s. This was not a permanent seat assigned to a woman's representative.

[13]Jean Stillman Long, interviewed by Dale Trelevan, 1974, Wisconsin Agriculturalists Oral History Project, Tape 589A, State Historical Society of Wisconsin.

[14]Many historians of urban women have equated women's equal contribution to family survival through productive work, such as existed on farms, with equality in the family and have argued that the loss of women's home production tasks led to a decline in women's status. Studies of farm women are beginning to show that the issue is more complex. The family had an essentially patriarchial form, and economic partnership and the importance of women's labor to family survival did not necessarily lessen its effects. See Osterud, "Strategies of Mutuality," 376-77, 575-88; and Janiewski, *Sisterhood*, 27-54, 196-97.

20

FARM WOMEN IN THE POLITICAL ARENA

Lorna Clancy Miller and Mary Neth [1]

Pointing to the starving families of Chicago and the wasted corn piled by the railroad tracks, a woman active in the Kansas Farmers' Alliance in the 1880s said, "Raise less corn and more hell." These words of Mary Ellen Lease – the "Kansas Pythoness," as she was called – reflect women's ability to be heard and remembered. One hundred years later, Lease's charge set the tone for the lively interaction of farm women, scholars, and policymakers at the Second National Conference on American Farm Women. "I think we have some sisters of Mary Ellen on our program," said Marcia Taylor as she introduced a panel of politically active farm women. "With the $1.25 cash corn prices, I'm sure some of the speakers are reviving that theme."

Although women were historically disenfranchised and formally excluded from political positions, farm women, like their urban counterparts, were not deterred from involvement in suffrage and other political movements. Most farm women used their community-building skills and resources to address local and state issues. Since farm people generally had limited access to political power, most farm groups were formed during the periods of agricultural recession and were organized outside traditional political institutions. This tended to give farm women a chance to share leadership with farm men and to define their own place within these less institutionalized grassroots organizations. Some farm organizations founded in less crisis-oriented times developed structures divided according to traditional gender interests. In either case, however, women practiced a leadership style that made these orgnizations responsive to the needs of their families and neighborhoods as well as the larger agricultural community.

The farm women on the "Farm Women in the Political Arena" panel at the conference echoed this historical context of farm women's political participation. As political institutions become more open to women, farm women are developing new approaches to operating in the male-dominated political arena. Farm women are still mostly involved in their local settings. But building on their experiences and the heritage of skills and resources that have been women's strengths, farm women are steadily moving into leadership roles in larger political settings where they search for creative solutions to the problems that confront agriculture today. They have expanded their community-building networks to state and national coalitions and have cooperated with long-standing institutions to increase women's power to influence the national farm policy agenda.

We will focus on four aspects of farm women's involvement in agricultural politics. After tracing the strategies that farm women have used to affect political change historically and examining the recent growth of women's participation in farm organizations from the grassroots to the national level, we turn to the words of the conference panelists to analyze the successes and obstacles women have met in the course of this transition and discuss the potential roles of farm women in defining agriculture's future. In their discussion, the panelists mention some gender-related handicaps – prevailing stereotypes of women's work, feelings of being patronized, internalized ideas of "women's place," and conflicts between activism and family responsibilities – that act as impediments to reaching their goals. But they also address gender-neutral obstacles such as entrenched farm leadership, top-down decision making, and division among farm groups as elements that limit the impact of farm people on agricultural policy.

HISTORICAL CONTEXT OF WOMEN'S PARTICIPATION IN FARM ORGANIZATIONS

Although women have always been active in politics, much of their effort has been at the grassroots level and has gone unrecognized. In response to their general exclusion from the formal political process and political roles, women adopted a volunteer approach to involvement. The grassroots, nontraditional origin of the Farmers' Alliance, for example, gave women like Mary Ellen Lease access to the political process and a political voice. The Alliance was outside formal two-party politics and so was less restricted by the customs and the constraints of that system.

But the name of this indomitable woman is one of but a few that have been recognized over time.[2] Until women's history and social history emerged in the 1960s and 1970s, researchers studying politics concentrated on men who had obtained formal positions of power. This "great men" leadership theory ignored the political activities of others who did not have access to formally institutionalized political roles. Feminist historians and theorists have developed a critique of this theory and begun to analyze the political process in ways that recognize women's participation (see Lerner 1979). These studies have found that women participated in politics throughout U.S. history. They formed coalitions to work for women's suffrage and rights, circulated petitions and spoke publicly about ending slavery, campaigned for temperance laws, struck for better working conditions, organized boycotts for consumer protection, lobbied for child welfare programs, campaigned for antilynching laws, participated in mass demonstrations for black civil rights, and were active in international organizations for peace.

The "great men" theory has also dominated the written record of agrarian politics. Today, scholars are beginning to study the political activities of farm women. For example, Jensen (1986) has found Pennsylvania Quaker farm women at the roots of resistance to slavery and at the very beginnings of the women's rights movement of the early nineteenth century. However, until this recent scholarship, little mention had been made of those women who articulated the vision, mobilized commitment, and fought for change within farm movements. Rather than having the direct access to power that comes with official positions, women have usually gained their leverage through what political historian James McGregor Burns (1978) terms transformational leadership – an open, responsive-to-the-follower approach that focuses on values, mission, qualitative thinking, and shared power.

Burns contends that by focusing only on top elected officials scholars have developed a distorted view of leadership. This limited vision of leadership needs to be corrected if we are to effectively govern our complex society. He writes, "As leadership comes properly to be seen as a process of leaders engaging and mobilizing the human needs and aspirations of followers, women will be more readily recognized as leaders and men will change their own leadership styles" (Burns 1978, p. 50). Men and women who practice transformational leadership will assist followers to envision higher goals, reach their potential, and integrate change into organizations and communities.[3]

Although men have held the formal offices of the general U.S. farm organizations and political institutions, women have often been the leaders who created understanding and provided social cohesion and group loyalty – all keys to the success of any organization.[4] These women have taken one of two approaches to the structure of their involvement – gender-integrated units or separate auxiliaries. For example, the Farmers' Alliance, Grange, and National Farmers Union were founded as protest movements during times of agricultural unrest. They developed structures that integrated women into the organization. The place of women in the American Farm Bureau Federation reflects their connections with male-dominated institutions together with the felt need to address issues of special concern to women. The National Farmers Organization, organized in more recent times, involved women through both approaches – full rights of membership and women's activities committees.

The Farmers' Alliance of the nineteenth century was the first grassroots agrarian movement to organize economic and political structures in response to grievances such as farm foreclosures and marketing abuses. Boyte and Riessman (1986) characterized the movement as neither abstract nor sentimental.

> Through the Alliances, ordinary men and women gained some power and came to believe that they might actually be able to save their farms and rural communities. They remembered the insight of Thomas Jefferson, that free government depends upon the free and voluntary association of ordinary citizens, joining together to fight concentrated power and privilege.

Built on a network of neighborhood chapters, the Alliance achieved effective use of power through the decentralization of leadership – not just a few leaders at the top but hundreds of men and women who were hired and trained to lecture and form new chapters. Starting in Texas, the Alliance rapidly spread to the South and Midwest. Mary Ellen Lease, a mother and teacher, directly experienced the pain of farm failure and became one of those lecturers. She studied law – "pinning sheets of notes above her wash tub" – and became one of the first women lawyers in Kansas. When Alliance leaders concluded that education and cooperation were not enough to rectify economic inequities, they began to engage in direct political action. Lease was one of several women who were important stump speakers for the Kansas People's Party (Burns 1986).

The Grange, founded in 1867 – and thus the oldest of the contemporary general farm organizations – mandated that women fill a certain percentage of the official positions. Local units of the Grange are autonomous and officially encourage their entire membership to participate.

Organized in Texas in 1902, the National Farmers Union (NFU) has also integrated women and men into one local organization and has granted the franchise to all members over sixteen. Some of the founders were linked with the then-defunct Farmers' Alliance, perhaps accounting in part for the NFU's strong populist traits. Women have held offices at the local and county levels of the Farmers Union from those earliest beginnings.

In contrast, the place of women in the Farm Bureau reflects its connections with the Federal Extension Service. From the outset, Farm Bureau women formed separate auxiliaries that were "naturally concerned chiefly with the home as stated in Home Bureau Creed." The first Farm Bureau Association was formed in Broome County, New York, in 1913. The intent of the founding group was to have a hand in directing the work of the Extension agent. The organization of Farm Bureau associations was greatly stimulated by the federal and state extension services, and the national federation was organized in Chicago in 1919 (Sanderson 1942). The auxiliary structure offered a platform for women to support or challenge the male mainstream leadership and to help maintain the organization's educational and social base.

The dual structure of the National Farmers Organization (NFO) reflects women's traditional roles in farm organizations and the need to address issues of special concern to women. It also recognizes women's increasing participation in the "male" political arena. Founded in the 1950s, the NFO has combined the two approaches, forming a women's activities department and encouraging full participation in the main unit.

But despite an extensive record of contribution by women to local and county units of the general farm organizations, they have rarely served on the elected state or national board of any of these organizations. Moreover, in spite of the differences in organizational approach, men dominated the public and political arenas, but the institutions they led were built on the structures that women created (see Chapter 18). Notwithstanding their near invisibility to the public eye, farm women's transformational leadership has contributed immeasurably to the tenacity and consistency of these general farm organizations.

WOMEN IN THE NEW FARM ORGANIZATIONS

In the traditions of the Farmers' Alliance, nearly 150 activist farm groups have been established within the last five years in response to the rural economic crisis (Boyte and Riessman 1986). But even before the upsurge of this populist activity, two new women's groups – American Agri-Women (AAW) and

Women Involved in Farm Economics (WIFE) – were created to expand the voice of women in U.S. agriculture. In the same period, producer groups advocating alternative production methods organized state and regional associations. The panelists at the Conference on American Farm Women were women active in these new farm organizations. The intent of these farm women is to be involved in a group that is more than an auxiliary or a social base for a male organization. These farm women address political issues traditionally considered appropriate for men only. This section describes the milieu in which their experiences can be understood.

The AAW was organized as a coalition of farm women's groups. It includes the auxiliaries of general farm organizations as well as agricultural commodity groups (e.g., American National Cowbelles [beef producers], National Porkettes [pork producers], Wheathearts [wheat producers]). Brought together in Wisconsin in 1974 at the first Farm Wife Conference sponsored by the periodical then called *Farm Wife*, now *Farm Woman*, AAW has both individual and organizational memberships. Its major concern is the well-being of the commercial family farm, and as an organization it is primarily engaged in education and networking. Most of the commodity group auxiliaries are an important segment of the coalition and concentrate their energies on promoting their respective commodities. But in spite of very divergent positions on many issues endemic to the coalescing groups, AAW considers and passes a range of resolutions on policy issues at biannual meetings. A recent example is the organization's call for the identification of food products according to the producing country.

The other recently created farm women's organization is Women Involved in Farm Economics (WIFE), chartered in Nebraska in 1976. Characterized by its national president as "a women's general farm organization," it has a policy orientation and has structured activities on local, state, and national levels. Local chapters address community concerns such as local taxes, social issues, schools, and roads. State associations focus on statewide issues like hazardous waste, taxation, and education. The national organization of WIFE, comprised of twenty state associations and free-standing memberships from thirty-five additional states, concentrates on lobbying for major farm policies. WIFE takes pride in the ties and open communication lines that its members and state associations have with congressional delegates.

The Iowa Farm Unity Coalition (IFUC) is an example of the recently organized activist farm group identified by Boyte. In these groups, as in the Farmers' Alliance, the less formal structure enables women to take active leadership roles. Organized in a bank basement in Iowa in 1982, the IFUC includes a coalition of organizations, such as the NFU, NFO, and the American Agriculture Movement as well as church, labor, student, and citizen action groups, and individual citizens whose goal is to foster communication on the farm crisis. The IFUC educates through citizen participation in legislative hearings, community meetings, rallies, press conferences, and sponsoring events such as the First Presidential Forum on Agriculture and Rural Life. Other projects include assisting financially troubled farm families through a hotline and lobbying for the state's farm mediation legislation and an agreement from the governor of Iowa for a moratorium on farm foreclosures.

The financial crisis together with a growing public concern over health and environmental issues related to agricultural production has encouraged the growth of groups like Kansas Organic Producers (KOP), which promote alternative production methods in agriculture. Organized in 1975, KOP was initially designed as a forum for the exchange of ideas among organic farmers. But, it has evolved into a concerted effort by farmers using organic practices to develop marketing opportunities to more effectively respond to national consumer demand for chemical-free produce. In addition, KOP engages in public education activities; initiates public policies, such as a Kansas legislative bill that would provide certification criteria for organically grown products; and attempts to develop alliances with other farm groups, such as the NFO, with plans to pool organically grown products and price them uniformly.

In summary, women were active in political organizations, especially at the local level, long before they were allowed to vote. Farm women generally gained the most influence and power through transformational leadership in the farm organizations and other community insitutions rather than through electoral activities. Most women took on roles within organizations that grew out of hard times in agriculture. Some women chose to form separate groups, initially to pursue gender-related interests, but more recently to influence overall agricultural issues and the special interests of single commodities. Some of the latest gender-separate activity was encouraged by the example of the women's movement. Underlining the struggle ahead, Sapiro made this important point: "The battle does not lie only in making women free to act; it also lies in making women free to be influential" (1984, p. 139). In the next section, statements of four farm women address the effectiveness issue by reflecting on the achievements of and obstacles to farm women's activism on the local, state, and national levels.

ACHIEVEMENT AND PROBLEMS OF LOCAL ACTIVISM

Rural women have been the social base and economic fund-raisers of community organizations such as rural churches and schools. They have also organized clubs to promote their own needs and interests and led youth groups. Individually and collectively, they have ameliorated problems for both family and community. Farm women, carrying on the traditions of the past, are turning their leadership skills to new issues and finding creative solutions. Panelist Denise O'Brien told conference participants about women rising to face the threat of losing the farm:

As the chronic condition has evolved in Iowa, women were among the first people to recognize that something was wrong. That probably has to do with the fact that many women do the accounting on the farms. What they began to see that alarmed them was when the interest rates started going up, the prices of the farmland were escalating, and the commodity prices were going down. They recognized when the books started to show an alarming imbalance.

Farm women are actively involved in the farm operation and recognize the harsh economic realities they face. The women admit that they have too little understanding of their legal rights and that they are not well enough positioned politically to attack the policies affecting agriculture's viability. They are moving to change those handicaps, much as earlier farm women did, through education and organizing. According to O'Brien:

> Education became very important. In farm policy, in bankruptcy laws, in what to do when the FDIC closes your local bank, they [women] needed to better understand. Many women realized that they had not been in positions of authority and in positions of policy making in the predominantly male organizations. This didn't deter them; this encouraged them. I think sometimes we rise to a challenge when there are more obstacles.

Women's traditional approach to community involvement through networking has become very useful:

> From these meetings, networks began to form phone trees. Women became very active in the nonpartisan aspect of getting out the vote. I see many women becoming very involved in the political arena. And I say nonpartisan, because they are involved with both parties. Many women have been active in going around in their local communities and distributing campaign literature, involving themselves in someone's campaign for public office.

Women use their community-building skills to increase local political participation and confront problems head-on.

Despite early proscriptions against public speaking by women, women have always taken stands in public arenas.[5] Once aroused, women have effectively corrected public misconceptions about issues. Sometimes these efforts can be frustrating. Panelist Connee Canfield related this story about a country western disc jockey from a large midwestern city who spoke disparagingly of farms over the air:

> One morning I had the misfortune to hear him. I didn't know this man existed on a country station. I was so infuriated by the time I got to work I called long distance and asked to talk to the program director. The program director said they were changing their program format on the station to make it more of a talk show. Well, he went on and said basically the same thing that my Congressman Stockman told me years ago: we don't need farmers. We can get this stuff from someplace else, where it's cheaper to grow it, they can use the labor down there, they can use the huge kind of machinery. If it means we have to export agriculture, fine and dandy. That's the basis of what he said. A farm woman from Wisconsin called in and tried to argue with

the jockey. It was like trying to argue with Stonewall Jackson or someone. I called in. And then he went on to call Willy Nelson everything but a pervert over the station. So I said, perhaps he doesn't know that his bread and butter comes from farming - that's understandable; we have a lot of ignorant people. I can understand that. But surely, he's on a country station. But he didn't care. He crucified them all. And this was over a major radio station. So no matter how much we have done, we still have a lot of disinformation out there. And I guess it's up to us to try to correct that in any way we can. But as we become fewer farmers, it gets harder and harder.

Confronting issues and educating the public continue to be traditions of female farm leaders. Women have also been able to recognize and analyze current farm problems and look for creative solutions. The issues they address show an interesting blend of traditional "women's" and "men's" issues and illustrate how family farm problems transcend barriers of gender. One cause of the farm economic slump threatening many family farms in the early '80s was the contraction of foreign markets and market dislocation. As farm women realized this, several groups looked for potential local marketing projects. Before World War II, farm women were very active in local marketing of such women's specialties as eggs, poultry, fruits, and vegetables. While most of this historic trading in local markets was informal and individual, today's farm women are meeting economic conditions by using cooperative strategies. The intentions of the Kansas Organic Producers, who are pursuing a marketing cooperative to achieve premium prices for their chemical-free produce, were described by panelist Nancy Vogelsberg-Bush: "The trend in agriculture is obvious. Either we choose to run a cooperative, or corporations will run us. Without control over our markets, we let others determine our prices."

Connee Canfield described activities of Women for the Survival of Agriculture in Michigan to improve their markets.

We started as an information group not only to get the price up for our products, but also to get the word out to the consumer about what we were about. I think we were fairly successful in that. We enacted the first state marketing and bargaining legislation. Our organization lobbied hard and long for that. We formed an organization that created the forum for the Benton Harbor Fruit Market, which was the largest open-air fruit market in the United States at one time. A forum was created to buy the market, so that it belonged to growers and to brokers and shippers together as a joint effort, because the city was going to close it down. They no longer thought it was necessary.

These farm women, like their predecessors, have used local markets to increase family farm income, and in doing so have entered the traditional male world of cash crop production and cooperative marketing.

Farm women also make connections between private family issues and public economic and policy issues. Concerns for family health and the future of their land have led some women to question the use of chemicals in farming. In Kansas, an unacceptable level of nitrate pollution in the wells led Nancy Vogelsberg-Busch to organize neighborhood action for control measures. She analyzed the pollution issue with the following statement:

> The health of our nation depends upon the health of our soils and water. Our modern technologies have created deadly chemicals to kill insects and weeds, but we don't have the technology available to know how to correct our contaminated water, nor do we know the long-term health affects of all the combined chemicals. I don't know about you, but I don't want to be one of the statistics proving that chemicals are harmful. Farming without chemicals today is not a matter of going back; it is a process of bringing forward knowledge left behind and adding our current appropriate research and knowledge for a sustainable agriculture. I define a farmer as a skilled steward striving for a sustainable agriculture. I would like to remind women here today to sustain means to nourish. We have deep, historical roots for providing nourishment. There is no question if women have a place in agriculture - rather we should question our current agriculture. Is it befitting to women? And if not, as stewards, we have a responsibility to change it.

Vogelsberg-Busch connects health issues to the economic question of increasing dependency on chemical inputs to achieve higher production. She described the marketing niche organic farmers have found:

> I don't know how many economists figure in the long-term health costs of agricultural chemicals in our society, or the cleaning up of the water, or the depletion of our soil, but I wonder if our get-big agriculture would be cost-effective if those costs were penciled in. I don't know about many of you, but I would rather farm less land and receive a higher price for quality products than follow current trends of farming more and more for less and less. And we do maintain average yields. At the county ASCS [Agriculture Stabilization and Conservation Service] office you can go in and find out how your neighbors are doing. It's real important in our neighborhood, for whoever gets out their first cuttings is like top dog and he always gets his picture in our local paper, and it says, so-and-so is yielding so many bushels. So then, you quick figure out, oh, well, gosh, this is what the current price is, and he's growing so many bushels. So you figure, "Wow, isn't he doing fine?" But I wish they'd publish what he's netting. I would like to know what his expenses are. Because of the demand, now we're getting into the economics, and because there's a demand for food that is raised without chemicals, we receive higher prices. And we do not depend on government subsidies.

On any farm, issues of family, land use, and economics are connected, and the role of farm women as family caretakers easily expands to include larger political issues.

Women not only recognize problems that affect the well-being of their family, farms, and community but use their community-organizing skills to confront them. For example, hazardous waste became a special local interest of WIFE as a result of an alert member, according to panelist Naioma Benson:

> There's another woman in Colorado, a member of WIFE who didn't feel that what was happening in her community was proper. She had a hazardous waste site that was proposing to move into prime farm land. But through that farm land ran a small river. And if something happened to the hazardous waste site, the river would have taken it on down into the next state. She simply began by calling people together in her neighborhood in her home to talk about it. And from that developed the Citizens for Eastern Colorado. And this group is still, after five years, holding at bay the hazardous waste site being proposed by the U.S.'s largest, least reputable toxic waste company.

Grassroots activism demands a great commitment in time and energy. If women's position in the family farm and community has given them unique insights and skills, it has also created problems. The burden of juggling families, farm work, and political activity has recently been compounded by the need to take off-farm jobs. Still, Naioma Benson sees this trend as an opportunity to broaden perspective:

> Farm and ranch women are moving into the work force. We're seeing also that many of our women are compelled to not only do their work at home, but to find employment off the farm. And this is giving them a broader base of experience from which to draw; an opportunity to look at and be among the public and to work with them and see what the public sector really needs.

Even without off-farm employment, the problem is one of finding enough time, as Nancy Vogelsberg-Busch explained:

> I'd like to thank the conference committee for asking me to come to Wisconsin. This is only the second time in the last eight years that I've been off the farm for two consecutive days. And the reason being that I milk cows; and I find that I'm more committed to my cows than I am to my kids, because I can leave my children on occasion, but it's real hard to find someone to milk. So, my husband is finding out just how valuable his wife is, because he's doing the chores. This is also the time for harvest in Kansas. We're trying to get the beans out. We've had a lot of rain. The sun was shining when I left. I have enormous guilt leaving, already. I have a lot of confidence in him; he is quite capable of running the machines and caring for the children.

And you never realize how valuable you are until you start writing out in longhand what all needs to be done while you are gone.

Farm women's multiple responsibilities in their homes, on their farms, and often in wage labor off the farm leave little "spare" time for commitments to political activism. Economic pressures compound these problems, as do the vagaries of nature. Connee Canfield told conference participants:

My husband and I began farming together twenty years ago. . . . We have vegetables ranging from asparagus to green beans and a second crop of green beans is completely under water in Michigan. There will be nothing realized from that crop at all. And it's a substantial part of our operation. We have soy beans, corn, both are in tenuous positions right now, due to the same flooding conditions. I'll be returning tomorrow, simply because I don't like to leave my partner in this alone, under these kinds of pressures and stress. What you hear about things happening out on the farm, it is true, it is real.

Women as farm partners share these burdens with their husbands.

Traditional women's roles have brought farm women skills to confront rural problems, but these traditions have also created obstacles. Naioma Benson sees slow but steady change occurring in age-old attitudes regarding women but recognizes that they remain a stumbling block:

I think the road to leadership for women can sometimes be rocky. Perhaps the largest single obstacle that is in the way is the "Good Old Boys" club. It is definitely alive and well, and it's functioning everywhere. There seems to be a mentality that some of the ladies need to do those menial chores, so we will have them fix the cookies and fix the coffee and clean up after the meeting. And we all know we can certainly rise above that.

Women continue to work from the strength of their heritage and against the restrictions this heritage spawned.

TRANSITION FROM GRASSROOTS TO MAINSTREAM POLITICS

The new sense of empowerment among farm women seems to arise from two sources: the devastating nationwide farm crisis that motivated women to seek strategies for survival and the women's movement of the 1970s. Economic and political opportunities and responsibilities are increasingly available to women. Many women now serve as school board and township officials, as extension advisory board members, and as representatives on other statewide policy-making bodies and commissions. But even for the highly motivated, taking that first step into national politics can be difficult. Benson described the turnabout after some small individual successes:

Although farm women are frequently involved in politics at the local level, politics at the national level is often perceived as foreign or mysterious. Writing that first letter to their congressman can be really difficult for some farm women. But getting the first reply back seems to ease all that up, and suddenly it's much easier to go on from there. Making that first phone call to a congressional office can be even more frightening. They're fortunate that the offices are often willing and able to help people and be receptive to those calls coming in from their constituents. We have instances where WIFE members sit on congressional advisory panels for their elected delegates.

Politicians cannot survive in an organizational vacuum. While important, the individual vote is only one step in influencing representation. The transactional relationship between the citizen and the candidate or political party is all important to influencing public policy. Women's active involvement in the party process can lead to thoughtful consideration of their views. Naioma Benson stressed this lesson:

> WIFE has become acutely aware that you have to work within the political structure. This country has a two-party political system, and that's the system within which action is accomplished. So we urge our members to attend their local caucuses, to be elected to their county caucus, to continue until they have someone in some states who gets enough seniority to go on to the state convention. To work within the political system means that you often will have to have access to that system and access to the lawmakers. Expect access to leaders when you want it.

Using the style and skill learned at the local level, women have organized to influence national politics through their increased access to the traditional political arena. Farm organizations are likely to have members active in both political parties facilitating congressional contact at the local level, and women are learning the importance of holding elected officials accountable. Denise O'Brien commented:

> We are very responsible people basically when it come to voting, although the average voter participation in the United States is a lot lower than in other democratic countries. We feel a responsibility to vote. But when it comes to holding our elected official accountable, we are lax. From our meetings, when we've had women coming out to the forefront, talking about politics and becoming more aware, we've also seen our politicians come back to our towns and hold their little town meetings. We encourage as many people as we can to go to those town meetings. We tell [the politicians] our problems, or praise them if they're doing well.

Naioma Benson elaborated on the importance of developing communications with elected officials through town meetings:

> Most of the state or local WIFE groups hold town meetings in the communities so that when a congressman comes back home, they're hosting the town meeting for him. And we find that this serves several purposes. It allows that member of Congress and the organization to develop a real working relationship together. It provides the congressman with the opportunity to see our members in their own environment and to really hear firsthand what their problems are. It also lets him know that the problems our members are carrying to him are shared by other members of the community. And finally, we have to recognize that it gives our congressman a chance for publicity and to be seen in the local community.

ACHIEVEMENT AND PROBLEMS OF STATE AND NATIONAL ACTIVISM

Looking for redress of agriculture's problems through public policy is a time-honored activity of farm organizations. In 1921, an unusual display of unity by the Grange, the Farmers Union and the Farm Bureau was instrumental in forming the Farm Bloc, a bipartisan coalition of legislators that gave farmers an effective voice in national public policy. Although the Farm Bloc disappeared as farm group unity disintegrated, these general farm organizations continue to have a presence in Washington and call on their membership to assist in that lobbying. For instance, since the mid-1940s, the National Farmers Union has conducted "Fly-Ins" of local leaders to Washington. New farm organizations and farm coalitions are following this model. Denise O'Brien related one such instance:

> As we organized around the farm bill, many solicited funds in their local communities. To pay for lobbying trips to Washington, D.C., they held hog roasts, bake sales, and solicited individual contributions to pay expenses. One woman in Iowa was responsible for getting over 300 farmers within a six-month period of time to Washington. After having been involved on this level, she is now running for a political office in the state legislature. A seventy-two-year-old women who remembers the Depression, and whose father was a political activist, has been in Washington four or five times – many times enduring very tiring, long bus trips. So, people felt that they were going to be effective by going to Washington and talking to congressmen and senators in their offices, and to pressure them into doing something about the current situation.

Before going to the Capitol, the farm men and women debated and wrote a legislative alternative to the farm proposal recommended by the administration and spent a great deal of time gaining their senator's support for their ideas. According to O'Brien:

> We were told in Washington that perhaps the people who came – not just the Iowa farmers, but those who came from all over the country – changed, actually brought about debate on the farm bill. Prior to that time, there was no alternative farm bill. These farmers' "farm bill" presented the senators with a viable alternative to the administration bill. If it hadn't been for the farming men and women in our country, that farm bill would not have been debated as heavily as it was. Senator Dole told Senator Harkin that when he started out with the alternative bill that he probably would be lucky to get ten votes. Harkin got thirty-six votes; we feel that was a very good representation. Harkin recently reintroduced the bill as the Save the Family Farm Act and has now been actively pursuing this around the country, finding support for it. He has been working very hard, and at this point, is a senator with backbone.

A few farm women have been effective lobbyists at state and national levels for years. However, with more farm women lobbying in state legislatures and Congress today, there has emerged a greater appreciation for women's grasp of agricultural economics and policy and for their ability to place facts into a community and family context. President of WIFE Naioma Benson reported:

> I have seen the power of women lobbyists. Maybe it's a surprise attack that congressmen think this sweet little farm lady is coming in and what can she know? And suddenly they find out that as they sit and listen, that she indeed knows the facts and figures and knows what's going on. Farm and ranch women are living the difficulties today, so who better to talk to them? And to speak about what's happening in agriculture? National WIFE meets in Washington, D.C., every June. We hold a legislative issues breakfast for members of the Senate and House Agriculture Committees. Last year, we had 160 attend this breakfast. Then our members go to the hill, keep their appointments, and visit with their congressmen. It allows us to tell them what's happening at home.

Working on all levels of government, exerting pressure and demonstrating heightened interest and expertise, farm women have been able to directly effect specific legislation. One noted achievement was the end of the Federal Widow's Tax in 1981. Another achievement at the national level was described by Naioma Benson as follows:

> In Colorado, recently, a woman who is a sugar beet producer learned that their final sugar beet payment was not going to come to them because Great Western Sugar had gone bankrupt. And that payment

had gone with Great Western, and they weren't going to give it to producers. She began a one-woman campaign, pointing out that the funds were to have reached on down to the farmer. And she convinced then-Senator Gary Hart and Senator Robert Dole to attach that amendment to the 1985 Farm Bill, and that provided the money to producers. She started that alone, a one-woman campaign. She got other people interested, and other people enthused, and moved forward.

At the state level, Michigan women lobbied for funds to improve seasonal labor housing, as recounted by Connee Canfield:

We very successfully got into the state legislature money appropriated for the construction grant fund – for growers who have migrant housing – so the migrant housing could be improved for seasonal farm labor in Michigan. That fund just came into effect this year. We had three-quarters of a million dollars put into that fund. More money has been appropriated for this next year.

However, farm women's political involvement has not evolved smoothly nor achieved as much as desired. The panelists indicated that they sometimes felt patronized because they were women. Connee Canfield summarized it this way:

When you go into a meeting with the USDA [U.S. Department of Agriculture] or whoever, they don't take you very seriously, at first, I've been doing this for fifteen years, and I don't know if it's my smiling, round face or what, but I would say as a whole that we are not taken very seriously. And I think that that is not necessarily a farm problem; I think that it's a female problem. I'll give you an example. Last year, I think it was Sissy Spacek and other of our female movie stars, went to Washington to testify as to their concern. As they had studied for their leading roles in the movies, they had learned so much about what was happening in agriculture, they went to testify. I don't believe their testimony was taken seriously. I think it was good media. I mean we all hear about it in all kinds of papers and such, but they were movie stars and pooh-poohed. At the same time, we have a President of the United States who is a male movie star who is taken extremely seriously. So, I would say that there still is this female-male kind of a thing.

Farm women with experience in national politics are also gaining insight into the problems of sustaining efforts for social and political change. Bellah (1986, p. 102) notes: "Populist politics suffers from the general problem of American voluntarism, namely, that it depends on the moment-to-moment feelings of individuals to make it go. Such personal motivation may bring excitement and vitality to politics, but it is also fragile and volitile." Canfield shared

Bellah's analysis and indicated possible remidies necessary to maintain long term involvement, including moving women into elected offices. Canfield put it this way:

> Throughout our history of fifteen years now, how a volunteer group ever stays together without any paid staff is beyond me. I don't know how we're doing it. We are restructuring ourselves, now, because most of our members hold full time jobs off of the farm. This is the transition that has occurred. It makes it very difficult to participate in events like this, to go to Washington to lobby, to go to your state capitol. It's an extremely different picture from what it was fifteen years ago. We, as women, are going to have to push those women into the leadership pipeline that can best make it in the next ten years, because there are going to be some of us that aren't going to be around. It's a ten year job. Tho women you choose to put into that [elected official] pipeline, make sure thay have staying power.

ORGANIZATIONAL DIFFUSION IN AGRICULTURE

The term "organizational diffusion of agriculture" draws attention to a widely accepted observation: organizations proposing to speak for the industry are widely spread, loosely connected, and moving in many directions. Farm organization representatives have had litle agreeement regarding appropriate public policy for agriculture. This "Babel effect" is often lamented by legislators and has led to short term, often conflicting policy. John Kenneth Galbraith (1983, p. 188) warns that when there is a proliferation of groups they may experience an illusion of power rather than real power. He wrote: "No one in a democracy should be in doubt as to the real effectiveness of organized opposition to concentrated power. But all must have an acute understanding of the weakness arising from the diffusion of power and the difference between illusion and practical effect."

As we described earlier in the paper, the past decade produced a proliferation of farm organizations. Farm women activists like our panelists have founded and joined these new organizations, all of which contributed to the fragmentation of the voice of American agriculture. It was on the issue of the diffusion of farm organizations that a question was raised by a participant from Canada: "Surely in the United States you must have had traditional farm organizations over the years. Why did you organize new groups rather than working within an existing one?" In response, each panelist and many speakers from the audience indicated they were members of one or more other farm organizations. Nearly all echoed Naioma Benson when she expressed her frustrations with entrenched leadership:

> I guess I have a short attention span; I did not feel that there was going to be a place for me very quickly [in established organizations]. They weren't moving fast enough for me. I've always had a project ahead. When I finish with one, I want to move on to something else. I wanted to be president of the county unit, but it has always been

passed on from father to son, brother to kids. I saw another place I could go. WIFE was organized just sixty miles from me, so I hopped onto the bandwagon. I find it interesting enough now that we're moving into a very cooperative and formidable role with the other agricultural organizations. One of them [a National farm leader] said, "Well, why aren't you over here in our group? You were active; why didn't you stay?" And I said there wasn't time for me. I needed to do something quicker. This is what's happened in my instance.

Referring to a different farm organization, another panelist said: "It's a real traditional passing on of the gavel. I find my inclination is that it's too much to deal with, trying to work with [long-established, general farm] organizations. Although input is still there in those organizations it is not necessarily in a decision-making or office-holding position."

The need for unity, cooperation, and democratic decision-making practices was stressed by another panelist:

In my case it was different; I did belong to the farm organizations – and I belonged to them all. And I encouraged my husband to belong to them all. I didn't come from a farm background, and I came from a labor movement background and understood the need for unity, a point on which farmers get really hung up – on labor unions and such. My uncle was a head of the AFL-CIO precinct, so I came from that kind of a background. It wasn't a matter of leadership; that wasn't the reason that I stopped going to the general farm organizations. It was the matter of the way it came down. It was the same reason that I got fed up with my education organization. I may be stepping on some toes here. When the decisions come from the top down to the bottom, instead of from the bottom up to the top, and there doesn't seem to be anybody who will listen, no matter what you do, it is time to move out and get started elsewhere.

Her plea for unity was underscored by another representative:

I agree we also have too much division among farmers to join one organization, rather than to choose several. We need to draw them together more, however. There's some good in all of it. We need to learn to work together to increase our price and to come up with ideas we all agree upon.

The debate continued from the conference floor. Not all participants agreed that a separate women's group is the way to be most effective, as is apparent in the following remarks:

I was elected to serve on the state policy and action committee of [my organization] in North Dakota for two years; last year I was elected on the state board of directors. I have to differ with these women, be-

cause I found that I could be very active in my organization and when
I was asked to join some other organizations, I refused. In [my orga-
nization] the women's place has always been important. Women have
always been in policy-making committees, so it was easy for me to
find my place there. So, I don't think that it's the same in all states
or organizations.

Another participant had a different reason for organizing outside the traditional
groups. She felt that farm organizations with long-standing policy positions
would not be flexible or responsive enough to address the concerns for economic
imbalance felt by some farm population segments – particularly where the office
holders were not active farmers or were less vulnerable to the crisis because of
factors like age and timing of entry into farming. This participant stated:

I think our sister from Canada has obviously struck a nerve. I would
like to address the fact that main-line organizations have a position;
they all tend to speak in the party tongue, whichever party it is. They
continue to pass on to the next generation the same old lines time
and again. What we're seeing now, in the crisis situation, that ideas
can come to the fore, but what we're seeing is that in some of these
organizations, people who think about different approaches to the
problems are being systematically thrown out of the organization;
they're being ostracized, they're being shunned. And consequently,
the entrenched leadership goes on. Some of those ideas are coming
from marginal farmers, and they may not be in farming two or three
years from now. Main-line organizations, consequently, often perpetuate the line they hold.

While some traditional farm organizations offer a structure of open opportunities for women's involvement, women have not always chosen to take this
route. Research on the reasons few women have sought political office has found
two significant constraints: family responsibilities and women's internalized
attitude about proper and improper behavior (Githens and Prestage 1977; Carroll
1984).[6] One participant felt that farm women have been too concerned about not
violating organizational norms and needed to have their consciousness raised.
She commented:

I guess I have to agree with most of what has been said thus far. I
work as a national women's coordinator for my organization. Women
have been very instrumental, there have always been active women,
but they [my policy groups] are male-dominated. Too many times we
may think we [women] have the answers but we don't want to seem
out of place and don't express them. We have to stand up and say we
do have some of the answers, and I'm not going to wait for my husband to say them. In North Dakota, in fact, a year ago, there was a

woman who had fine ideas, who kept whispering them to the man sitting next to her; and it wasn't even her husband sitting next to her. And he would introduce them. It's time we stand up and tell them "We're sick of what's happening to our families and to our farms." It's time we say you owe us X amount of power positions for all those cookies we baked.

Another participant pointed out the differences in official leadership tenure experienced by main-line organizations with professional staff and those led by volunteers. She recognized the value and need for both types:

There are two kinds of things you can see here. When we as volunteer organizations volunteer our time, volunteer our money, we can only endure this job for a couple of years. That is why the positions are only for two years. We see that there is a changeover all the time, with new people coming in with new ideas and the organization changes; whereas some of the other agricultural organizations maintain their presidency for a long length of time, and the change doesn't happen as quickly. Although they [main-line organizations] establish our credibility in Washington because they're there for years, going back, we also have new ideas; so there's some good in both of them.

Another participant also compared general farm organizations and the newer farm groups which depend on volunteerism. She contrasted the continuity and consistency of institutionalized organizations' policy positions with the fluidity of positions assumed by movement leaders.

You're basically talking about two different kinds of organizations. One is an organization that has become institutionalized with a long tradition and with enormous responsibilities to its membership, including maintenance of business enterprises and permanent staffs. It has a process of developing resolutions, starting from the grassroots and moving up, and many years of a track record, old mistakes they have to carry as old baggage. The other side which moves faster, that you are attracted to, is really a movement, rather than an organization. It comes up, it can say whatever it wants to say off the top of its head, and it doesn't have to live with it; it can move on. It's quite a different matter to be a leader of that kind of organization. You can indeed shoot from the hip and say things that you don't have to live with or get kicked off the national board because you've made a mistake, or you've disappointed your membership. We did a conference once and I asked a young person to serve on the panel who came from the movement rather than from one of the traditional organizations. One of the traditional presidents said to me, "I don't understand why you've asked him to sit on the panel." And I said because he has a lot of interesting ideas and he represents a lot of people; he's got a voice that should be heard. And he said, "Well, he can say whatever he pleases, and it doesn't matter. But I have to live with what my organization says, and has said, for many years."

It seems both approaches, established organizations and movements, are needed, especially when agriculture is under such stress, but there must be more communication and cooperation.[7]

Each of the panelists recognized the need for cooperative linkages with established institutions to achieve their organizations' goals. As mentioned before, all of their organizations are involved with churches, labor unions, and other community groups as well as the main-line farm organizations, demonstrating an intuitive appreciation for the point made by Bellah (1986, p. 103): "No politics beyond the level of spontaneous protests can exist without some degree of institutionalization. It is institutions that provide the principles and the loyalty of ongoing memberships that again and again are the indispensable resources for successful social movements." Naioma Benson, underscoring Bellah's observation, expressed her appreciation for both types of groups:

> I want to make it clear that I think we do need the old long-line farm organizations, that they are necessary; they have the Washington offices, and they can maintain them there full-time. I find those staff members willingly provide valuable resources that I do not have access to. But what we're talking about here is the involvement of women in politics; and for women to move ahead quickly, we have to find a place where we will be allowed to have that leadership.

Stockdale (1980, p. 325) called for research to determine who is involved in what ways in shaping food and agriculture policy. He asked: "To what extent are traditional farm organizations being displaced by commodity groups? Whose interests are reflected in the policy? Whose interests are neglected or subverted?" It seems apparent that as specialization in agriculture has increased, so has the power of commodity organizations. Some commodity groups include only the farmer/producer (e.g., the National Association of Wheat Growers). But most are vertically integrated with industry-wide representation for all commodity segments. These types of commodity groups may include feed, seed, and farm supply companies, processors, and shippers as well as producers. In such groups, producers have little influence (Hadwiger 1982). Not surprisingly, there are not only conflicting interests among commodities (e.g., effects of cheap grain policy on grain producers versus livestock producers) but also between the producer and the associated agribusiness entities of a particular commodity (Meier and Browne 1983). To illustrate, it may be to the farmers' advantage to engage in low-input farming practices or to support mandatory quotas as each of these could reduce price-depressing overproduction and increase profitability. However, low-cost production or cuts in production would likely reduce the business volume for both farm input suppliers and commodity handlers. These tensions make it nearly impossible to develop a coherent food and fiber public policy.

Notwithstanding these conficts, commodity-based organizations have become quite powerful in Washington and do produce special-interest results for particular commodities. Marcia Taylor, the panel moderator, ended the debate on farm organization diffusion by discussing these commodity groups as power actors in the policy arena:

> As a Washington editor, one of the observations I'd like to make, after watching the wheeling and dealing in Washington last year about the farm bill and about some of the deals being cut in the last minute of this current session of Congress . . . is that quite a lot of the terms of the farm legislation in the 1985 farm bill were not dictated by the main-line farm organizations, but by the commodity groups. If there is anyone here who is a cotton or rice producer, you should give your congressmen gold stars, because they followed the commodity groups' suggestions right down the line. The same for the corn growers and wheat growers, as well; much of the technical language was drafted by those commodity organizations – behind closed doors. Much of it's also done at the last minute. For example, as we were leaving Washington on Wednesday, the cotton growers inserted provisions in the commodities-futures trading reauthorization bill that would exempt some types of cotton from the cross-compliance feature of the farm bill. The wheat growers were successful in getting a provision in that same bill that would allow the wheat deficiency payments to be made by December of this year instead of waiting until later next year. None of these bills have had any public hearings, no public debate, no public testimony; they're all attached as riders to unrelated legislation. It's very difficult for farm women's organizations to have any influence over last minute deals when there's really no one there who's watching out for their interests.

The increasing importance of commodity groups in determining policy may point to a special opportunity and responsibility for members of American Agri-Women. This coalition cuts across the organizational lines of traditional farm organizations, commodity auxiliaries, and some crisis-oriented groups. The dual participation offers members communication networks that could facilitate movement toward a political agenda substantially influenced by women, as well as open new possibilities for shaping a more coherent food policy.

CONCLUSION

To have power, women must be present in the political arena. Collecting data over a ten-year span, the National Women's Political Caucus (NWPC) found there had been only slight increases (four to five percent) in the number of women elected to national-level offices. However, a significant increase in the number of women elected at the state level – almost tripled from a decade ago – and increased numbers of county clerks, treasurers, county commissioners, and other local officials indicate that many women, including rural women, are pro-

gressing up the political ladder. Naioma Benson reiterated the NWPC's observation: "Women political leaders are now in the pipeline."

Mary Ellen Lease, the symbol of farm women's participation, and other
women Populist Party leaders were referred to in an early historical reference as
"a band of female orators led by the bony-handed Mary Ellen Lease speaking
with unladylike ferocity about unladylike topics" (Goldman 1956). Even the official history of the People's Party founding convention at Omaha seemed to
disclaim the contribution of women outside traditional roles. Describing the
family life of their 1892 presidential candidate, the party historian referred to his
"neat and tasty" home, his "chic" daughter, and his wife who stayed away from
public platforms (Goldman 1956).

Ninety-five years later, historians choose a different image for Mary Ellen
Lease, perhaps illustrating better acceptance of women in the political arena. "A
tall, stately woman," in William Allen White's recollection, "she had a golden
voice, a deep rich contralto, a singing voice that had hypnotic qualities." But she
could also "hurl sentences like Jove hurled thunderbolts" (Burns 1986, p. 186).

Rural women have demonstrated that they can be effective transformational
leaders and that this leadership style is important to lasting institutions and social change. Now they need to better learn how to translate their efforts into
more identifiable and focused power. As Connie Canfield put it, "We have to
learn to recognize power and use it to our advantage. Rural women look at power
as kind of nasty; we are nurturing and compromising. But we have to learn to
speak out, take a stand, and look at issues in a strategic way."

These highly motivated farm women have turned the farm crisis into a
learning and developmental opportunity and have had some success in penetrat-
ing the political arena. They recognize the need for institutional support for their
essentially volunteer organizations and have developed cooperative endeavors for
their newly created groups. They are making the transition from supportive and
organization-building roles in their general farm organizations, to a voice of their
own. It would seem that women offer some hope of unifying rather than further
diffusing public policy positions for agriculture, thereby providing a major influence on the voice of farm families in the political arena.

NOTES

[1]The achievements of contemporary farm women as political leaders and the
impediments they experience were the focus of the opening session of the
Conference. This chapter is based on transcripts from that panel, moderated by
Marcia Taylor, Washington editor of the *Farm Journal*. Panel members included:
Naioma Benson, National President of Women Involved in Farm Economics

(WIFE), is a 26 year partner of her husband on a third-generation ranch near Sterling, Colorado. She is the bookkeeper for the farming operation which produces winter wheat, small grains, and yearling cattle, a Governor's appointee to the Colorado Agriculture Commission, and chair of the Rural/Urban Action Campaign, a nationwide coalition of farmers, workers, consumers, religious teachers, and community leaders. *Connee Canfield*, represented American Agri-Women, a coalition of farm women organizations. She is president and founder of Women for the Survival of Agriculture, an active advocacy group, and is a Michigan green vegetable and small fruit grower. *Nancy Vogelsberg-Busch*, of Kansas Organic Producers,farms 320 acres with her husband. They, along with Nancy's father and her two brothers, use organic farming practices on over 1800 acres of land. They raise alfalfa, red clover, soybeans, wheat, feed grains, and calves. *Denise O'Brien*, of Iowa Farm Unity Coalition, has farmed for eleven years in southwest Iowa on a diversified dairy farm with a you-pick-it strawberry operation. She is presently employed full-time with Prairie-Fire, an advocacy group credited with the passage of a farm bank mediation bill in Iowa.

[2]Lorna Miller had heard the Mary Ellen Lease quote repeated often while working with farm groups over a thirty-six year span, yet the first time she heard it attributed to a woman was at this conference. Mrs. Lease's correct name was Mary Elizabeth Lease. However, at her many appearances for the Farmers' Alliance People's Party during the 1890 presidential campaign she was erroneously introduced as Mary Ellen, and that name has found its way into many sources.

[3]Githens and Prestage (1977) also write that the "assessment of the input and impact [of women] on public policy is made on the basis of criteria devised for male office holders." Further, they suggest that women and American blacks have three characteristics in common that contribute to their marginality in the political arena: absence of an electoral political tradition, an acute sense of frustration, and the society's stereotyped conceptions of women/blacks that are in conflict with cultural and political contributions.

[4]Historians searching for examples of transformational leadership may be interested in researching Gladys Talbott Edwards of the National Farmers Union. Her contribution was especially notable in the area of civil rights and civil liberties.

[5]See Sapiro (1984) for research findings on the effect of communications on women's basic ability to participate in politics.

[6]Lynn and Flora (1977) found that motherhood had the strongest impact on political participation of women from rural areas. The lack of child care facilities in rural areas, as well as rural women's more traditional views of maternal obligations, were underscored in their findings.

[7]Many young male farmers have also expressed frustration with farm leaders who seem insensitive to the special concerns of beginning farmers and those whose venture into agriculture was affected by the recent economic recession. They also find it difficult to attain positions of leadership and are working outside the establishment to bring about redress.

BIBLIOGRAPHY

Bellah, Robert N. 1986. "Populism and Individualism." In *The New Populism: The Politics of Empowerment*, ed. Harry C. Boyte and Frank Riessman, pp. 100-107. Philadelphia: Temple University Press.

Boyte, Harry C., and Frank Riessman, eds. 1986. *The New Populism: The Politics of Empowerment*. Philadelphia: Temple University Press.

Burns, James MacGregor. 1978. *Leadership*. New York: Harper & Row.

_____.1986. *The Workshop of Democracy*. New York: Vintage Books.

Carroll, Susan J. 1984. "Feminist Scholarship on Political Leadership." In *Leadership: Multidisciplinary Perspectives*, ed. Barbara Kellerman, pp. 139-156. Englewood Cliffs, New Jersey: Prentice Hall.

Galbraith, John Kenneth. 1983. *The Anatomy of Power*. Boston: Houghton Mifflin.

Githens, Maranne, and Jewel L. Prestage, eds. 1977. *A Portrait of Marginality: The Political Behavior of the American Woman*. New York: Longman.

Goldman, Eric F. 1956. *Rendezvous with Destiny*. New York: Random House.

Hadwiger, Don F. 1982. *The Politics of Agricultural Research*. Lincoln: University of Nebraska Press.

Jensen, Joan M. 1986. *Loosening the Bonds: Mid-Atlantic Farm Women, 1750-1850*. New Haven, Conn.: Yale University Press.

Lerner, Gerda. 1979. *The Majority Finds Its Past: Placing Women in History*. New York: Oxford University Press.

Lynn, Naomi, and Cornelia Butler Flora. 1977. "Societal Punishment and Aspects of Female Political Participation: 1972 National Convention Delegates." In *A Portrait of Marginality: The Political Behavior of the American Woman*, ed. Maranne Githens and Jewel L. Prestage, pp. 118-149. New York: Longman.

Meier, Kenneth, J., and William P. Browne. 1983. "Interest Groups and Farm Structure." In *Farms in Transition*, ed. David E. Brewster, Wayne D. Rasmussen, and Garth Youngberg, pp. 47-55. Ames: Iowa State University Press.

Sanderson, Dwight. 1942. *Rural Sociology and Rural Social Organization*. New York: Wiley.

Sapiro, Virginia. 1984. *The Political Integration of Women: Roles, Socialization, and Politics*. Urbana: University of Illinois Press.

Stockdale, Jerry D. 1980. "Who Will Speak for Agriculture?" In *Rural Society in the U.S.: Issues for the 1980s*, ed. Don A. Dillman and Daryl J. Hobbs, pp. 317-327. Boulder, Colo.: Westview Press.

Tweeten, Luther, 1979. *Foundations of Farm Policy*. Lincoln: University of Nebraska Press.

AUTHORS' BIOGRAPHICAL DATA

Janet Bokemeier is an Associate Professor of Sociology at the University of Kentucky. She received her Ph.D. from Iowa State University with specializations in family and community studies. Her research interests are in the areas of family relations and processes, and gender differences in career patterns and work experiences. She has published articles on rural women's labor force experiences, their self-identity and decision-making in *Rural Sociology* and other scholarly journals. She is co-directing a study of Kentucky farm women and agricultural cooperatives.

Kathleen Cloud received her doctorate in Public Policy Research from Harvard University in 1986 and is Director of the Office of Women in International Development at the University of Illinois at Urbana-Champaign. From 1970 to 1983, she was on the faculty of the University of Arizona, where she was responsible for a series of conferences and publications on women's roles in world food systems. Her current interests center on shifts in gender roles during the structural transformation of agriculture, and their implications for public policy; she has published extensively in this area.

Karen Davis-Brown has a Masters' of Science Degree in Human Development and Family Ecology from the University of Illinois at Urbana-Champaign and works as a church Education Coordinator. Her current research interest is the instrumental and emotional support exchanged among women.

Sarah Elbert is Professor of History at The State University of New York Binghamton. The author of numerous articles on farming families and farm women, she is also the author of *A Hunger for Home: Louisa May Alcott's Place in American Culture*, Rutgers University Press, 1988. The Cornell Farm Family Documentation Project, a fifteen-year study of farming families is the subject of a new book, *Farming*, presently in draft by Professor Elbert and Professor Gould Colman. Sarah delivered the keynote address at the Conference.

Deborah Fink received the Ph.D. in anthropology from the University of Minnesota in Minneapolis. She has done research and has published on women in rural Denmark, Iowa, Nebraska, and Nicaragua. *Open Country Iowa: Rural Women, Tradition and Change* was published in 1986 by the State University of New York Press. She is currently working on a book on rural Nebraska women and family.

Virginia Fink is a Ph.D. candidate in the Department of Sociology at the University of Virginia. She is interested in women's work roles, rural women, gender stratification, and the impacts of technological change. Her dissertation focuses on the connections between the indispensability of women's work roles and the trend towards greater external control by the state over women's bodies in the birthing process by legal precedent and recent innovations such as regulation of surrogate parenting.

Cornelia Butler Flora is a Professor of Sociology at Kansas State University and holds a research appointment with the Kansas State Agricultural Experiment Station. She has published extensively on women and agriculture and on community change and rural development in the United States and overseas. She is President-Elect of the Rural Sociological Society and the first recipient of its Award for Excellence in Research.

Lorraine Garkovich, an Associate Professor of Sociology at the University of Kentucky, received her Ph.D. in Sociology from the University of Missouri-Columbia with a specialization in demography. Her research has focused on family and work roles in farm households and the consequences of population change in rural communities. She has published articles on farm women's self-identity, work, and decision-making roles and on migration and population change in rural America. Currently she is co-directing a study of Kentucky farm women and agricultural cooperatives.

Wava G. Haney is an Associate Professor of Sociology in the University of Wisconsin Centers where she teaches in the undergraduate liberal arts program. She chaired the planning committee of the Conference. Her published research on rural women in the U.S. and Latin America and on small town businesswomen has appeared in a vareity of journals and books. She completed a doctorate in Sociology at the University of Wisconsin-Madison.

Mary Harmon, a native of West Virginia, received her Masters of Arts Degree from the University of Kentucky. Presently, she is a graduate student in the Department of Rural Sociology at Pennsylvania State University. Her primary areas of study are demography and environmental sociology; she plans to work in the public health area.

Julia Hornbostel, an Associate Professor of English at the University of Wisconsin Center-Rock County, teaches literature courses such as American Women Writers, Images of Working Women in American Literature, and the Literature of Chicago. Her research interests center on the images of women in fiction, women's autobiographies, and women's diaries. Currently, she is working on a Midwestern women's diary project.

Dolores Janiewski is a Visiting Assistant Professor of History at Mount Holyoke College. In a few months, she will assume a Lectureship at Victoria University of Wellington in New Zealand. She published *Sisterhood Denied: Race, Gender, and Class in a New South Community* in 1985 with Temple University Press. She is working on two research projects: one dealing with issues of gender and ethnicity in the Inland Northwest and the other investigating the politics of suffrage in the New South.

Jacqueline Jones is Professor of History at Wellesley College. Her book, *Labor of Love, Labor of Sorrow: Black Women, Work and the Family From Slavery to the Present*, won the Julia Spruill Prize awarded by the Southern Association for Women Historians in 1987. She is currently working on a study of sharecroppers and seasonal and migratory laborers in the American South, from 1860 to the present.

Jane B. Knowles is both Assistant Director of International Agricultural Programs and Associate Director of the Land Tenure Center at the University of Wisconsin-Madison. A major part of her international work for the last decade has been concerned with women's roles in economic development, especially in agriculture. Holder of a Ph.D. in American Civilization from the University of Pennsylvania, Knowles has a long-standing interest in women's economic roles in the agricultural development of the U.S., and particularly in how women have been served by the Cooperative Extension Service.

Seena Kohl is a Professor of Behavioral and Social Science at Webster University in St. Louis. She received her Ph.D. in cultural anthropology from Washington University. Her dissertation examined family and household dynamics in small-scale family agricultural enterprises in southwestern Saskatchewan, published in 1976 as *Working Together: Women and Family in Southwestern Saskatchewan* by Holt Rinehart and Winston of Canada.

Mary McCarthy is an Assistant Professor in the Department of Agricultural Economics at the University of Wisconsin-Madison. She received her Ph.D.in economics from New York University in 1986. Since then she has developed a research program and taught in the area of rural labor markets, farm labor allocation, and wage differentials. In 1987-88, she was on sabbatical leave to University College at Cork in her native Republic of Ireland, near the farm where she was born and raised.

Lorna Clancy Miller is a Specialist in the Department of Rural Sociology at the University of Wisconsin-Madison. In this role, she develops and provides a continuing education program in the areas of community and organizational development and the sociology of agriculture for a statewide audience. She served as an editor and contributing author of *Needs Assessment: Theory and Practice*, Iowa State University Press, 1987. Previously, she was an Assistant to the Chancellor of the University of Wisconsin-Extension and an education and policy officer with a major farm organization.

Mary Neth is Assistant Professor of History at Virginia Ploytechnic Institute and State University where she teaches U.S. social history. Neth completed her dissertation, "Preserving the Family Farm: Farm Families and Communities in the Midwest, 1900-1940," and received the Ph.D. from the University of Wisconsin-Madison in 1987. She also served on the planning committee for the Conference. Neth grew up on a farm in Missouri.

Nancy Grey Osterud teaches American History at San Jose State University in California. The project upon which her chapter is based began with an exhibit on rural women's history at the Nanticoke Valley Historical Society in Maine, New York, became a Ph.D. dissertation in American Civilization at Brown University, and is currently being extended from 1900 to World War II for publication as a book.

Rachel A. Rosenfeld is a Professor of Sociology and a Fellow of the Carolina Population Center at the University of North Carolina at Chapel Hill. She is the author of *Farm Women: Work, Farm, and Family in the United*

States (University of North Carolina Press). Her research interests include women's work and careers, the integration of work and family, and higher education.

Carolyn Sachs is Associate Professor of Rural Sociology and Women's Studies at Pennsylvania State University. Her research interests include the sociology of agriculture and women's work in agriculture. In 1984, her book on women farmers entitled *The Invisible Farmers: Women in Agricultural Production* was published by Rowman & Allanheld.

Sonya Salamon is an anthropologist and Professor of Family Studies at the University of Illinois at Urbana-Champaign. Her research has documented how Illinois farmers reflect in their family organization, inheritance patterns, farm persistence, land tenure, and rural communities the influence of ethnic values.

Priscilla Salant was an economist with the Economic Research Service, USDA and is now a Research Associate at Washington State University. In her current work, she is developing resource materials for rural community organizations. Her project, which is funded by the Rural Economic Policy Porgram of the Aspen Institute, is designed to build the research capacity of groups involved in rural development.

William Saupe is a Professor in the Department of Agricultural Economics at the University of Wisconsin-Madison. His professional work addresses the economic well-being of rural persons, including research and extension programming about the changing structure of family farms, farm financial stress, and the economic issues surrounding farm families, their businesses, and the communities in which they live.

Leann M. Tigges is an Instructor in the Department of Sociology at the University of Georgia, Athens. She received her Ph.D. from the University of Missouri-Columbia and is the author of *Changing Fortunes: Industrial Sectors and Workers' Earnings*. Her research interests include women and work, industrial and regional change, and social inequality.

MaryJo Wagner is on the faculty of the Center for Women's Studies at The Ohio State University and is also the Editor of the National Women's Studies Association Journal. She received her Ph.D. in American history from the University of Oregon. Currently, she is working on a book-length manuscript on women in the Populist Party and writing a biography of Luna Kellie, the state secretary of the Nebraska Farmers' Alliance.

INDEX

312019